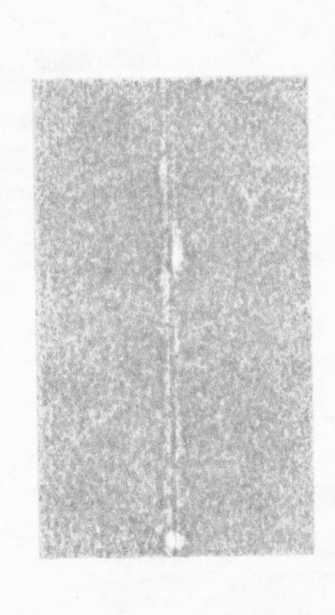

The Descent of Icarus

The Descent of Icarus

Science and the Transformation
of Contemporary Democracy

Yaron Ezrahi

Harvard University Press
Cambridge, Massachusetts
London, England
1990

Library of Congress Cataloging in Publication Data
Ezrahi, Yaron.
    The descent of Icarus : science and the transformation of
contemporary democracy / Yaron Ezrahi.
        p. cm.
    Includes bibliographical references.
    ISBN 0-674-19828-X (alk. paper)
    1. Political science. 2. Authority. 3. Democracy. 4. Legitimacy
of governments. 5. Science—Political aspects. 6. Technology—
Political aspects. I. Title.
JA80.E97 1990   90-4197
320'.01'1—dc20   CIP

To my father
who taught me how to fly
and to the memory of my mother
who taught me how to land safely.

Preface

My initial interest in the relations of science and politics in the mid-1960s was motivated by the desire to understand how scientific knowledge can render the actions of democratic governments more rational and effective. I was also interested in exploring the ways in which the integration of science and technology into the making and implementing of government decisions could be reconciled with liberal-democratic values and practices. In time, however, I became increasingly convinced that the story of the relations of science and politics in the modern democratic state is not an account of the progressive rationalization of politics. It is, rather, a process through which liberal-democratic ideology and politics selectively appropriate and adapt science and technology for constructing political authority and legitimating the exercise of political power. I came to view the role of scientific knowledge in the rationalization of politics largely as an occasional, secondary consequence of what primarily are the uses of science and technology as political resources. What emerges in this book is, therefore, not another account of how the attempts to realize Enlightenment visions of a politics rationalized by science have either succeeded or been dashed by the forces of unreason nor of how public policies can still be guided by functionally relevant scientific knowledge. It is instead a study of the specifically political and ideological role of science in upholding modern liberal-democratic conceptions of action, authority, and accountability.

A book as long in the making as this one collects many debts to teachers, friends, students, and family. While as its author I am responsible for all its flaws, its merits should be shared more widely. The notes which constitute a major portion of this study contain a specific account of my intellectual debts. Some, however, warrant special mention.

Don K. Price was responsible for my initial fascination with the role of science in modern politics and culture. His book *The Scientific Estate* (Cambridge, Mass.: Belknap Press of Harvard University Press, 1965), which he generously sent to a young graduate student at the Hebrew University whom he had met only briefly, was a decisive influence. The impact of his book and his presence deepened during my years at Harvard University as his student and assistant and in the intervening years as his colleague and friend. Judith Shklar has had a sustained influence on the development of my thinking and work from my first day as a graduate student at Harvard to the present. She has been an invaluable source of suggestions and criticisms. Whatever weaknesses this book may have are probably due to my not having followed all of her advice. I owe a profound debt to Robert K. Merton for a series of precious exchanges over a period of almost twenty years and for his constant encouragement. I have been rewarded by an ongoing dialogue with Shmuel N. Eisenstadt, especially during the two years we taught a faculty seminar together at the Hebrew University on "Cultural Traditions and Worlds of Knowledge." Eric Cohen and Michael Heyd have been constant partners in many discussions on science, culture, and politics. In this context I also mention my late student Emil Greenzweig, who was a brilliant and most promising scholar. I cherish the memory of the many conversations we had and continue to miss the conversations we might have had if not for his assassination during a "Peace Now" demonstration in February 1982.

I also owe special thanks to my teachers and colleagues at the Hebrew University: the late Benjamin Akzin, the late Joseph Ben David, Shlomo Avineri, Yehezkiel Dror, Immanuel Gutmann, Elihu Katz, Martin Seliger, and Ze'ev Sternhell. At Harvard I incurred many pleasant intellectual and personal debts to Edward Banfield, Harvey Brooks, Peter Buck, I. B. Cohen, Erwin Hibert, Stanley Hoffmann, Gerald Holton, Arthur Maass, Barbara Rosenkrantz, Michael Walzer, and James Wilson. I am especially grateful to Everett Mendelsohn for his support and for his inspiring direction of an informal seminar of faculty and graduate students in the History of Science Department. Many of the students who sat around that table have become prominent scholars in the history, philosophy, and sociology of science.

I had many useful conversations during the writing of this book with Lee Cronbach, Robert Kargon, Joshua Lederberg, Timothy Lenoir, Simon Schaffer, Steven Shapin, Arnold Thackray, Stephen Toulmin, and Harriett Zuckerman. My thanks especially to Dan Eldar for his generous and vital help.

This book was conceived and planned at the Center for Advanced Study in the Behavioral Sciences, Stanford, California, during the 1977–78 academic year. I want to thank especially the center's former director Gardner Lindzey and my colleagues there: Sacvan Bercovitch, Louis Diamond, Richard Epstein, Daniel Kahneman, Alfred Kazin, Robert Keohane, Anthony King, Theodore Lowi, Caroline Merchant-Iltis, Joseph Sax, and Paul Sniderman.

During a sabbatical at Duke University I received many useful comments on early drafts of some chapters of this book from William Ascher, James Barber, James Booth, William Coats, Michael Gillespie, Seymour Mauskopf, Thomas Spragens, and Edward Tiryakian. I am also grateful to Allan Kornberg and Eric Meyers, among others, for the exceptional hospitality extended to me at Duke.

My friends, colleagues, and students at the Hebrew University Department of Political Science and the Sidney M. Edelstein Center for the History, Philosophy, and Sociology of Science have provided a stimulating intellectual environment for working on this book. Many thanks to all of them.

I am grateful to the Ford Foundation, the National Science Foundation, the Bath-Sheba de Rothschild Foundation for the Advancement of Science in Israel, and the Russell Sage Foundation for supporting various parts of the work that led to this book. I am indebted to Yael Wyant for her skills and devotion in editing the manuscript. I would also like to thank the readers for Harvard University Press for their astute comments; Aida Donald, Editor-in-Chief, for her good advice along the way; Elizabeth Suttell for her thoughtful handling of the manuscript; and Carol Leslie for her valuable editorial suggestions.

Throughout the years of working in this field I have received sustaining intellectual companionship and moral support from my friends Yehuda Elkana, Baruch Kimmerling, Hillel Levine, and David Shulman. Hillel's support was invaluable particularly during the last phase of writing *The Descent of Icarus*.

In certain respects, of course, writing about the relations between culture and politics is never a neutral act. Living in Israel, a community undergoing a painful process of renegotiating the very premises of its existence, one is constantly reminded of the precariousness of the liberal-democratic order. The ongoing conversation with my children, Talya, Ariel, and Tehila, and their varied responses to the moral and political dilemmas of this community gave me invaluable insights into many of the problems treated in this book and touched the deeper layers of my engagement with the subject.

My wife, Sidra, has been my indispensable copilot in this rather long flight. As the most incisive and careful reader of my work and the vital source of the love and faith that sustain its author, she has a very large share in the writing of this book.

Mt. Scopus, Jerusalem
January 1990

Contents

The Descent of Icarus

Introduction

Edmund Burke warned his contemporaries against those who in their zeal to extend experimental philosophy to politics would be prepared to "sacrifice the whole human race to the slightest of their experiments."[1] Alluding to a famous scientific experiment performed by Joseph Priestley, who was also an enthusiastic supporter of political "experiments" such as the American and the French revolutions, Burke suggested that "these philosophers consider men in their experiments no more than they do mice in an air pump, or in a recipient of mephitic gas."[2]

The historical record of the fascist state and the communist dictatorship has more than confirmed Burke's fears of political engineers who would treat people like gassed mice. And, for their part, modern liberal-democratic governments have not been free of dreams of political engineering nor innocent of the morally and humanly costly uses of science and technology to augment their power to ameliorate, reconstruct, control, and manipulate. This aspect of the relations of science and politics has often eclipsed a deeper level of relations between them: the less dramatic yet no less important process through which science and technology have been harnessed to the development of modern liberal-democratic concepts of action, authority, and accountability. What has been widely ignored are the efforts to use scientific knowledge and skills not so much to enhance the instrumental effectiveness of democratic governments as to ideologically defend and legitimate uniquely liberal-democratic modes of public action, of presenting, defending, and criticizing the uses of political power.

It is this role of science and technology in the production of modern liberal-democratic politics—particularly the American variant—and its decline toward the end of the twentieth century that are the subject of this book. The changing role of science and technology between the early and later parts of the twentieth century in the liberal-democratic state has certainly been deeply affected by their place in the ideologies and politics of the fascist and communist dictatorships. But underlying these changes is a deeper sociocultural interaction between modern science and technology and liberal-democratic politics. It is necessary to examine this dynamic in order to understand how the cultural premises of the ideal of an enlightened democracy, and in particular of rational technical political action, came to be questioned towards the end of this century and what the broader implications of this development are for the place of science and the nature of liberal-democratic ideology and politics in late twentieth-century society.

In the background of the modern view of the role of knowledge in politics has been the modern notion of politics as a human enterprise inherently exposed to the disruptive effects of contingent forces and events. This view contrasts with earlier views which held collective as well as individual lives as dependent upon the will of a supreme agent, the only truly autonomous and free actor, and upon the laws of a divinely ordained universe. By extending the divine faculty of voluntary action to human agency, Renaissance humanism laid the foundations of the modern view of political action as consisting of human attempts to impose order, govern, and control public life and the contingencies or uncertainties which continually resist and limit these efforts. The principal constraints on the realization of human schemes, according to this view, is no longer a supernatural will but nature, including human nature, and the inherently limited human capacity for understanding, predicting, and controlling the conditions for a stable political order. To the moderns who denied the presence of divine guidance and rediscovered human freedom of action, it is ignorance of the causes of the sudden rise and fall of empires, nations, and leaders that limits human political ambition and it is, on the other hand, the acquired knowledge of these causes that supports it. But the inherent partiality of the knowledge of politics and history was already acknowledged by the early moderns. For Machiavelli the use of knowledge to guide political action is largely a matter of trying to tame chance, of only partly and temporarily controlling *fortuna* through the intelligent and forceful imposition of the will on the resistant materials of political life. A deeply pessimistic view of human nature led Machiavelli to distrust the relevance or efficacy of Christian or moral virtues for stabilizing the political order. Such stability, which he regarded as the highest aim of politics, was to be temporarily achieved not so much through moral conduct but by means of the skillful and effective use of power. Judging political action by its effectiveness as distinct from (although not necessarily opposed to) its morality, Machiavelli makes room for the special functions of knowledge in politics. He anticipates the modern instrumental concept of politics and the role of knowledge and technology in shaping and justifying the use of power to achieve specific objectives. In *The Prince,* he develops such an instrumental concept of politics from the perspective of the autocratic ruler and stresses the value of the "knowledge of the deeds of great men."[3] In his *Discourses,* the idea that actions should be directed and judged according to their effects is the basis of republican politics in which esteem should be granted to "those who would know how to govern states, rather than [to] those who have the right to govern, but lack the knowledge."[4]

In the ensuing four centuries, attempts to fuse an instrumental concept of politics with a political commitment to a humanistic conception of freedom became one of the central features of the Western political tradition. As a result, the role of knowledge and technique in directing and justifying action has become central to modern Western liberal-democratic notions of authority, accountability, and order, thus providing independent political rationales for the uses of knowledge, or claims of knowledge, in public affairs.

The rise of modern science and especially the development of an experimental natural philosophical tradition since the early seventeenth century has provided an additional impetus to this process. Inspired by the visions of the ideologues of the Enlightenment, such goals as the advancement and the diffusion of knowledge became integrated into liberal-democratic notions of political power checked by and accountable to an enlightened public. All along, to be sure, the belief that knowledge can temper human passions and civilize the common life has had its critics. Thomas Hobbes, Jean-Jacques Rousseau, or Karl Marx, despite the many differences among them concerning the possible and desirable forms of government or the place of knowledge in politics, share a common distrust of the use of science to rationalize public action and secure human happiness.

In the early twentieth century, the question of whether knowledge can liberate society from the burdens of scarcity and conflict persists: whether Icarus' flight to the sun is feasible, whether science can carry politics on its "wings" to spheres where collective human existence is free from chance, prejudice, and arbitrariness. The debate between

J. B. S. Haldane and Bertrand Russell is illustrative. In his *Daedalus, or, Science and the Future* (1924), Haldane, encouraged by his sympathy for the optimistic socialism of the time, presents a progressive view of human conquests ranging from space, time, and matter to the "dark and evil elements" in the human soul.[5] Bertrand Russell, in a response entitled *Icarus, or, the Future of Science* (1924), takes issue with Haldane's "attractive picture of the future as it may become through the use of scientific discoveries to promote human happiness."[6] Icarus, having been taught to fly by his father Daedalus, "was destroyed by rashness," writes Russell, invoking the ancient myth. "I fear," he concludes, "that the same fate may overtake the populations whom modern men of science have taught to fly . . . science is not a substitute for virtue . . . Technical scientific knowledge does not make men sensible in their aims . . . [and] science has not given man more self-control, more kindliness or more power of discounting their passions."[7]

Toward the end of the Twentieth century, Russell's pessimism about the force of science to transform politics appears more in tune with the sensibilities of the age than Haldane's optimism. This century's record of the massive attempts to apply scientific and technical knowledge in the making and implementing of public policies does not seem to support Haldane's vision of progressive control over the sources of social conflict and political upheaval. It also largely disconfirms the more specifically democratic variants of this view, such as John Dewey's, according to which "the operation of cooperative intelligence as displayed in science [is] a working model for the union of freedom and authority which is applicable to political as well as other spheres."[8] The point, of course, is not that scientific instrumentalism has not affected modern liberal-democratic politics and that competence or technical integrity has not become a relevant standard for judging political actors along, and at times competitively, with moral and ideological ones. It is rather that a skeptical attitude toward an instrumental-scientific conception of public actions which was confined earlier to limited counter-enlightenment circles has now become a nearly universal state of mind.

Although this study focuses primarily on the modern American and, to a lesser extent, the English experience, it is also concerned with general questions about the changing role of science and technology in modern liberal-democratic ideology and politics. The book is divided into three parts. The first consists of an analytical discussion of the principal latent political functions of science in the liberal-democratic polity. The second examines the cultural foundations of instrumental paradigms of action and the political uses of science and technology in the Anglo-American variants of liberal-democratic ideology and politics. The third and last part of the book explores late-twentieth-century trends toward the deinstrumentalization of public action and the corresponding decline in the role and authority of science and technology in the production of liberal-democratic political systems of action, authority, and accountability in America. It is the descent of Icarus rather than the ascent of Daedalus which, toward the end of the twentieth century, characterizes this latest phase of the American and, more broadly, the Western effort to mesh political power with knowledge and freedom. The book concludes with a speculative discussion of some possible wider implications of this development for science and politics in the late-twentieth-century liberal-democratic state.

Part I

The Political Functions of Science in the Liberal-Democratic State

1. The Balance between Free Agency and Causation in the Liberal-Democratic Theory of Action

As a cultural enterprise, science, like religion or art, is a distinct cluster of forms of authority, discourse, and action which, while differentiated from politics, can be deployed and adapted as elements of particular political worlds. But the socio-cultural "repertoire" of any political world—the range of norms, institutions, or behaviors upon which it can draw—is determined in each case by the available cultural materials, that is, socially established traditions, beliefs, and practices. The following is a study of the changing role of science and technology as cultural resources in the construction of liberal-democratic politics: the appropriation of science and technology by modern liberal-democratic ideology and politics as means for shaping and legitimating the uses of political power in America and, to a lesser extent, England during the first two-thirds of the twentieth century, and the declining role of science and technology in serving these ends toward the end of the century.

Just as in any period architecture is constrained both by authoritative ideas of design and available materials, politics is constrained by acceptable ideas of order and available sociocultural materials, the values and practices with which political orders are constructed. Clifford Geertz makes a pertinent observation when he notes that religions, ideologies, and other kinds of symbolic universes are "extra-personal mechanisms for the perception, understanding, judgment and manipulation of the world . . . [they] are 'programs' [which] provide a template or blueprint for the organization of social and psychological processes."[1] It is as if in each political world actors had a tool kit of available resources for symbolically and institutionally shaping and justifying action and of available strategies for synthesizing values, "facts," perceptions, and interpretive codes into meaningful and working systems of social behavior.[2] While ideas of political order determine which of the available cultural materials are relevant to the task of supporting particular political "world making," these materials determine in turn the range of supportable forms of politics. Historically, ideals and images of a liberal-democratic political order have been articulated in many societies but only in a few have local sociocultural traditions and practices supported the evolution of a liberal-democratic state. Still, the political histories of those countries, such as France, England, and the United States, which have been hospitable to the growth of liberal-democratic forms, reveal the extent to which liberal-democratic ideas of political order can, when they interact with different sets of opportunities and constraints, lead to different political configurations of liberal-democratic politics.[3] In the following discussion I shall try to examine the role of science and technology in the construction of liberal-democratic forms of public action and accountability and in the encounter with a host of tensions and contradictions inherent in liberal-democratic politics.

Science and the Production of
Liberal-Democratic Politics

To view science and technology as "resources" for the construction of liberal-democratic forms of action is to carry the inquiry into the relations of science and politics beyond the limits commonly imposed by a narrow casting of the problem in terms of an encounter between knowledge and power, rationality and irrationality in politics. The traditional view of the relations of science and politics as a struggle between reason and unreason has led to two principal omissions. One concerns all those sociocultural aspects of science which are regarded as extrinsic to the properties of rational knowledge. The other concerns what may be called the inner logic and the ideological construction of political action. Ignoring such key aspects of the interaction of science and politics has often been fatal to the attempts to understand such complex phenomena. I believe that regarding science as a cultural resource in the "construction" of the political order should help to overcome this difficulty and enlarge the scope of the elements that can be integrated in the analysis.

The character and dimensions of the interaction of science and politics are more fully appreciated if beyond the cognitive aspects of rational knowledge and its production one considers science as a cluster of symbols, languages, orientations, institutions, and practices, of ways of seeing, describing, and judging experience or—if one also includes technology—of acting in relation to it, which can be at least partially deployed and used in the political universe. Correspondingly, the potential role of science in politics is more likely to be understood if one recognizes political action and speech not just as meeting or failing to meet the requirements of "rationality" or "irrationality" but also as complex configurations of value commitments and forms of behavior, authority, and discourse. This point is clarified when one recognizes that in politics action is not just the performance of a task but a mode of political and ideological communication, that action is always a gesture which has a rhetorical dimension, and that certain properties of political action are more likely to be determined by their rhetorical-ideological import than by their instrumental effects. In other words, what counts are their latent functions in validating and legitimating action and the authority of the agent within a particular political community rather than the substantive instrumental relation of the action to the manifest ends it is meant to serve. I shall argue that shifts between defining political actions in religious, moralistic, or legalistic terms and defining them in instrumental technical terms are often more the expression of a change in the rhetoric than in the substance of action, more a change in the terms of reference in the exercise of political power than in the actual tasks or goals to which it is directed. To assess, value, and reconstruct the rhetorical dimension of political action is, therefore, very different from assessing and valuing its effectiveness or moral justification, its legality or its intellectual or scientific rationale. What makes actions morally or legally defensible, intellectually rational, or technically effective does not necessarily correspond with what makes them self-authorizing or acceptable within a given community. The logic of the political rhetoric of action is not derivative of moral theory, legal doctrine, science, or instrumental rationality, although all these elements may function as factors in the rhetoric of action. Choices from among such alternative rhetorical strategies are in fact also choices from among alternative models of authority and accountability. In public life, internally inconsistent actions, like internally inconsistent statements, may have at times certain virtues over internally consistent ones. Consistency in political speech like consistency in political action may force a choice among equally cherished values which inconsistency and ambiguity may avoid; it could expose the readiness of actors to adopt specific policies at the expense of rejecting certain other principles or interests. An ineffective action can therefore be preferable to or more self-legiti- mating than an effective one when a commitment of the relevant audience to a principle which the actors manifestly seek to enhance coexists with a degree of ambivalence toward the actual consequences of its application—as, for instance, in the case of the principle of equality when it is applied to school desegregation or the principle of free immigration when it seems to contribute to unemployment. In such cases a political action which would constitute a symbolic gesture expressing a commitment to such a principle, without the substantive behavior which would expose the contradictions in the attitudes of those who subscribe to it, may be more politically self-legitimating, more rhetorically agreeable.

Such attributes of political action as its perceived morality, legality, or instrumental effectiveness *can*, of course, reinforce its rhetorical powers. The point, however, is that this is not necessarily the case. The rhetorical valence of attributes such as coherence and effective- ness can at times be negative. Science and technology can become fac- tors in political actions often despite—and not because of—their association with such values as coherence and effectiveness since they may reinforce other, more politically desirable, objectives. Once we see the interaction between science and politics without the strictures of an exclusive focus on issues of rationality and effectiveness, we may discover that "science" or technical modes of action can be employed to enhance a host of political objectives such as winning an ideolog- ical contest, restructuring jurisdictional boundaries among actors, redistributing political power between actors and their spectators, or presenting action as indifferent to personal interests or as politically neutral.

A study of the role of science and technology in the rhetoric of lib- eral-democratic political action is, therefore, not exclusively a study of the role of truth or rational knowledge in public affairs any more than a study of the place of religion in public affairs exclusively con- cerns the pursuit of salvation in politics. It is rather an inquiry into the role of science and technology in political strategies of defining and legitimating actions as well as holding actors accountable in the con- text of public affairs.[4]

Just as one can ask how miracles or holy scriptures were used in certain political contexts to authorize the claims and legitimate the actions of political actors apart from the question of whether such claims or actions were tenable, one can examine the uses of science and technology as means of authorizing and legitimating political actions within the particular context of the modern liberal-democratic state. Concentrating only on the intellectually warranted uses of science to the exclusion of its "abuses" is, therefore, to unnecessarily limit and probably also distort the answers to the questions of why and how science and politics interact in the modern society.

In the following discussion I shall concentrate on the uses of science as a political resource in redefining the relative place of the "agent" and the "situation" in shaping the course of action, enhancing the status of action as an observable social event, distinguishing between arbitrary and nonarbitrary forms of free action, and presenting the actions of political actors as public and impersonal rather than private and subjective. I shall further examine the uses of science in depersonalizing or "depoliticizing" the exercise of political power and in rationalizing government actions as actions taken not only on behalf of but also supposedly for the sake of the people. As such, I shall argue, scientific—and technical—standards of action have become relevant in meeting the strategic political requirements of liberal-democratic accountability and in supporting the credibility of direct observation as a principal factor in liberal-democratic rituals of legitimation.

I do not wish to deny that such technologies as the atomic bomb, the space vehicle, or the birth control pill have had important consequences for the changing place of science and technology in twentieth-century liberal democracies. But in the attention they have received, they have eclipsed other, no less significant, dimensions of the interactions of science and politics which can no longer be overlooked. I shall try to show that it is precisely the factors which become salient from a more comprehensive perspective that in the end help account for the fact that toward the end of the twentieth century, when science can show an unprecedented record of spectacular technological successes, its status as a source of social ideals of rationality, as well as its authority as a source of standards of public political discourse and action, is being widely questioned. In the closing decades of the twentieth century the intellectual and technical advance of science coincides with its visible decline as a force in the rhetoric of liberal-democratic politics.

This state of affairs can be largely attributed to a process of separation between science and the public sphere of the polity which is in some respects comparable to the earlier separation between church and state. This process, what I shall call the "privatization" of science, is, therefore, just as compatible with the continued and even growing influence of science in society as the separation of church and state has been compatible in some societies with the spread of the social influence of religion. The privatization of science, like the privatization of religion, is not so much a diminishment of the place of science in society as it is a redefinition of the terms of its freedoms and constraints.

The privatization of modern science, which is viewed by some as an aspect of the movement toward greater freedom,[5] is regarded at the same time by others as the deterioration of science as a source of authoritative constraints on discourse and action and a major breakdown in the cultural "materials" available for the construction of the modern political order. Science has been used, indeed, to support a host of modern political structures, including some which are clearly authoritarian. The political history of societies with scientific traditions is partly a record of the uses and deployment of science as a cultural resource in the political world making of monarchies, aristocracies, and modern dictatorships. In recent decades, a variety of historical and social studies of science have contributed to a substantial deepening of our understanding of the ways in which science has been used as a cultural and a political resource in such diverse contexts as monarchic and revolutionary France,[6] aristocratic, middle- and working-class England,[7] Weimar and Nazi Germany,[8] democratic America,[9] and the Soviet Union.[10] The modern erosion of the belief system that made science a valuable cultural resource is, therefore, potentially the decay of a cultural resource for a variety of political programs and structures and not just the liberal-democratic ones. Just as the decline of the belief in—and fear of—hell during the seventeenth century undermined a powerful sociocultural mechanism of social control,[11] a decline of beliefs in the existence of objective external reality, in the possibility of universally valid scientific knowledge, can deplete the cultural materials of a whole range of political constructions. Scientific and technological paradigms of rational action have, of course, been assimilated into democratic and authoritarian political structures in quite different ways, and serve quite distinct political values and objectives. Each of these kinds of political programs selects for its purposes different aspects of science and uses them differently. But across such differences, the declining cultural force of science itself may still constitute an impoverishment of the general reservoir of cultural materials available for both democratic and nondemocratic political universes.

My study concerns the foundations, as well as the later decline, of the role of science and technology in upholding modern forms of liberal-democratic politics. I shall advance the argument that an "instrumental concept of politics," which encouraged the receptivity in America—and some other liberal democracies—to scientific and technological paradigms of public action, especially between the closing decades of the nineteenth century and the late 1960s, has been discredited toward the end of this century with profound consequences for the role of science and technology in the modern liberal-democratic state.

My concentration on the American variant of liberal-democratic politics requires, of course, a consideration of the unique and ungeneralizable features of the American political experience. Yet as the most scientifically and technologically advanced modern democratic state, America also furnishes the opportunity for gaining insight into more general aspects of the relations between science and modern liberal-democratic ideology and politics.

The Instrumental Concept of Action

"Those who make a practice of comparing human actions," observed Michel de Montaigne in his essay "Of the Inconsistency of Our Actions," "are never so much at a loss as to put them together in the same light; for they commonly contradict each other so strangely that it seems impossible that they have come from the same shop."[12]

Difficulties in discovering consistency and coherence in the actions of an individual actor are multiplied, of course, when consistency and coherence are sought in the actions of a multitude of individual actors or in collective social or political behavior. The inconsistency of our collective actions is a particularly persistent problem in a political universe in which order must be generated without undermining a commitment to the freedom and autonomy of individual persons.[13] The problem of converting the actions of individual persons into legitimate public actions without denying the integrity and autonomy of the actors can be regarded as the liberal-democratic problem of action. In order to discern the particular uses of science and technology as cultural resources for coping with this problem, it is necessary first to examine the political elements of what I shall call "instrumentalism" as a way of making the actions of individual actors appear both internally consistent and public.

Montaigne thought that what gives the actions of any individual their coherence is the decision of the agent to aim toward a definite goal. "No wind," he observed, "serves the man who has no port of destination."[14] The formulation of an instrumental perspective on action such that discrete actions can cohere when they are viewed as a means to further a certain goal is, of course, pervasive in modern theories of action.[15] Within the liberal-democratic polity, however, the instrumental concept of action raises the question of whether making discrete, particular actions consistent as means to an end is compatible with protecting the integrity and autonomy of individuals as voluntary agents. Modern liberal thinkers such as John Dewey and Karl Popper characteristically reject deterministic variants of instrumentalism which assume the goals of human action to be inherent, respectively, in nature, history, or society. These—and other—thinkers differ, however, with respect to how far free agents can fix and share collective goals and whether such goals can be specific and clear enough to direct public actions. Such variations, as we shall see below, have consequences for the degree to which instrumentalism can be assimilated into voluntaristic theories of political action. Different views of whether and how voluntary agents can share the goals which make their actions consistent have, therefore, important consequences for the acceptability of instrumental concepts of public action as well as for the value ascribed to science and technology in the context of liberal-democratic politics.

An instrumental paradigm of action within which actors are held accountable in terms of the perceived consequences of their actions is likely in turn to favor goals which actions can visibly advance. One of the most important political functions of science in the modern liberal-democratic state has been, indeed, to delegitimate and criticize objectives which cannot be achieved by practical action. Galileo, who conceded to religion the task of teaching us "how to go to heaven," thought it necessary to leave it to science to teach us "how the heavens go."[16] Humanizing the goals of political action, that is, separating politics as the field of this-worldly concerns from politics as a way to an other-worldly salvation, has been one of the principal impulses behind the liberal-democratic idea of order. Historically, of course, science both discouraged and inspired utopian politics.[17] But the affinities between science and the objectives of predicting and controlling nature and human behavior, the technological success of science, have, in the long run, furnished some of the most powerful rhetorical resources for justifying and legitimating a form of politics confined to actions directed by practical, instrumentally attainable goals. As a way of putting, to use Montaigne's language, actions "together in the same light," instrumentalism has been therefore most congenial to the liberal-democratic political temper. One can in fact make a case for the assertion that especially, although not exclusively, in America a particular variant of the liberal-democratic creed accounts for a good part of the receptivity to scientific-technical modes of public action. This possibility has been neglected in the literature, which typically ascribes the impact of science and technology in liberal-democratic politics to such extrapolitical factors as the industrial revolution, technological development, a progressive historical rationalization of social and economic life, the spread of literacy and education, and other aspects of the process of modernization in Western society.

The focus of this study is, then, quite different. Although such historical processes as secularization, industrialization, or modernization remain, of course, important aspects of my topic, I shall concentrate on instrumentalism as a political-ideological response to the liberal-democratic problem of action. The diffusion and institutionalization of instrumental paradigms of action in the public sector of the modern liberal-democratic state are accounted for from this perspective in terms of their manifest or latent *political* functions. By political functions I mean the uses of instrumentalization to make the coercive powers of the state acceptable to people touched by modern consciousness, to institutionalize and validate public actions and claims in terms of liberal-democratic values, and to overcome the tensions between the requirements of public action and the values of voluntary individualism.

Accounting for the rise of instrumentalism in American and other Western democracies as a political response to the liberal-democratic problem of reconciling public action with a commitment to individualism and voluntarism is distinct from at least two alternative, widely held accounts. The first has been that instrumentalization is a process of rationalizing public affairs and enlightening democratic politics.[18] The second, inspired by the criticism made by people such as Jacques Ellul and Lewis Mumford, is that technicalization both dehumanizes the citizen and subverts liberal-democratic values. A variant of the latter account has been advanced by critics of capitalism, such as Herbert Marcuse, who consider the technicalization of state actions to be an expression of the true character of capitalism as a nondemocratic system of control and domination.[19] The former account has been consistent with the attitude which regards the scientific and technical rationalization of the handling of public affairs as a feature of truly democratic politics.[20] The latter tends to associate the influence of science and technology in public affairs with nondemocratic systems of political action and control.

In this study I maintain that one need not choose between these two accounts. Each refers to the uses and adaptations of science and technology as political resources in a different political universe. As a political or ideological resource science can be made to support distinct and contradictory objectives. I shall concentrate, therefore, on the various ways in which science and technology have emerged as valuable political resources for coping with key problems in the liberal-democratic system of action, and on the uses of instrumentalism as an ideological-political strategy. In order to clarify the particular functions of science and technology in liberal-democratic politics and ideology, I shall make occasional comparative references to the interaction of science, technology, and politics in nondemocratic states. I should emphasize, however, that the purpose of the illustrations used in the discussion is not to reconstruct historically the development of these relations in the modern liberal-democratic state but to understand the ways in which science and technology have been incorporated into liberal-democratic ideological strategies for presenting, justifying, and criticizing the exercise of political power.

In the following discussion I shall concentrate on three key aspects of the political role of science in upholding instrumental paradigms of public action in the modern liberal-democratic state. The first concerns the need to reconcile a commitment to freedom with the necessities of order. The second has to do with the objective of partially depersonalizing the exercise of political power while preserving the status of agents as responsible actors. The third concerns the need to ensure that the actions of public agents are taken "for the sake" of the citizens and that these agents can be held publicly accountable.

Although I have found it analytically useful to distinguish between them, all these aspects of public political action are, of course, closely interconnected in the sense that science and technology are engaged as political resources for dealing with the tensions inherent in liberal-democratic ideology between the commitment to voluntary individualism and the requirements of public action.

Science and the Rationalization of Freedom as a
Principle of Political Construction

Liberal-democratic political actors must always reckon with the kind of criticism that Edmund Burke directed against the French Revolutionary Assembly. "They have a power given to them, like that of the evil principle, to subvert and destroy; but none to construct, except such machines as may be fitted for further subversion and further destruction."[21] One of the principal difficulties of modern liberal-democratic theory and practice has been to find a way to move from the idea of freedom as a rationale for undermining oppressive government and protecting the private sphere of the individual against the interventions and invasions of authoritarian actors, to the idea of freedom as a means of generating alternative systems of order and authority. As is illustrated, for instance, in the political philosophy of Montesquieu, liberal-democratic theory has been preoccupied with the need to affirm against the kind of arguments advanced by Machiavelli and Hobbes that it is not fear but liberty which is the principle of a good and stable political order.[22]

Through its evolution the liberal-democratic tradition has tested several conceptions of freedom as a principle of order. I shall concentrate on the role of science in the three primary ones. The first consists of the idea that spontaneous interaction among free, self-serving actors can generate a balanced system of actions whose aggregate results are publicly beneficial. The notion that competing egotists can, involuntarily, advance a collective goal, that private vices lead to public benefits, assumes that freedom can generate order without the requirements of cooperation or purposeful public-mindedness on the part of the participants.[23] According to Adam Smith, the individual actor generally "neither intends to promote the public interest, nor knows how much he is promoting it. By pursuing his own interest he frequently promotes that of the society more effectively than when he really intends to promote it."[24] Friedrich Hayek echoes this philosophy when he writes that "the only alternative of submission to the impersonal and seemingly irrational forces of the market is submission to an equally uncontrollable and therefore arbitrary power of other men."[25] Hayek accepts the liberal-democratic concept of freedom as a principle of political creativity but insists that it is blind creativity. Human institutions are made in the sense of being "entirely the result of human actions," but at the same time "they may not be the designed [or] the intended product of these actions."[26] Social institutions are not the products of "conscious control"[27] and do not arise as the intended results of deliberate actions; any process which deserves to be called social or distinct from the actions of individuals is, according to Hayek, not deliberate. Denying the possibility of conscious social action, Hayek develops an anti-instrumentalist conception of action according to which freedom and order are reconciled by voluntary adherence to general rules: "The demand that every action should be judged after full consideration of all its consequences and not by any general rules is due to failure to see that submission to general rules, couched in terms of immediately ascertainable circumstances is the only way in which, for man with his limited knowledge, freedom can be combined with the essential minimum degree of order. Common acceptance of formal rules is indeed the only alternative to direction by a single will man has yet discovered."[28]

The second conception of freedom as a principle of order replaces the invisible hand of a marketlike supermechanism of coordination with cooperation and adjustment guided by enlightenment. This view of political action rests on the assumption that action can be both informed and voluntary. The public sphere is upheld, according to this approach, by individuals who can reach consensus or generate majorities through processes of learning and rational persuasion. If, in the case of involuntary equilibrium, constraints are supposedly inherent in the "natural" logic of human interaction, in the case of voluntary rational adjustment constraints are acknowledged and self-imposed by the agency of "informed" individuals. Whereas in the market the arbitrariness of collective action is supposedly checked by the operation of the "laws of the market," in a system of reciprocally informed adjustments arbitrary behavior—the destructive aspect of freedom—is checked by the normative status of rational standards of conduct. The idea of public enlightenment as a means of decentralized coordination of free individual actions was articulated in the eighteenth century by Condorcet, in the nineteenth century by John Stuart Mill, and in the twentieth century by thinkers such as Karl Popper and John Dewey.

The liberal-democratic political tradition has developed a third conception of freedom as a principle of order which is in fact a centralized variant of the conception of order as a product of enlightened interaction. According to this concept, order is generated and maintained not through public enlightenment but through the actions of the enlightened few. What supposedly ensures that the actions of the few are not arbitrary or subjective are the publicly established—extrapolitical—standards of adequate performance. Because the actors must justify their actions before free citizens, they must appeal to publicly trusted indicators of their claims to act in the public interest. What appears to reconcile such centralized structures of actions with democratic political values is, then, a decentralized structure of accountability. Among the theorists who contributed to the development of the idea of the centralized democratic administrative state are Thomas Hobbes, Alexander Hamilton, Jeremy Bentham, Sidney Webb, Beatrice Webb, and, in the early decades of twentieth-century America, Herbert Croly and Charles Merriam.

Common to all three conceptions is the assumption that freedom is a creative principle, that it is a condition for the generation of order. What makes science central to the liberal-democratic idea of politics is its versatility in supporting these three variants of freedom as a creative yet disciplined principle of order. In the first conception, according to which the structure of the public order is not an intended but an involuntary outcome of spontaneous interaction, science is a principal means for discerning and authoritatively certifying that such spontaneous interaction is governed by patterns, laws, and regularities which ensure that freedom does not lead to chaos.[29] Science fulfills its political function in this model not so much as a method of deliberate action but as a rhetorical resource, a rationale for justifying freedom and constraining state intervention on naturalistic grounds. The latent political function of science in this context stresses the classical ideal of contemplative knowledge as a mirror of necessary natural truths. As such, however, it provides the basis for rationalizing freedom as an element not only compatible with but in some respects even inherent in the extension of natural regularities to the social sphere. In this view, it is when human action is not subject to artificial constraints that the lawfulness which upholds the social and the political order is revealed. It is largely due to such an attitude that society has come gradually to be regarded as a distinct system which sets limits to what political actors can do. In the context of involuntary coordination, a scientific outlook helps, then, to enlist a naturalistic argument to defend a liberal-democratic theory of constraints on state actions. Newtonian mechanics has generated the key metaphoric vocabulary for this model of order as equilibrium, and Adam Smith's concept of the market has extended it from physical nature to society.[30]

The second liberal conception of freedom as a creative principle of order that enlists knowledge to justify purposeful voluntary public action is in some respects both more instrumental and more democratic. Here the principal political function of science is seen not as providing the constitutive metaphor of order as an involuntary mechanical equilibrium but as exemplifying the method through which a community of free, rational individuals can generate "objective" knowledge and define truths which are in turn established as authoritative constraints on all rational speakers and actors. The political function of science as a model of enlightened interaction focuses not on any particular scientific body of knowledge but on the "republic of science" as a socio-organizational model of liberal-democratic principles according to which freedom can advance both knowledge and peace, a system in which self-development and collective progress can harmonize. Michael Polanyi has noted the special affinities between the sociological principles of the republic of science and the classical economic theory of the market.[31] Still, insofar as science produces rational consensus and advances "public knowledge,"[32] it supports decentralization as a system of voluntary rational adjustments or enlightened accommodation rather than as a system of blind involuntary coordination. The symbolic rhetorical force of the scientific enterprise in this model of the liberal-democratic polity lies in the fact that by comparison with the market mechanism it leaves more room for the role of reason and purposefulness in the construction of public actions.

In the liberal-democratic state, the freedom of scientists and academics, like the freedom of citizens, is commonly defended in this model as a necessary condition for the generation of such public goods as knowledge and order, of authority legitimated by informed voluntary consent. In totalitarian states, where science is cultivated largely as a means to confirm a particular view of the world and to augment state power and control, the idea of the republic of science as an example of the creative potential of freedom for enlightened decentralized accommodation is discarded or suppressed.[33] In the liberal-democratic polity, where individual creativity is celebrated as the basis of general social, technical, and cultural enterprises, the scientist symbolizes the general political justification of freedom as a condition that enhances the public good.[34] Whereas the liberal-democratic state extends to the political sphere the example of the republic of science as a demonstration of the potential of freedom to be a creative source of order and discipline, the totalitarian state extends to the political

sphere the scientific idea of order as a foundation for, and rationalization of, its idea of freedom as adherence to certain imperatives or
adaptation to a certain concept of necessary reality. Consistent with
these distinctions, public definitions of truth and knowledge in the
liberal-democratic society can serve on both the side of the state and
the side of the individual, who can act as a potential adversary and
critic of established claims and authorities. In the totalitarian state,
public definitions of truth and knowledge tend, by comparison, to be
on the side of established corporate authority vis-à-vis any potential
individual or group challengers.

The third variant of the conception of freedom as a principle of
order retains the commitment to the role of knowledge as a guide to
action but diminishes the role of decentralized interaction. As we shall
see, this approach actually relies on the assumption that rational actors
are sufficiently transparent to warrant not so much the possibility of
reciprocal adjustment and coordination but rather the capacity and
the right of a third party to discern and act upon an aggregate, or an
average, of the revealed preferences of all individual actors.[35] In this
model, knowledge and rationality are not regarded as the ingredients
which lead discrete individuals to enlightened accommodation or
cooperation, nor as what bring a multitude of free individuals to
decide and act jointly; instead they are seen as the means by which
the results of voluntary interaction can be anticipated and therefore
supposedly simulated by a third party so as to avoid the "waste" and
"inefficiencies" of decentralization. The function of science in this
model of liberal-democratic action is not to rationalize control and
manipulation but to establish public knowledge as a constraint upon—
and therefore also a defense of—centrally directed public actions.
Within the modern liberal-democratic state, science has indeed helped
to justify centralized structures of action by appearing to ensure the
exposure of actors to objective public tests of effectiveness and by suggesting that legislative or executive actions according to natural principles or scientific knowledge are nonarbitrary and disciplined. While
in the first conception the political function of science rests on the
uses and elaborations of the metaphor of spontaneous or involuntary
mechanistic equilibrium and in the second on the republic of science
as a model of order based on enlightened and purposeful voluntary
interaction, in the third approach the political function of science
focuses on presenting and justifying centralized actions as technical-
instrumental and therefore as public and accountable actions.

In all three variants of the idea that free actions generate and sustain the public order, knowledge is supposedly used to ensure that freedom does not degenerate into arbitrariness or disorder but is employed to enhance the public good. These three variants of the liberal-democratic ideological formulation of the idea of freedom employ science in three distinct senses, respectively, as the application of scientific-mechanistic metaphors of nature to society and politics, as a system of socio-institutional practices, and as a paradigm of action. In the political contexts of decentralized coordination, of the involuntary as well as the voluntary kind, science serves, among other things, to substantiate the claim that decentralization does not necessarily lead to chaos. In the case of centralization in the context of democracy, science serves the idea that certain kinds of centralization can be democratically accountable. In the first instance, science is employed to combine free individual actions so that their spontaneous consistency with the public good is sufficiently established to rationalize freedom from state intervention. In the second, science is employed to substantiate the claim that informed individuals can voluntarily and deliberately act together to further public objectives. In the third, science is employed to rationalize the claims of a centralized authority to be accountable to the public and to ensure that its power to act is not employed arbitrarily.[36]

Of the three variants of the idea of freedom as a principle of political creativity, only the last two can be regarded as consistent with instrumentalism. In the first, where no shared public goals are granted, the conversion of private into public actions, the process which makes them internally consistent so that private actions and public benefits harmonize, is supposedly spontaneous and not purposeful; it is an impersonal adjustment inherent in the nature of the situation. In the last two variants this result and objectifying and depersonalizing actions are deliberate. One assumes that a multitude of rational individual actors can agree on the objectives of public policies or actions and therefore can also fix joint means of action. The other assumes that the same grounds which can lead a multitude of actors to join in common courses of action can be transparent to a third party, which can deduce the appropriate public courses of action from revealed individual preferences and therefore supposedly combine them in joint acts directed to serve the public interest. Such claims are defended in democracy by tying the political standing of public actors to the publicly perceived consequences of their actions. Although action proper is centralized, the nonparticipatory feature of such a structure of action is rationalized by reference to conditions which supposedly ensure that the principal actors are continually exposed to external criticism and judgments.

Despite the obvious differences between the involuntary or spontaneous equilibrium of a multitude of discrete actions, the deliberate coordination resulting from voluntary accommodation, and the central direction of public action, there is much continuity in the role of scientific knowledge in these three variants of the idea of free action as a source of a disciplined order. In the first, marketlike, variant, knowledge mirrors the supposedly immanent harmony of individual actions which add up to lawful regularities and in turn rationalize the constraints on state intervention. In the second, knowledge and understanding permit autonomous actors to be sufficiently transparent to each other and assume sufficient regularity and predictability in the field of action to warrant the possibility of persuasion and horizontal coordination. In the third or centralized, variant, the same transparency, regularity, and predictability are used to warrant the claims of a third party to deduce the course of public actions from the relevant facts, including the revealed—or calculated—preferences of the individuals, and to conduct public affairs as a "neutral" agency for the advancement of an ideal of the public good such as the "greatest happiness for the greatest number."

In the three variants knowledge permits free actions to be regarded as structured relations of cause and effect and separates freedom as a principle of creative political construction of liberal-democratic order from freedom as a source of arbitrary actions. In all three variants the principal function of scientific knowledge is to "externalize" actions as patterns, "to put them together in the same light." What changes among the three forms is the perspective from which actions are seen to cohere and the political implications of such different perspectives.

This point can be clarified perhaps by a hypothetical illustration. Imagine that actors, like fireflies, emit light which illuminates their paths in the darkness. In the market variant of freedom as voluntary action by autonomous egotists, the actors who emit light unknowingly enable a "God's eye view"—or a scientific view—of the patterns which indicate how the paths of all individuals aggregate, as if by an invisible hand, to form a harmonious whole. In the second variant of freedom as an enlightened voluntary adjustment it is as if the actors—the fireflies—could observe each other's illuminated paths and mutually adapt their movements to form a collective pattern. Knowledge here allows for reciprocal transparency, which makes coordination and coherence in collective action possible. While in the case of blind interaction light is a condition for the outsider's knowledge, in the case of enlightened interaction knowledge is a means of mutual adjustment and cooperation. In both variants the liberal state has minimal functions as a guardian and facilitator of smooth interaction. The state fixes and standardizes such things as words, rules, coins, weights, and measures in order to ensure the stability and regularity of the system.[37] In the modern liberal-democratic state, the role of government in fixing and guarding standards such as weights and measures has been extended to cover ever new categories of standards relating to matters such as health, safety, and product labeling.

The third variant of freedom as actions taken by a few elected officials on behalf of the public combines elements of both marketlike spontaneous equilibrium and enlightened decentralized coordination. The claim of the government to act on behalf of the public rests on the presumption that the preferences of citizens are transparent to the government. The "eye of God" in the first model is replaced here by the eye of the state, but the authoritarian potential of such a condition is supposedly checked by the equal transparency of liberal-democratic government to the citizens as spectators. The principle of reciprocal transparency among citizens, which is the main feature of the second model, the model of decentralized enlightened coordination, is transformed in the third model into reciprocal transparency between the citizens and the government. Inasmuch as witnessing and viewing as the prerogative of all actors is decentralized, the transparency of government actions appears to limit the centralization of power ("power observed is power devalued").[38] In this variant, then, the supposed visibility of citizens' preferences to the government, the assumption that the government can know and anticipate the desirable course of public action, is used to rationalize the claims of the state to act for the citizens, and the visibility of the state to the citizens is used to mitigate centralized structures of state action through the decentralization of accountability. The government employs science to substantiate the claim that a synoptic view of the entire "system" empowers it to provide rational direction and to act for the general good while in turn the public and its authorized—or self-authorized—agents outside the government enlist science to make government actors accountable in terms of public standards of technical competence and integrity. In each of the three variants of liberal-democratic public action (involuntary aggregation, voluntary adjustment, and publicly accountable centralized direction), a distinct distribution of visibility—or the property of being transparent to the other—presupposes a particular distribution of the power to control action. What makes the centralized variant still consistent with liberal-democratic values is that contrary to authoritarian-technocratic centralism, democratic instrumentalism implies a government which remains visible and therefore exposed to the citizens as independent spectators.[39]

Although each of the three main variants of liberal-democratic action have been in certain times and contexts more central than the others, the modern liberal-democratic state combines all three in a mixed system of action. Their coexistence lends the liberal-democratic polity its exceptional flexibility in shifting between involuntary and voluntary modes of decentralized collective action, as well as between decentralized and moderately centralized ones. It is the persistent notion of public action as a product of decentralized interaction which checks the periodic justifications of centralized structures of action in the liberal-democratic state. Liberal-democratic rationales for strengthening the role of the executive branch are closely linked with the persistent operation of mechanisms of decentralized interaction which furnish indicators—like prices in the market system—for rationally guiding and planning action. They also rely, of course, on the role of a free press as a means of exposing the executive to public tests of adequate performance. A liberal-democratic polity is in fact a political pendulumlike system where disenchantment with radical decentralization leads to periods of moderate centralization and reaction to the fears of overcentralization leads to periods of redecentralization.[40]

Although fluctuations between spontaneous equilibrium, decentralized voluntary coordination, and rational democratic centralization as paradigms of public action entail corresponding shifts in the level of knowledge required as the basis of public actions, science plays an important, albeit distinct, role in all three. This fact reflects the centrality of science in the theory and practice of modern liberal-democratic action. It is in light of this role that trends and countertrends toward instrumentalizing and deinstrumentalizing public action are connected with shifts in the political functions of science and changes in the values attached to science and technology as political resources for constructing and maintaining the liberal-democratic idea of order. While spontaneous equilibrium or involuntary coordination is compatible with a non- or even anti-instrumentalist conception of public action, a paradigm of public action conceived as voluntary coordination or as democratic administrative centralism, instrumentalism assumes that there is sufficient knowledge to make actions consistent as means to designated ends and that the ends of collective action can be fixed in a society of autonomous individuals. Both these assumptions are subject to constant changes in the liberal-democratic state. Since even the noninstrumental notion of liberal action as the spontaneous equilibrium of a multitude of discrete individual acts has been rationalized—in classical economic theory for instance—by the claim that spontaneous interaction has an inherent economy, that it has a logic discernible from the synoptic perspective of the scientist, the radicalization of the "limits of knowledge" argument can undermine not only decentralized or centralized variants of instrumentalism but also liberal laissez-faire rationales against instrumentalism.

A progressive willingness to accept a measure of irreducible uncertainty in human affairs has indeed contributed to the erosion of instrumental paradigms of public action and the decline of science as a political resource in late-twentieth-century liberal-democratic America as well as in other Western democracies. The place of scientific knowledge in liberal-democratic theory and practice is therefore thoroughly protean. On the one hand, as I have already indicated, claims of knowledge underlie the defense of freedom as a condition capable of generating order and the assertion that politics based on freedom does not necessarily lead to chaos or to the arbitrary exercise of power. On the other hand, the argument about the limits of knowledge, which has become more salient toward the end of the century, has proven to be one of the most powerful attacks on any claims of a special authority to act. This fact highlights the contradictions inherent in the dual presumption of scientific knowledge as a solvent that can rationalize freedom as a positive basis for the political construction of order and, as thinkers from J. S. Mill to Karl Popper and Paul Feyerabend note, a basis for illegitimate claims to power and authority. This ambivalence indicates the persistent dilemma of liberal-democratic politics: how to integrate knowledge into its idea of freedom not only as a negative principle limited to the protection of individual rights from the invasions and intrusions of arbitrary external authority but also as a principle of political creativity and a basis for the construction of the public order.

Science, Causation, and the Depersonalization of Political Power

Giovanni Sartori exaggerates only slightly when he observes that "the depersonalization of power has indeed been a task to which western man has devoted all his political ingenuity."[41] Law, bureaucracy, and technology are all potent instruments which the modern state has used to depersonalize the uses of political power. The concern with the depersonalization of power relates to the historical origins of the modern state in the monarchy. It reflects the impulse to replace the personal principle of monarchic authority with impersonal principles such as office, law, and function.[42] As a fighting creed in its revolutionary stages, liberal-democracy attacked the principles of monarchic despotism inherent in personalized arbitrary power that hides behind a facade of splendor, honor, and paternalism; as a ruling ideology, however, its focus has shifted to the corruptive effects of power personalized by elected or appointed officials as well as by the passions of the masses of newly enfranchised citizens. I shall concentrate here on how, against this ongoing concern with the corruption of political power by personalization, the three principal types of liberal-democratic public action imply three distinct strategies of employing science to depersonalize the exercise of political power.

Concerns about the corruptive effects of personalized, capricious exercise of political power have been accentuated in modern political worlds with the spreading belief in the individual as the ultimate source of action and in individual freedom as a sacred principle. As Walter Ullmann notes, the humanistic tradition of the Renaissance, by focusing on the personal, subjective dimensions of human experience, in fact exposed and accentuated the tensions between the subjective and the objective dimensions of political action. "Precisely because virtually all medieval public life rested on the distinction between the office and the personality of the office holder, the objective norms held sway and had great success. The concentration on the humanity of man . . . on his personal features gradually undermined these objective standards because the new humanist's attention released forces which, in any case, had been latent."[43] It was precisely the growing appreciation of human subjectivity, creativity, and capacity to choose that generated new anxieties concerning the vulnerability of politics to corruption and decay by subjectivization. The possible uses of modern concepts of freedom and individualism to support partisanship, pluralism, and even anarchy have challenged the modern state to devise methods of generating impersonal, neutral public forms of power which could constitute a legitimate constraint in a free polity. The problem faced by the modern liberal-democratic state therefore has been not only to depersonalize political power but to do it in ways consistent with its commitments to individualism and freedom. By contrast with its authoritarian counterparts, the liberal-democratic concept of action can accept depersonalization of political power only within limits set by voluntaristic theories of action.

It can be shown that within the respective frameworks of both decentralized and centralized variants of public action in the modern liberal-democratic state, scientific knowledge has been conceived and used as a means to uphold democratically acceptable modes of depersonalizing the exercise of political power. It is important to note, however, that along with science and technology the modern liberal-democratic state has employed other, no less powerful means for satisfying the need for a "neutral power," for democratically acceptable constraints on the freedom of public actions. The most important one is, of course, the law.

The law is employed in the liberal-democratic state as a means to balance the need to hold agents accountable for their actions with the requirement of introducing some impersonal, even apolitical, grounds for the exercise of political power. The legal system permits restrictions on the discretion of agents without contradicting the voluntary premises of public action. By stressing the need to evaluate the relations between actions and established rules, the legal framework restrains the political predisposition to evaluate actions in relation to the intentions or the manifest personality traits of the actors. Contractual theories of the polity, conceived as the creation of the citizens, ensure in the liberal-democratic tradition that legal constraints on the discretion of public or political actors are not too independent of the acts of free individual actors to threaten the harmony between order and voluntary theory of action.

While the key to the legal strategy of depersonalizing the grounds of public actions or their judgments is the imperative that actions conform to authoritative rules, the instrumental-scientific strategy of depersonalizing the exercise of power focuses on the relations between actions (conceived as causes) and their consequences in a world of at least partially knowable facts. In their different ways both legalism and instrumentalism pin down actions within respectively simple formulas, the application of which provides easily identifiable criteria for judging actions and holding actors accountable. The former conceives actions as something which can be consistent or inconsistent with rules while the latter conceives actions as adequate or inadequate means to further specified ends. These formulas offer perspectives from which discrete and partially indeterminate actions can be put together and can cohere as objects of public inspection and even partial control.

While both legalism and instrumentalism stress the relations between actions and impersonal public referents while diminishing the significance of the relations between actions and the actors' personality or inner states, the former *formalizes* actions as rule-governed behavior while the latter *rationalizes* actions as the selection of means to further specified ends.

Despite such differences, there have been important affinities and convergences between legal and scientific perspectives on action, as the history of the concept of "natural law," Montesquieu's notion of the "science of legislation," or modern instrumental approaches to legal theory suggest.[44] Nevertheless, guided by modern scientific and technical norms, instrumentalism has emerged as a distinct central strategy for depersonalizing the uses of political power in the modern state. To examine how instrumentalism has been integrated into liberal-democratic politics and adapted to serve liberal-democratic values is, therefore, to look into the foundations of the modern liberal-democratic political theory of public action.

An essential aspect of the political import of the influence of scientific-instrumental norms of political action in the liberal-democratic state has been to ensure the external public nature of power without denying notions of voluntary action and accountability. According to the modern democratic variant of instrumental action, the causal relations revealed and established by (natural or social) science are not used to replace or subordinate voluntary action. They are used instead to add an "objective" observable dimension to voluntary action and to define it within a system of impersonal constraints which exposes it to continual public tests of adequacy. The compatibility between instrumentalization as a strategy for depersonalizing political power and liberal-democratic values has been secured in part by the idea of freedom as a positive principle of political construction. The notion that voluntary actions may have discernible structures, that under conditions of freedom voluntary individual behaviors form lawful social patterns, has contributed to the view that coherence among actions, employed as means to an end, need not imply authoritatian concepts of political action. Because instrumental modes of public action presuppose purposeful agents who deliberately act to promote the public good, I suggested earlier that the instrumental norms which apply in the case of intended public actions belonging either to the decentralized or centralized variety do not apply in the case of spontaneous coordination. The idea of involuntary aggregation of individuals into collective public actions is nevertheless central to the role of science in both early and later forms of liberal-democratic actions. The characteristic function of science in early forms of liberalism is indicated in the centrality of the mechanistic metaphor of the market, the attempts to extend it into the public sphere in order to make the actions of a multitude of citizens appear consistent as involuntary means to equally yet usually "good" unintended ends. In some respects, the metaphor of the "invisible hand" fitting the individual acts of many discrete individual actors represents the most radical depersonalization of public action in the liberal-democratic tradition. It achieves the integration of naturalistic and voluntaristic notions of action by allocating them respectively to the public and private spheres. Although it grants the individual the freedom to act as an autonomous agent, it subordinates the public sphere to involuntary lawful regularities. It was along such lines that during the first half of the nineteenth century Adolphe Quetelet, one of the founders of statistics as a social science, could conceive the possibility that the heterogeneity, the freedom, and the unpredictability of individual behaviors can coexist with the possibility of social laws.[45] The use of science to "naturalize" the realm of politics—and society—and present it as a sphere of necessary laws was what, among other things, provoked the attack by Karl Marx and Friedrich Engels on political economy as a tool of capitalist domination and led them to develop an alternative conception of politics which rests on a different distribution of the deterministic and voluntaristic elements of action.[46]

While classical liberal theories of action often attempted to balance a commitment to voluntary individualism and to causal conceptions of behavior by confining freedom to the sphere of the individual and lawful regularities to the level of the group, their modern variants have progressively tended to extend the voluntary sphere of action to the public realm. For J. S. Mill, John Dewey, and Karl Popper, liberal-democratic political institutions are deliberately created and sustained. Subject to certain constraints, they are the fullest expressions of the exercise of freedom as the capacity for political creativity. By reasserting the status of agency in political action, this attitude has accentuated the dilemma of checking the oversubjectivization of political action without denying the conditions of voluntary action. It is in this connection that science and technology have become vital resources for the political rhetoric of the modern liberal-democratic state. The move away from the market metaphor of spontaneous equilibrium required that the assumption of blind convergence or aggregation of individual actions be replaced by an assumption of deliberate, face-to-face interactions. Such a shift was bound to accentuate anxieties about the possibilities of personal conflicts, personal dominations, and the loss of personal dignity. The voluntarization of public action and the politicization of individual interaction increased the need for a method of checking the subjective, potentially arbitrary aspect of the behaviors of actors who function as agents of public actions. As cultural clusters of symbols, norms, and practices, science and technology have furnished a perspective, an epistemology, a vocabulary, and a set of socio-organizational strategies by which actions can be separated from actors and objectified as "means" to stated ends without sacrificing the idea of the agent as free and responsible. Just as scientific discourse has furnished a model of a conversation in which utterances and propositions are evaluated independently of the personal traits of speakers, so models of scientifically informed technical action have provided a politically attractive strategy for defining, observing, and evaluating the effectiveness or the instrumental adequacy of actions independently of the subjective traits of the actors. Science and technology have provided sociocultural techniques for conceiving actions as alienated from their agents without absolving the latter from responsibility for their effects. Quite the contrary, as we shall see, this alienation, the exposure of actions to independent external judgment, has made it possible to impose upon actors even more stringent standards of accountability.

The alienation of actions from actors, the depersonalization of actions as means to given ends, has opened up the possibility of conceiving public action as an aggregate of alienable individual actions, as a form of collective action which does not require individual actors to actually cooperate or form a group. As a science of the interplay of aggregates of individual actions, economics, using such concepts as "supply," "demand," "prices," and "productivity," demonstrates the power of the conceptual alienation of actions from persons to depersonalize the view of collective actions and define them as the features or the performances of a whole "system." It illustrates how individual actions can be thought of as elements of public action without denying the integrity of their agents as autonomous actors. The citizens of the liberal-democratic polity can appear to combine their detachable actions while keeping their personal selves apart; they can be construed as voluntarily or involuntarily uniting their actions without surrendering ground as independent persons.

Both voluntary decentralized and centrally directed coordination, as variants of public liberal-democratic political action, politically appropriate scientific knowledge and adopt an instrumental perspective to make actors appear reciprocally transparent. In contrast to magic, alchemy, and other esoteric forms of instrumentalism, science and technology appear to rationalize actions with reference to a realm of observable public facts.[47] Liberal-democratic instrumentalism has tended, therefore, to encourage political actors to choose actions which are rationally and publicly justifiable in technical terms, or at least to present them as such. It has predisposed actors to claim for their actions visible factual indicators of adequacy.[48]

The role of science and technology in the modern democratic state has been no less crucial in depersonalizing public action in the context of "administrative centralism" than in the context of decentralized interaction.[49] If in the latter depersonalization aims at checking the oversubjectivization of face-to-face interactions and at restraining the dependencies and vulnerabilities which undermine trust and reciprocal adjustments among equal actors, in the context of democratic forms of administrative centralism depersonalization is a necessary condition for legitimating the claim of the one or the few to act for the many. The alienation of actions from actors, which in the context of decentralized interaction facilitates coordination and cooperation among autonomous individuals, is enlisted by the democratic administrative state to substantiate the claim of state officials that inasmuch as their actions are based on consideration of the objective facts of the situation, including the aggregates of revealed or anticipated citizens' preferences, they are "representative actions." In the contexts of both decentralized and centralized public actions, conceiving action as a technical means separable from its agents as persons and viewing action in terms of roles, tasks, functions, and consequences have provided a way of handling the potential moral and political conflicts that could evolve in the shaping and directing of public actions.

Instrumentalism, when it encourages the use of science and technology to construct public action as a technically disciplined application of measures to achieve certain ends, furnishes the means to transform the loaded rhetoric and dramaturgy of moral, political, and personal confrontations into the cooler rhetoric of techniques used in the human struggle to conquer a world of facts and objective constraints.

Such a transformation is compatible with democratic values, especially insofar as it promises to expose the principal actors to more rigorous public tests of performance over which they have—as I hope to show—but little control. It is a specific feature of liberal-democratic variants of instrumentalism that they imply the freedom of the relatively independent, decentralized social carriers of scientific and technical knowledge to advise both the government and the public, to integrate knowledge into—as well as publicly assess and criticize the adequacy of—public actions, to apply their skills to policy problems, and to judge the competence of public servants. They supposedly provide, in short, the basis for a neutral power or authority in a democratic, highly politicized society. Even when the claims of public authorities that their actions are technically sound elude conclusive expert judgment, even when the facade of instrumentalism as a paradigm of action is not backed up by substance, instrumentalism can still support decentralized democratic accountability structures. Even when it is just a ritual of legitimation, democratic instrumentalism forces political actors to publicly defend their actions against the potential criticisms of relatively independent expert professional communities. The authority and power of the former are partly conditional upon what the latter do or say. Even when instrumentalism in the field of public affairs is just a form of political theater, in a free society it is a democratic political theater in which spectators and critics have considerable power over the life expectancy of the show and over the actors' ability to stay on stage. I would stress again that, contrary to authoritarian, and particularly totalitarian, variants of centralized instrumental action, in the liberal-democratic polity, because of the political function of depersonalization in exposing action to public assessments, the centralization of action appears to be at least partly mitigated by the decentralization of accountability. Depersonalization is licensed in the liberal-democratic state as a dimension of a process of making the actions of individual agents publicly transparent, of externalizing the indicators of adequate performance, and *not* as a way of discarding voluntaristic theories of action by appeals to determinism or elites of skill. Detaching actions from the inaccessible subjective dimensions of agents as persons is in a democratic society a way to expose actions to the judgment of others. In an authoritarian polity no such autonomous public forums or independent outsiders exist to render depersonalization of government actions or neutral standards of adequate action an aspect of a decentralized public system of accountability. In totalitarianism the constraints on the personalization, particularization, or arbitrariness of centralized action are considerably weaker. What legitimates action in such a context is not so much its apparent technical effectiveness or practical success, which is manifest in a supposedly politically neutral public sphere of observable facts outside the privileged jurisdiction of established political authority.[50] It is rather the condition that actions are undertaken by certain authorized persons or institutions. Actions are authoritative more by virtue of references to their source than to their intended or manifest consequences.[51]

Although in fact the ignorance of certain agents may free their actions from the strict discipline of technical rationality, even in its form as a ritual of justification, democratic instrumentalism imposes significant constraints on the freedom to act arbitrarily. In both its substantive and ritualistic forms, the instrumental paradigm of action has provided powerful means for mitigating the tensions and anxieties inherent in "voluntarizing" public action as an open-ended interaction among free agents. Such a theory of public action, which balances the respective commitments to individualism and restraint, has been particularly in tune with the political temper of the rising middle class. David Schneider and Raymond Smith note that whereas the individualism of both the lower and the upper classes is congenial for "a dramaturgical view of social action," middle-class individualism encourages a view of social action as something "predominantly determined by the application of technical rules."[52] Instrumentalism has provided a framework for structuring and disciplining public action without relying on personal authorities and without negating its basis in a decentralized system of voluntary interaction.[53]

A significant feature of the instrumental ends-means scheme as a framework for the presentation or judgment of public actions in instrumental terms has been its power to relate technical-factual aspects of behavior to normative ones. Linking objective with subjective aspects of action has provided, in the context of the liberal-democratic polity, a most valuable way of furnishing partially objective or external referents for the "invisible" ends and motives of actors. In a society that cultivates the values of individualism, the attribution of particular motives and goals to actors is an inherent predisposition. The instrumentalist assumption that discrete actions can cohere as consistent means in relation to a particular goal has suggested, therefore, a way to render actors' motives partially transparent. Of the goals that may be imputed to actors, those which make their actions appear more coherent as means are likely to appear more valid to observers than those which do not. Considering the fact that the goals and motives of actors are epistemologically more elusive and less directly accessible than their overt actions, it is no wonder that the possibility of regarding actions as reliable clues for imputing motives or ends to actors could reinforce the harmonization of instrumentalism with liberal-democratic structures of accountability. Constructing the "real" ends of actors on grounds of observable yet voluntarily chosen actions has provided a nondeterministic, partly teleological, conception of causality as a feature of public action. Instrumentalism could, therefore, ground a perspective from which coherence, public accountability, and voluntarism can appear to be coexisting, and even mutually reinforcing, features of public action.

To safely impute ends and motives to actors on the basis of what makes their actions appear consistent as means requires, however, that the relevant body of knowledge be sufficiently advanced to suggest that for each end there is only one best knowable course of action. The conditions which permit maximum technicalization of a given action are therefore the very conditions which, within a means-end scheme, permit the most reliable imputation of goals to actors. Only when it is perceived that there is but one optimal way to act in advancing a given goal can deviance from that course of action be visible and reliable enough to challenge actors' publicly stated motives or question their competence.[54]

In the context of the liberal-democratic polity, however, neither the ends of actors nor the means devised to enhance them are, for the most part, clear and determinate enough to support a rigorous framework for using the actions of agents as a means for the unambiguous imputation of goals and motives. There are, nevertheless, areas of public policy and public action where relatively high degrees of consensus on goals and general levels of knowledge and information restrict actors and expose them to approximate, yet publicly credible and politically consequential, imputations of motives and values. This, again, is one of the most important latent political functions of instrumentalism in the liberal-democratic polity: to externalize the invisible, inward domain of motives in a visible domain of observable, knowable, rationally reconstructible actions and to subordinate the credibility of words and arguments to the apparently more public and objective tests of deeds and actions.

The framework of Keynesian economics, for instance, purports to force economic policymakers to choose between appearing to give priority to preventing massive unemployment at the cost of risking higher inflation and appearing to prefer the risks of unemployment in order to contain and lower inflation. Although the imputation of motives to actors is based in many such cases upon unwarranted attributions of causation, varying levels of actors' knowledge and responsibility, or untenable notions of which kinds of action serve which ends, instrumentalistic orientations still encourage such schemes for attributing motives to actors and holding them accountable with reference to both the perceived and the anticipated consequences of actions. As a way of externalizing and depersonalizing aspects of the behavior of public actors, instrumentalization, therefore, enhances distinct features of the rhetoric of liberal democratic action and satisfies important requirements of liberal-democratic accountability.[55] *The physicians, physicists, chemists, engineers, economists, psychologists, and other professionals who are massively deployed at all levels of government action in the modern democratic state help institutionalize instrumentalism not only as a substantive mode of action but perhaps even more as a political strategy for constructing, legitimating, and criticizing public action.* Even when lay political leaders lack the competence or the desire to subordinate their actions to substantive instrumental standards and the lay public lacks the capacity to hold actors responsible in instrumental terms, experts who advise and criticize the government are often trusted as reliable, politically neutral representatives of the "public interest."

Some of the analytical devices employed by the instrumental approach to public action have been simplified enough, however, to be incorporated into "common sense" judgments of action. "Rational choice models" devised by the social sciences can illustrate the point. Economics, sociology, political science, psychology, and strategic studies are just a few of the principal social sciences which have developed such models of rational choice that, in more simplified, generalizable form, have penetrated the common perception of action and behavior in the context of public affairs. The central role of considerations of technical feasibility and predictable results in public discussions and journalistic accounts of policy choices, such as the Strategic Defense Initiative or measures to reduce the national budget deficit, illustrates the point.[56] Such simplified formulas of instrumental judgments of action are in fact more authoritative among laypeople than among the experts who devised them and who are aware of the uncertainties inherent in the determination of causal chains in human behavior or in the imputation of goals to actors. The integration of such standards of instrumental performance is, of course, a powerful means of depersonalizing the presentation and assessment of public action in liberal-democratic political contexts and of shifting attention from the question of who has authority to act to the question of what actions can be authorized. It is an important aspect of the move from dramaturgical to technical paradigms of political action.

Instrumental views of action, and particularly the depersonalization of aspects of human action as technical means to specific ends, have been criticized, to be sure, by advocates of various rival perspectives on public action. The moralistic criticism of instrumentalism is perhaps the most prominent one. From the moral perspective of J.-J. Rousseau, an instrumental concept of politics is thoroughly suspect. The process of alienation of actions from actors, which makes instrumentalism such a potent strategy for converting individual actions into public ones in the liberal-democratic state, appears to Rousseau as a prescription for undermining the moral quality of politics and with it human freedom and dignity. Rousseau subscribes to an entirely alternative view of politics as the realm of virtue and moral sentiments. Instrumentalism, as I have already implied, can be equally suspect from the legalistic and constitutional perspective, which stresses the need to depersonalize action by reference to rules whose authority derives from their source rather than from their anticipated effects. The moralistic and legalistic criticisms of instrumentalism indicate its limits in liberal-democratic politics. They also reflect the ambivalence inherent in the status of the depersonalization of political power both as a liberal-democratic objective and as a condition inimical to other equally central liberal-democratic values. As is manifest in the central position of the chief executive (the president or the prime minister) in modern liberal-democratic states, despite the pressures to depersonalize public actions, liberal democracies cannot entirely dispense with "personality" as a principle of political action and accountability. Hence, even as a strategy of action which enhances particular liberal-democratic values, instrumentalism remains vulnerable to serious criticism that calls attention to the liberal-democratic values which it represses. As such, the uses of instrumentalism to depersonalize the exercise of political power tend to expose the tensions produced by the inherent conflict between liberal-democratic individualism and its commitment to public order free from the arbitrary uses of power.

2. Science and the Making of Representative Actions and Accountable Actors

Technicalizing actions, in the sense of rendering them impersonal, disciplined means to designated ends, has generated ways not only to purify public action from personalized uses of political power but also to enhance it as "representative." As a method for alienating actions from their agents, for making actions detachable from persons, instrumentalism has given support to the claim that individuals can be trusted as agents "acting for" other persons, that individual actors can generate public actions.

Functionally Representative Actions

There is perhaps no more instructive expression of the power of technicalization to make the actions of private agents trusted as means to promote public objectives in the modern liberal-democratic polity than the growing role of private business entrepreneurs in providing the scientific and technological components of government actions in such diverse areas as defense, space, communications, energy, and conservation. Since World War II, government contracts with private firms have emerged as a principal technique for the scientific and technological modernization of vast areas of public action in America and, to a large extent, also in other Western democracies.[1] The point is that this development is not just a practical matter. It has a powerful symbolic function connected with the liberal-democratic ideology and particularly with its concept of legitimate public action. The following episode can illustrate the point.

Anyone who visited the Kennedy Space Center in the late 1970s or early 1980s may recall this familiar scene. You join a group of enthusiastic Americans who have come to visit the site. A competent guide leads you through the enchanting relics of one of the greatest adven-

tures of all times, the space odyssey. Perhaps the most important arti-
fact is the body of a Saturn 5, a gigantic space leviathan whose carcass
lies wide open in a didactic gesture toward curious taxpayers always
eager to be informed. The anatomy lesson proceeds smoothly as the
guide moves his stick quickly pointing to the various distinctly painted
organs of the rocket. This, he says, is a device made by the . . . electric
company in Texas! Suddenly, a thunder of applause erupts from one
corner as several proud citizens clearly feel that they share a piece of
the action. This, he continues, moving his stick upward, was made by
. . . in Nebraska; this in New Jersey and this in California! The guide's
voice disappears again in a thunder of applause. By the time the
anatomy lesson is over, there is almost no American from a near or
remote part of the country who remains excluded from the enterprise.
Meticulously enveloped with the language and rhetoric of democratic
participation, the space leviathan emerges suddenly as a monument to
the ingenuity of an entire people, the creativity and contributions of
many private American citizens and firms spread all over the United
States. Like the original drawing of Thomas Hobbes's leviathan,[2]
Saturn 5 has emerged as an icon of public action consisting of an
aggregate of many small private actions, a collective enterprise carried
out by individual agents. The curious harmony achieved in such a
democratic ritual of legitimation between the rhetoric of participation
and the coherence of action is hardly conceivable without the possibilities opened up by technical, instrumental paradigms of action. In
this particular case a period of wide national consensus on the objective of advancing American space ventures, combined with the availability of a sufficient scientific and technical base, made it possible to
radically instrumentalize this segment of public action and divide
it into a multitude of specialized technical tasks and operations.
Because of their technical-instrumental form, such actions can be separated from public agents, become diffused across the entire private
economic-industrial sector, and reassembled again as a scientifically
and technically coherent piece of public action. It is as if once a field
of public action was defined in technical-instrumental terms it permitted the decentralized allocation of pieces of action without the fear
of their corruption or loss in a maze of personal orientations or private interests.

The temporary political consensus and the technological confidence
which were congenial for the instrumentalization of the U.S. space
program between the 1960s and the early 1980s are not characteristic

of many other fields of public policy in post–World War II America. The space program illustrates, nevertheless, the power of instrumentalization to integrate private actors as agents of public actions. It is precisely because, and insofar as, the scientific-technical components of public action appear to force rigorous discipline upon individual agents and subject them to objective tests of adequate performance that public authority can entrust them to private agents without fear of corruption or overpersonalization. Moreover, as the government is the largest buyer of products and services in the free market, private firms have strong incentives to establish a reputation of reliability and integrity. Thus, ironically, the alienation of technical actions from the private-subjective dimensions of their agents, the extraordinary mobility of technical actions among diverse agents of action, the very condition which has always been condemned in humanistic critiques of the role of technology in our culture, enables the modern liberal-democratic state to expand its responsibilities in the field of action without a corresponding increase in the size of government agencies and the public sector.[3] Through the technique of contracting out pieces of public action to private firms, relying heavily upon the private sector, the government can more easily reconcile its expanding responsibilities with liberal-democratic norms of action and accountability.

In a pioneering work on this subject, Don K. Price analyzed the growing postwar use of contracts to enlist private firms and universities to contribute to public government programs and services. Price sees the evolution of a large-scale system of contracts between public and nonpublic agencies—a development which he calls the rise of "federalism by contract"—as leading toward a "considerable diffusion of central authority." "[It] has destroyed the notion that the future growth in the function and expenditures of government, which seems to be made inevitable by the increase in the technological complexity of our civilization, would necessarily take the form of a vast bureaucracy, organized on Max Weber's hierarchical principles, and using the process of science, as Julian Huxley predicted, to answer policy questions."[4]

Such amalgamation of private actors and public actions, a process which has blurred earlier demarcation lines between the private and the public sectors, would have been impossible without the deployment of instrumental scientific standards that could make the actions of private economic firms appear as trustworthy as the actions of public servants. Scientific-technical norms have made it possible to substitute technical discipline for moral, organizational and political controls as socially trusted guarantors of the integrity of public actions.

The institutional expansion of government contracts with agents in the private sector indicates the centrality of science in structuring and legitimating public action in the modern liberal-democratic polity. The same scientific and technical knowledge which facilitates a rational division of labor and decentralized participation in public action by bringing in competent private agents also constitutes a basis for rationalizing a partial yet crucial role for centralized public authority which coordinates and harmonizes the various elements of a system of action. What allowed the various mechanical elements of Saturn 5 to be developed by such a diverse group of private and public agents were the scientific and technological principles which provided the basis and generated the trust that made it possible to fit and to keep all these pieces together. A program of action could not be broken up into numerous specialized tasks without analytical and calculative techniques which discipline the relations of these parts in an integrated whole. Technical and instrumental accountabilities tie public and private actors to shared professional tests of adequacy and to shared notions of how discrete actions fit into coherent programs of collective action.

The very science and technology which authorize decentralization by specialization, because they substantiate instrumental rather than arbitrary or political grounds for unifying parts of action, can also authorize centralization. In a totalitarian state where no autonomous private sector exists, the employment of science and technology to legitimate centralized political control in terms of necessary technical unity is not mitigated by the ideologically sanctioned decentralizing effects of specialization, the authority of nonpublic bodies, and the public nature of science as an intellectual enterprise.

The coexistence of free enterprise and the public sector in the liberal-democratic polity creates, then, the conditions for the development of a specific form of instrumentalism in which decentralizing and centralizing functions are complementary and combine to balance the values of participation and discipline.

The interpenetration of the private and the public spheres to which such a system inevitably leads, however, provokes fears about the respective integrity of those sectors. The instrumentalization of government actions can appear to lead toward the unrestrained extension of the public sector into the private domain and such developments as "federalism by contract" can appear as facilitating a process by which private interests can corrupt the discipline of civic public norms. The fact that in the United States such fears have not been intensive or extensive enough to curtail the development of federalism by contract, nor to drastically restrain the effects it has in blurring the boundaries between the private and the public sectors, indicates the power of instrumentalism to instill trust in the integrity and discipline of both private and public agents of government policies. In the American case, the participation of private actors in carrying out public programs—the incorporation of private initiative, individual creativity, and economic competition—is construed in fact as a way of mitigating the coercive, centralizing, and often bureaucratically conservative features of state actions. As means for fusing elements of the private and the public sectors, science and technology come, therefore, to symbolize a classical liberal idea: voluntary private actions which are amalgamated into collective actions are a trusted vehicle of public benefits.[5] Federalism by contract is indeed in some respects a partial reintegration of the "market" as a means of public action. In this case, however, the fears of the egotism of the "economic person" are mitigated by belief in the restraining effects of science and technology as objective, public rationales of action.[6]

Transposed into the sphere of political action, the presuppositions of representation and the idea that experts can optimalize the technical effectiveness or efficiency of public actions imply that the actions of public officials, like the actions of physicians or engineers, can be made sufficiently detachable from the subjective values of their agents to warrant trust in their integrity as functionally representative. Engineers, unlike artists, are expected to act such that their actions are alienable from their personal selves. Walter Benjamin points out that "the whole sphere of authenticity is outside technical and, of course, not only technical reproducibility."[7] To the extent that authenticity presupposes uniqueness and the reflection of the singular and the particular in action it negates the very idea of alienable, reproducible actions and likewise the status of such actions as representative. Artistic acts valued as authentic expressions of their particular agents cannot, therefore, be representative in the sense in which technical actions can. The ethos of the "creative process" in art in fact celebrates the value of unrepeatable, irreproducible acts of creation. Reproductions of originals are always less valuable and, in a basic sense, antagonistic to the very spirit of art as the sphere of authentic actions.

Benjamin was indeed concerned with the danger the extension of instrumental values poses to art as the sphere of authentic actions. Those who include the political sphere in the domain of authentic actions show similar concerns with the corruptive effects of instrumental values on politics.[8] While the view of action as the authentic expression of the agent, rather than as an instrumentally conceived means to further a particular end, may be consistent with certain variants of participatory democracy, it is clearly incompatible with the liberal-democratic idea of representative actions as actions taken for, or on behalf of, other persons. According to this idea, people who act for or on behalf of others must be able to alienate their own actions from their subjective personal worlds.[9] The notion that public acts can be totally alienated from the acting agent is, of course, almost as illusionary as the notion that public acts can be unqualifiedly authentic expressions of individuals. But a scientific-instrumental perspective on human action furnishes a framework which upholds the possibility of conceiving and presenting political actions as sufficiently alienated to be functionally representative without denying the status of the actors as agents.

Whereas instrumental actions are defended with reference to their ends not their agents, works of art are typically validated as authentic with reference to a particular agent (the artist) whose personal characteristics are legitimate, though not necessary, referents in the interpretation and assessment of his or her enterprise.[10] In some respects, artistic works are—especially in the context of modern artistic sensibilities—icons, representations or expressions of the inner worlds of particular persons. By contrast, technical actions are evaluated with reference to goals and circumstances. The personality of the technician who acts is usually irrelevant.[11] What is relevant in light of the goal of action is the adequacy of the relations between certain aspects of action viewed as means, and the pertinent "objective" facts of the situation. Within any technical instrumental framework the relation between *actions* and *situations* which are mediated by *goals* are characteristically standardized. Standardizing the structure of technical action like the standardization of legal actions in terms of rules serves, therefore, as a powerful means for emancipating actions from the elusive, hidden domain of personal motives and carrying them into the visible space of observable causes and effects where they are both partly impersonal and potentially representative. Standardized impersonal responses to relevant situations can appear as representative in a way that personal or subjective responses to the relevant situations cannot. Insofar as they can be separable from the personalities of their agents, technical actions can be sold and transferred among agents and therefore also stand as actions which some persons authorize others to take in their name. Elements of the very alienation of labor, which Marx condemns as dehumanizing, underlie the authority of the professional in modern society as an agent of representative actions. In the context of technical actions, singularities are commonly treated as capricious, deviant, and irrational.[12] Technicians guilty of such conduct are considered to be irresponsible. Octavio Paz, writing about North American culture, captures an important aspect of the latent functions of science when he notes that "the universality of science (or what passes as science) justifies the elaboration and imposition of collective patterns of normality . . . the imposition of rules that condemn all singularities."[13]

As the spheres of economic, medical, or mechanical action illustrate, notions of technical rationality presuppose that individuals are in some fundamental sense *equal before nature*. Once such basic human goals as health, material well-being, or security are taken as universal and the knowledge of the facts relevant to action is sufficiently advanced, it is expected that the optimal means are largely the same with reference to different people. The mass production and marketing of technical means like cars, typewriters, optical glasses, and personal computers are based on this notion of standardized means for the advancement of technically defined individual goals which can involuntarily add up also to collective ones.

There are fundamental impersonal bases for technical solutions to human problems which do not require alteration with each change in the personal identity of the individuals who are facing the situation. The presupposition of equality before nature or reality facilitates the evolution of technical practices which are based on matching the standardized relations between actors and situations. Once fundamental goals are taken as common to different people and such equality before reality is an accepted premise, professionalization can evolve as a form of authoritative instrumental "representation." Professionals can be viewed as agents who have a mandate to represent clients in the sense of systematically matching *for them* available knowledge and skills with the standardized situations to which they are applicable.

Medical treatment can serve as an illustration. The doctor always treats a particular instance of the universal human body. The aspects of the human body which medical knowledge usually incorporates into a conception or strategy of treatment are first of all the universal, representative aspects, not those which are particular to an individual human body. The entire drug industry, and the production of other medical technologies, rest on statistically worked out and established standardized relations between classes of pathologies and matched categories of diagnosis and treatment. Doctors are expected, of course, to take into consideration the particulars of any individual patient in modulating levels and schedules of treatment. But the adjustment for each particular case is made in the context of generalized types of well recognized pathologies and their respective treatments. On a spectrum of illnesses between the pole where the symptoms and treatments of an illness are easily formalizable and the pole representing symptoms and treatments which are hard to formalize and codify, the closer an illness is to the former, the more technicalized is the treatment.[14] The more technical the treatment, the easier it is for a doctor to match prescriptions to a patient's condition. In highly standardized contexts it is easier for both doctors and patients to view treatment as action which represents what the patient would have liked to do in the given situation if he or she only had the skill or resources. It is in this sense that technicalization of action enhances its "representativeness."

Scientific constructions of regularities in phenomena are in fact a powerful instrument for standardizing vast fields of experience for the purpose of establishing technical, and in the above sense representative, modes of action. Categories such as "heart patients," "diabetics," and "schizophrenics" in medicine, or "average I.Q.," "low-income families," and the "functionally illiterate" in other fields, stand for regularities which are extensively used in our society to establish instrumental rationales for standardized (representative) treatments, policies, and programs. What Daniel J. Boorstin aptly calls "statistical communities"[15] can be regarded as modern devices for substantiating the deployment of standardized instrumental modes of action in the public (and private) sphere of modern societies. In addition to statistical communities that warrant specialized standardized policies and procedures, some such as "consumers," "television viewers," or "taxpayers" are sufficiently encompassing to facilitate the extended application of certain generalized standard instrumental orientations almost to the entire society. Such large problems as environmental pollution and health hazards are often handled even with reference to "humanity" as the relevant statistical community.

In their attempts to devise methods for controlling the environment, reducing health hazards, or advancing the technologies of transportation, communication, or energy production, scientists are commonly perceived as acting for all people, like a vanguard army in the human struggle for survival against common obstacles. The assumption underlying the representativeness of technical action is connected, therefore, with the notion that science, as the intellectual construction of general regularities, is both a universal enterprise and—at least potentially—the ground of universal actions. Technical modernization has been typically regarded from this perspective as a chapter in human history, not just in the history of a particular society.[16] The potential representativeness of technological action in this sense is indicated by the fact that great technological breakthroughs such as the invention of the steam engine, electric power, the smallpox vaccination, or the space rocket are commonly viewed as achievements of human civilization, as indicators of human progress, stages in the universal drama of the human encounter with natural forces. It is largely because of the wider cultural validity ascribed to actions based on science and technology that political actors so often attempt to present their actions as consistent with universally shared values by appealing to the authorities of science and technology. As we shall see in Part III, the validity and social influence of this perspective has been seriously challenged in the closing decades of the twentieth century by a view which tends to regard technology as the embodiment of particular cultural and political values rather than the mirror of a common extracultural natural base.

The literature on the relations between representation and professional authority is surprisingly sparse. Harold F. Gosnell is one of the few who has made the point that professionals represent, in some sense, the people on behalf of whom they act. Gosnell suggests that "any specialization of functions involves the idea of representation . . . A specialist is one who takes better care of certain of the peoples' interests than they could if they assumed the task themselves."[17] The people may not wish, says Gosnell, to undertake the inconvenient investment of resources required in order to exercise the necessary skills themselves. "An engineer," he notes, "represents his clients in his work, as does a doctor his patient."[18] Representing an individual in society is a condition which exists "when the characteristics and the acts of a person in a position of power . . . are in accord with the desires, expressed and unexpressed, of the individual."[19] From the perspective of liberal-democratic theory and practice, this concept of representation is, as Hanna Pitkin notes, problematic. When experts or specialists act as superior guardians of other persons in the way that adults look after small children, she asserts, they do not act as representatives. The liberal-democratic notion of representation implies equivalence between the representative and the represented, a condition without which the former cannot be conceived as substituting for the latter.[20]

Still, the notion that experts are in some sense representative adds, as Pitkin suggests, a dimension to classical concepts of representation which stress formal authorization. What formal authorization usually leaves out are the substantive criteria for evaluating the extent to which the actions of authorized agents are adequate.[21] Such substantive criteria are relevant for determining whether representative actors are indeed "acting for" those who authorized them. The distinction between formal and substantive representation suggests a distinction between representing persons and acting in their interests. I would subscribe to Pitkin's view that in liberal-democratic political theory representing is a mixture of formal and substantive factors, of valid authorization of representatives and of substantive actions they take "for" the represented. "A true expert taking care of a helpless child is not representative," notes Pitkin, "and a man who merely consults and reflects without acting is not representing in the sense of substantially acting."[22]

There are some tensions, however, between representing persons and acting for their interests, between Madisonian and Burkean concepts of representation.[23] To stress, along utilitarian lines, that representing is substantially acting for rather than standing in place of, mirroring, or substituting for other persons is to stress action as a means to advance interests. Instrumentalism is clearly biased in this direction, engaging the concept of representation as acting for interests rather than as reflecting persons. Insofar as the concept of individual interest could be thought of as allowing a notion of the public interest as an aggregate deducible from individual interests—without requiring that individual persons actually form a corporate body—public actions could be regarded not only as substantively instrumental, but also as representative in a sense consistent with liberal-democratic principles.

Often, of course, the substantive concept of representation has been invoked to defend the representativeness of instrumental actions even when conditions of formal authorization are lacking. In a constitutional democracy, however, substantive representation through concrete actions is inevitably checked by the imperatives of formal authorization through established political and legal procedures.

Instrumentalism has then an ambivalent theoretical and practical significance in the context of representation. Substantive representation may clash with formal representation; what makes government actions instrumental in relation to public goals can undermine what politically and legally authorizes the government to act. Still under some circumstances instrumental effectiveness or functional representation becomes a part of political legitimation, and "technicalizing" public action can contribute to the political rhetoric and claims of representation, particularly when it facilitates the alienation of actions from agents so that these actions can be seen as "owned" by others for whom the agents supposedly act.[24]

The credibility of instrumental actions as representative is limited, however, by conditions which ensure a degree of stability and consensus in both the goals of action and the body of knowledge which is used to objectify actions as means. Frequent shifts in the normative and cognitive parameters of public actions can diminish the authority of instrumental norms in the context of public action. Dissent over the goals of public policy, as well as controversies among experts concerning the appropriate measures to advance such goals, undermine the power of scientific and technical norms to substantiate the claim of the public authority that it is acting for the public as a dispassionate agent. Once the resources for depersonalizing and objectifying public actions are depleted, actors find it more difficult to persuade their audience that their actions do not stem from personal or partisan political considerations.[25]

In the context of public affairs, technical actions, to be sure, have always been a species of political action. The uses of science and technology to "depoliticize" action have been among the most potent *political* strategies in the modern state. The authority of this strategy has been sustained by the illusion that social and political problems like scientific problems are inherently solvable. As Bertrand de Jouvenel indicates, however, political problems can never be solved; at best they can only be settled.[26] Yet the authority to settle rather than to solve implies the exercise of discretion and judgment beyond the constraints of calculations and mechanical applications. It constitutes therefore a weaker basis for assuring citizens that their leaders, like their doctors, act for them, that their actions are sufficiently alienable from the personal subjective values and interests of the agents to ensure their representative qualities. What makes strictly mechanical, nondiscretionary actions acceptable to modern sensibilities is the assumption that the actors who carry them out do not exercise personal authority; that insofar as they follow an algorithm rather than a judgment they are just carrying out a task within a system of functional divisions of labor and not of hierarchical authority. Considerations of political legitimation at least partly underlie the modern tendency to substitute functional-instrumental for personal or political rationales of action and replace hierarchy and political patronage by expertise and technical competence as the basis for the modern civil service. If patronage disciplines action through personal and political loyalties, modern professionalized civil service has suggested an alternate way to ensure the capacity of public agencies to act for the citizens by depersonalizing and depoliticizing their actions as objective measures. Again, then, the uses of science and technology in the context of public action suggest their latent political and ideological function in upholding instrumentalism as a basis of authoritative and accountable structures of action, and in resolving the liberal-democratic problem of making individual persons appear as trustworthy agents of public actions.

The function of science and technology in securing the discipline and integrity of the actions of both private and public agents has had a profound impact on the very concept of politics in the modern liberal-democratic state. The instrumental concept of politics and its complementary ethic of public action have often been taken to suggest that as distinct from *technical* action, *political* action is inherently nonfunctional, nonpublic, and partisan. Paradoxically, instrumentalism has succeeded in partially reversing the relative status of private and public actors, making the former appear at times the more "apolitical" and trusted agents of public actions. The tendency to equate political with subjective partisan motives and the readiness to view experts, technicians, and even business executives as trusted modern agents of public action have in fact empowered instrumentalization as a strategy for restraining political actions and enveloping them in the rhetoric and morality of politically disinterested public actions. The virtues of the dispassionate skillful expert have come to be at least partially generalizable as the ideal virtues of political actors. This trend has encouraged a separation between the public and the political aspects of action, thus opening the way for depoliticization as a modern way of making public action virtuous. Replacing professional external for moral internal controls as guarantors of the public character of action has at least temporarily made science appear in wide circles as a more adequate and reliable standard of impersonal-representative public action than politics.

In the long run, however, the depoliticization of public action in the liberal-democratic state was bound to generate new tensions. The substitution of competence and skill for morality and personality could not be regarded as an improvement by those democrats who, with Rousseau, seek to base the good polity on "noble actions."[27] Although instrumentalism has furnished a method to discipline decentralized actions, and to democratically rationalize centralized ones, when carried too far it seems to undermine the humanistic moral perspective on politics and the commitment to the centrality of agency in the theory of action, a perspective which has remained a fundamental liberal-democratic commitment. Such diverse writers as Hannah Arendt, Bernard Crick, Moses Finley, and Hans Eulau have found it necessary to defend the integrity of the moral political grounds of public action against the excessive invasion of instrumental norms.[28] Supported by the humanistic strain in the liberal-democratic tradition, the impulse to reassert the primacy of the political over the apolitical component of public action has, particularly since the 1960s, become a principal force behind the attacks on the role of science and technology in public affairs and the reassertion of the value of authentic political participation with its implicit distrust of representative instrumentalism. Against earlier trends to instrumentalize, this new orientation has supported countertrends to repoliticize public action. The new pressures to "politicize" and "ideologize" the role of science in our culture indicate a *loss* of trust in the force of scientific and technical standards to secure the "objectivity," "impersonality," "representativeness," and "public-regardedness" of actions. From a historical perspective, such trends and countertrends to instrumentalize and deinstrumentalize public action imply different concepts of what constitutes a politically legitimate action. As we shall see presently, they also represent different notions of how to hold public actors accountable.

Science and the Accountability of Democratic Political Actors

The functions of science—and the authority of knowledge—in depersonalizing actions or in rendering them instrumentally representative relate to the ways in which particular individuals, in both the private and the public sectors, can generate trust as agents of public actions. Underlying these processes, of course, is a larger liberal-democratic theory of political accountability which specifies the conditions for the authorization of public agents and the legitimation of their actions. Distinct political worlds give rise to distinct modes of conceiving and of describing political action, to different methods of pinning blame on actors or of crediting them for what they do or do not do. Such differences reflect variations in the ways actions as cultural, political constructs become factors in the distribution of authority, power, and reputation among political actors. To reconstruct the ways in which actors, actions, and their perceived effects and relevant social groups are connected is to discern the accountability system which regulates action in a given polity. Accountability systems are clusters of behaviors, epistemological commitments, metaphors, values, and institutional practices which give meaning to what actors do and sustain the processes through which actions are attributed to agents and then legitimated or criticized. In any given political world, therefore, the ascription of causes and responsibilities in the field of action reflects the particular beliefs and attitudes with which this political world is put together. To "trace" the accountabilities of actors is in each case to reconstruct the particular ways in which actions are integrated into the ascriptions of credit or blame in the political sphere.[29]

As a cultural method of blaming or crediting actors, witchcraft, for instance, has been acceptable in some and not in other societies. But in any social context in which it has been employed, witchcraft is adapted to fit particular commitments and conditions. In the Azanda society investigated by Evans Pritchard, "It availed a bad craftsman nothing to claim that a witch made his tools slip. To blame witchcraft for bad technical performance would only arouse laughter. And the same for moral responsibility. It availed an adulterer nothing to protest to the injured husband that a witch caused him to commit adultery . . . the kind of disasters that could be charged to witches were limited so as not to drain personal responsibility out of the system."[30]

As a way of connecting actors, actions, and their supposed effects and publics, scientific concepts of causality, like those of witchcraft, are modified, edited, and therefore partly transformed in any given sociopolitical context of action. In modern democratic societies, for instance, attempts to trace the "causes" of differences in average I.Q. levels to genetic-hereditary factors have been met with fierce resistance.[31] An entrenched commitment to the values of equality has imposed severe constraints on the acceptability of hereditary biological accounts of individual or group differences in intellectual performance.

Similarly, in the Western legal tradition, a commitment to view society as a system of interactions among autonomous agents has restricted the penetration of scientific notions of causation. Legal theorists recognize that when raised in courts, questions about causal links are not purely questions of fact but a blend of fact and policy.[32] The tracing of causes in the judicial context is restricted, for instance, by concern for attributing and distributing responsibilities and doing justice within certain time limits. No such constraints limit the reconstruction of chains of causes and effects in the context of scientific research. There may be a deadline for doing justice but there is no deadline for ending the intellectual search for truth.

Within the particular limits imposed by social and political conditions, modern science has played a central role in the development of liberal-democratic modes of holding political actors accountable. No doubt the belief that science, unlike magic, astrology, or theology, is a form of public knowledge has contributed significantly to this development.[33] Noting the declining trust in magic and the triumph of mechanical philosophy in seventeenth-century England, Keith Thomas observed that "the new science carried with it an insistence that all truths be demonstrated, an emphasis on the need for direct experience and a disinclination to accept inherited dogmas without putting them to the test."[34] Since the early modern era the notion that practical experience constantly tests the relative standing of competing claims or arguments has made it possible to integrate the field of action into humanistic disciplines such as philosophy and rhetoric, thus investing it with a new dignity. Early humanist writers already rejected the Aristotelian dichotomy of action and speculation and the hierarchy of philosophy and the arts, intellectual and manual enterprises. They valued "knowledge in use," both to improve and perfect life and to enhance the spiritual significance of action.[35] As Paulo Rossi notes, this shift in the perspective on the relations between knowledge and action was associated with the idea of knowledge as construction, an idea advanced by Giambattista Vico that "we hold to be true in nature only that to which by way of experiment, we succeed in constructing something similar . . . We demonstrate a truth to the measure that we make it."[36] "Just as God is the artifice of nature," notes Vico, "so is man of the things formed by art."[37]

The partial fusion of natural philosophy with the subculture of craft and practical action has given rise in the Western tradition to a concept of action which both dignifies manual labor and forces abstract ideas to undergo the "lower" practical test of experience. As a meeting ground between theory and practice, "head and hand," technical action could be integrated as an element in the rhetoric of truth while natural philosophy (science) could emerge as an element in the rhetoric and the justification of practical action. The idea of knowledge as construction could support the idea of action both as an expression of higher human capacities for freedom and reason and as a kind of performance which functions as a rhetorical device for persuading a public of observing spectators to adopt certain claims and to reject others.[38]

The perceived historical role of experiments in the advancement of knowledge, and later of machines in the industrial revolution, has socially enhanced the rhetorical power of instruments and technical operations to authorize claims not only in the context of science but also in wider areas of discourse. The idea of knowledge as something developed and demonstrated in building and operating machines, an idea that has rationalized action as an integral ingredient of modern modes of persuasion, has increasingly challenged earlier rhetorical traditions according to which knowledge is something that emerges in contemplation, in discourse, or in texts. The modern idea was central to the works of humanist masters such as Alberti, Agricola, and Vesalius, who combined natural philosophy with the mechanical arts, the intellectual goals of contemplation, and the pursuit of control. In his De re metallica (1556), Agricola sought to dignify art by insisting on its philosophic and scientific aspects;[39] Vesalius used the anatomist's hand to extend the domain of the eye and bring into the open the hidden truths about the fabric of the human body. Similarly, for Alberti and Palladio architecture was the art of embodying cosmic principles in material objects.[40] The fusion of philosophy and craft empowered fields such as mechanics, anatomy, and architecture to serve the rhetoric and pedagogy of truth. These arts were increasingly considered, therefore, as superior to alchemy, magic, and astrology, which Bacon criticized for drawing "little light from philosophy" and for holding "much more of imagination and belief than of sense of demonstration."[41] Consistent with this tradition, a thinker like Andreas Libavious stressed in the early years of the seventeenth century a civic humanistic notion of the public character of knowledge.

He criticized Paracelsus and Croll for cultivating the affinities between technical knowledge and traditions of religious enthusiasm and political radicalism, and he objected to Tycho Brahe's associating the pursuit of knowledge with secluded contemplation and aristocratic aloofness.[42]

Instrumentalism as a modern paradigm of political action and the derivative methods by which political actors are held accountable in liberal-democratic systems draw upon these converging traditions of "philosophizing" the technical arts and subordinating philosophy to the practical tests of action. Political action could emerge therefore simultaneously as the expression of human freedom and a rhetorical enterprise, the realization of the human capacity for generating voluntary actions disciplined by knowledge, and the casting of action as a "performance" that tests ideas and has objective features rendering it open to the "judgment of history," or the judgment of an observing public. The humanistic response to the tendency to downgrade this-worldly materialistic dimensions of experience in the classical, Christian or aristocratic traditions was to appropriate the material domain as a theater for the expression of the individual's divine capacity to shape and construct and to render human freedom and knowledge visible by means of observable things and operations. The significant rhetorical function of visible actions and operations was already stated by Francis Bacon who held that, as a method of presentation and persuasion, "examining" is superior to "telling."[43] Bacon also stressed the pivotal role of action in substantiating the rhetoric of knowledge claims, or of truth, in his assertion that "works must be esteemed more as pledges of truth than for the comforts of life they afford."[44] From Machiavelli through Hobbes and Bentham to Dewey and Keynes, the character of action as a technically disciplined expression of the freedom to shape sociopolitical realities becomes also a potent rhetorical means for the self-legitimation of action. Once the expression of power in action appears to be governed by knowledge or instrumental logic, it projects itself as restrained and nonarbitrary, respectful of the strictures imposed by natural and social realities and assuming, therefore, a public character.

As long as access to the power to manipulate the natural "materials" of politics, and the authority of individuals to serve as witnesses to such actions, remained confined—as in Machiavelli's *Prince*—to the privileged few, as long as the idea of instrumental politics could combine skill and freedom of action without forcing the actor to become publicly exposed, political instrumentalism could still be compatible with monarchic or aristocratic political structures. Similarly in the case of science, the "public space" of the experiments performed and witnessed during the second half of the seventeenth century in scientific forums such as the Academia del Cimento or the Royal Society was at first confined within a reciprocally trusting yet sharply bounded community of gentlemen.[45] In the contexts of both science and politics, however, a progressive social expansion of the public spaces in which actions are performed and witnessed led eventually to the emergence of technological and political actions as public spectacles.[46] As I shall show in greater detail, the standardization of modes of visually presenting, observing, and reporting actions and the expanding, progressively inclusive community of spectators have defined and institutionalized the modern democratic sociocultural space—the public stage or the site—of the public actions and events which have become the focus of common life in liberal-democratic societies.

Contributing to the latter development has been a process of separating the skills required for performing public actions from the simpler ones for judging by the perceived consequences of these actions whether they are successful or not. It is in conjunction with the sociocultural formation of the modern "public space" that technological success has become a more readily "democratic" basis for judging the acceptability of claims than metaphysical referents, logic, refined empirical analysis, or mathematical proofs. Visible technological events such as the dramatic balloon flights, which made Lavoisier's claims about invisible gases publicly acceptable, have demonstrated the rhetorical force of materialist referents.[47] In the case of politics, any visible instrumental indicators of success have furnished similar advantages. The instrumentalization of public actions, their embodiment in technical operations, has provided more democratic modes of addressing the public, of socially validating claims, and of depersonalizing and legitimating the uses of political power. Instrumental orientations have made it possible to present and perceive public actions and events as a series of encounters between agents and a world of facts in which they try to advance certain goals. As distinct from the way actions are presented and perceived within a dramaturgical orientation toward politics as a clash of personalities, in the context of instrumental orientations actors are perceived as performing tasks which require both respect for impartial judgment of circumstances and the mastery of skills. Insofar as the results of such instrumental actions are not fully predictable, and as long as competent actors are presumed capable of learning from their experience, the open-ended context of action, like the context of scientific experiments, subordinates the authority of claims made by agents to their ability to render actions into persuasive demonstrations of the adequacy of their performance and their ideas. The authority of the inherently invisible ideas thus appears to be at least partly dependent upon the force of visible referents in a public-perceptual space.

While scientific instrumentalism elevates the actor as agent vis-à-vis the world of objects, political instrumentalism implies a problematic distinction between the agent who acts and other persons who are the subject of these acts. Political experimentalism encourages a manipulative orientation toward other persons who are treated more as facts or objects to be reckoned with than as moral agents. In the context of the liberal-democratic commitment to the idea of citizens as free moral agents, the manipulative orientations implicit in instrumental-experimental approaches to public action therefore constitute a problem.

The liberal-democratic justification of instrumentalism has been constrained by the need to reckon with this perceived association of an instrumental approach to public actions with manipulative orientations toward other persons. Machiavelli and Hobbes were widely interpreted as saying that in order to anticipate and effectively influence political behavior one should not be distracted by an idealized moral view of humanity. One should recognize instead human beings' true ugly nature, egotism, and propensity to violence, as well as the influence of fear on their conduct. The integration of instrumental values into liberal-democratic concepts of authoritative and accountable action has required, therefore, that the association between instrumentalism and negative images of humanity, as well as manipulative orientations on the part of rulers, be balanced, neutralized, or reinterpreted. Such attempts to reconcile instrumental (scientific and technical) approaches to political action and liberal-democratic values have been made at least since the early modern era. Key elements in these attempts can be found already in early (including nonliberal or nondemocratic) articulations of the instrumental approach to politics. They include, among other arguments, the utilitarian justification of instrumentalism, the assertion that instrumentalism upholds a democratic epistemological notion of action as socially accessible fact, and a behavioral rationale for instrumentalism as a form of nonarbitrary restraint on conduct.

For Machiavelli and Hobbes, for example, a negative image of humanity is compensated by the belief that insofar as the image reveals the true logic of human behavior, it opens the way for checking the influence of chance in public affairs and for rationally, that is, instrumentally, promoting shared goals such as order, stability, and security. In the early noninstrumental model of liberal, public action, what I called above involuntary equilibrium or spontaneous aggregation of individual actions into collective acts as imagined in Mandeville's *Fable of the Bees* (1723), it is not the moral virtues of individual actors that ensure the public good but private vices (egoistic behavior) which, although not deliberately, are causally connected so that they bring about public benefits. In the instrumental models of liberal-democratic public action (both the decentralized and the centralized ones), the assumption about the causal links between what is regarded as the true principles of human behavior and public benefits persists. The difference is that such links are not conceived as automatic but as dependent upon deliberate interventions on the part of free yet knowledgeable agents. Voluntaristic concepts of action and utilitarian rationales could thus be integrated into such a framework in order to defend the democratic character of instrumental approaches to public actions despite the association with negative images of human nature and manipulative orientations toward other persons.

Such attitudes still leave open the question of how the actions of instrumentally oriented actors could be acceptable in terms of liberal-democratic values while the role of moral restraint in checking arbitrary action is discarded as unnatural or utopian. One way of coping with this problem has been to imply that while morality is not a force that can be counted on to check arbitrary actions, technical-instrumental discipline is. The virtues of the "good" prince according to Machiavelli are not the noble qualities of a good person but the ones congenial for an effective actor.[48] Moral restraint is characteristically replaced here by technical skill and discipline. A good prince is not the personally honest one but the one whose acts are disciplined by instrumental considerations for the enhancement of effectiveness. Politically the replacement of moral restraint by technical discipline made it possible to endorse instrumentally guided actions as a category of actions which, consistent with liberal-democratic norms, are neither arbitrary nor controlled by passions or personal caprice. The implied shift from judging actions in terms of their agents to judging them in terms of their more apparent ends, or consequences, has opened the way for legitimating political instrumentalism not only as the rationale of the actions of the prince, or other privileged actors, but also as a rationale of democratic political participation.

Once "those who would know how to govern" are preferred over those who merely have the "right to govern,"[49] once acquired skills and techniques become relevant to the exercise of political power, aristocratic prerogatives of special access become more vulnerable. Moreover, the negation of supernatural powers and the demystification of action, the assumption that any human mastery and control are inherently limited by the "resistance" of nature, further undercuts maximalist claims of authority.

Beyond the utilitarian justification of instrumentalism as serving the public good and the rationale for instrumentalism as a form of non-arbitrary, restrained action, the attempts to harmonize instrumental values and liberal-democratic political concepts of action and accountability were supported also by the epistemological justification of instrumental actions as publicly observable. Appearing to shift the focus of political action from the drama of clashing agents to a disenchanted confrontation between rational actors and an at least partly knowable, lawful world of facts, instrumentalism has implied that political actions are transparent and discernible. Actions conceived as causes chosen to produce desirable results could be presented as demystified and accessible events without the burden of hidden motives and sinister agents. As technical actions they could appear to render agents more publicly accountable than personally, morally, or religiously motivated ones.

While within the religious paradigm of action, accountabilities are typically traced to transcendental referents, and invisible agents and conduct are judged with reference to the socially elusive inner motives of actors, within the instrumental paradigm of action what becomes relevant are the external aspects of behavior. Underlying the religious paradigm is a vertical, not horizontal, structure of accountability: "For the Lord seeth not as man seeth; for man looketh on the outward appearance, but the Lord looketh on the heart" (I Sam. 16:7).

The rise of modern natural—and later social—sciences authorizes human knowledge based on observing the outward surface of things, their external appearances. Once extended into the political field of public affairs, this perspective empowers instrumentalism because it "externalizes" human action as a relation of causes and effects, thus defining it as an enterprise which people can "see" and therefore judge. As such, instrumentalization democratizes the epistemological status of political public actions. Instrumentalizing political action together with the wider trend—evident especially in the tradition of English liberalism since Locke—to "materialize" or "concretize" politics by references to "outward things" (such as private property) can be regarded, from this perspective, as complementary attempts to ground politics in the domain of common sense perception and substitute this-worldly horizontal accountabilities for other-worldly vertical ones.[50]

The accent on the materiality and the visibility of action is associated closely with the evolution and authorization, in the context of modern scientific forums, of novel modes of persuasion which, in the words of Thomas Sprat, prefer the "silent force of experiments" over the "pomp of words." The inscription on the coat of arms of the Royal Society of London, *Nullius in Verba,* is perhaps the most explicit articulation of the ideal of a "rhetoric of action," persuasion based on visible operations, as distinct from and superior to the rhetoric of speech or texts.[51] The authority of instrumentalism draws upon this tradition, which enlists operations to support claims made in public forums. As such, instrumental action has rhetorical force lacking in legal action, which draws its authority from the increasingly demystified human scriptures of legal texts. It is useful to recall in this connection that the word "fact" comes from the Latin *factum,* denoting a deed or an act. The force of the word "fact" in the Western tradition reflects to a certain degree the superior powers attributed to acts relative to words in representing persons.

This stress on the factual, the outward visible aspects of action as a referent for authorizing claims and behaviors in the contexts of science and politics, is meant not only to differentiate fields of discourse and action from the invisible referents postulated by religious authority but also to protect horizontal accountabilities from their susceptibility to degenerate through overpersonalization, excessive subjectivity, arbitrariness, and fantasy. The function of visibility in checking the "corruptive" effects of grounding action in subjective, publicly unaccountable referents is illustrated in the ambivalence shown in the liberal-democratic tradition toward authorizing actions as the dictates of one's own conscience. In some contexts, of course, the subjectivity of individual conscience is tempered by socially conventionalized models of conscience-governed behavior. The social authority of conscience can depend on the presence of "a motive beyond self-interest."[52] But the fact that even a nonanarchistic, nonradical concept of the moral conscience is a concomitant of political pluralism suggests the difficulties of integrating it into liberal-democratic systems of horizontal accountability.[53] As is illustrated in cases of conscientious objection, conscience is not so much a bridge between the actor, a subjective individual, and the public realm of political action as it is a fence protecting the integrity of the individual as the ultimate source of judgment against the invasions of external authorities. To the extent that the liberal-democratic conception of the public sphere is grounded in a multiplicity of such private domains of individual judgment, individual conscience cannot be rejected as a principle of action underlying the accountability of the individual to oneself, but neither can it be endorsed as a satisfactory framework for holding actors accountable to their peers, which is the principal form of accountability in democracy.

The power of instrumentalism as a structure of accountability lies precisely in substantiating accountability to one's peers as an alternative to accountability to one's superiors and as complementary to the self-referential standards of accountability to oneself, thus affirming, beyond individual conscience, the authority of impersonal external referents of action. Insofar as the scientific-instrumentalist approach stresses the moral neutrality of the world as a body of public facts, it creates a sociocultural space for action as something constrained by impersonal external givens and something observable and assessable by persons who are at least partly conceived as detached observers. These features stand out when one juxtaposes the cultural norms of scientific and technical enterprises with those of art in our society. Whereas scientific and technical works are normally validated in modern society with reference to "impersonal" bodies of knowledge, the value attached to artistic works and their interpretations are often mediated by references to the personal traits and the unique individual features of the artist. Unlike scientists and engineers, artists are not under comparable pressures to depersonalize their claims and actions by reference to impersonal public facts. Unlike scientists and engineers, artists represent the license in our society, within certain confines, to subordinate functional adequacy and instrumental values to aesthetic values and the free entertainment of fiction. It is precisely this lack of disciplined referents in the external world which suggested to people who lived in interbellum Europe, such as Karl Kraus and Walter Benjamin, that the aestheticization of politics can lead to corruption and irresponsibility, and that the legitimate sphere of art is the domain of individual experience where one does not have to be answerable to others.[54]

The modern tendency to view art and science as representing the polar opposites of the private and public realms, this contrast of subjectivity, imagination, and temporality with objectivity, reason, and timelessness, was clearly stated by Turgot when he asserted that "the knowledge of nature and of the truth are as infinite as they are. The arts, whose object it is to please us, are limited as we are."[55] (Of course, the sociocultural status of art as a domain of subjective self-expression, the "unaccountability" of modern artists, is a feature of art in a particular historical moment. Renaissance masters operated within an entirely different cultural framework.[56])

I have suggested that, while in the context of the decentralized variant of liberal-democratic public action, instrumentalism plays an important political role in suggesting a way to cement the actions of discrete agents, in the context of the centralized variant, its primary political role is to ensure that the few who act remain significantly dependent upon the many who can only observe. In the contexts of both the decentralized and centralized variants of liberal-democratic public action, instrumental norms imply a commitment to the idea that public actions are deliberate, that their agents are free, and that their freedom is constrained by at least partly knowable causal chains. Underlying the integration of instrumental and liberal-democratic political values, then, is the belief that objective causal connections both constrain the subjectivity and arbitrariness of free agents and permit them to objectify their acts and render them public in a universally accessible world of facts.

The presumption of the human ability both to understand causation and to be a cause furnishes here a basis for a concept of action which integrates scientific notions of necessary causality with voluntaristic theories of action. The image of the state as something constructed like a machine could be reconciled, from this perspective, with a humanistic view of human action.[57] Whereas Christian thinkers often ascribed righteous government to divine grace, Renaissance humanists tended to stress the dependence of politics on the human being conceived in anti-Augustinian naturalistic terms and on the exercise of human faculties.[58] Like the figures in Giotto's paintings—

so remarkable against the backdrop of contemporary medieval conventions—the citizens in the modern polity are conceived as natural, not idealized persons. In the Renaissance imagination, human beings are neither totally free to construct the polity according to their will nor fated to complete submissiveness to external causes. They are not completely autonomous nor fully determined. Poised between these two polar states, human actions emerge as part of the drama of humanity's struggle against fate, a series of relentless attempts to assert and exercise freedom and intelligence in the face of implacable necessities and contingencies, a story both of conquests achieved by the successful exercise of practical wisdom, skill, and will and of defeats exposing the limits of man.

This dualism of agency and world, of freedom and causation, has been essential to the possibility of assimilating an instrumental concept of action and an idea of humans as free makers of things, without denying the tragic element of their fate as creatures partially chained by necessities. According to Hobbes, the state is a voluntary artificial construct aided by "devices and designs taken from nature and driven by natural necessities." [59] Man becomes lord of nature, according to Bacon, only insofar as he is its servant and interpreter. [60] Thus, people have a measure of responsibility for their fate. Failure, which is blamed not only on the objective limits of human knowledge and control but also on rashness, frivolity, or lack of humility before the facts, was mythologized in Icarus' misguided flight. It was illustrated also by such earthly equivalents as the French engineer Bertrand de la Coste, who in 1671 was humiliated by the French Academy of Science after failing to back up his claim to have discovered the secret of perpetual motion. [61]

Machiavelli applies similar standards of "realistic" instrumentalism in the political sphere. Acknowledging that the materials of political world making condemn political actors to a relentless struggle against the resistance of natural forces and the uncertainties imposed by chance on the possibilities of order, he too notes that "our free will may not be altogether extinguished. I think it may be true that fortune is the ruler of half our actions, but she allows the other half or thereabouts to be governed by us." [62] Politics can be at least partly tamed and directed. Machiavelli compares the violent forces of chance and disorder to "an impetuous river that when turbulent, inundates the plains, casts down trees and buildings, removes earth from this and places it on the other; everyone flees before it and everything yields to its fury without being able to oppose it; and yet," he insists, "though it is of such a kind still when it is quiet, man can make provision against it by dykes and banks so that when it rises it will either go into a canal or its rush will not be so wild and dangerous."[63] As a political crafts-man, Machiavelli's trained prince can construct and control within limits imposed by fortune. Like a craftsman his actions, informed by knowledge, mediate between freedom and constraint, ideas and matter.

Religion, morality, law, art, and science furnish, then, distinct cultural models of accountability and different modes of connecting actors, their actions, their publics, and the procedures employed for distributing credit, reputation, or blame. I have tried to show how by upholding instrumental paradigms of public action science and tech-nology have come to play an important role in the construction of modern liberal-democratic actions and accountabilities. The force of instrumentalism as the extension of scientific-technical standards of action into the public sphere of the liberal-democratic state has largely stemmed from this latent political function of science and technology to externalize the grounds of action and uphold hori-zontal rather than hierarchical or self-referential accountabilities. But as an orientation to the organization of public action, scientific instru-mentalism does considerably more than support liberal-democratic forms of accountability. It has, in fact, supported the rise of demo-cratic politics as "a view," as an ongoing series of performances in the domain of public perceptions. The emergence of the public domain as the theater of democratic politics, conceived as an ongoing spectacle, is inseparable from the rise of the modern public as a political force.

3. Science and the Visual Culture of Liberal-Democratic Politics

The liberal-democratic tradition has generally rejected claims of certain historical, social, or political knowledge. The criticism of such claims has been associated with liberal-democratic commitments to an open society, freedoms of speech and association, tolerance, and the decentralization of political power. Still, liberal-democratic concepts of representative and accountable political authority have tended to encourage—and be supported by—optimistic theories of political knowledge. The possibility of knowing other persons and of understanding and judging their actions has been an important condition for the belief that some persons can act as representatives for others and that political agents can be held accountable to the public. This faith has been upheld in the liberal-democratic tradition by an optimistic political epistemology, according to which politics consists of actions or events that are observable and reportable as public facts.

Viewed from this perspective, what makes political action public in the liberal-democratic polity has not been merely that it is an action taken to further public goals or action taken by public agents. A public action is also that which is accessible in some sense to the perception of the wider public.

The perceived need to make political action public in this sense has increased with the decline of the early, liberal faith in the idea that the political order is the product of "natural" spontaneous equilibrium among discrete actors or institutions. The growing recognition of the necessity of continual intervention—actions calculated to maintain the political order and to advance particular objectives—posed the need for a new synthesis between the liberal-democratic commitment to voluntary political agencies and the desire to ensure that their actions are not arbitrary, capricious, or destructive to shared goals. This shift between passive and active, or what John Dewey called "old" and "new" liberalism, implied a change in the role of science as a political resource.[1] Whereas in the context of the old liberalism science served to rationalize conformism to "natural regularities" and therefore to delegitimate government interventions as "artificial" acts which may disrupt the natural equilibrium, in the context of the new liberalism the ideological and the political uses of science have shifted toward legitimating such "artificial" interventions as technically disciplined, rational measures to correct or improve imperfect natural states. This change in the direction of a more activist-interventionist theory of political or state action has inevitably increased the perceived gap between the liberal-democratic ideals of universal political participation and the realities of government by the few. It is in this very context that making the actions of a few politically authorized agents publicly transparent could acquire so much importance as a condition for ensuring that those agents be both representative and accountable.

Such gaps between ideals of equal participation and the realities of the unequal distribution of power have existed even in small local democratic communities, such as the New England town or the Israeli kibbutz, where size did not constitute a serious constraint on universal participation. The significance of making actions in some sense publicly visible has become more acute, however, as the growing size of the body of citizens and the territories over which they are dispersed has made the idea of government by the people appear increasingly impractical.

Such concerns for the feasibility of instituting a democratic system of government in a populous and territorially vast state were expressed by the early founders of the American republic.[2] The Federalists considered the principles of representation and divisible sovereignty as means to partially mitigating the tensions between the requirements of government in a populous and territorially extensive state and the imperatives of democratic accountability. I suggest that a no less important, although much less discussed, measure of reconciling the realities of an unequal distribution of power with the ideals of democratic participation has been the attempt to make politics a matter of, to use Thomas Paine's words, "simple facts, plain arguments and common sense."[3] This attempt rested upon one of the most central beliefs in modern Western culture, the belief that seeing is knowing, that visually experiencing the world is in some sense directly contacting its reality, that the truth about the world is largely inscribed, as it were, on the visible surface of the objects of our perception.

In many respects modern democracy is based on the extension of this belief to the domain of politics, that is, on the idea that politics is transparent, that political agents, political actions, and political power can be viewed. The notion of politics as an observable fact, "a view," an object of public perceptions, has become a central liberal-democratic ideological commitment despite the difficulties of defending it intellectually or sustaining it in practice. In some respects the acceptance of this idea has furnished an alternative both to utopian theories of participatory democracy and to nonparticipatory politics based on skeptical political epistemology.

The specifically Enlightenment variant of the liberal-democratic idea of politics as something "out there" which, like the physical world, can be at least partially known—scientifically—as a fact has had, of course, to compete with alternative views. Its distinctiveness stands out against such visions of politics as the one stressing the creative status of the agent in producing the political order while negating the "distance" required by the notion of the individual as a spectator.[4] It is in fact precisely against the difficulties of treating political acts as visible facts, like physical objects or events, that the extraordinary cultural construction of politics as something observable, and reportable by means of a designative language, assumes its full significance.

My purpose here is to examine the relations between authority, representation, and accountability. It is through these relations, I suspect, that we can understand the emergence of political action in modern mass democracies like America's as an ongoing public spectacle. I shall argue that the attempts to define the actions of public agents in technical instrumental terms can be construed as an integral part of a wider strategy to externalize and objectify political actions in the visual space of publicly perceived facts. I shall further suggest that the centrality of the eye and of acts of seeing and witnessing in liberal-democratic political discourse, and their metaphorical extensions in discussions of authority, representation, and accountability, are inseparable from the attempts to define politics as a realm of plain observable facts which are accessible to all the citizens conceived as spectators.

The Theatrics of Liberal-Democratic Action

In some sense, of course, all forms of politics exploit the field of perception for viewing the enactment, representation, and legitimation of political authority. Different strategies of political "world making" involve equally diverse ways of exploiting the sense of sight in order to concretize, project, and evoke support for authority. Tribal chiefs, kings and queens, presidents, prime ministers, and military dictators are all actors in distinct political theaters. As a dimension of the establishment and legitimation of political authority the theatrics of political spectacles is an integral part of the art of government. Statecraft is in some respects inseparable from stagecraft, and failures and successes in the latter often lead to respective failures and successes in the former.

The political spectacle of authority, the theatrical aspect of politics, is not so much a gloss over what is real in politics but very much the articulation of the norms and commitments underlying the political order. Even a brief examination of the kind of cultural codes that in any given political world fix the political functions of visual experiences and govern the meanings attributed to the relations between the visible and the invisible can provide important clues to the particular norms of seeing, observing, and displaying which have shaped liberal-democratic politics and influenced the latent political functions of science and technology in the modern democratic state.

It is important to note at the outset that our own ability to view the theatrical aspect of political action as the substance of politics, and not as just a representation or misrepresentation of political reality, has been inhibited by a predisposition in the Western cultural tradition to distinguish between the real and the fictitious and to classify the theatrical with the latter. It is largely on the basis of these distinctions that democrats such as Thomas Jefferson used to disparage monarchic politics as "theatrical." Like other democratic critics, Jefferson views monarchic stagecraft as the art of concealing political truths from the eyes of a public which can be "dazzled by the glittering of crowns and coronets."[5] Liberal-democratic criticism of nondemocratic systems of authority has typically attacked splendor and pomp as illegitimate theatrical means with which leaders try to conceal the truth.[6] Consequently, liberal-democratic authority has often tried to distinguish itself as being untheatrical in the sense of being honest, of rejecting the massive use of aesthetic persuasion and affective gestures for purposes of self-mystification or self-adornment. The self-presentation of authority as a neutral agent of instrumental public actions is in many ways the ultimate expression of this strategy of self-legitimation by claims of honest exposure; it is a particularly democratic genre of the theatrics of political action.

Inasmuch as we recognize the objective, real, factual, or technically rational to be just as culturally constructed—a sort of "collective hunch"[7]—as the fictitious, personal, and theatrical, we must recognize that the "realism," "instrumentalism," and "publicness" of liberal-democratic political actions are equally culturally and theatrically produced. The "real," in Clifford Geertz's apt observation, "is as imagined as the imaginary."[8] Liberal-democratic politics is neither a realm of incontestable publicly observable facts nor a "realistic theater" which can be judged in terms of its success or failure in mirroring such objective facts. The point is that in the liberal-democratic political universe "reality," as a strategically central, political construct, is defined as the aspect of an action that constitutes a neutral (supposedly apolitical) public check on the arbitrary—and theatrical—conduct of all agents. As such, factual reality is used in the liberal-democratic political universe to decentralize and restrain political power. It is precisely because reality in the context of nondemocratic political discourse serves other purposes, such as buttressing the claims of a hierarchical authority or any other "superagency" to have extraordinary—sometimes even magical—powers, that it is a profoundly different cultural construct. In nondemocratic political worlds the sense of sight would typically be employed not to establish factual reality as a potential check on the claims of political authority but rather to uphold epistemologically and adorn aesthetically as well as to celebrate its powers to defy the limits imposed by any extragovernmental social or public norms like "common sense" reality.

In some political orders the theatrical enactment of the structures of, and the links between, the cosmic and political universes is the controlling end of state spectacles. The spectacles of the nineteenth-century Balinese "theatre state" are an instructive illustration. According to Geertz, these seem to exemplify "power serving pomp rather than pomp power."[9] They project hierarchy in which rank derives from genealogy, not from deeds. "The state ceremonials of classical Bali were metaphysical theatre designed to express a view of the ultimate nature of reality."[10] They were designated to present, actualize, and enchant hierarchy.[11] The public space in which the political theater of the Balinese is visually enacted is not public in the Western sense, which, as Hans Speier notes, signifies the extension of the space of mass political participation, or, as Keith Baker puts it, the space of the tribunal of public opinion.[12] It is not an extension of the space of the people from the bottom up but "the extension of the sanctified space of the royal palace transformed into a temple." [13] The logic of the spectacles of the modern liberal-democratic state is based, by contrast, on a metaphysical theater designed to employ a disenchanted, demystified concept of public reality in order to "humanize," check, and level all political actors.

In the spectacles of state designed and produced by Inigo Jones for the Stuart kings, the controlling purpose is still the glory and extraordinary powers of the king.[14] As a means of monarchic ideology and propaganda, the Stuart court theater employs architecture, choreography, and technology in order to celebrate the king's extraordinary powers and project an enchanted public image, even in the face of the political and historical facts which may appear to contradict it. "If we can really see the king as the tamer of nature," writes Stephen Orgel, and "the queen as the goddess of flowers, there will be no problems about the Puritans or Ireland or ship money. Thus the ruler gradually redefines himself through the illusionist art, from a hero, the center of a court and of culture, to the god of power, the Center of the Universe." [15]

The visual field is used to display and celebrate hierarchy and is therefore controlled by the king's designer and architect. The hierarchic principle is manifest also in the placement of the spectators in relation to the show. Orgel stresses the fact that after 1605 perspective settings were used only when royalty was present. With such settings there is only one focal point, one perfect place in the hall from which the illusion of a single total vision achieves its fullest effect. This is where the king sat, and "the audience around him," in the apt language of Orgel, "at once became a living emblem of the structure of the court. The closer one sat to the monarch the 'better' one's place was, an index of one's status." [16] Except for the king each spectator has, therefore, only a partial visual scope. Orgel notes the importance the king's advisers ascribed not only to the king's seat as the only place from which there was such a perfect view but, even more important, to the other spectators' ability to view and recognize the king's privileged view of the stage.[17] In the monarchic theater, the uniquely privileged position of the king is further reflected in the fact that unlike all the other spectators he, the principal spectator, is also the only one who can take the stage and assume the role of the principal actor. This free crossing between the spaces, or the loci, of seeing and displaying reflects the central role of the king in controlling the spectacle.[18] The structure of the court theater implies, then, that a full vision does not consist of an aggregate of partial individual perspectives but is the superior, all encompassing vision of one person. This approximates, of course, a Platonic model of a hierarchy of perspectives which centralizes the claims of knowledge and authority at the top. Machiavelli articulates such a hierarchical view of knowledge when, in the dedication to *The Prince,* he notes that "in the same way that landscape painters station themselves in the valleys in order to draw mountains or high ground, and ascend an eminence in order to get a good view of the plains, so it is necessary to be a prince to know thoroughly the nature of the people." Machiavelli alludes, however, to the possibility of another kind of knowledge when he says that it is also necessary to be "one of the populace to know the nature of princes."[19] The point about the liberal-democratic notion of politics as a view is, indeed, the stress on the public's view of the government rather than on the government's view of the public.

As the visual enactment of an idealized image of the monarchy, the Stuart court theater exemplifies what may be called a *celebratory* visual frame, a "culture" of vision organized to induce wonder and admiration toward the powers and magnificence of authority. A central and most influential tradition of celebratory visual culture in the West has emerged, of course, in the Catholic church, which has employed the visual arts as a principal device for the glorification of divine authority and its earthly agencies. It is noteworthy, therefore, that in the context of the cultural and political conflict between court and country in seventeenth-century England, Charles I was a "High Anglican" who was very responsive to Catholic cultural strategies, and that the spread of the cultural and visual orientations which countered the court culture in English society was related to the country's opposition. The country's opposition, which was supported by puritans and moderate Anglicans, was an important force in the English revolution and the legitimation of anti-Catholic cultural orientations.[20] While, as can be instantly recognized by any visitor to St. Peter's Basilica in Rome, Catholicism brought to near perfection the art of producing aesthetic visual experiences which dwarf the spectators and fill them with awe toward superior powers, anti-Catholic and anticourt cultural orientations shifted powers from privileged performers to spectators.

While the visual cultural code which has governed the representation of monarchic authority is mainly "celebratory," I would like to suggest that the one which has come to govern the representation of liberal-democratic authority is by contrast largely "attestive." The principal orientation of the latter is not adulatory but descriptive and testimonial; the intention is not to glorify but to attest, record, account, analyze, confirm, disconfirm, explain, or demonstrate by showing and observing examples in a world of public facts. The stress is on displaying and seeing as elements of the enterprise of persuading critical spectators, not of swaying trusting worshipers. Socially supported by the norms of the successful modern experimental-scientific tradition as exemplified, for instance, in the philosophical theater of the Royal Society of London during the second half of the seventeenth century, the attestive visual code defines the eye as a dispassionate skeptical—rather than credulous—witness of facts. The attestive eye testifies to the existence of the observable world and its properties. It disconfirms claims which cannot be corroborated by what can be seen. It is not an eye that wonders or celebrates the magnificence of superagents or "wonderful" objects. The integrity of the attestive eye lies in its resistance to the evocative force of aesthetic visual experience and its ability to focus only on what is relevant to the confirmation or disconfirmation of statements about the state of the world.

Attestive visual culture presupposes, of course, a host of norms, ideas, institutions, and practices. It implies epistemological commitment to the reliability of seeing and its relevance to acts of knowing; it fixes standards of admissible visual evidence and acceptable testimonies and separates them from unacceptable ones; it determines which forms of displaying are consistent with the integrity of liberal-democratic canons of persuasion and which are not, what forms of language-use and rhetorical style are appropriate in discourse, which kinds of testimony are reliable, how acts of seeing enter into the confirmation or disconfirmation of the claims of agents, what the appropriate relations are between the performers of public acts and their spectators, and finally what qualities are demanded of the public as an aggregate of trustworthy spectators and witnesses. Attestive visual culture is implicitly committed to particular notions about the nature of the public space of visual perception and its legitimate uses for demonstrating and testing claims of knowledge.

"The Union of Eyes": The Experimental-Scientific Tradition and the Attestive Gaze

W. V. Quine notes that, like the Homeric view of the world, the scientific view of the world as a physical object is but a myth. Still, he goes on to observe that the "myth of physical objects is epistemologically superior to most in that it has proved more efficacious than other myths as a device for working a manageable structure into the flux of experience."[21] As a bundle of social practices science and technology have, no doubt, played a crucial role in proving the efficacy of this myth and in authorizing it as a paradigm of viewing and interpreting the world outside the context of science.

One can make a "strong" or a "weak" claim about the relations between the elements of what I have called attestive visual culture— the view of the world as a bundle of observable facts, which is discernible within the traditions and practices of Western science and technology—and the attestive visual cultural norms which underlie liberal-democratic concepts of action, authority, and accountability. The strong claim is that the formation of the visual culture of modern liberal-democratic politics has been affected by the social diffusion of norms and practices of displaying and witnessing that have developed within the subculture of science since the middle of the seventeenth century. The weak claim does not require that science be established as a cause (or a source) of liberal-democratic modes of presenting, accounting for, or witnessing actions. It settles on the more minimal claim that science functions as an authoritative cultural model which socially validates the normative status of attestive visual codes. In the following discussion I will make the weaker claim without discarding the stronger one. The weaker claim is, as we shall see, sufficient to establish the importance of science and technology as a political resource, and their role in upholding liberal-democratic notions of agency, action, authority, and accountability.

It is with an eye to supporting the weaker claim that I shall examine the articulations of attestive visual norms in the experimental-scientific tradition. Regardless of its genesis, the role of science (and later modern technology) in socially validating forms of discourse, action, and accountability, which rest on the myth of politics as a view, an observable factual reality, becomes particularly evident toward the end of the twentieth century with the increasing signs of its decline. If democratic citizens were to know all along how poor our theories of causation in politics really are—how uncertain our knowledge of the causal links between actions and their effects in the context of public affairs, how precarious the assumption that seeing political agents acting or speaking yields reliable knowledge of political processes or events—if they were to recognize that observable facts are but complex cultural artifacts, they would have great difficulties maintaining their beliefs and directing their actions in the political universe which they inhabit.

As I indicated above, however, it has been an important feature of liberal-democratic politics to ignore such doubts and enact politics as a "real" view which implicitly denies its own theatricality. This, in fact, is the blindness in the democratic mode of seeing and knowing politics. It is largely in supporting this "naive realism" toward politics conceived as a matter of "simple facts," and in defending politics against the potential destructiveness of epistemological skepticism, that the cultures of science and technology have had their greatest significance in liberal-democratic politics.

There is perhaps no sharper expression of the faith in the power of observable facts to speak for themselves, in the superior force of the eye over the tongue in conveying the truth, than the inscription on the coat of arms of the Royal Society, *Nullius in Verba,* thus instructing the fellows to distrust language. This attitude, the deverbalization of the way to truth, reflects the commitment to the autonomy and independence of the eye, to the superior validity of seeing over hearing, to an idea of knowledge as something manifest in visual experience outside discourse. The notion that seeing can be independent of interpreting, an idea which has become increasingly discredited in late-twentieth-century culture, represented in the middle of the seventeenth century a fundamental shift in cultural values.

There has been, of course, a rich religious tradition of employing a discerning sense of sight as a means for demonstrating the existence and celebrating the power and intelligence of God. The emergence of natural theology with its stress on the display of divinity in the works of nature,[22] and the fact that early physicists such as Robert Boyle, Isaac Newton, and Joseph Priestley were religiously inclined to consider science as a means of testifying to and celebrating God's power and presence, suggest that celebratory and attestive visual orientations were not necessarily separable and mutually exclusive, especially in the early phases of the scientific revolution in the sixteenth and seventeenth centuries. The attestive-descriptive mode was no doubt subservient in some contexts to the celebratory visual rhetoric of religious authority, to religious testimonies to the presence of God. Hence the historical emancipation of attestive norms from celebratory modes of seeing and displaying is an important aspect of the cultural development of modern science as well as of its cultural role.

While the court theater was the characteristic site of celebratory visual culture, the philosophical theater was the most important site for the development and articulation of attestive visual norms. Bishop Sprat's *History of the Royal Society* (1667), records of Robert Boyle's experiments and Robert Hooke's works, reflect this phenomenon. Relevant historical studies of the role of sight in the culture of modern science include the works of Steven Shapin, Simon Schaffer, David Gooding, and Owen Hannaway.[23] Most illuminating, of course, are Sprat's references to the fellows of the Royal Society as equal and "sincere witnesses" who reject all mediating authorities and remove all the veils between man and the world. Sprat insists on the superiority of the "union of eyes" over the "glorious pomp of words."[24] Consistent with this general orientation, Robert Hooke wrote in his *Micrographia* (1665) about the need for a "sincere Hand and a faithful Eye, to examine, and to record the things themselves as they appear."[25] Preferring direct contact with the "book of nature" the fellows of the Royal Society are said to direct their gaze to "perfect originals" rather than to "corrupt copies."[26]

The potential democratic import of the attestive visual norms was evident already in the early experiments. In the course of one experiment made in the Academia del Cimento in Florence in 1660, the fellows who were concerned that their own testimonies might be corrupted by self-deception called on many people, including illiterate persons, to observe the experiment and make sketches of what they saw.[27] This event illustrates the belief in the universality of the attestive eye. In fact, of course, attestive seeing was increasingly subject, in the context of the emerging science, to special discipline and required specific skills and training. Upon receiving the reports of Cotton Mather (who was elected a fellow of the Royal Society in 1713), the Royal Society deemed his account of meteors observed in New England most acceptable but dismissed his reports on monstrous birds, as well as his ventures into psychosomatic medicine, as accounts which "relate little to natural philosophy"—"begging pardon of the Reverend Gentleman that attested it."[28] Such criticisms by the Royal Society of a fellow who "remained a cleric at heart" illustrate the attempts of the principal agents of the new science to differentiate a rigorous scientific mode of seeing and reporting from religious and common sense modes which are guided by celebratory and other nonrational, nonattestive visual orientations.[29]

Robert Boyle's attempts to validate knowledge claims by means such as the air-pump experiment and to perfect it as a technique of settling disputes and establishing knowledge are in many respects paradigmatic of the functions of attestive visual orientations in strategies of persuasion devised by experimental philosophers. Shapin and Schaffer's instructive study gives a close examination of Boyle's ideology of experimentalism, its practice within its sociopolitical setting, and its wider implications. A principal feature of Boyle's approach is the insistence that matters of fact are constituted by the "multiplication of witnesses,"[30] the aggregation of individual testimonies.[31] As such the constitution of experimental knowledge is perceived as a public process, a process which evolves in a public space of witnessing.[32] The observers are, therefore, not just passive spectators but witnesses.[33] Compared with spectators, witnesses have a greater role in authorizing and deauthorizing the claims of performers. Acts of seeing by witnesses represent, therefore, a distribution of authority which implies more power to the public relative to the performer.[34]

The ethics of the experimental situation require that the experimenters and the witnesses who attest to their actions and their effects be modest and humble so as to ensure their respect for the facts and a tempered mode of discourse.[35] Eighteenth-century experimental philosophy as practiced by Joseph Priestley or nineteenth-century experimental philosophy as practiced by Michael Faraday tended to project an image of knowledge as something advanced by common, often untrained, and theoretically or mathematically disinclined observers, not as something discovered by a few geniuses.[36] These ideas are meant, of course, to ensure seeing as a public, not a private, experience. The status of the experiment in deciding the distribution of authority among competing claims has from the very beginning required, in addition, that both experimenters and witnesses, the performers of experiments and the observers, act freely. Free action has been a condition for the integrity of the experiment as a public "philosophical" event, as a means of establishing factual truth. The notion that experiments consist of performers who—unlike alchemists, for instance—are ready to expose their actions, and through their actions their claims, to public tests of honesty and competence, this readiness to take the risks of an open-ended interplay between self-exposure through transparent action and a voluntarily constituted community of witnesses, is particularly pertinent to our concerns. It is precisely the supposed public nature of instrumental action, as exposed performance in which the actors' success or failure is open to public tests, that would later render it such an attractive model or genre of democratic action. As a form of "honest" conduct, instrumental action could appear as having features congenial to self-legitimation in terms of liberal-democratic values.

It is crucial in Boyle's conception of the power of the public experiment that the experimenters, the actors, may fail and that their failures are just as exposed as their successes.[37] By taking—or appearing to take—risks, the humility of the actors before the superior "authority" of nature is demonstrated and the nonarbitrary, impersonal integrity of the test and its results are socially confirmed.

The status of public witnessing as constitutive of authority and the status of actions as transparent objects of public judgment are precisely what Thomas Hobbes, perhaps the most formidable critic of Robert Boyle's experimental program, denies. Despite some observations to the contrary,[38] Hobbes on the whole rejects Boyle's technique of persuasion on the grounds that neither witnessing nor manipulating instruments and machines in the interrogation of nature can constitute a firm basis for distinguishing public from private experience and for enlisting the former for the purposes of separating valid from invalid claims.[39] The reliable technique of settling disputes and conflicts is not factual witnessing, according to Hobbes, but a deductive mathematical-geometrical mode of resolving uncertainties. Certain knowledge does not lie in the relation of people to facts but in their relation to their own operations and products. Whether it is geometry or state authority, it is the individual's role in the very constitution of a thing which opens the possibility of a certain knowledge of that thing. Humans can fully know only that which they have made. Hobbes is skeptical of the possibility of a public space of perception in which conflicting opinions and authorities can be decisively settled and replaced by a consensus.[40]

For Boyle, by contrast, the experimental community is a model of an ideal polity, an example, as Shapin and Schaffer observe, "of how to organize and sustain a peaceful society between the extremes of tyranny and radical individualism."[41] Hobbes's rejection of witnessing as an authority-constituting procedure must have been an important aspect of his subscription to an authoritarian solution to the problem of settling social conflicts. The alternative model presented by an experimentalist conception of political action had to be defended, however, not only against the anti-empiricist rationalist criticism of thinkers such as Thomas Hobbes but also against the widespread distrust generated by unreliable witnesses, that is, uncritical empirics, and the quacks or charlatans who manipulate instruments not to decide between contending truth claims but rather to create effects, to entertain, to impress, and to win the admiration of the public. Trying to instill "reverence for experience, in comparison of authority,"[42] Boyle is led to criticize "unskillful beholders" whose "sensuality and lusts and passions darkened and seduced their intellects."[43] The principal method he uses to discredit the alchemists is to challenge them to move from their inaccessible private spaces into the open space of the public laboratories in which they can be exposed to collective critical witnessing.[44]

The inculcation of trust in disciplined testimonies and the institutionalization of a public space which rests on reliable witnesses was, however, a very slow and complex sociocultural process. The initial creation of such spaces by the kind of people who were associated with the Royal Society, and the later social expansion of such public spaces as a sociocultural device for constituting and challenging claims of authority in fields outside science, depended upon a host of developments and transformations in basic canons of action and persuasion.

Shapin shows the extent to which in early forms of "reliable" witnessing, the social scope of the public space where the early experiments were performed was restricted to gentlemen whose social affiliations and status certified them as trustworthy witnesses.[45] The authority of gentlemen as reliable witnesses, and performers, of experiments was also connected with the assumption that truthful testimonies can be made only by free and independent individuals.[46] Freedom in this context implies a combination of features including not only the condition of being independent vis-à-vis others but also the virtues of restraint and moderation, of not being a slave to one's "lusts and passions," as Boyle put it. In seventeenth-century England such features were associated with the gentlemanly class. Later it took the powerful force of social and political reforms, guided by the ideas of liberalism and democracy, to expand the social scope of reliable witnesses and ascribe the potential for the virtues of freedom and reasonable judgment to all individuals. Thus, liberal-democratic ideas did more than encourage the notion that public witnessing of scientific experiments is an inclusive category which refers to all individuals, that true knowledge is knowledge possessed by the whole public. They also opened a possibility for defining instrumental actions in democratic terms as the kind of actions which, like experiments, are subject to inclusive public witnessing and therefore, depending on the adequacy of any given performance, to public confirmation or disapproval. The expansion of the social space of witnessing was therefore a sociocultural and political development which substantiated the partial convergence of scientific and political norms of witnessing and authorizing claims, a development which underlies much of the impulse of the Enlightenment and its profound impact on Western notions of the relevance of truth and rationality to politics. In this context, debates on the competence of citizens as voluntary yet rational judges of facts, and on the prospect of educating the "lower classes" to think scientifically, were inextricably associated—in mid-eighteenth-century France and mid-nineteenth-century England, for instance—with the discussions on the very prospect of a liberal-democratic political order. What was regarded as the vulnerability of the uneducated to the "corruptive" effects of evocative spectacles and the tricks of demagogues was a source of great concern for those who feared that the public which can establish authority by means of attestive critical gaze may degenerate into a mob.[47]

There was, therefore, a strong ideological incentive to protect and reinforce the norms of what I have called attestive visual culture as an integral element not only of modern science but also of the cultural and educational programs of modern liberal-democratic politics. Seventeenth-century fellows of the Royal Society deliberately attempted to establish experimental philosophy as something distinct from the activities of mystics, empirics, and enthusiasts, no less than those of scholastics.[48] Public fascination with such things as early demonstrations of electricity was easily exploitable for cultivating beliefs in miracles and supernatural accounts of phenomena as well as for diffusing a scientific outlook. Schaffer indicates how eighteenth-century French natural philosophers had to defend the disciplined uses of the effects of electricity to substantiate naturalistic-scientific accounts against their exploitation by quacks and charlatans.[49] In eighteenth-century America, people such as Isaac Greenwood, Charles Town, and Archibald Spencer cultivated and perfected a genre of public scientific lectures which employed instruments for the production of electric phenomena and used them for scientific demonstrations and naturalistic expositions of electricity.[50] Inspired by Benjamin Franklin, Ebenezer Kinnersley (1711–1778), who emerged as one of the most popular public lecturers of colonial America, reportedly toured the colonies giving lectures accompanied by public demonstrations, which he repeatedly revised in light of current research.[51] The success of such popular lectures must have been influenced by their appeal, beyond the exclusive circle of cultivated American gentlemen, to peasants and artisans, and by the democratic character of the situation.[52] In England, the French Huguenot refugee Jean T. Desaguliers used mechanical devices in public lectures to illustrate the Newtonian laws of motion and employed illustrative engravings in his influential *A Course of Experimental Philosophy* (London, 1725) to "prove experimentally what . . . Newton has demonstrated mathematically."[53] Still, the attempts to use experiments to validate a rational attentive orientation toward nature had to overcome resistance often encouraged by religious speakers who employed nature and science to terrorize sinners or celebrate miraculous powers.[54]

The struggle to enlist experiments to the inculcation of the attestive-scientific mode of seeing and judging phenomena was reinforced by such major cultural and technological developments as the mass printing of pictures. Although the printing machine is usually assessed with regard to its impact on the diffusion of texts, William M. Ivins, Jr., indicates that through the mass printing and diffusion of pictures the printing machine also had a powerful impact on the shape and function of visual communications.[55] The possibility of exactly reproducing pictorial images, and of standardizing images of things, enhanced the reliability of visual communications and lent pictures the power to convey the reality, continuity, and objectivity of the things depicted.[56] As such, printed pictures that were controlled by scientific sensibilities could facilitate the social diffusion of "attestive visual codes" of presenting and looking at objects. One of the most influential illustrations of this development is, of course, Diderot's *Encyclopedia*.[57] The *Encyclopedia* is a most instructive document of attestive visual strategies of persuasion and their functions in the social rhetoric of science in eighteenth-century Europe. Most interesting, for my purposes here, are the plain, unornamented pictures of machines and instruments intended to extend through print some of the values of display and witnessing in public experiments.[58]

An important indicator of the universalization of attestive visual orientations, and their incorporation into the rhetoric of power and authority outside science, is the frequent eighteenth-century employment of "light" or "enlightenment" as a metaphor for knowledge and its social diffusion, implying a wider public participation in the cultural and political orders.[59] The Enlightenment reflects the rise in the normative status of attestive seeing in the authorization of claims of both knowledge and power. Although Condorcet's concept of knowledge reflects in some respects his "mathematical" preoccupations, he expressed the spirit of the day when he advocated enlightenment as a way to decentralize political power. "The more men are enlightened," he wrote, "the less those with authority can abuse it and the less necessary it will be to give [people of authority] social powers, energy and extent. Thus truth is the enemy of power, as of those who exercise it. The more it spreads, the less they will be able to mislead men, the more force it acquires the less societies need to be governed."[60] Such faith in the force of knowledge to democratize politics underlay Condorcet's and many of his disciples' faith in the democratic political effects of public instruction.[61] An ideal of universal education which includes the diffusion of experimental knowledge came to be closely associated here with the ideal of universal political participation.

Not all forms of education, of course, were instruments of the social diffusion and authorization of the critical attestive visual orientations which were so intimately associated with the culture and the authority of experimental science. But some of the most influential educational reforms in nineteenth-century Europe and North America were inspired by people such as Heinrich Pestalozzi who held that the proper method of teaching rests on first *showing* the students the objects or things to which words refer and only then teaching them the words and their appropriate use.[62] Nevertheless in nineteenth-century America, the spread of attestive visual orientations met with persistent resistance from celebratory religious orientations which were inclined to present "nature lessons" as religious lessons.[63] Toward the end of the nineteenth century, however, the influence of scientific orientations toward nature significantly increased in American text books.[64] Pestalozzi's "object method" implied a profound transformation in the terms of reference of the teacher's authority. From unchallengeable readers and interpreters of texts, teachers, under Pestalozzi's tutelage, were turned into mini-experimentalist-performers appearing before a group of younger, and potentially skeptical, witnesses. The particular effectiveness of Pestalozzian methods in fields such as geography, geology, and physics, and consequently the growing significance of such subjects in the curriculum, corresponded with the diffusion of attestive cultural codes of vision in the educational system. The specific American stress on the value of useful knowledge provided another powerful motive for the introduction of scientific education and its anti-elitist cultural strategies. The new stress on the value of seeing and displaying represents, then, a profound shift in social canons of persuasion.

It is against this background that the rhetorical value of machines and instrumental operations became so significant in the course of the nineteenth-century industrial revolution. The public appeal of mechanical spectacles was, as I indicated above, anticipated well before the industrial revolution. The mechanical wonders employed by Inigo Jones in the Stuart's court theater in the early seventeenth century and the spectacular balloon flight in Metz, France, in October 1773, are illustrative.[65] But it is largely due to such cultural institutions as the great international exhibitions of science and industry (the Crystal Palace Exhibition of London in 1851, for example) and the modern public science museums that the rhetorical force of machines and instruments was systematically "tamed" and enlisted to the social authorization of attestive scientific orientations. If in earlier centuries collections of the kind assembled in the "curiosity cabinets" of the nobility, which characteristically included both natural and "magical" objects, were used to entertain and to project power and wealth, the modern science museum is a visual dictionary of a democratic attestive visual culture. It offers authoritative classifications of objects and it teaches the appropriate modes of looking at the world as an object of knowledge.[66] But its authority, like the authority of the experimentalist, is subject to public scrutiny and criticism on the part of both professional and lay audiences.

The attestive visual orientation, which Boyle, Priestly, Faraday, and other experimentalists codified in the performance of public experiments designed to substantiate claims of knowledge and to settle conflicts of scientific opinions, underlies also the rhetorical force of machines in the social context. The socially accessible machine can function as an ongoing informal experimental demonstration of claims of knowledge. One historian observed aptly that the factory has become "a victory for pure science and not a degradation of the mind."[67] The factory, like the science museum, furnished a readily accessible space in which, as Bacon already anticipated, works and their effects testify not only to their significance for the conveniences of life but also to the truth.[68] The rising significance of the laboratory, the workshop, and the factory, relative to the library, as referents with which public speakers have sought to substantiate their claims no doubt represents changes in Western canons of persuasion with implications far beyond the context of science. Walter Ong suggests that the very ideals of "clarity" and "distinctness" so stressed by Descartes are "conceivable in terms of some analogy with vision and a spatial field." The emphasis on such ideals marks, according to Ong, a turn from a concept of knowledge "enveloped in disputations" to one associated "with a silent object world conceived in visualist diagrammatic terms."[69]

The significance of visible mechanical effects in validating scientific claims of knowledge has grown, particularly since the end of the nineteenth century, due to the progressive professionalization of science and the concomitant decline in the status of the amateur scientist, who was formerly welcomed in scientific forums as a useful participant in measuring and reporting natural phenomena and in collecting "documents of nature." As scientific theories and ideas have become more abstract and more esoteric, and as scientists have had to master complicated skills in order to engage in research, the social rhetoric and legitimation of science have come to depend more heavily upon the power of easily perceived effects of the kind associated with drugs, flying machines, weapons, and, later in the twentieth century, computers.[70] The discrepancies between the levels of professional and lay knowledge have tended, of course, to encourage also the popular perception of machines and the visible effects of scientific instruments as magical devices rather than as icons of rational knowledge. The power of machines as, to use Bacon's words, "pledges of truth" has depended on whether the machines were observed within the visual culture of attestive rather than celebratory or other alternative orientations.[71] On the whole, however, in modern Western societies machines and instruments have been enlisted to support cool, functional claims of knowledge presented in the context of attestive visual orientations. During the nineteenth century, the Royal Institute of London, the Mechanics Institutes, and the American Lyceums and Academies were principal institutional agents for the diffusion of such attestive-visual orientations as well as for the concomitant practice of enlisting the rhetorical powers of machines, instruments, and experiments to back up claims and arguments.[72]

Like Robert Boyle and Joseph Priestley in the seventeenth and eighteenth centuries, respectively, Michael Faraday is perhaps the most central nineteenth-century experimental scientist to employ instruments and experiments as ways to cultivate the view of scientific knowledge as something produced and confirmed through acts of the public witnessing of objects, operations, and effects. David Gooding's study of Faraday's science and lecture techniques indicates how effective he was in moving his discoveries from the contingent context of the private space of experimental research to the public forum of demonstrably self-evident facts.[73] This move from the private space of discovery to the public space of demonstration and certification corresponded in the case of Faraday with his moving from a laboratory in the basement of the Royal Institution to the lecture theater on the first floor. Faraday's techniques of public persuasion were designated to belittle his own role as well as the impact of his instruments in order to present the results as self-evident "natural facts."[74] The power of Faraday's technique of experimental demonstration derives from the presuppositions of attestive visual culture according to which facts are something seen and witnessed as independent of theory or concepts. His mastery of the art of public demonstration made it difficult for his public to realize the enormously complex interventions and decisions which in fact underlay his practice. "The very invisibility of the enabling techniques," observes Gooding, "is what made the demonstration experiment so effective as a means of disclosing nature directly to lay observers. Faraday knew that an experimentalist preoccupied by practicalities or encumbered by problems with his apparatus will make his audience very much aware of them as well."[75] Professing to distrust vision when it is mediated by theoretical orientations, Faraday recognized the relations between the accessibility of effects and their social status as "real facts." He exemplifies the scientist's technique of establishing his authority through manifest humility before nature, the capacity to appear as having contributed nothing to the outcome. It is by means of such practice that the authority of science has been enlisted for the social validation of the myth of the world as an observable given and of unmediated attestive seeing as a source of reliable knowledge. As a historian of Faraday's experimental techniques, David Gooding's own analysis is informed by the ability to apply late-twentieth-century reflexive orientations toward facts, which recognize the status of visible objects and effects as constructs, to describe and expose Faraday's public demonstrations. He shows that the rhetorical force of Faraday's operations depended upon a prior social commitment to the norms of what I call attestive visual culture, and the mastery of techniques of presenting and demonstrating knowledge, which renders invisible the process through which facts are fabricated.[76]

One of the consequences of the growing force of visible examples in the rhetoric of modern science has, of course, been a tendency to socially grade fields of knowledge according to the degree to which their claims can be visually demonstrated. The concrete visual referents which socially substantiate the scientific claims of physicists, geologists, astronomers, or medical scientists are not usually available for visually less articulate fields such as mathematics.[77] The difficult struggle of the social sciences to acquire the status of science along with fields of knowledge such as physics and astronomy, especially since the late nineteenth century, reflects the inferior accessibility of visual effects of the kind available to most natural sciences.[78] As we shall see below, the social sciences nevertheless succeeded in rationalizing qualified deployment of attestive visual orientations in the sphere of human behavior. As a result, they have played an important role in culturally and socially validating the authority of the liberal-democratic conception of politics as a view, as a particular kind of spectacle.[79]

Politics as a Public Spectacle and Liberal-Democratic Ideology

Once the norms of attestive visual culture, which are manifest in the practice and, even more sharply, in the ethos of modern experimental science, are deployed in the context of public affairs, they appear to uphold central liberal-democratic values. The codes of attestive visual orientations which underlie the concept of politics as a view, as an observable series of events, implicitly confirm the emergence of the public as an aggregate of individual spectators. The idea of public opinion as a convergence of a multitude of independent individual testimonies has furnished a way of reconciling the liberal-democratic commitment to the individual as the ultimate source of authority with the commitment to the public as the political expression of the association of individuals in a group. A concept of the public as a collective, which is compatible with the values of individualism, provides here a liberal-democratic rationale for the public as a legitimate and legitimating agency. The cultural construction of politics as a view, together with the validation of the public as the viewer who has the authority to attest and define political reality, furnishes a normative framework for integrating politics as a spectacle with liberal-democratic principles.

In some respects this development can be seen as a particular instance of a wider cultural trend that was noted—and criticized—by

Martin Heidegger. He pointed out that the metaphysical construction of the world as an observable object is inseparable from the rise of the individual as a viewing subject. In Heidegger's moral and aesthetic anthropology, the object and the subject, the view and the viewer, are complementary categories. It is because the attempt to understand the world as a view relates, according to Heidegger, to the affirmation of the subject as a viewer that he can state that "humanism arises only when the world becomes a view." [80] In the political context, the idea of politics as a view similiarly affirms the position of the individual citizen as a viewer.

No less significant in the context of liberal-democratic ideology is, of course, the sense in which the concept of the public implicit in attestive visual modes of witnessing politics distinguishes itself from alternative notions of the public, for instance, as organic unity, enthusiastic-passionate mob, or passive crowd. As an agency of attestive viewing of politics, the public, which can gaze silently and coolly, which can have a clear vision free of the distortions caused by emotional and aesthetic appeals, is less vulnerable to the critics who equate democratization with the politics of unreason. [81]

In the political context the kind of criticism directed by Robert Boyle against "unskillful beholders," whose sensuality, lusts, and passions "darkened and seduced their intellects," [82] stresses the importance of self-discipline and distance in securing the reliability of seeing and witnessing. While a view of the world as a creative construct of our imagination, as invoked by Blake or Coleridge, for instance, tends to dissolve the boundaries between the object and the viewing subject, [83] the attestive gaze balances the freedom of the subject by lending independent weight to the object. In upholding the distinction between object and subject, attestive visual culture allows the world as an object to function as a sort of nonarbitrary, impersonal (and therefore democratically acceptable) constraint on the freedom of the subject. By rejecting the extremes of both unrestrained enthusiastic engagement and radical detachment, liberal-democratic visual culture, consistent with the attestive visual orientations in the experimental-scientific tradition, grooms the eye of the democratic citizen as an instrument of detached engagement. Attestive visual culture allows, therefore, the generation of forms of political discourse in which designative modes restrain expressive or subjective uses of language. In the context of liberal-democratic politics, attestive visual culture becomes, therefore, an instrument of appropriating "factual reality" to secure the authority of "external" over "internal" referents for political discourse and action, thus checking arbitrariness and rendering agents more publicly accountable.

The humility of the experimental scientist before the facts of nature translates in the context of liberal-democratic political culture into the deference of political actors before the public facts of social and political "realities." It is the kind of respect for facts which supposedly binds technical experts in the various professions. From the perspective of the citizen as a spectator-witness this attitude implies the readiness to subject political actions to detached judgment. The distinction, on the one hand, between "factual reality," as shareable experience, and unshareable subjective events such as dreams and, on the other, between modes of objective and subjective discourse and action provides the basis for a host of cultural strategies for disciplining and tempering politics.

From the perspective of liberal-democratic ideology perhaps the most significant implication of witnessing public facts as a means of confirming or disconfirming political claims is the supposed inclusiveness of this procedure. As the development of free press and political journalism in liberal-democratic societies has shown, especially since the mid-nineteenth century, the idea of political reality as a view, as an object of the observer's report, has served to decentralize the vested authority to judge, criticize, and influence the actions of political agents.[84] An important, indeed crucial, feature of reality as a cultural device for cementing decentralized liberal-democratic concepts of action, authority, and accountability, and for upholding the normative superiority of public external referents of political actions and discourse, is the assumption that there is no certain but only probabilistic knowledge of reality.[85] From the perspective of political performers, the inherent constraints on the full knowledge of reality guarantee that they can never fully control and manipulate their own actions and their consequences. Insofar as no certain knowledge of reality is possible (including knowledge of how the public will respond to actions and gestures intended to mislead it), political actors like experimental scientists cannot fully anticipate the course and effects of their own actions.[86] They remain, therefore, always vulnerable to failure. As attestive visual orientations force political actors to be exposed to the public eye, the inherent limits on the knowledge of the relevant facts practically ensure that they must constantly take the risks of publicly exposed failures. Just as experimental scientists are vulnerable to the possibility that an experiment could fail to confirm their claims, so political actors may not be able to sustain their claims against the visible import of their own actions. In a world where actors are publicly exposed and the contingent character of action, as well as the limits of knowledge, constantly humble and occasionally destroy the reputation of actors, there are formidable constraints on the centralization of political power and authority. Reality constantly exposes the limits of human agency and the fragility of all human enterprises.

As a mechanism for constantly establishing and disestablishing political leaders, the inherent vulnerability of political authority to exposed failures ensures a kind of public political accountability which does not depend on the actual capacity of the citizens to guide and control their governors. When the force with which publicly exposed failures can diminish or undermine political leaders is ignored or misunderstood, the character of democratic politics as a mass spectacle is often unwarrantably construed as a degenerative shift in the democratic tradition.[87] Once we recognize that the vulnerability of democratic political actors—within the cultural framework of attestive visual orientations toward politics—does not require rational, competent, participatory citizenry, that public witnessing effectively redistributes political reputations and power even where—as is usually the case—the witnesses can claim to have neither the knowledge nor the consensus to pinpoint the "right" course of action, then we need not subscribe to the idea that when classical models of participatory or representative democracy are not realizable the only alternative is degenerative forms of democracy, where the few try, and often succeed, to deceive the many. Insofar as what is important for checking and keeping leaders democratically accountable is unremitting exposure and vulnerability before an inquisitive gazing public, the failure of "public opinion" as a coherent guide for public policymakers may not be as damaging to liberal-democratic political institutions as some scholars have thought.[88] The irony, of course, is that in liberal-democracy the very vulnerability of actors to publicized failures instills trust. The early experimental scientists were apparently aware of the fact that reporting unsuccessful experiments has the effect of establishing their credibility as objective and humble scientists.[89] In the context of attestive visual culture, exposed failures confirm both the limitations of agents and the power of spectators to control the reputation of performers.

Another democratizing element in the notion of politics as an observable factual reality is its implicit commitment to the normative superiority of the present over the past and the future.[90] Attestive visual orientations toward politics imply a conception of politics as a series of actions, events, or processes unfolding within the confines of the present tense. Insofar as seeing consists of acts of immediate contact between viewers and the viewed, seeing implies also the possibility of instant public accountability on the part of performers. Political worlds in which invisible referents have normative superiority in authorizing claims or actions over visible referents, in which celebratory visual orientations enlist the past and the future to authorize superhuman or privileged agencies, tend to weaken the living relative to the dead and the unborn. By contrast, attestive visual culture engages spectators as participants in politics as a live performance. By replacing the "inner light" of divine illumination, or of reason, with the "external light," which enables the physical eye to contact the outside world, attestive visual cultural codes substitute democratic for hierarchical concepts of political knowledge. Liberal-democratic political epistemology assumes that that which the public cannot witness has a lesser claim to the status of "fact" and, therefore, inferior authority to validate or invalidate claims and actions.

The conception of politics as a publicly observable yet partly contingent reality, a reality manifest before a live audience which rewards successful and punishes unsuccessful performers, is one of the factors which distinguishes liberal-democratic from nondemocratic and particularly totalitarian political systems. Modern totalitarian states, such as the Soviet Union, Nazi Germany, Franco's Spain, and fascist Italy, have repressed attestive visual culture because they could not accept its political implications. The totalitarian state cannot acknowledge the status of the public as an independent and authoritative political agency, the power of the citizens to participate in defining the facts of the political world, or the inherent vulnerability of political authority to manifest failures. Totalitarianism cannot permit the epistemological and ontological commitments which ensure the vulnerability of political actors in the liberal-democratic state. Unlike democracy, totalitarianism constructs politics on the fantasy of certain knowledge, total control, and no risks. It enlists epistemological optimism to rationalize sacrifices as worthy investments in a better future and to justify the centralization of political power in instrumental terms.[91] Moreover, where totalitarianism aestheticizes, mystifies, and absolutizes authority, democratic attestive visual orientations tend to deaestheticize, demystify, and relativize it. While, as I indicated above, both communist and fascist dictatorships have rejected and repressed the deployment of attestive visual cultural norms in the political realm, the fascist variant seems more predisposed to pursue this goal by the aestheticization of politics whereas the communist variant proceeds more by scientistic bureaucratic centralism.[92] Still both variants of modern totalitarianism have relied on a concept of certain objective reality to foreclose all doubts and criticism on the part of the citizens. Both, in addition, have employed the evocative aesthetics of mass state spectacles to weaken their citizens' powers to distance themselves critically from the government. Their purpose in doing so is to arouse the loyalty of their citizens and protect the government from the kind of citizen's detached engagement which continually subjects democratic leaders to merciless scrutiny.

Differences in the norms which regulate seeing and displaying in discrete nondemocratic political universes are, of course, as instructive as variations among democratic systems or between democracies and nondemocracies. Such differences concern us here because they help distinguish political universes in which science and technology function as ideological and political resources from those in which they do not. They also help illuminate the diverse ways in which science and technology indeed function as ideological resources in the former.

Although both the modern totalitarian state and premodern feudal-aristocratic societies leave no room for attestive visual orientations toward authority, the latter lack the sociocultural conditions in which attestive visual attitudes flourish, while the former tends to repress the autonomy and freedom of spectators who could be witnesses. In the feudal or aristocratic society, both the people and the government remained largely invisible while the space of the visible was employed primarily for the ceremonial display or the celebration of hierarchy.[93] In the feudal society, writes Marc Bloch, "the material world was scarcely more than a mask behind which took place all the really important things."[94] But this reality could not be made public, as the inherent heterogeneity and hierarchical features of such a society did not furnish support for commensurable individual points of view in relation to which objects of experience could emerge as publicly visible, as objects confirmed by shared yet independent perceptions. There was no concept of a publicly "objective" world of facts which could in turn confirm the existence of a multitude of discrete yet equal subjects, of spectators or witnesses whose observations would spontaneously aggregate to form a public view. The hierarchical-heterogeneous structure of such a society tended to support different layers and definitions of reality whose relative cultural positions depended on the hierarchical distribution of power and authority. In modern democracy it is, however, precisely the presumed equality of a multitude of individual spectators and the spontaneous convergence of their testimonies which underlie the construction of the "public" and of "reality" as a shared experience. The modern totalitarian state is not so much a variant of the hierarchical-heterogeneous culture of seeing and displaying in the feudal society as it is a transformed, or distorted, variant of the democratic uniform public vision based on the equality of spectators. In place of the spontaneous aggregation of voluntary individual testimonies, the unity of the world as an object is obtained in the totalitarian state by centralized control over acts of seeing and displaying, although the state does use the rhetoric of attestive visual culture to claim the autonomy of its concepts of reality from the structure of political power and authority.

Ultimately, however, the difference between democratic and totalitarian conceptions of factual reality is not that the former is committed to an autonomous-objective notion of reality which the latter distorts through the manipulation of public perceptions. The difference is rather between centralized and decentralized methods of *constructing* reality or of *producing* concepts of the factual world. In late-twentieth-century society, it is more widely recognized that reality is a sociocultural construct which depends on prior commitments to values that determine what kinds of experiences are objective, what kinds of testimonies count, and what assertions and claims about the world are admissible as certified facts for social currency. Whether reality is an attribute which is assigned only to observations or testimonies that seem spontaneously to converge or only to those observations and testimonies which can be ascribed to a few authoritative agents, in both cases there is no body of context-free given facts against which sociocultural constructions of reality can be checked. Although Hobbes maintained that centralized definitions of reality are more effective and reliable as means of settling social disputes than decentralized definitions of reality, which are based on collective witnessing, both possibilities are compatible with his view that ultimately our knowledge, our conceptions of reality, are made rather than found.[95] What varies among distinct political-cultural universes is not the degree to which, as the positivist would have it, these systems can actually discover and recognize the same objective truths. It is rather the processes through which certified "pictures" of reality are made and diffused. In the liberal-democratic polity, the stress on the spontaneous convergence of a multitude of voluntary individual testimonies serves, among other things, to harmonize a concept of reality as a universal constraint with a commitment to freedom. Once facts are established by free individual witnesses, the generative powers of freedom are affirmed. If free individuals can agree on certain constraints, if freedom can be self-limiting, then freedom can be reconciled with order. In a totalitarian state no such values or requirements guide the authoritative definitions of reality. The need to objectify the assertions and claims of a centralized authority in fact tends to repress the authority of witnesses and attestive visual orientations. Totalitarianism prevents the voluntary formation and articulation of perceptual and cognitive majorities. Instead, it binds individuals to preestablished definitions of reality. Totalitarianism undermines the cultural and institutional matrix which in the liberal-democratic society ensures the independence and, therefore, the authority of the individual eye as an instrument for securing the public status of knowledge and reality. It destroys the sociocultural conditions of public visibility that force all actors into a public space in which they are equally exposed. It represses any recognition of the uncertainty inherent in experience because of its implied acceptance of the possibility of total control. Insofar as what is recognized as a fact is intended to support the authority of the state, the totalitarian orientation toward reality is celebratory rather than attestive. Modern totalitarianism is from this point of view not simply an abuse of democratic concepts of representation or law but, more fundamentally, a distortion of the democratic concept of politics as a public spectacle regulated by attestive rather than celebratory visual culture. Totalitarian censorship in the cultural, communications, and political fields does not allow for the principles, practices, and institutions of which the democratic political theater is made. Only in the liberal-democratic polity do public spectacles actually expose performers to unpredictable tests and the educated eye mediate a decentralized system of accountabilities rather than a centralized system of controls. One of the most significant signs of the breakdown of totalitarian government is, therefore, the substitution of official celebratory spectacles of state by public displays and discussions of the failures of government actions and suggestions for their remedy.[96]

In democratic—unlike totalitarian—states, political actors are, therefore, caught up in a dilemma. On the one hand, their capacity to enlist support and exploit effectively the rhetoric of democratic action depends on the extent to which they can attach their actions to positive, visible indicators of success in the sphere of factual reality where actions appear to be subject to objective tests. On the other hand, because the realm of visible facts is underdetermined and has an ineradicable residue of uncertainty, and because liberal-democratic actors have neither the authority nor the instruments to monopolize the certification of facts or their social representations, their political reputations remain dependent upon uncertain and unpredictable events.[97]

Public blaming or crediting of democratic actors is, of course, only rarely based on intellectually warranted links between their actions and the events which the public perceives or construes as their effects. Ultimately the uncertainties, inconsistencies, and ambiguities which characterize public perceptions, images, and evaluations of political actors are more relevant to the fluctuations in their political reputations than the substantive features or impact of their actions. This system succeeds, however, in preserving the uncertainty of democratic political actors about the impact that their actions might have on their political reputations. Even when public judgments of instrumental success or failure are misguided or distorted, the presumed transparency of actors to such public judgments of their performance ensures the power of democratic rituals of legitimation or delegitimation—the power of the public—in the establishment or disestablishment of political authority.

Science and technology have fulfilled, then, a series of key functions in the ideological construction of modern liberal-democratic politics and, more particularly, in the justification of instrumental paradigms of public action. By furnishing authoritative means to define political action in instrumental impersonal public terms, science and technology facilitated a shift from early liberal-democratic notions of public action as an aspect of involuntary "natural" regularities to notions of public action as the result of deliberate voluntary choices. As political resources, science and technology provided social validation for metaphors, vocabularies, behavioral norms, and practices which were used to construct public actions as voluntary yet causally determined, as dependent upon human agency yet partly impersonal, as politically and functionally representative, and as partly contingent yet publicly visible displays of the competence or incompetence of political actors.

The extent to which science and technology could have such latent political functions in the modern liberal-democratic state has depended also upon the existence of certain traditions, values, and social practices which were congenial for the partial convergence of the subcultures of science and technology and liberal-democratic politics. We will now turn to key aspects of this convergence and its expressions in the modern American democracy. My purpose here is to identify and analyse both the particular features of the interactions of science, technology, ideology, and politics in the American democracy and the more general, or generalizable, features of the American experience within the larger category of liberal-democratic states. For purposes of comparison, I shall continue to refer selectively to differences between American and other democratic as well as nondemocratic modes of using science and technology as ideological and political resources.

Part II

The Dilemma of Private Persons and Public Actions in the American Democracy

4. Science, Experimental Politics, and the Culture of Democratization

Perhaps more than any other modern liberal democracy, America has sustained and "literalized" the fiction that, much like physical phenomena, politics is something that can be seen and described with the designative language of factual reports, that actions can be observed like movements and agents described like objects. The notion of politics as something observable has come to uphold in America a conception of accountability which rests on the complementary requirements (not equally respected in other variants of liberal democracy) that actions taken by political agents be made transparent to the public and that the citizens act as competent witnesses and judges of the exercises of political power.

While the Western experimental-scientific tradition developed and refined cultural strategies which could be enlisted to uphold the concept of politics as an observable body of facts, the reception of these strategies and their deployment in the political sphere have been affected in each social context by a host of local cultural factors. Sociocultural contexts vary with respect to both the acceptability and the interpretation of distinctions that are required for the diffusion and institutionalization of attestive visual orientations toward politics, such as between objects and subjects, performers and spectators, facts and fictions, and between designative and expressive languages. A comparative explanation of the factors encouraging or inhibiting attestive visual orientations in the political cultures of America, England, France, and Germany would highlight, therefore, the particular characteristics of the American variant.

Cultural Styles of Seeing and Displaying

One can detect wide cultural variations in the meanings attached to visual experience, including the status of seeing and representing not only among distinct political traditions but also among distinct scientific ones. Pierre Duhem, for one, held that while the French tend to persuade mainly by (mathematical) reasoning, the English characteristically try to persuade by relying upon examples.[1] J. B. Bernal concurred with this view when he noted that in contrast with French and German science, English science is "practical and analogical." More than in any other country, he added, in England "science is felt rather than thought."[2] The English imagination tends, according to Bernal, to be concrete and visual, as is illustrated among other things in the tendency of the English scientist to focus on the question, "How does it work?"

Pertinent differences between French and English orientations toward the role of instruments and experiments in validating claims of knowledge have been noted by Peter Dear. For a French scientist like Pascal, he observes, an experiment is more an element in a mathematical reasoning and is characteristically construed as a contrived measure to establish the normal general course of nature. In the English experimental tradition, however, an experiment is more a singular historical event. Much greater attention is given in the latter than in the former to describing the particular time, place, and structure of the experimental situation and to establishing the integrity of unique acts of witnessing as a part of certifying scientific claims.[3] Another historian observed that while French engineers attempted to elicit trust in the idea of the suspension bridge by mathematical demonstration, their English counterparts relied characteristically on the eloquence of physical models.[4] We shall see below that if, compared with the French, both the English and the American scientific traditions have developed respectively strong commitments to attestive visual norms, the deployment of those norms in the political realm has encountered much less resistance in the United States than in England (or, for that matter, in France and Germany).

Cultural variability in the tendency to rely on attestive visual norms of the kind associated with the English and American experimental scientific traditions can be discerned also in various traditions of visual art. Svetlana Alpers notes that in seventeenth century Dutch painting it is expected that "pictures document or represent behavior."[5] Alpers traces some links between what one can call the attestive impulse in seventeenth century Dutch painting and scientific traditions connected with people such as Francis Bacon, Johannes Kepler, and the fellows of the Royal Society of London. The Dutch way of seeing reveals the commitment to a "deanthropomorphized" vision which secures a measure of detachment consistent with rational discipline. Alpers alludes to yet another related feature of Dutch painting as the tendency to conceive the picture as an "aggregate of views," an assemblage of partial aspects which add up to a larger whole.[6] These traits of Dutch painting stand out, according to Alpers, when juxtaposed with the distinct visual strategies of Peter Rubens whose pictures are a sort of visual historical narrative which (to use my own terminology) stresses celebratory rather than attestive visual orientations. Whereas in mainstream Dutch painting there is, as Alpers notes, a partial convergence between painting and mapmaking, in Peter Rubens' work the stress is on paintings as a means of adoring and validating certain moral ideas and religious dogmas.[7]

A comparison of the visual norms which, according to Alpers, govern seventeenth-century Dutch painting and those attributed by Michael Fried to eighteenth-century French painting can be very suggestive. According to Fried, it has been characteristic in France to expect that the gaze, and especially a public gaze, produces inauthentic theatrical behavior on the part of subjects aware of being observed. The expectation that the knowledge of being observed distorts conduct implies, of course, that seeing is a very problematic way to psychological, social, and political knowledge. Inasmuch as personal, social, or political truths are embodied in human conduct they cannot be witnessed, according to this approach, except under the most extraordinary circumstances where the agents observed are unaware of being gazed upon. Fried notes that such considerations at least partly account for the frequency with which eighteenth-century French painters chose to paint figures in states of sleep or absorption of the kind which, according to this notion of the interaction between visual exposure and behavior, diminishes the deauthenticating impact of theatricality.[8] Among the great painters who were active between the end of the eighteenth century and the end of the nineteenth, Goya provides a striking illustration of the shift from celebratory to attestive visual orientations. In his portrait of the royal family of Charles IV, Goya breaks away from the convention of theatrical idealization of the sitters and produces a portrait free of the earlier artistic devotion to the celebration of kings and the royal family's virtues. Goya thus tempers his vision with detached, attestive values. Fred Licht shows how Goya distances himself and avoids facing his subjects directly by painting their reflections in a mirror. The mirror, like the camera a

few decades later, depersonalizes and objectifies the act of representation, thus allowing the Spanish painter to minimize the personal risks
of painting truthfully rather than ideally.[9]

I have already noted the possibility, to which I shall give much more
attention below, that the apparent authority of attestive visual norms
in the English experimental-scientific tradition has not been matched
by their respective authority in the political field.[10] Although one
may discern some general trends which cut through and differentiate
between whole cultures, such differences in the propensity to adopt
or reject attestive visual norms between various spheres of the same
culture can be equally significant. William Blake's attack on the Newtonian mode of viewing the universe and his alternative religio-
imaginative vision is a pertinent illustration. For Blake the factual
reality assumed (or constructed) by Newtonian science is a hindrance
to the creative imagination.[11] James Engell notes the differences
between Blake's, Coleridge's, and Shelley's emphasis on the creative
function of the imagination, a position which dissolves the boundaries between object and subject, and William Hazlitt's tendency to
regard the objects of our perception as legitimate constraints upon
what the eye can experience. Engell goes on to suggest that American
literary discourse shows lesser trust in, and assigns lesser value to, the
"creative imagination" than its European counterpart.[12]

Although attestive, celebratory, and other types of visual orientations may coexist in the same society or culture, various studies of
American culture and society, especially of the period since the mid-
nineteenth century, suggest the uniquely powerful presence of attestive
visual codes in American science, art, technology, and education, as
well as in politics. It may be instructive to examine briefly a few such
wider cultural articulations of attestive visual norms before we go on
to explore in greater detail their expressions and functions in American ideology and politics.

Since its first appearance in 1839, the camera as a machine for producing images of reality has played a uniquely important role in culturally deploying and validating attestive visual orientations in the
larger social and political spheres in America. As Alan Trachtenberg
shows, the making, collecting, and diffusing of photographs for the
purpose of accurately documenting and representing reality has
appeared together with the uses of the camera for aesthetic, moral, or
ideological purposes.[13] Nevertheless, the massive use of photographs

as visual historical documents, the role of the camera in scientific surveys of the physical and social environments, in the making of medical records, in modern journalistic reports, and in political communications appeared to confirm the belief that photographs "can be seen, handled and swapped as if they were tokens of an absolute reality."[14] As such, photography helped sustain the belief that the visible surfaces of things as well as the exteriors of persons tell us what is inside, that the eye is a reliable instrument of knowing and even contacting reality. Photography could appear, therefore, as upholding the notion of the world as an object of knowledge through eyesight against such powerful challenges as the notion that reality is an infinitely elastic aesthetic-imaginative construct or that far from constituting a unified object of our knowledge it is a chaotic, largely accidental assortment of particles of experience.

While the association of photography with automatic machinery made it particularly congenial as a cultural vehicle of attestive visual orientations, the wider force of the attestive-documentary gaze is manifest in the extent of its penetration into the very domain of art. The works of the influential nineteenth-century American painter Thomas Eakins and of the poet Stephen Crane are illustrative.[15] Eakins' well-known *The Gross Clinic* (1875) and *The Agnew Clinic* (1889), like Rembrandt's *The Operation of Dr. Tulp,* show close affinities to the attestive visual values which were cultivated in early modern European anatomic theaters.[16] Philip Fisher interprets Eakins' pictures as expressing wider cultural trends. "Eakins brings surgery into public view by means of these paintings," he observes, "in the same way that the novelists of Realism and Naturalism or the journalistic muckrakers would bring into the light of public scrutiny the normally invisible and often deliberately concealed affairs of political and economic life."[17] Fisher stresses the links between Eakins' repeated attempts to depict "the performance of a skilled master before an audience"[18] and the emphasis on the importance of the audience and the "art of observing and witnessing."[19] Fisher alludes to the links between the rise of the public and the development of a public visual space in which exposure demystifies and disenchants agents and their actions. In the context of this cultural development, the audience is no longer thought of as a mob but as a disciplined public. "The audience for art is not the audience that gapes and stares at wonders or sensations but the alert, serious bank of students whose intelligence and learned respect for the skilled hand translates back into veneration for the grey-haired master who commands the performance." [20] It is within the framework of attestive visual culture that skill manifest in instrumental performance is rewarded, as incompetence and failure are penalized.

It was in the context of a public space regulated by attestive visual norms of displaying and witnessing that, as the great fairs in Philadelphia, Chicago, and St. Louis prior to World War I showed, the industrial world of the machine could convert knowledge into visible exhibitions. It was also in such cultural settings that instrumental politics conceived as publicly observable performance could become a variant of modern liberal-democratic politics. An American readiness, to which Daniel Calhoun alludes, to believe that the true nature of things is inscribed, as it were, on their surface, a tendency manifest in such discrete fields as nineteenth-century American engineering style and religious rhetoric, spread also to the sphere of politics. [21] Fisher observes that "the new materials of personality and action suitable to be made conspicuous were only slowly discovered in different realms of culture." [22] In the field of democratic politics, he notes, it was Theodore Roosevelt who pioneered the first concentrated effort to employ the mass media in order to enhance political leadership. He explored, tested, and demonstrated the new cultural materials and strategies with which political authority could now define politics as an ongoing performance before a national audience.

Noting the centrality of visibility and exposure in the work of Eakins and Crane, Michael Fried sees a connection between the development of such artistic values and cultural influences as Heinrich Pestalozzi's ideas of education in mid-nineteenth-century Philadelphia high schools and the importance they ascribed to drawing as a means to train the eye and the hand to respect accurate representations of the external world. [23] The above illustrations are not sufficient to warrant any solid generalization about the relations between modes of displaying and seeing in the cultural contexts of science, art, and politics in America. Nevertheless, attention to the potential analogy between the cultural structures of the anatomic theater and the theater of democratic action, to the wider cultural role of the disciplined gaze in balancing the subjective and the objective, the engaged and the detached, the private and the public, should further our understanding of the role which the objectification of politics as a realm of observable facts can play in checking the freedom and the potential arbitrariness of agency in the liberal-democratic theory of action.

Visibility and Accountability of American Governments

In late-nineteenth-century America there were, of course, direct expressions of the affinities between the idea of politics as a spectacle for engaged spectators, the experimental-instrumental orientations toward politics, and the norms of attestive visual culture cultivated in the American experimental-scientific tradition. Henry Rowland, who as the head of the Johns Hopkins research laboratory in the closing decades of the nineteenth century was perhaps the most influential research director and science teacher in the United States at the time, articulated an American cultural ideal when he stated that "to produce men of action, they must be trained in action . . . If they study the sciences they must enter the laboratory and stand face to face with nature; they must learn to test their knowledge constantly and thus see for themselves the sad results of vague speculation; they must learn by direct experiment that their own mind is liable to error. They must try experiment after experiment and work problem after problem until they become men of action not of theory."[24]

The person of action is, as Robert Kargon points out, not just a kind of scientist but a model of a citizen capable of seeing for himself or herself and having respect and humility before the facts of experience; one whose experimental approach to action is suffused by a deep recognition of both one's powers and one's own limitations and propensity to err. There is in this view a close relation between the integrity of what I call attestive visual orientations and the experimental approach to action. The mind which the "physical laboratory is built to cultivate," notes Rowland, is the very mind "which is destined to govern the world in the future and to solve problems pertaining to politics and humanity as well as inanimate nature."[25]

When Henry Rowland saw a link between the education of the experimental scientist and the democratic citizen, when still another leading American scientist, Robert Millikan, advocated at the beginning of the twentieth century the application of the scientific method to civic problems,[26] they were echoing a powerful American ideological commitment already articulated by Thomas Jefferson. Perhaps the most significant feature of Jefferson's *Notes on the State of Vir-*

ginia (1785)[27] is the fact that a book which employs the designative language of science to describe the geography, geology, climate, and population of the state of Virginia unapologetically applies the same language to a description of the constitution, laws, and government of the state. A scientific perspective on political phenomena was consistent in Jefferson's view with faith in the "Science of Government."[28] An experimental-scientific approach to politics as well as to other subjects was essential to liberty, just as liberty was essential for the substitution of knowledge for prejudice. The freedom which permits a true knowledge of facts allows in return the kind of action which— insofar as it is based on knowledge rather than on command—is grounded in liberty: "Newton's principle of gravitation is more firmly established, on the basis of reason, than it would be were the government to step in, and to make it an article of necessary faith. Reason and experiment have been indulged, and error has fled before them. It is man alone which needs the support of Government. Truth can stand by itself."[29] This Enlightenment notion about the autonomy of truth which extends also to the facts of state and society underlay the notion of free politics governed by the judgment of competent citizens. Jefferson held that the assertion that the king of England is a despotic ruler is something that can be proved if the relevant "facts be submitted to a candid world."[30]

In his second inaugural address Jefferson articulated some of the key elements of an experimental approach to politics, which relies on the citizens as witnesses, when he referred to American public life as "an experiment" which would determine "whether freedom of discussion unaided by power is not sufficient for the propagation and protection of truth."[31] Describing citizens as witnesses, Jefferson stressed the virtues of the kind of detached gaze which I have associated with attestive visual orientations. He praised the judgment of "our fellow citizens [who] have looked on *cool and collected*" (my emphasis).[32] Their judgment proves, according to Jefferson, that "truth and reason have maintained their ground against false opinions . . . the press confined to truth, needs no other legal restraint, the public judgment will correct false reasonings and opinions."[33]

Jefferson's reliance on the "cool look" implicitly rejects the employment of affective or evocative strategies of persuasion. In order for seeing to ground rational judgment and action it must be a disciplined individual act—and, in the aggregate, also a nonarbitrary social act. Jefferson trusted the act of witnessing, the direct experience that citizens can have of their leaders, as a source of true notions about leaders. He was also aware of the difficulties. He observed that "of the various executive duties no one excites more anxious concern than that of placing the interests of our fellow citizens in the hands of honest men, with understanding sufficient for their station. No duty at the same time is more difficult to fulfill." [34] Despite the difficulties, he insisted that ultimately citizens must pass verdicts on their leaders (as in his own case) guided by "what [they] themselves will have seen, not what their enemies and mine shall have said." [35] Such trust in the superior power of seeing over hearing implied, of course, a preference for reports or utterances made by eyewitnesses rather than distant or hidden agents. Jefferson's concept of a science of politics is connected with his commitment to the democratic ideal of politics as something that can be known as a view, provided the facts are brought before the eyes of the citizens who can act as cool and collected witnesses. In order to defend this view of politics, Jefferson needed to insist on the competence of the public. "The general spread of the light of science," he noted, "has already laid open to every view the palpable truth that the mass of mankind has not been born with saddles on their backs." [36]

Jefferson's notion of politics as something observable shows, of course, strong affinity to Montesquieu's ideas in *The Spirit of the Laws* (1748). Jefferson read the book and promoted its publication in America. [37] While the idea of a science of politics encountered much resistance, especially on the part of Catholics and aristocrats in Europe, it had enthusiastic followers among the founders of the American republic. Such ideas could be employed in the American context both to debunk the despotism of the European regimes and to provide a new basis for establishing political authority without relying on the past. For Alexander Hamilton and James Madison, faith in the possibility of a science of politics, of the knowledge of the principles of good government, was necessary in order to defend the assertion that democratic political order can be established not only in a small community but also in a populous and territorially vast state. It was important for the Federalists to present the ultimate political acts of structuring a government as a matter of knowledge and reason, not tradition, contingency, or chance. [38] The Reverend J. Witherspoon, who was, *inter alia,* a teacher of Madison, observed that "whereas there is nothing new in governments settled by caprice or accident . . . to see government in large and populous countries settled from its foundation by deliberate counsel and directed immediately to the public good of the present and future generations is certainly altogether new."[39] Gordon Wood notes that as a part of the American political culture American political science, the search for the scientific principles that can account for people's political actions, was uniquely empirical, stressing—to use Hamilton's own language—"the evidence of fact itself."[40] For Madison, America was indeed "a workshop of liberty,"[41] as for John Adams, politics was a continual experiment.[42]

In his "A Defense of the American Constitution," Adams observed that such people as Jefferson, Paine, Barlow, Franklin, and Rittenhous saw legislation as a science.[43] No wonder the Anti-Federalists felt it necessary to deal with the appeal of their opponents to the authority of science. One of them, Luther Martin, wrote that "if the framing and approving of the constitution now offered to our acceptance, is a proof of knowledge in the science of government, I not only admit, but I glory in my ignorance."[44] This line of attack could have had a powerful appeal for a democratic public insofar as ignorance appears to be distributed more equally than knowledge. Still, in the climate prior to the professionalization of American science in the latter part of the nineteenth century,[45] the faith in a universally accessible science of politics, promoted by people who held that everyone can contribute to the advancement of science, appeared widely plausible and more consistent with the melioristic optimistic temper of the new republic. Inasmuch as American exponents of a science of politics rejected Montesquieu's view that republican government cannot be established over a vast and populous territory, perhaps the most important implication of faith in the possibility of a science of government was, as I have already indicated, that politics is a realm of objective observable facts that permits citizens to function as participant-spectators.

Stripping Off the Veils of Power

The most immediate appeal of a science of government based on public observation and judgment was, of course, its power in debunking the monarchy as a political order based on the governors' deception and theatricality and on the subjects' credulity and deference. No wonder the introduction of an attestive visual perspective on politics was associated with a recurrent preoccupation with the need to "strip off" political authority so that the citizens could see what was hidden beneath the garments of the king. The shift between monarchic and democratic concepts of government from credulous, celebratory to skeptical, attestive visual orientations toward political authority was captured in Hans Christian Andersen's famous story "The Emperor's New Clothes."

> "But he hasn't got anything on!" cried a little child. "Dear me! Listen to what the pretty innocent says!" cried his father. And it was whispered from man to man what the child had said. "'He hasn't got anything on' says a little child, he hasn't got anything on!" "Why but he hasn't got anything on!" they all shouted at last. And the emperor winced, for he felt they were right. But he thought to himself: I must go through with the procession now! And he drew himself up more proudly than ever while the chamberlains walked behind him bearing the train that wasn't there.[46]

The last paragraph of Andersen's fairy tale contains some of the key elements of the revolutionary debunking power of an attestive visual orientation, of an inspecting public, when it is interjected in the context of celebratory visual representation of political authority. As in this case, the critical force of the attestive eye threatens to completely undermine celebratory state spectacles. It is significant that Andersen stresses the force of the innocent eye of a childlike observer who has not been, as yet, "socialized" by convention. The fact that it is the innocent eye of a child which can lead to a total redefinition of the situation indicates the democratic implications of attestive vision, and the rhetorical powers of the autonomous witness. The story captures also the power of "realistic" description of the exposed truth to command public attention and to spread within the social space. It notes further the pain of the monarch at the moment of exposure and his attempt to hide his recognition in order to delay the collapse of the celebratory spectacle in the face of the sudden transformation of credulous celebrating spectators into skeptical witnesses.

These important features of Andersen's fairy tale are discernible in key documents of modern liberal-democratic ideology, such as those composed by Thomas Paine and Joseph Priestley. Perhaps because they were Englishmen who came to play significant, albeit different, roles in the formative stage of the American democratic creed, both Paine and Priestley are particularly instructive when they juxtapose the democratic idea of politics as a view of "simple facts" and monarchic politics as the employment of pomp and splendor to cover the "true facts" behind the theatrics of the court. In his *Rights of Man,* for instance, Thomas Paine notes that "what is called monarchy always appears to me a silly contemptible thing. I compare it to something kept behind a curtain about which there is a great deal of bustle and fuss, and a wonderful air of seeming solemnity: but when by accident, the curtain happens to be open and the company see what it is they burst into laughter."[47]

That laughter is, of course, devastating to political authority. It is triggered by a sudden realization of the discrepancy between what is claimed and celebrated and what can be attested to. The idealized heroic status which celebratory orientation accords political actors makes them vulnerable to such satirical exposure.[48] In both words and illustrations an English contemporary of Andersen, William Makepeace Thackeray, fully exploits the satirical force of the incongruities between the idealized and the real king. In his *Paris Sketch Book* Thackeray writes, "But a King is not every inch a King." In his regular clothes he appears as he really is, a "little lean, shrivelled, paunchy old man, of five feet two . . . Put the wig and shoes on him, and he is six feet high;—the other fripperies, and he stands before you majestic, imperial, and heroic! Thus do barbers and cobblers make the Gods that we worship . . . Majesty is made of the wig, the high-heeled shoes, and clock, all fleurs-de-lis bespangled."[49]

Bursting into laughter is, of course, only one of several ways by which free citizens can break the rules of celebratory state spectacles and undermine the solemnity and dignity which uphold monarchic authority. Once the public sees the nakedness of the emperor, the effects of scorn, contempt, and degradation are equally devastating. Machiavelli, who recognized the dependence of monarchic authority upon the theatrical projection of splendor and self-assurance, recommended that the prince should always conduct himself with an eye to "upholding . . . the majesty of his dignity which must never be allowed to fail in anything whatever," that "his actions [should] show grandeur, spirit, gravity, and fortitude."[50] It is partly for undermining the celebratory orientation of citizens toward authority and partly for their diminishing respect for the king or the queen that Burke criticized the French Revolution as well as its radical supporters such as Thomas Paine and Joseph Priestley. Dwelling on the degradation of the Queen of France, Marie Antoinette, whom some years earlier he had seen in Versailles "glittering like a morning star,"[51] he observed that "the supreme majesty of a monarch cannot be allied with con-

From William Makepeace Thackeray, *The Paris Sketch Book of Mr. M. A. Titmarsh* (1840) (New York: Charles Scribner's Sons, 1904), opposite p. 404. Reproduced by courtesy of the Houghton Library, Harvard University.

tempt."[52] Like Thomas Paine, Edmund Burke recognizes, of course, that once the garments of kings and queens are torn off it becomes evident that "a king is but a man [and] a queen is but a woman."[53] But, unlike Paine, Burke sees the exposed nakedness of kings and queens as leading toward the degeneration of civilized politics, rather than as a progressive shift. According to his logic, the public does not rest with the discovery that a queen is but a woman. It goes further and excuses the capital crime of regicide by presenting this woman as nothing better than an animal.[54] Commenting on the effects of the French Revolution, Burke regrets that "all the pleasing illusions which made power gentle [and which] . . . incorporated into politics the sentiments which beautify and soften private society, are to be dissolved by this new conquering empire of light and reason."[55] To demystify monarchic authority and to do away with the salutary effects of "taste and elegance" is, for Burke, not to humanize but rather to dehumanize politics and risk its degenerating into barbarism. Burke's approval of the seeming solemnity of political authority as a condition for making power gentle would have put him on the side of the emperor in Andersen's tale. He regrets that, as a result of the French Revolution, "all the decent drapery of life is to be rudely torn off. All the super-added ideas, furnished from the wardrobe of a moral imagination, which the heart owns, and the understanding ratifies, as necessary to cover the defects of our naked shivering nature, and to raise it to dignity in our own estimation are to be exploded as a ridiculous, absurd and antiquated fashion."[56]

To explode the seeming solemnity of the monarchy, to demonstrate that a king is but a man is, of course, precisely what motivates Thomas Paine to guide the eyes of the citizen to observe and expose what is behind the "pleasing illusions" which make power gentle. The establishment of attestive visual orientations toward the government is clearly a fundamental element of Paine's program of democratization. There is ample evidence of the affinities between Paine and the subculture of science and technology, which probably account for his trust in the power of visual display and disciplined observations, to establish socially the distinction between true and false claims. From his familiarity with itinerant scientific lecturers such as Benjamin Martin and James Ferguson as well as from his own experience in addressing London's and Philadelphia's artisans, audiences with a special interest in science, Paine might have learned the power of concrete examples to persuade. His impulse to persuade by reference to concrete and observable facts is expressed among other things in his attempt, with the assistance of Benjamin Franklin, to promote his plan for a bridge by presenting a physical model of the bridge in the state house of Philadelphia.[57]

Paine tried to be equally concrete in the context of political discourse when he insisted, for instance, that the invisible English constitution had less authority than the visible American Constitution. "A constitution," he wrote, "is not a thing in name only but in fact. It is not an idol, but a real existence; and wherever it cannot be produced in visible form, there is none."[58] Government which is readily observable and understandable must be as rational and orderly as nature, according to Paine. Hence democracy, in his view, is more natural than monarchy. Whereas "nature is orderly in all her works" the monarchy, he observes, "is a mode of government that counteracts nature."[59] Again Paine relies on the analogy between the scientific observation of nature and the attestive viewing of a government which, insofar as it is democratic, is visible.

Paine's close contact with people such as Joseph Priestley, Benjamin

Franklin, Thomas Jefferson, and Benjamin Rush could have provided much encouragement both for his faith in the public's potential to witness and understand the simple facts of politics and for his conviction that every "illiterate mechanic" could judge the nature of government.[60] It was in line with such ideas that Paine could claim that democracy is a kind of government which "presents itself in the open theatre of the world in a fair and manly manner. Whatever are its excellences or its defects, they are visible to all. It exists not by fraud or mystery."[61] Ultimately, then, it was politics as transparent facts which according to Paine distinguishes democratic government from "the puppet show of State and Aristocracy."[62]

For Joseph Priestley, a scientist, preacher, and supporter of the American and the French revolutions, and an advocate of an experimental concept of politics, what is reprehensible in Burke's defense of the pomp and majesty of royal authority is that these are precisely the conditions which encourage kings to forget the people. "So fascinating is the situation in which our kings are placed, that it is of great importance to remind them of the true relation they bear to the people, or, as they are fond of calling them 'their people.'"[63] He criticizes Burke for spreading the "poison" of "respect for princes" which makes the latter "apt to imagine that their rights are independent of the will of the people."[64] We are not . . . to be governed by names," continues Priestley, "but by things . . . The more respect for a king in consequence of his person being held sacred—does alone in some countries render his person and his power inviolate."[65] He sees such "superstitious respect for royalty" as largely undermined in France by the revolution.[66]

For Priestley, as well as for Paine, then, once the celebratory orientation toward authority is discredited, authority is more likely to come to depend upon its perceived actions as an agency with a mandate to act for the people. "The only rational end of the power of the king," says Priestley, "is the general advantage, that is, the good of the people."[67] A fundamentally instrumental-experimental concept of public action combines in Priestley's thought with the requirement of the governor's exposure to the critical gaze of "well informed," "well disposed," and concerned spectators to form a kind of authority which without the protection of "pleasing illusions," majesty, splendor, and celebration becomes publicly observable and therefore democratically accountable.[68]

Alexis de Tocqueville made some of the most insightful observations on what can be characterized as the centrality of attestive-critical witnessing in the constitution of democratic authority. "It is on their own testimony," he said in regard to democratic citizens, "that [they] are accustomed to rely . . . They like to discern the object which engages their attention with extreme clearness [and] they, therefore, strip off as much as possible all that covers it; they rid themselves of whatever conceals it from sight, in order to view it more closely and in the broad light of day. This disposition of mind soon leads them to condemn forms which they regard as useless or inconvenient veils placed between them and the truth." [69]

As the very logic of attestive, inquisitive visual orientation, "stripping off" reflects the special power of the citizens not just as spectators but as skeptical witnesses. Stripping off the body politic is, therefore, a fusion of attestive visual orientations and the democratic impulse to hold the government accountable and continually exposed to the judgment of the citizens. The democratization of witnessing has, of course, important implications for the nature of visual persuasion and its role in the rhetoric of political power and authority. "Equality," notes Tocqueville, "begets in man the desire of judging of everything for himself, it gives him in all things a taste for the tangible and the real." [70] The operation of the same principle affects acting on both the political arena and the stage. "It is difficult," Tocqueville continues, "for an aristocracy to prevent the people from getting the upper hand in the theatre. The literature of the stage . . . even amongst aristocratic nations constitutes the most democratic part of their literature." [71] There is, then, a relation between elevating or recognizing the status of spectators as witnesses and the rhetorical strategies most effective in winning their approval. In both the theater and the polity, democratic spectators lend very special force to that which can be made observable and concrete with reference to "reality." According to Tocqueville, in a society where the citizens are "placed on equal footing, they readily conclude that everything in the world may be explained, and that nothing in it transcends the limits of understanding. Thus they fall into denying what they cannot comprehend, which leaves them but little faith for what is extraordinary and almost insurmountable distaste for whatever is supernatural." [72]

The significance attributed by Tocqueville to the role and authority of the citizens in stripping off the veils of political authority, and by people such as Jefferson, Paine, Priestley, and many others to the power of citizens to observe and expose their governors, indicates the extent to which attestive visual norms in the American democracy were explicitly or implicitly stressed in connection with the role of citizens as spectators and of the government as the object of their gaze.

In contrast with the American case, when attestive visual orientations and their power to expose and discipline the observed are discussed in the context of European politics there is a characteristic tendency to stress the functions of seeing as means of control employed by the governors vis-à-vis the citizens. This is, of course, Bentham's perspective when he advances the principle of the "panopticon" as an all-encompassing inspection which serves hierarchical control of conduct in prisons, hospitals, schools, and "other establishments."[73] He is even attracted by the possibility of adapting the architecture of such establishments in order to subject inferiors to visual inspection. The essence of the panopticon principle, according to Bentham, is in "the centrality of the inspector's situation, combined with the well known and most effectual contrivances for seeing without being seen."[74] Bentham senses the novelty of using sight as an instrument of social control. Inspection, he notes, is "a new mode of obtaining power of mind over mind, in a quantity hitherto without example."[75] His model prison is built as a rotunda—a circular structure—with the cells along the circumference and the inspector at the central point, able to see all the prisoners. By the use of "effectual contrivances," Bentham seeks to ensure that the prisoners themselves would not enjoy similar advantage vis-à-vis the inspector. His objective is to combine the omnipresence of the inspector with his or her own invisibility to the inspected.[76] It is precisely this asymmetry between observing the many and being invisible to them that renders Bentham's panopticon principle an instrument of hierarchical authority. In this context, the observer is not interested so much in knowing the inner state of the observed as in disciplining their overt behavior.[77]

If one reverses the roles and makes the governor exposed to the constant inspection of the prisoners, the panopticon is transformed into a democratic principle of inspection. Although Bentham does not quite reverse the roles of governor and prisoners as inspector and inspected, the tyrannical character of one-sided inspection of subordinates by their superiors is tempered in the panopticon by exposing the latter to the gaze of *visitors*.[78] In the larger political context, a principle of reciprocal inspection—the possibility of a flexible shifting of roles between the observer and the observed—implies, of course, a more equal distribution of the power to control or discipline behavior through inspection. Still it is with an eye to the role of the government as the spectator, or rather inspector, and to the role of the public as the object that Bentham analyses the role of seeing in the polity. Michel Foucault, who discusses Bentham's panopticon at length, generally ignores the democratic implications of the power of reciprocal inspection indicated in Bentham's concept of the visitors who inspect the inspectors when he chooses to focus on Bentham's notion of inspection primarily as a technique of hierarchical surveillance over subordinates, "an ingenious cage," a form of subtle coercion.[79] Because he regards the eye mostly as a means of inducing discipline from above, Foucault is intrigued by the fact that the same Enlightenment which discovered the liberties also discovered these new soft, noncorporal techniques of coercion.[80] This is, however, more an apparent than a substantive contradiction. As Jefferson, Paine, and Priestley recognized, once the same technique of inspection is applied by citizens to their governors rather than the reverse, once it is the government itself which becomes an object of increasing observation, inspection as a technique of control is transformed into a democratic instrument for holding authority publicly accountable. As such, inspection is perfectly consistent with the Enlightenment concepts of liberty, accountability, and politics. Popular surveillance of the government could in fact emerge as a principal technique of checking arbitrary power in the modern liberal-democratic state. It becomes evident that techniques of inspection can furnish a way to economize the costs of control not only from top to bottom but also from the bottom up. While such techniques allow the state to observe the citizens without actually convening large assemblies, they also allow the citizens to entrust a skillful few with the power to expose the government to a public gaze. Governors exposed to the public eye are disciplined through the pressures of anticipated as well as unanticipated public reactions, and are thereby motivated to make their actions appear agreeable to their citizen-spectators. When they fail or when the public discovers discrepancies between the public presentations and the observable facts of the governors' conduct, their authority and powers can be fatally diminished, as the fate of many modern democratic political leaders demonstrates.[81] In totalitarian states, as George Orwell illustrated with particular acuity,[82] one-way seeing from the top down, seeing without being seen, centralizes power at the top. In the liberal-democratic state, the attempts are directed primarily at ensuring the visibility of the governors to the lay public, the omnipresence of the "public eye," as well as, in the name of citizens' rights for freedom and privacy, to render the citizens at least partly invisible to the government.[83] In America the force of inspection, as a democratic means of holding governors accountable, and its corresponding weakness, as a means of hierarchical control, relates to the unwillingness to consider any individual or institution—including the president—as having a privileged overview of the entire society while considering all others as having but partial views. The American rejection of hierarchical authority structures and the commitment to the principle of divisible sovereignty imply that a comprehensive view is not accessible to privileged outsiders but is largely an aggregate of the equally authoritative yet partial views of all participants. Against this background, it should be easier to understand the significance of the fact that in liberal democracy political action becomes an ongoing public spectacle in which political actors and institutions clash or cooperate under the gaze of the public eye. As Bentham understood, the key to the panopticon principle as a source of power is not that the objects of inspection are continually under the eye of the inspector, which may be impractical. The point is rather that the observed "should feel themselves as if under inspection."[84] This condition is satisfied when the observed have no way of knowing or anticipating when they are going to be under surveillance. Consequently, even in moments in which they are not observed, they must feel exposed. They feel themselves, to use Bentham's language, "living and acting under view of an all-observing though human eye."[85]

Experimental Instrumentalism as a Genre of Democratic Political Theater

"Human abilities," notes Joseph Priestley, "are chiefly conspicuous in adapting means to ends."[86] Considering the role of attestive visual orientations in the definition of political actions as facts or objects of perception, decisions to instrumentalize or technicalize public actions take on a new meaning. They may reflect the response of political performers to the demand of liberal-democratic spectators for acts which can be made conspicuous by being externalized and concretized as visible material relations between causes and effects, acts whose direction, structure, and consequences are manifest. From the perspective of Priestley's claim that human abilities are manifest in actions when they are defined instrumentally, it is precisely by hiding the instrumen-

118   Private Persons and Public Actions

tal logic of their actions behind a facade of pomp and splendor that monarchs can cover their incompetence or disregard for public interests. In contrast to this use of pomp and splendor, the stark, factual display of the grounds and course of public actions can appear to be central to democratic notions of politics, authority, and accountability. Although the technicalization of public actions is often defended as a means of enhancing their effectiveness in the realization of defined objectives, their very exposure as overt, publicly inspectable acts, whose adequacy can supposedly be judged independently of the more elusive, invisible, inward traits of their agents, already satisfies the principal requirements of liberal-democratic accountability as it is defined within an attestive visual culture. Actors who cast and defend their actions in instrumental-technical terms can therefore appear to expose themselves, in some respects at least, to public judgments of their competence in terms of the external visible effects of their actions. They seem to be renouncing some measure of personal, institutional, or ideological power to define or control the indicators of their successes or failures as performers. As such, the features of liberal-democratic political action as a public spectacle involve the demystification of politics as a series of "performances" in both senses of the word—as carrying out, executing, or implementing decisions as well as exhibiting skills and competence before a gazing, judging public. Both the carrying out of functional tasks and the exhibition of technical skills reinforce a separation of actions from persons parallel to the distinction between the visible realm of public life and the invisible one of subjective life.

I have already argued that, as a form of liberal-democratic political action which combines claims of knowledge and authority with a public performance of certain actions, instrumentalism shares important features with the experimental-scientific tradition. Those affinities are again most instructively manifested in the positions and activities of Joseph Priestley and in Edmund Burke's criticism of Priestley and what he represents in his attempts to transfer the spirit and techniques of experimental science into the sphere of politics. The general focus of Burke's attack is the manipulative implications of an interventionist approach which applies materialistic-mechanistic metaphors in the political sphere. He is concerned that, like chemists, political experimentalists will "mingle," "blend," and "sift" social institutions as if they were convertible matter in order "to crystalize [them] into true, democratic explosive insurrectionary nitre."[87] Burke warns of the "enormous evils" of "dreadful innovation[s]" which render "knowl-edge . . . worse than ignorance."[88] He fears that experimental phi-losophers will "sacrifice the whole human race to the slightest of their experiments,"[89] that "geographers and geometricians . . . want new lands for new trials,"[90] that they seek to substitute the principles of mechanic philosophy for "love," "manners," wisdom, and experi-ence,[91] that they substitute "mechanical balance" for the moral basis of power.[92] He is concerned that through their "smithery," political experimentalists like Priestley strive to create "new fancied and new fabricated republics."[93] Against these attitudes, Burke insists that in politics the subject of demolition and construction is not brick and timber but sentient beings who "by the sudden alteration of [their] state may be rendered miserable."[94] Against the instrumental political experimentalism of his opponents, Burke insists that "no discoveries are to be made in morality, nor many in the great principles of govern-ment."[95] He attacks "the fabricators of governments"[96] and defends the primacy of experience and the need to follow precedent. Although he acknowledges causes in political life, Burke doubts that history can "furnish grounds for a sure theory on the internal causes which neces-sarily affect the fortune of a state" because he finds these causes to be "uncertain" and "difficult to trace."[97] Contrary to radical reformers like Priestley, who held that the effects of causes in the construction of a commonwealth can be demonstrated through visible "crucial" experiments, Burke believes that "the real effects of moral causes are not always immediate" and that "in states there are often some obscure and almost latent causes, things which appear at first view of little moment, on which a very great part of its prosperity or adversity may most essentially depend."[98] One must therefore approach the "faults of the state" with great caution, treating them like "the wounds of a father, with pious awe and trembling solicitude."[99]

By contrast to this Burkeian anti-instrumentalism, Priestley insists that although the fabrication of a new government is not desirable, "it may nevertheless be necessary" that the people "make many experi-ments of new forms of government without much inconvenience; and though beginning with a very imperfect one, they adopt a very good one at last."[100] Whereas Burke insists that causes and effects in polit-ical matters are often latent and obscure, Priestley holds that histor-ical events such as the American and the French revolutions can demonstrate which of the competing theories of government is valid. Using the language of experimental philosophy, Priestley claims that "such events as these, teach the doctrine of liberty, civil and religious, with infinitely greater clearness and force, than a thousand treaties on the subject. They speak a language intelligible to all the world." [101] Once freedom is granted to all persons, says Priestley, "society would have the benefit of all the experiments they would make" and adopt the scheme "which should appear to be most conducive to the good of the whole." [102]

Priestley's tinkering orientation to politics clearly presupposes a mechanistic conception of the state. "When a state," he observes, "cannot be preserved by the universal, or very general, desire of the people, it may be saved by the *balancing* of those powers which would tend to destroy it." [103] He acknowledges that there are constraints on political experimentalism. It is not feasible, although it would have been very instructive, he maintains, to try the French constitution in England and vice versa. [104] But, consistent with the principles of experimental philosophy, he asserts that "we are so little capable of arguing *a priori* in matters of government, that it should seem experiments only can determine how far this power of the legislature ought to be extended, and it should likewise seem that, until a sufficient number of experiments have been made, it becomes the wisdom of the civil magistracy to take as little upon its hands as possible and never to interfere without the greatest caution." [105]

For Priestley, experiments are not simply the means to justify and rationalize the actions and interventions of the state. As a framework for holding governors accountable for their actions, the ethics of political experimentalism prefers instrumental actions through which the efficacy and skill of the actors, not their character, morality, or rank, can be made publicly manifest and tested without the mystifications and affects of splendor and majesty. "If the pride of nations must be gratified," he writes to Burke, "let it be in such things as [canals, bridges, and noble roads; public buildings, libraries, and laboratories] and not in the idle pageantry of a court calculated only to corrupt and enslave the nation." [106] Just as the dominant social image of Priestley as a scientist was of "the inductivist hero par excellence," of an "untutored amateur" who made great discoveries by simple careful observations, [107] so the temper of his political experimentalism suggests an antielitist approach according to which every person "retain[s] his natural powers of speaking, writing [and] especially [of] proposing new forms of government." [108]

Simon Schaffer points out that Priestley subscribed to an epistemology which "connected assent to political and religious authority with assent to matters of fact. If such matters of fact were properly constructed and reproduced for others through the network of enlightened contacts, then corrupt authority and false belief would be overthrown and replaced by virtue. By linking free individual assent with virtuous politics, Priestley revealed his own allegiance to the civic humanist concept of knowledge." [109]

Like Jefferson's and Paine's, Priestley's career illuminates the links between various strains of eighteenth-century experimental science and liberal-democratic politics. It is the diffusion of the kind of concepts of political action conceived in Priestley's political experimentalism that made instrumental paradigms of public action normative in America and in other modern liberal-democratic states. Furthermore, it is largely due to the perceived public nature of instrumental success—or failure—as something attested to with reference to widely accessible facts and events rather than to the judgment of hierarchical authority that political actors faced with the need to enlist public support and satisfy the requirements of accountability before modern democratic publics have so often been motivated to adopt the instrumental style of action as a way to externalize their actions and make their competence "conspicuous" in terms of such visible referents.

Instrumentalism as a genre of "performing" in the sense of exhibiting a certain mode of acting may nevertheless take precedence over instrumentalism as "performing" in the substantive sense of carrying out. The impulse of democratic citizens to trust, as Tocqueville observes, the tangible and the real, may encourage actors to act in a way that satisfies these conditions even when such actions are not substantially effective. Whether the theatrical and the substantive dimensions are united or separated, "technicalizing" or "instrumentalizing" action is precisely such a strategy of implicitly claiming that actions are subject to objective public assessments. In a society in which scientific and technical standards are not monopolized by exclusive elites and in which professional communities are open and autonomous vis-à-vis political authority, such acts of technicalization are compatible with the rhetoric of democratic action. Hilary Putnam may have sensed this special relation between the political authority of publics in the democratic polity and the propensity to tie public actions to visible technical referents when he noted that "both instrumentalism and majoritarianism are powerfully appealing to the contemporary mind. The contemporary mind likes demonstrable success." [110] Whereas majoritarianism and instrumentalism may combine to invest "demon-strable success" with persuasive powers across diverse sociopolitical contexts, only in a democratic polity are they integrated into both dom-inant ideology and practice. In dictatorships where "public" action is inherently invisible to the citizens, governments can much more easily conceal failures from their citizens or prevent them from translating such failures into powerful political processes of delegitimation.

As I have indicated above, instrumentalism as a strategy for exposing actions as performances in a shared field of visual perception can also be transformed into technically empty but politically substantive rit-uals of legitimation. What actors present and even more what spec-tators perceive may be incongruent with the certifiable causal links between the involved actions and their consequences.[111] To the extent that the politically ritualistic efficacy of such presentations and per-ceptions does not depend on substantive instrumentalism, "ritualistic instrumentalism" can still control the actual distribution of political credit or blame among competing actors. Ritualistic instrumentalism may be, therefore, a less costly political resource than substantive instrumentalism. It satisfies the external form of the requirement of attestive visual tests of accountability but does not satisfy their func-tional logic. This is probably the most important persistent reason for the predilection of political actors for the form or style of instru-mental action as a ritual of legitimation and their tendency to ignore it as a substantive (and considerably more costly and demanding) mea-sure for enhancing rationality and technical effectiveness whenever the two can be kept apart.

Although in a theatrical production of the appearance of instru-mentalism actors are free from the harsh tests of substantive efficacy, they remain constrained by the public expectation that insofar as they claim or appear to act on scientific-technical grounds their compe-tence or incompetence is expected to be publicly manifest in at least certain features of their actions. If the actors could predict which aspects of their performance in a particular situation would generate public trust or distrust and if they could then find the measures to suffi-ciently control these features, they could substantially reduce the risks that accrue from presenting their actions in instrumental-functional terms that expose them to potentially damaging criticism from inde-pendent, and occasionally expert, observers. There is no such knowl-edge base, however, which can grant actors the desired control. Political, like commercial, advertising cannot be informed by sufficiently certain social-scientific knowledge of consumers' responses to alternative stimuli (products or actions) to furnish actors with effective means of eliminating the uncertainties of public responses once they act or appear in the public field of perception.[112] Hence, paradoxically, whether the claim that actions are guided by scientific and technical considerations is warranted or not, it contributes to the vulnerability of actors to external public criticism.

The metaphysical construction of political actions as events in the world of sense perceptions and observable facts has drawn upon a powerful drive to materialize politics as a this-worldly activity. This drive can be recognized among diverse early modern political and social thinkers including Machiavelli, Hobbes, Locke, Condorcet, Jefferson, and Bentham. One of the principal motives of these thinkers was the rejection of the fusion of politics and religion which they tended to regard as a principal source of political conflict and instability. In the late nineteenth century the reaction to the role of religious orientations and sensibilities in politics, as well as to some cultural trends that mystified and spiritualized society as a corporate entity, was a powerful motive for the rise of the social sciences, as one can discern in the enterprises of thinkers such as Emile Durkheim and Max Weber.

Resisting such tendencies in their earlier manifestations, Hobbes was very direct when he stated that the authority of "power invisible" diminishes the obedience of the citizens to the sovereign power.[113] Materialistic concepts of politics serve in Hobbes to consolidate the powers of the sovereign to govern and secure order. For Locke, to confine politics to "outward things" was similarly a part of a strategy of defining politics as activity outside the sphere of religion which was increasingly confined to the private domain.[114] For Scottish thinkers such as David Hume and Adam Smith, a science of politics was a means to check the destabilizing effects of superstition and enthusiasm.[115] Just as the new chemists forced the alchemists to subject their claims to public tests, so modern liberal-democratic political ideologues have enlisted materialistic and instrumental notions of political action to render political authority dependent upon acts open to public observation and judgment.

As I have already indicated, the metaphysical construction of politics as consisting of material-like observable public facts has drawn also upon the Western empirical scientific tradition which has grounded knowledge in sense perception. The commitment to empirical and, therefore, inherently probabilistic knowledge of "reality" further implied that no concept of political facts can be certain and determinate enough to end all debate. While empirical-materialistic epistemology has been congenial, therefore, to the democratization of politics by placing it in the domain of socially inclusive sense experience, the probabilistic concept of political knowledge made it impossible to absolutize any particular view or concept of politics. John Stuart Mill understood this empirical view of politics as implicitly classifying politics with physics and ethics in the domain of open-ended discourse, unlike mathematics where "all the argument is on one side [and where] there are no objections and answers to objections."[116]

An empirical probabilistic concept of knowledge enabled liberal-democratic theory to conceive political reality as something which continually emerges from the convergences of a multitude of discrete individual testimonies without ever freezing into a fixed given. As a public construction such a definition of reality can neither be easily imposed from above by the privileged few nor used by them to avoid public exposure and criticism. Such an open-ended empirical concept of reality is more compatible with a voluntary theory of action and with a concept of accountability according to which arbitrary actions appear to risk visible failure in a neutral world of facts. Like the concept of the "market" in early liberal ideology, the concept of "reality" in modern liberal-democratic ideology has required that reality be neither deliberately produced by privileged agents nor just the result of blind necessities. Reality, like the market, has derived its authority in the context of liberal-democratic ideology from the special balances of freedom and causation, voluntarism and necessity, agency and situation. The crucial point about the market as a liberal principle of order and discipline has been that so long as there are no monopolies and the various actors can be taken to be roughly equal in their powers to influence the results of its operations, the market could be, at least relatively, regarded as a morally and politically "neutral" mechanism for distributing opportunities and constraints or rewards and penalties among actors. Reality in the context of public affairs is in some respects the extension of the socioepistemological principles of the market into the political sphere. Just as the market is conceived as a product of the spontaneous convergence of a multitude of free actions, so reality is conceived as something established through the convergence of independent individual testimonies. Hence reality could emerge as a dynamic, open and nonpartisan check on political discourse and action.

Underlying the fusion of an experimental-empirical orientation toward politics and liberal-democratic values is also the assumption that the reality to which scientists refer is the same as the reality with which laypeople are familiar in their ordinary experience. This assumption has supported the tendency to ignore the inherent discontinuities between "public knowledge" in the sense of scientifically established knowledge, which is replicable, systematic, dependent upon theoretical arguments, and impersonal, and "public knowledge" as common sense, publicly shared opinion. Historically the authority of scientists to function as intellectuals, sages, moralists, technicians, teachers, and advisers has rested in the Western tradition on this belief in the basic continuities between the worlds of science and ordinary experience.

The particular force of television as a medium of visual political communications in the modern Western polity must be understood in this wider cultural context of the trends to materialize politics in the this-worldly sphere of observable facts and the social diffusion of the cultural codes of attestive visual orientations. It has been largely due to the regulatory authority of attestive visual codes in the political sphere that acts of seeing and witnessing have become so central to the functions of the citizens in legitimating and delegitimating their rulers and that publicly acceptable visual indicators for the honesty and the competence of political leaders have become so central in the determination of their fate. Ultimately it is the absence or weakness of the norms and practices of attestive visual culture which distinguishes totalitarian from democratic politics. It is because attestive visual norms empower acts or experiences of seeing to validate claims about reality that in the Western liberal-democratic state what is seen on the television screen can have such an impact on the distribution of trust among competing agents. This observation is sustained even when, as is often the case, what is seen bears only a remote, indirect, or even negligible relation to what is politically said or done. While the social distribution of televisions, the spread of visual technology, has integrated visual and mass political communications in many modern societies, the particular norms of a culture define the status, meanings, and standards of acts of witnessing political events and political agents and determine much of the political effects of such acts in both liberal-democratic and nonliberal-democratic states.

Changes in the character and status of the norms of dominant visual codes like those of attestive visual culture are bound, therefore, to have important political consequences. In the closing decades of the twentieth century the democratic political spectacle, which at least in America has been upheld by faith in the "informed" eye posited by attestive visual culture, seems indeed to become increasingly vulnerable to the combined effects of the growing influence of subjectivist and relativistic notions of perception, the revival of fundamentalist religious sensibilities, which encourage in wide circles the reintroduction of variants of celebratory visual orientations, and the tendency to reestablish the primacy of the invisible and the fantastic over the visible and the "factually attestifiable." As we shall see, the epistemological relativism which has spread especially among late-twentieth-century intellectual circles undermines the confidence of the modern Western intelligentsia in defending attestive visual norms against religious, spiritual, and ideological assaults on the status of the visible. In the context of an increasingly reflexive visual culture which regards scientific and religious views of the world as equally, although differently, constructed, and which holds the objects of attestive vision to be no less dependent on a process of structuring and interpreting experience than the objects of celebratory vision, it is more difficult to insist that speakers and actors show "respect for facts" or stand the tests of empirical confirmation and instrumental efficacy.

An important aspect of this development is the spreading recognition that photographs are not the product of a neutral machine, they do not simply mirror given objects, but are more like cultural artifacts which reflect a host of selective strategies built into the camera and the decisions to employ it in specific times and places. We have come to recognize that photographs do not just depict objects; they also mirror the camera or more accurately the culture that produces them.

The transition from attestive to reflexive visual orientations, like the transition from celebratory to attestive ones, involves, then, a significant and potentially revolutionary transformation of the relations between the observers and the observed as well as of the concepts of political persuasion, authority, and accountability which depend on these relations. I have alluded already to parallels between Hans Christian Andersen's fairy tale, "The Emperor's New Clothes," and the regard of democratic advocates such as Thomas Paine and Joseph Priestley for the power of attestive visual orientation once it exposes what is behind the seeming solemnity of monarchic authority. If we were to rewrite the end of Andersen's story not as an illustration of the transition from celebratory to attestive but from attestive to reflexive visual codes, the boy's real discovery would not be that the king is naked but that it is his, the boy's own, eye which dresses or undresses the king. The object is demystified not by exposing its true features but by recognizing the role of the beholder's eye in the construction or deconstruction of the object. Such recognition implies as well an appreciation by the individual of the difficulty of transforming private subjective visual experience into publicly admissible evidence, a difficulty which in some respects is just a special instance of the problem of socially establishing any individual interpretation of experience as a neutral description of objectively given facts.

The transition, to which I shall return later, between attestive and reflexive visual orientations instantly raises the question of whether the liberal-democratic commitment to a concept of order based on the ultimate value ascribed to the individual can be sustained. What liberal-democratic concepts of political action, authority, and accountability can survive in a society of skeptical reflexive observers?[117] Can such a society develop and sustain a public realm? What is the status of science and technology in a political context in which the fragmentation of formerly shared cognitive and normative bases of public action exposes their historicity and limitations as local cultural artifacts? What can be the role of scientific knowledge in a political universe in which it is recognized that the world viewed carries on its "face," so to speak, the "eye prints" of a particular "period eye," a particular episteme, the cultural "software" which programs the eye (or the camera) to follow particular modes of seeing, producing, or interpreting the world as a view?

5. The Aesthetic and Rhetoric of the Machine and Its Role as a Political Metaphor

Whereas the Christian doctrine of natural theology conceived of the invisible God as known and celebrated through visible nature or through His works as the Divine Engineer,[1] modern liberal-democratic ideology has enlisted the sense of sight to make invisible political power known and accountable through the actions of the state. As the works of thinkers such as Jefferson, Priestley, Paine, and Tocqueville suggest, and the criticisms of Edmund Burke illuminate, modern liberal-democratic ideology has been committed to the notion that the state is an object of attestive visual orientations and that the intentions and skills of political actors can be made publicly manifest through their actions.

In the preceding chapter I suggested that within the visual culture of modern democratic politics the instrumentalization of political action has emerged as an attractive strategy for legitimating action. By supposedly externalizing the tests of adequate action as visually manifest connections between certain features of action, its causes, consequences, and objectives, instrumentalization implicitly confirms the role of the public in judging the actions of government and in holding its agents accountable.

It is in connection with these developments that one should understand the emergence of the machine as a key political metaphor in the modern liberal-democratic tradition. Imagining the state and its actions in mechanistic terms, as well as viewing political actors as competent or incompetent technicians, has furnished a framework for "externalizing" political action in the public space of visual perception, for conceiving and presenting the exercise of political power as both a publicly observable and rationally assessable operation.

In the following two chapters I shall examine the various ways instrumental concepts of action and the implicit commitment to mechanistic images of the state, which have been reinforced in America by attestive visual orientations in the political sphere, were supported by the particular modes of respectively aestheticizing and moralizing the machine. I shall juxtapose some of the distinct features of the cultural validation of instrumentalism in American politics, such as the aesthetic and moral approval of the fit between form and function, with the more ambivalent and often antagonistic attitudes of the English.

Celebrating and promoting the idea of scientific progress and the values of industrialization, the Great Exhibition of the Industry of All Nations held at the Crystal Palace in London in 1851 constituted a most instructive display of national variations in the assimilation of technology into culture.[2] Benjamin P. Johnson, who was sent by the state of New York to attend the exhibition and to report on the reception of the American display, notes that many English visitors sensed a lack of splendor, grace, and ornamentation in the American objects. During the first three weeks, while admission to the exhibition was open only to the "wealthy classes," reactions to the American exhibit were not favorable compared with reactions to the displays of European countries such as France, Austria, and England. While European countries exhibited "costly articles wrought with exquisite taste, silks, statutory, diamonds and jewelry," those displayed by the Americans were "mainly of a character of utility in the implement and machinery department." There was nothing from this country, according to Johnson, "to compete with those splendid articles, designed only to minister to human pride which composed so large a portion of the exhibition." The "wealthy classes . . . hastily passed over" the American exhibit.[3] Johnson was not entirely discouraged, however. "As an American," he notes, "I rejoiced that this was so, and it will be, in my opinion a sad day for our country when articles of this character shall attain a preeminence here, over the useful and the necessary as they do in the old world."[4]

These initial reactions already reflect important differences between American and European cultural and political orientations toward machinery and utility. The juxtaposition of these orientations indicates the kind of attitudes which have, particularly since the mid-nineteenth century, underlain American receptivity and English ambivalence, or even resistance, vis-à-vis the "machine" as a political metaphor and vis-à-vis the deployment of instrumental modes of action in the political sphere. The main features of these differences become evident when one examines the distinct American and English responses to a set of strategic cultural questions. Can the useful be regarded as beautiful? Does the expression of function in form make machines or actions more, or less, agreeable? Do machines represent materialistic, as distinct from spiritual or moral, values or are they invested also with spiritual and moral significance?

The American society, permeated by republican-democratic values that are untempered by the European legacy of a feudal past and a traditional political order, and the English society, with its hierarchical class system and strong aristocratic cultural legacy, constitute two very distinct contexts of response to the above issues. They indeed exemplify two sociopolitical modes of assimilating the cultures of science and technology and of trying to develop and establish instrumentalism as a paradigm of public action.

Whereas, with the important exception of the Crystal Palace itself, Europeans revealed in the 1851 exhibition a tendency to use art and craft to hide or sublimate the useful and the necessary, the Americans appeared more favorably disposed to allow the useful and the necessary their full honest expression and to regard splendor and ornaments as diversions inspired by aristocratic sensibilities. Where the Victorians, for instance, were more inclined to dress their machines with the garments of tradition and make them more acceptable to the upper classes by masking their utilitarian uses, in America the affinity for such traditional European sensibilities was increasingly challenged by what was emerging as an indigenous tendency to aestheticize the simple, the plain, and the functional.[5] The exterior of machines, which was often cultivated and ornamented in England in order to perfect a sense of dignity and aloofness vis-à-vis the useful and the necessary, was increasingly enlisted by Americans to reveal the full logic and character of the machine as a functional device. While many commentators criticized the undecorated and plain shape of American articles as manifesting the poor taste and the lack of culture of a new nation, there were already others who appreciated the association between the "functional simplicity" of American products and democratic values such as the provision of large quantities of articles at a low price to suit the needs and means "of a whole people."[6]

The elaborate and costly decorations, which suggested to the Victorians that technology can be tempered and civilized by art, conveyed to many of their American contemporaries luxury and catering to the taste and means of the privileged few.[7] Ralph Waldo Emerson

made a characteristic observation when he noted that "outside embellishment is deformity [and] any real increase of fitness to its ends, is an
increase of beauty."[8] In the Chicago world's fair of 1893, the facades
of the buildings still indicated, however, the persistence in America of
the aesthetics of the cultivated European taste. Steel frame buildings
were dressed with the "illusion of marble and classic monumen-
tality."[9] The touch of an architect more responsive to indigenous
democratic American values like Louis Sullivan, who insisted that
"form follows function" and that there is harmony rather than conflict between "the beautiful and the useful," was not yet encouraged
to challenge fully the aesthetics of the cultivated tradition.[10] At the
same time, however, the aesthetics of the plain and uncultivated style,
which was noted already in the American display at the Crystal Palace
exhibition, had become more pronounced in the field of industrial
design. The competitive coexistence between the two approaches continued in America until the second quarter of the twentieth century,
when the readiness to lend aesthetic value to "clean functional form"
and "unadorned engineering" became more vigorously articulate and
American defensiveness in the face of the charge that the American
character is, like American taste, uncultivated and materialistic, was
balanced by a new confidence in the positive value of American
plainness.[11]

John Kouwenhoven suggests that those who, like Thomas E. Tall-
mudge, argued in the 1920s that the beautiful must be useless,
appeared more and more to be defying local American sensibilities and to be revealing a predisposition to adopt European cultural
identity.[12]

The differences between the aesthetics of the ornamental, the embel-
lished and the monumental, and the aesthetics of "clean functional
form" partly correspond, of course, to the distinctions I have made
between celebratory and attestive visual cultures. The "cultivated tradition" which lends aesthetic values to the idealized, refined, and elevated is compatible with the celebratory impulse to glorify and adorn
the real, while the tendency to lend aesthetic value to the functional
and see with Emerson any "outside embellishment [as] deformity" is
consistent with the attestive visual orientation that ascribes value to
that which is visually manifest and which demonstrably works. It is
not surprising, therefore, that in the American case the principle that
"form follows function" was particularly pronounced in the context
of industrial design where the attestive visual norms which develop in

the subcultures of experimental science and engineering could exert special influence.

Despite the challenges of the "cultivated taste," the aestheticization of the instrumental and the functional have gradually come to be more self-consciously identified with distinct American sociopolitical traits. Although influential Victorian representatives of modern English attitudes toward the relations of aesthetics and industry, such as Henry Cole and his circle, did not reject utility as a principle of ornamental design and directed their criticism particularly against excess in ornaments, they clearly endorsed moderate ornamentation as a means of "civilizing" the machine. Constructions, they believed, should be decorated and the public should be educated to appreciate art.[13]

While in America one detects a more natural and less restrained convergence between the functional and the aesthetic, between science and art, in England the practically useful and the beautiful are more sharply demarcated as norms and domains.[14] A sense of continuity between subjective-aesthetic and impersonal-instrumental orientations toward objects has come to suggest a distinct American attitude which does not fear the assimilation of scientific and technical norms on the grounds that they facilitate or represent the encroachment of the objective or the public on the subjective or the private. In the context of action, such sensibilities are more trusting of the possible accommodation between human agency and the logic of technical necessities.

Kouwenhoven appropriately labels an American predisposition for simplicity, plainness, functional realism, and honest, explicit serviceability in industrial design as expressing the elements of "a democratic technological vernacular" style.[15] Juxtaposed with the style of the cultivated European tradition, it prefers manifest functionality to the unique, personalized, artistic expression of master craftspeople. The vernacular style of design, he suggests, reflects the particular American closeness to nature and a characteristic American tendency to lend cultural status to the common ordinary objects of daily life. The notion that form should follow function does not mean in this context that the useful and the necessary are permitted to eclipse the beautiful and the graceful. In America, attestive visual culture does not undermine closeness to nature but alters its cultural significance.[16] The earlier accent on a celebratory religious orientation toward nature is tempered in modern America by the stress on a concept of nature as a demystified, rational order which reveals the actions and designs of the Divine Engineer. The economy of functional organization and the fitness of form to function have therefore been interpreted in America as having a higher and nobler sanction. What Kouwenhoven defines as a democratic technological vernacular style could represent for Louis Sullivan, for instance, "a principle of structure . . . plainly inculcated in the works of the creator."[17]

Such aesthetic, spiritual, and moral reconciliations between the useful and the natural were, of course, at odds with the view of the machine as the characteristic embodiment of the artificial conceived as antagonistic to the aesthetics, spirituality, and morality of the purely natural.[18] But the attempt to reconcile industrialization and nature was sufficiently forceful and encompassing in America to invest machines and technical feats with moral-spiritual meanings and regard them as signs of progress and of the divine within the human. John Augustus-Roebling, the engineer of the Brooklyn Bridge, thought, for instance, that the American capacity to understand nature which is demonstrated in its engineering achievements is "proof positive that our mind is one with the great universal mind."[19]

Combining the qualities of contemplation and creation, science and technology came to symbolize the individual's virtues as both a spectator, a worshipper of the cosmic order, and a courageous maker and shaper of things.[20] The steam engine, the most celebrated piece of technology in the nineteenth century, seemed an icon of both mind and nature.[21] As a product of mind tuned to the secrets of nature, technology could be integrated in America with the values ascribed to freedom, divinity, and the natural order. Note, for instance, the poetic image of the locomotive in Emily Dickinson's poem of 1862:

> I like to see it lap the Miles—
> And lick the Valleys up—
> And stop to feed itself at Tanks—
> And then—prodigious step
>
> Around a Pile of Mountains—
> And supercilious peer
> In Shanties—by the sides of Roads—
> And then a Quarry pare
>
> To fit its Ribs
> And crawl between
> Complaining all the while

In horrid—hooting stanza—
Then chase itself down Hill—

And neigh like Boanerges—
Then—punctual as a Star
Stop—docile and omnipotent
At its own stable door—[22]

In England, where William Blake juxtaposed "England's green and pleasant Land" with "dark Satanic mills,"[23] where already in the 1830s and 1840s a city like Manchester had become a disturbing icon of the degradation of life and the filth associated with mechanization, where technology was regarded more as a product, a cause, and a symbol of alienation from nature, the machine was more readily construed as a menace, an intrusion into the organic order idealized in pastoral landscapes and reflected in hierarchical social structure.[24]

English ambivalence toward the machine, particularly toward its symbolic association with amoral power, is forcefully articulated in Charles Dickens' works. In *Dombey and Son* (New York, 1892), for instance, the train is associated with destructive energies.[25] The different American response to the culture of industrial machines is illustrated in Lowell, Massachusetts, which was cultivated as a counterexample to Manchester. The American town was supposed to demonstrate the possibility of humanized and aesthetic assimilation of technology and industrialization into society.[26] While in America, then, science and technology characteristically conveyed the possibility of fusing the machine and the garden,[27] of meshing the factory with republican values and love of nature, in England the machine raised more sharply and more polemically the issue of a cultural-political choice between competing identities of England as a garden or a workshop, a polity whose culture is dominated by country gentlemen or by scientists, engineers, and industrialists.[28] If in America nature was characteristically appropriated in order to discard the authority of the past, and the ideas of history and progress were blended with the ancient pastoral dream of recovering the Golden Age of harmony with nature,[29] in England nature was largely invoked by tradition to block a future which breaks from the past and embraces change and innovation.

The tendency during the latter decades of nineteenth-century America to blend the machine and the garden in an equilibrium between society and nature was reflected, among other things, in the value accorded in literature and in painting to the "middle land-scape" as a compromise between the radical ideals of primitive nature unspoiled by human manipulations and the equally radical ideals of nature totally transformed by humanity.[30] Powerful English spokesmen such as Thomas Carlyle and John Ruskin saw a conflict between nature and technical civilization, whereas Americans saw the two as more amenable to being welded together. Technology was considered both as partially embodying the necessary laws of nature and as a human power which could be applied to civilize and socialize the wilderness. Discovering the principles of automatic machines could assume in this cultural climate the valence of a lesson in how to tame primitive nature as well as in how to harness it for human benefit. In Emerson's and Whitman's America, machines could be conceived as harmonious with pastoral life.[31] Nature and artificial machines could be seen to reciprocate by mutually checking each other so that nature limited the ambition of people as makers or creators while machines domesticated the often wild and unruly forces of nature.

The experiment in Lowell, Massachusetts, is a case in point. Even when socialist criticism of the textile mills of Lowell as a form of capitalist exploitation directed attention to the negative, degrading features of such things as overlong workdays, members of a visiting committee of legislators found it edifying to discover in the window-sills in the rooms of factory workers plants such as geraniums and roses attesting to the peaceful coexistence of industry and nature.[32]

For John Roebling, the suspension bridge was a microcosmic reflection of the macrocosmic order. Like Alberti and Palladio, those early Renaissance humanist architects who regarded their art and science as the deployment of the geometrical-mathematical principles of divine design in the artificial world of human creations,[33] Roebling held a humanistic conception of technology. Works, he notes in 1864, are the expressions of the spirit in matter. "There is no essential antagonism in creation . . . [or] absolute opposition to the fulfillment of the Creator's design."[34] To Roebling, who equated "evil" with "transgression of the laws of [one's own] being,"[35] technology appeared to represent a state of accommodation between humanity and nature, a commerce of mind and matter within a regime of respected boundaries.

In Victorian England, where the machine suggested the operation of a more menacing, potentially unrestrained impulse in humans as seekers of material things, machines were not as readily regarded as fit to mirror such lofty things as the principles of cosmic architecture or the harmony between the human mind and divine design. To find beauty in that which is uniquely technological was a discovery an Englishman could most appropriately make in America. "There is no country in the world where machinery is so lovely as in America," Oscar Wilde told his British audiences; "I have always wished to believe that the line of strength and the line of beauty are one. That wish was realized when I contemplated American machinery."[36] The more typical English response to American technology, one more consistent with European ambivalence toward the affirmation of the convergence of the beautiful and the useful, was to disparage the American synthesis of technology and aesthetics as an exemplification of middle-class materialism unchecked by the elegance and refinement of a cultivated taste. In Victorian England, machines were often negatively regarded as icons of detested middle-class values. To Dickens, who became uneasy about the spirit of commerce and industrial production, steamboats did not represent the divine in human action. They suggested, rather, "restless beatles," an image loaded with connotations of a Darwinian struggle for existence and of middle-class activism.[37] For those who equated "Englishness" with the idealized countryside and the idea of organic order, America as a "workshop in the wilderness" was an unsettling example of an antagonistic alternative.[38] For Victorians like Sir Henry Cole the art of design was a means of restraining the machine and checking its tendency to encourage vulgarity, materialism, and excess. Fearing that the "poorer classes," lacking the self-restraint and the cultivated tastes of the upper classes, would be further brutalized by machines, Cole and his companions sought to encourage cultivated industrial design which would "obtain as much beauty and ornament as is commensurable with cheapness,"[39] and secure a measure of refinement and containment for the workers.[40] It is as if machines, like the working class and the lower middle class, were themselves classified as belonging in the domain of low material culture and the fine arts socially associated with upper-class culture were enlisted to the mission of investing them with some of the virtues of upper-class taste.[41] Such didactic-evangelistic attitudes, the mission of refining the lower classes, inculcating discipline, and preventing the reign of mediocrity, were, of course, advocated also by American "Victorians" who saw themselves as protecting high culture and standards of excellence in defiance of the corrosive effects of mass taste and populist democracy.

In this respect, the clash between the cultivated and the vernacular

traditions of design is only one of many recurrent outbreaks of the conflict between "high" and "low" culture and of competing approaches
to the "democratization of culture" in America. As I shall show in
greater detail, the tension between Victorian and vernacular tastes
is, therefore, also a cultural dimension of the continual process of
defining and redefining authority in America.[42] During the second half
of the nineteenth century and the first half of the twentieth, similar
tensions between "elite" and "mass" cultures manifested themselves
in the fields of literature, art, and education.[43] Still, by contrast with
English and other European democracies, such distinctions between
lower- and upper-class cultures were less entrenched and more socially
and politically objectionable in America; science and art, as representing the useful and the beautiful, respectively, could appear, therefore, more naturally as complementary aspects of the same general
experience. Perceived as modes of contact with the immutable laws of
the cosmos, science and technology could also be more easily reconciled with a conception of art as an imitation of nature inspired by
"respect for nature as evidence of God's handiwork."[44] Such was the
view of James Jackson Jarves, who, in his *Art-Idea* (1864), pointed
out that the modern landscape is God's "sensuous image and revelation through the investigation of which by science or its representation by art men's hearts are lifted towards Him."[45]

A view which harmonizes science and art in a common exploration
of the outside world, rather than separating them between low- and
high-class cultures, is not congenial, however, to an appreciation of
craftsmanship as the embodiment of the unique artistic "signature" of
particular individuals. This latter view, so central to the "cultivated
tradition of craftsmanship," entails notions of art that are too personalized and elitist for democratic sensibilities. The sense that machines
are not so much the unique works of individuals as that they reveal to
those properly attuned to nature, and in principle to all humanity, the
secrets of cosmic design made machines more culturally compatible
with democratic values.

In the American political and cultural context, democratic values
have encouraged the notion that religion, as well as art and science,
allows inclusive rather than exclusive access to important truths. It
was in accordance with these American values that the articles of the
American exhibit in the Great Exhibition of 1851 in London were
described as showing the "enterprise, energy, skill and ingenuity [of
the] citizens themselves."[46] *The ability, manifest in the vernacular tra-*

dition of machine design, to combine the aesthetic and the practical permitted technology to appear in America as a composite of the realms of freedom and necessity, as an activity which blends creative engagement with the physical world and detached recognition of the limits nature imposes on the human will. Machines could project simultaneously the process of adaptation to external constraints imposed by the structure of the universe and the capacity to interpret this adaptation as an aesthetic harmony, which finds its expression in the intelligible convergence of function and form in the realm of voluntary human enterprise.

Whereas, as a cultural enterprise of the imagination and of the senses which is unrestrained by material facts or practical needs, the fine arts appear responsive to the values of the upper classes, the aestheticization of the functional and the useful, which is more responsive to middle-class values, rationalizes a role for knowledge of the material world in disciplining the imagination and the senses. As such, a disposition toward the aestheticization of technology in America has been consistent with a liberal-democratic commitment to the dualism of freedom and restraint. It suggests that material culture is compatible with sensations disciplined by the logic of function and that utility can have an aesthetic and therefore a spiritual dimension. The aesthetics of the functional and the instrumental translates into the language of art the republican dialect of freedom and restraint, that is, free will and respect for lawful regularities. Thomas Ewbank, an Englishman who emigrated to America in 1819, articulated the value of the aesthetic fusion of technology and republican sensibilities in America when he praised the inventor as the "artist of the real" and the steamer as "a mightier epic than the Iliad."[47]

By viewing articles of the industrial age as reflecting the ingenuity of an entire people, and not just of a few privileged master craftsmen, Americans were able to place both tool making and the aesthetics of the functional within the domain of the common experience. "Ingenuity," as the fitting of forms to functions, could appear as a kind of universal response to necessities that does not lower but positively elevates humanity. It celebrates people not only as beings who must adapt to necessities but also as creators capable of freedom and autonomy. The equation of the beautiful and the useful could therefore have the double effect of democratizing art as well as aestheticizing (and hence also dignifying) technical and industrial work.[48] Where leading English spokespersons conceived of art as a way to refine and check the bad effects of mechanized culture on the temper, manners, and sensualism of the lower classes, their American counterparts came more and more quickly to find intrinsic artistic qualities in the very process of industrialization and technological advance. While for Americans science and technology were often a medium for a dialogue between humanity and nature, for Victorian Englishmen such as Carlyle, Ruskin, and William Morris, they suggested more a force of moral corruption, a danger of losing rich inward spirituality, and a potential for destroying the balance of culture.

A very instructive expression of Victorian ambivalence toward the "artificial" can be found in the aesthetics of the Pre-Raphaelites. Influenced by the ideas of both Carlyle and Ruskin, this group of English artists, including Dante Gabriel Rossetti, Holman Hunt, and John Millais, were committed to anti-instrumentalist concepts of nature as a visible record of divine revelation.[49] Consistent with the seventeenth- and eighteenth-century idea that the "book of nature," like Scripture, is written by God and suffused with transcendental meaning, the Pre-Raphaelites combined realistic and sacramental orientations toward nature. They held that the artist, like the scientist, has a religious and moral mission to represent and make more manifest the visual details which convey sacred meanings. Such an effort to appropriate visible nature, undistorted by humanity, for the purpose of tracing divine language, this fusion of "mimesis and revelation,"[50] was bound to regard the machine as an intrusion, a threat to the mission of visible nature as a religious and moral document. Within this worldview, the balance of engagement and detachment is ultimately achieved through a religious encounter between human and divine agencies and not through the encounter between humanity and nature.

Reflecting orientations which enlist visible nature to the rhetoric of religious and moral preaching, the Pre-Raphaelites represent in pure form the kind of sensibilities which inhibited in England the harmonization between mechanization and religious or moral values. In nineteenth-century America, such inhibitions were more vulnerable to the competing, mainly Protestant, predisposition to find profound religious and moral meanings not only in the works and words of God but also in the works of men and women. Reinforced by the democratic celebration of human creativity and spirituality, these attitudes were congenial for integrating the machine and its culture into the deeper layers of American civilization. "Machinery and transcendentalism agree well," wrote Emerson in his journal.[51]

Although it was often challenged by competing orientations and values, the vernacular aestheticization of function in form also implied American legitimation for the didactic use of the surface to communicate "useful knowledge," to invite the public to gaze at machines in operation and understand what makes products useful. While the cultivated tradition charges art with the task of distancing the useful and diverting attention away from the necessary, the vernacular tradition expresses the powerful democratic ideal of the morality of exposure. It is this morality of the honestly exposed function that integrates manifest utility with both the rhetoric and the theatrics of legitimate action. It is here that one can find a most suggestive connection between the distinct perceptions of the machine in the two cultures and the respective differences in its employment as a metaphor in politics. In England a thoroughly entrenched aristocratic tradition, which survived the actual decline of the aristocracy itself, has sustained the ideal of politics as the domain of trustworthy actors, of uniquely capable individuals whose actions need not be fully transparent and comprehensible to warrant public approval. English political leaders and public servants are not usually expected to explicate the grounds of their decisions or actions to the extent that this is expected of their American counterparts. A political culture still deeply steeped in the legacy of monarchical values, England allows its political leaders much greater leverage in using secrecy as a prerogative.[52] In England class, character, personality, and other such "ascriptive" features are more acceptable referents of credibility, relative to actual competence demonstrated in actions, than in America.[53]

Such attitudes are persistently reflected both in English orientations toward the organization of the civil service and in English styles of public action. In 1968, the Fulton Commission on the Organization of the British Civil Service recommended that scientists and managers be granted a greater role in the civil service. The Fulton report, however, did not significantly alter the situation any more than had former attempts to enhance the role of science and scientific expertise in the British Civil Service. Twelve years later, *Nature* magazine still complained that little attention was being paid to the adequacy of civil service recruits who get their training in "Oxbridge." The civil service, noted *Nature,* still tends to rely "on gifted generalists . . . without particular expertise." These generalists are "almost proud of having no expert knowledge of the fields of the public service they administer."[54]

There is, of course, a widely shared view in England which approves of the conditions which are criticized by *Nature* and by other advocates of the scientific and technical modernization of government operations. According to this view, the enhancement of the role of experts in public affairs is not conducive to good government. Michael Oakeshott, an English conservative political philosopher, echoes this Burkian view when he attacks the attempts to introduce in England a managerial-scientific approach to public affairs as reflecting a negative American influence. Oakeshott criticizes what he calls the "American technical problem-solving approach" to public affairs, the faith in "the sovereignty of technique" and the role of such faith in encouraging "adventures in the rationalist reconstruction of society."[55] The notion that public service is something which requires skill and competence of the kind that can be acquired by technical training seems to Oakeshott both baseless and dangerous. It overrates knowledge and underrates "experience," "judiciousness," "character," and moral and cultural education all of which are, in his opinion, more likely to be inculcated in "the good home" than in technical schools. This notion, according to Oakeshott, gives the "inexperienced" a license to enter the domain of public affairs.[56] Such criticism of the relevance of acquired competence and skills in the context of public affairs is deeply at odds with pervasive American views which, although far from indifferent to their relevance, regard "experience" and "moral character" as too elusive and class-dependent to command unqualified trust.

Where social or political trust are not generated in a hierarchical class system the authority of the public actor tends to depend more upon the transparent publicly manifest instrumentality of action, on the expression of its function in its form, than upon the fitness of the form of action to the class or personality of the actor. Trust in actors draws in America more upon what people appear to do than upon who they are, upon the perception of a visible fit between means and ends, the voluntary surrender of autonomy to technical-functional discipline and respect for the realm of facts. English aristocratic sensibilities link the freedom and autonomy of actors with the invisibility of the grounds and causes of action. What supposedly controls and disciplines public actions is not so much a gazing, informed, constantly guarding public but rather the character and restraint of trustworthy political leaders. More profoundly suspicious of political power and constantly preoccupied with the dangers of personalized authority, arbitrariness, and self-interest,[57] Americans have cultivated and institutionalized forms of accountability according to which actors in the public sphere are encouraged to "depoliticize" the exercise of discretion in action by voluntarily subordinating (or appearing to subordinate) their personal considerations to public goals and to "neutral," scientificlike standards of adequacy. In such a culture, the instrumentalization of political actions and the subordination of public decisions and programs to the scientific-technical logic of functional values could be made to agree with the epistemological and moral basis of democratic accountability. In contrast to the English, the American tendency to blur the boundaries between the natural and the artificial and the willingness to accept technology as an ingredient of the common experience have supported closer affinities between instrumental and democratic styles of politics. Less inhibited by a characteristically aristocratic cultural dichotomy between the realms of necessity and freedom, between the domain of lower- and upper-class life, and boosted by the aestheticization of technology, the technicalization of political action in America is relatively less burdened by the stigma that technical values have had in culturally stratified societies. Relegating politics to the domain of public, technical actions was therefore less likely to entail for Americans the dangers of enlarging the sphere of necessity at the expense of the sphere of freedom, of permitting deterministic material forces to "arrest" the fantasy of voluntary actions. If in England the sphere of politics was protected as a particular domain of actions guided by the aristocratic values of insular autonomy, character, will, and uniqueness, in America the suspicion of the implications of these values in the political sphere encouraged technicalization and instrumentalization as a means of checking the overpersonalization of political action, the potential effects of overstressing independence, autonomy, will, and uniqueness as the virtues of political actors. It encouraged the tendency to use science and technology to depersonalize the exercise of power and hold public actors accountable in functional terms. Again, the fact that Americans do not usually share the European predisposition to view machines as threatening extensions of the realm of material needs and necessities into the domain of freedom, morality and the spiritual quest has facilitated in America the integration of science and technology into voluntaristic concepts of political action. Inasmuch as the machine was regarded as a servant of humanity, a way to harness the secrets of nature and to tame wild natural forces, and as an expression of the "ingenuity of the people," technicalization in the political sphere could appear compatible with the humanistic and republican features of politics as a domain of creative human action.

A poetic view of the machine, explored and cultivated in America by people such as Thomas Ewbank and Ralph Waldo Emerson, certified it as a political metaphor of action that fuses human creativity with respect for the constraining laws of nature. In America it appears that the fear of technology as a invasive and dehumanizing force corruptive of human freedom was further mitigated, at least until the latter part of the twentieth century, by the notion of the machine itself as a civilizing force deeply rooted in both the social and the natural worlds. This attitude has been consistent with an American disposition, explored below, to view the inner and the outer person, the private person and the citizen, as belonging in the same common plane of reality rather than in two separate and insulated planes.[58] Such an attitude does not support the view of technology as belonging in a sphere where action springs from needs and necessities rather than from the values and moral choices of free agents. It accepts instead the possibility that the inner person can find public expression without necessarily denying autonomy, individuality, or authenticity. The transparency which Europeans have tended to ascribe to shallow and nonautonomous actors came to be associated in American political culture with the virtues which enable independent actors to coordinate their actions or hold each other accountable without being humiliated by arbitrary hierarchical authority. Furthermore, as a feature of actions carried out by government officials, transparency has been consistent with the particularly stringent standards of performance which Americans have tended to impose on their public servants.[59]

Just as the vernacular aesthetics of design has represented trust in the externalization of functions and structures in visible surfaces, democratic politics has supported a form of instrumental action in America in which motives, choices, and ends are made manifest in the visible, perceptual domain of the common experience in terms of the relations between observable causes and effects. Actors who overtly subordinate personal discretion to method, who prefer to validate their action by referring to public knowledge rather than personal experience and who depend for trust upon competence manifested in action rather than upon the more elusive virtues of character or moral personality, could appear as more "honest" and "sincere," as more trustworthy actors. Just as the vernacular aesthetics of machine design makes form appear constrained by function, instrumental political action could appear to suggest actions restrained by the objective logic of the situation. In each case, reason and knowledge appear to impose limits on the arbitrary use of the freedom to shape and create. The tendency to judge actors by referring to the "objective" properties of their actions, those aspects of actions which are publicly perceptible, implies, as I suggested before, a bias for action as the public performance of technical tasks. This bias reflects the operation in America of powerful political incentives to temper the politics of personal conflicts and partisan interests with what Henry Adams called the politics of impersonal forces;[60] it has supported the extension of the instrumental paradigm of political leadership to vast spheres of action, such as public health, communications, energy, transportation, economic policy, and city management, where science and technology appear to have prepared the ground for "objectifying" political actions as forms of technical public actions. The notion that the technicalization of action renders the conduct of actors objectively visible and accountable has encouraged the belief that instrumental accountability—accountability in terms of adequate technical performance—can replace, or at least complement, moral discipline.

The view of mechanical discipline as an alternative to moral discipline was characteristically cultivated among late-nineteenth-century American engineers. As one historian notes, "in response to a few demands for a code of ethics, engineers developed the idea that since the actions of the engineer were checked at every point by the immutable laws of God and nature, there was no possibility for undetected malfeasance. This concept was developed in conjunction with the idea that the traditional professions despite their fancy codes of ethics had far greater opportunity to cheat and defraud the individual client and the public."[61] The comparison with the traditional professions here recalls Galileo's defense against the Church, when he insisted on the nondiscretionary character of the scientist's stance: "The demonstrated conclusions touching the things of heaven cannot be changed with the same facility as opinions about what is legal or not."[62] Essential to the argument advanced by the engineers was not only that *objective reality* can check the engineer where ethical codes check the lawyer, but also that the conduct of the engineer is visible even to the uneducated. As one engineer put it, "a mere tyro can recognize a poor roadbed, defective machinery or a dangerous bridge."[63] Cecilia Tichi notes the "engineers' imperviousness to corruption" as a theme in early-twentieth-century American literature. As a symbol of integrity, the engineer appears often as a noble fighter against the villains of politics, business, finance, and, more generally, corporate capitalism.[64] If there was one thing the average American considered himself, notes Monte Clavert, "it was a mechanic and as such he was qualified to judge engineering design and correctness."[65] Machines and techniques have been associated, then, with the possibility of externalizing action and, therefore, also with the potential for observing and controlling it from the outside. Again, depending on the sociopolitical context, the standardized externalization of action through technicalization, rendering actions transparent, could be conducive either for unmediated cooperation among autonomous actors or for the enhanced exposure of a few actors to a multitude of spectators.[66]

The tendency to discern the functions of action in what is publicly visible could also encourage the theatrical production of instrumentalism in political conduct, maintaining the facade of technical discipline without its substance.[67] The theatrics of instrumentalism as a ritual of legitimation are probably more pervasive than substantive instrumentalism. The political "aesthetics" and the moral "hygienics" of technical decisions and actions could, as it were, detach themselves from technical criteria as actual ingredients of action and function merely as rhetorical resources for eliciting support. The appearance of a fit between means and ends could be employed as a way of mobilizing political approval and legitimacy, especially where the absence of the more costly substantive fit could at least temporarily be hidden from the public eye. Just as any norm, such as honesty, defines also the forms of its violation,[68] so the uses of scientific and technical norms of public action invite their own specific kind of deliberate or nondeliberate distortions.

The political rhetorical value of technical instrumentalism, when it is detached from its real structures, cannot be discarded, however. Even when politics is mediated by the metaphors and rhetoric of instrumental action without the substantive technical discipline of instrumentalism, it is shaped significantly differently from politics mediated by the metaphors and rhetoric of religion, morality, law, or ethnicity.[69] Particularly from the end of the nineteenth century through the first six decades of the twentieth, the cultural norms of science, technology, and politics have partially converged to reinforce in America certain modes of legitimating actions and holding actors accountable so that actions have come to be defended or criticized in terms of visible indicators of their adequacy or inadequacy as means of furthering certain ends.

The idea of action having a structure or a function which can be transparent as an observable relation between cause and effect, the machine as a metaphor of political action, has been supported in America by what Daniel Calhoun sees as a general tendency "to think in terms of surface and appearance." "Throughout the culture," he notes with reference to late-nineteenth-century America, "attention was directed more and more to surface, to external structure, to what could be symbolized by wordless images, to what could be produced by observing form."[70] Again, such an idea must have encouraged the spread of the vernacular aesthetics of industrial design which stresses the relationship of form and function and implies that the surface of machinery can and should represent the logic of its inner structure. In the context of political action, these sensibilities could very well have encouraged the tendency to believe that surface articulates substance, that there are visible, observable aspects of action which can represent its inner "essence."

Calhoun suggests that this American tendency to think in terms of surface appearance may give priority to spatial imagery over analysis. In the context of political action this suggests, of course, the possible discrepancies between the surface and the substance of instrumentalism, between the theatrics of instrumental public action and the very substance of action. But the fact that what appears as a technical-instrumental action is often not fully constrained by substantive technical standards, that surface instrumentality may coexist with substantive deviation from scientific and technical standards of action, can only indicate the extent to which the power of the machine as a constitutive metaphor in the rhetoric of liberal-democratic political action could extend beyond the limits set by the practice of science and technology. Even when the belief in the visible surface of action—its transparent form—as representing its true function is untenable, the attitude that actors who act "instrumentally" are exposed to the public gaze can still be sustained. The conviction, exploited by modern commercial advertising, that seeing is a contact with true reality, is, of course, in many respects just a myth. But even as such it is a substantive building block of liberal-democratic action and accountability. I have tried to show how, as a basis for the theatrics of liberal-democratic action, instrumentalism is politically significant independent of its efficacy as a basis for making political action functionally effective.[71] Even as the mere facade of public action, the form rather than the substance of technical action, instrumentalism has been a potent rhetorical resource for legitimating liberal-democratic action. It has made it possible to present, and talk about, public action as an external, objective, visible relation between means and ends, thus defining it as impersonal, lawful, and constrained without denying the individuality and the responsibility of its agents.

The record of modern liberal-democratic governments suggests, indeed, that technical effectiveness is most often subordinated to political utility, that in the liberal-democratic polity the theatrics of public action are often primary whereas the substance of action is derivative.[72] Because effective techniques of action—such as powerful weapons or drugs—produce substantive visible results, they may be, of course, more visually persuasive than less effective ones and therefore also have superior value in the theatrics of political authority. This suggests that the theatrics of action are not necessarily independent of their substance and may in fact rationalize the preference for techniques that manifestly work over those that do not. The dramaturgy of instrumentalism in liberal-democratic rituals of legitimation has probably been, at times, an even more important factor in the rise of the vernacular, technical style of political action—of political action which is overtly, and occasionally also substantially, rationally technical—than a genuine appreciation for the actual utility of knowledge.[73]

In the context of politics as a continual mass spectacle, the theatrics of instrumentalism, the presentation of public action as a scientifically and technically controlled means of bringing about certain substantive results, convey the appearance of self-exposure, of readiness to step into the public space of visible actions and become transparent and publicly accountable in a world of "objective" factual constraints. As such, theatrics indicate the political uses of science and technology in liberal-democratic rituals of legitimation, including the rhetorical and dramaturgical political value of substantive instrumentalism when it is visibly effective.

Unlike its American counterpart, the English system, in which the emphasis is on the will and autonomy of political actors, does not base the theatrics of public action on the trust given to transparent actors and visible actions. Even English business executives, whose successful performance is most perceptible in the material world of practical action, have characteristically tried to withdraw to an inaccessible space, to evolve an inner unobservable dimension which aristocratic culture postulates as a necessary condition of upper-class dignity and freedom.[74] English styles of action in comparison with American ones, therefore, have been less hospitable to the machine metaphor and to instrumentalism as a means of externalizing action in a realm of observable causes and effects, of making action transparent in a visual public space, or of projecting it as a balance between voluntarism and determinism, engagement and detachment, freedom and accountability.

6. Machines and Images of Order

Since the early modern era, Western attitudes toward the machine reveal the complexities of a dualistic vision. On the one hand, the machine is viewed as an artificial extension and embodiment of necessary natural laws, an icon of humanity's servitude to the inexorable regularities of nature. On the other hand, the machine is viewed as the human expression of the divine capacity to create and manufacture things, as a vehicle of the human dream of transcending the limits of nature. According to the first view, the machine, as a mirror of nature indifferent to humanity, represents the individual's tragic fate as a prisoner of implacable necessity.[1] The latter view links the machine with humanity's power to break loose from the chains of natural necessity and fly to ultimate freedom.

The Clock, the Flying Machine, and Iconographies of Necessity and Freedom

The clock is perhaps the most appropriate icon of the tragic view of technology as expressing the human imprisonment within a cosmic system of necessary regularities while the flying machine is the icon of technological idealism, of the dream of transcending natural limits.[2]

In the early fourteenth century, western Europeans put astronomical clocks not only outside but also inside their churches, less to tell time than to demonstrate visually the orderliness of God's cosmos.[3] According to Lynn White, this general idea of the machine as a mirror of the cosmic order found its way during the fourteenth century into the visual representation of the virtue of Temperance. If, by the eleventh century, Temperance was characteristically represented in the figure of a woman pouring water into a cup of wine to dilute its potency, fourteenth-century Italian representations of Temperance take the form of the mechanical clock.[4] The essential elements of Temperance—measure, balance, and regularity—are identified with machines, thus investing the new mechanical arts with virtue and religious sanction.[5] This concept of the machine as a balanced, self-regulating mechanism persisted throughout the industrial revolution as a metaphor of the market mechanism.[6] While as mechanism the clock became an icon of orderliness and regularity, as a timepiece it has come to function in Western culture as a reminder of mortality, as a symbol of human temporal finitude, of the ultimate limits of life.

Coexisting with the clock as an expression of human limitation and the machine as the embodiment of the principle of orderly balance, the flying machine represents both the risks and the rewards of technological idealism, of the dream of freedoms acquired beyond the gifts of nature.[7] The story of aviation includes the catastrophic flights of Eilmer of Malmesbury (1066), Domiani (1506), and the Challenger explosion (1986), as well as the ultimately successful realization of Leonardo da Vinci's visions of the flying machine in the pioneering flights of Otto Lilienthal and the Wright brothers and those who followed. This record combines the tragic experience of limits with the triumph of ascendance. The tragic dimension is, of course, most powerfully expressed in the myth of Icarus' fateful flight to the sun which melts his waxen wings, a myth which anticipates the nemesis of utopian engineering, the arrogance of humanity unrestrained by humility before natural limits, fantasy undisciplined by knowledge of facts, will uninformed by the real, rashness which leads to disaster.

Together, however, the clock, as a mirror of necessary regularities, and the flying machine, as the fantasy of escape from necessity to freedom, represent the two poles of a spectrum of Western attitudes toward science and technology; oscillating between the ideals of rational adaptation ·to given natural limits and the appropriation of ungiven freedoms, these attitudes at times converge dialectically, as in Francis Bacon's injunction that man can be the lord of nature only insofar as he is her servant.[8]

The complexities and richness of this dualistic view in the Western tradition are preserved in the deployment of the machine as a political metaphor, as an element in the rhetoric of liberal-democratic action. The modern idea of scientific politics, the notion of politics as the art of the possible, contains both the imperatives of "Realpolitik," which tie effective actions to the capacity to appreciate the "realities" and the logic of power, and the idea of politics as a melioristic enterprise, a deliberate attempt to improve and perfect the political order. At times science and technology are enlisted to rationalize the existing order and at times to direct its radical reconstruction.

One of the central features of the Western liberal-democratic political tradition is that it assimilates both these poles of the spectrum rather than only one, thereby excluding its counterpart.[9] Liberal-democratic politics characteristically consists of a constant unresolvable tension between freedom and restraint, voluntarism and determinism, the spirit of the flying machine and the clock. The temper of liberal-democratic ideology is recognized neither in Hobbes's artificial and coercive state nor in Hume's conservative skepticism about political reconstruction nor in Montesquieu's, Condorcet's, Paine's, Priestley's, or Bentham's politics of rational meliorism, Rousseau's criticism of progress, or Kant's vision of a progressive movement toward freedom. It is not manifest in John Dewey's experimental politics, Meynard Keynes's rational management of the economy, or Friedrich Hayek's distrust of deliberate change. It lies rather in the constant pendulum movements between the skeptical and the meliorist visions, in the unresolvable conflicts between the imperatives of conforming or adapting to necessity and the dreams of freedom to create, shape, and reconstruct. The temper of liberal-democratic politics is manifest in the constant attempts to change without losing respect for limits and to accommodate necessity while leaving room for freedom.

It is this view of technology as a balance between the principles of freedom and necessity, an embodiment of the duality of the flying machine and the clock, that characterizes liberal-democratic orientations toward the machine as a political metaphor and distinguishes them from alternative orientations such as, for example, those of Italian and German cultural ideologues who inspired fascism. For reactionary German modernists,[10] technology was the expression of the triumph of the will over necessity, of spirit over body, of creativity over passive conformity. The flying machine that fired the imagination of F. T. Marinetti or Ernst Jünger was not a machine which balanced freedom and necessity, will and external constraints.[11] It was rather an embodiment of the ideal of breaking loose from all restraints, the ideal of the flying machine without the clock. Both Italian and German prophets of fascism rejected the liberal-democratic view of the machine as a product of intellectual discipline, requiring scientific deference to external limits and regularities, and assimilated it into the sphere of artistic freedom. Ernst Jünger was drawn to technology because he believed it could help "aestheticize politics."[12] Both the futurists and the German fascists romanticized and appropriated the artist-engineer Leonardo da Vinci as their ancestor.[13] Both celebrated Leonardo's contributions to the engineering of war machines and idealized war as the context in which art and technology can merge in human action as the noblest expression of free will and spirit. "The reactionary modernists," writes Jeffrey Herf, "succeeded in incorporating technology into the symbolism and the language of Kultur—community, blood, will, self, form, productivity and finally race—by taking it out of the realm of Zivilisation—reason, intellect, internationalism, materialism and finance."[14]

From the ideological perspective of this tradition, the alienating language of economic calculation and rational consideration of objective limits subvert technology as the expression of spirit in matter. Many Germans identified what they viewed as soulless technological materialism with Americanism, with an attitude that allows the economy to repress culture and spirit.[15]

Such a merger of technology and scientific detachment is what the aestheticization of technology, its identification with the spirit of art, was supposed to counter. Precisely, however, because aesthetics without inner restraints was unacceptable to liberal-democratic sensibilities as a principle of action, do we find mid-nineteenth-century Americans such as Thomas Ewbank and John Kimball already preferring technology to art. They thought that insofar as the fine arts deal only with aesthetic perfection they deceive and corrupt, while technology requires obedience to God's physical laws.[16] Inasmuch as American orientations toward technology have reflected the balanced dualism of freedom and restraint, of the flying machine and the clock, the tendency, particularly from the end of the nineteenth century, to aestheticize the machine has assumed different meanings and characteristics in America and in continental Europe. For one thing, as we shall see, it was not an attempt to shift technique from the realm of material Zivilisation to the realm of Kultur. The American engineer was not celebrated as a poet of the soul but, to borrow Ewbank's phrase, as the "artist of the real."

Insofar as liberal-democratic orientations have appropriated the machine as a political metaphor which embodies the balance of freedom and necessity, the primacy of either free will or determinism was denied. The function of the machine as a liberal-democratic political metaphor has been both to uphold freedom as a principle of political order—rather than anarchy—and to enlist lawful regularities, the constraints of the objective world, for the purpose of depersonalizing political action as a public instrumental performance which exposes its agents to public tests of technical adequacy. The temper of liberal-democratic political action is that of "voluntary instrumentalism" with its dual commitment to freedom and to the lawfulness which, once respected, can render free actions restrained, effective, and accountable. The spirit of voluntary instrumentalism is manifest in the constant interplay between political idealism and the periodic crushing experience of limits, between such extremes as the dreams of revolutionaries and conservative prudence, as the ideals of a welfare state, or a "great society," and the criticisms of arrogant reforms. Samuel Huntington captures this dialectical movement in American politics when he notes the constant shift in American political history between periods of "creedal passion," like the rise of the progressive movement, and periods of pessimism and disenchantment in the face of harsh realities like the great Depression.[17] American politics, he notes, constantly fluctuates between "promise and disillusion, reform and reaction."[18] Science is similarly enlisted alternately to justify technological idealism focused on objects ranging from the locomotive to the space vehicle and to warn against the hubris of the human violation of nature.[19]

The capacity to balance technological optimism and instrumental conservatism, idealism, and realism is, however, unevenly distributed among liberal-democratic countries. In various European societies, historically entrenched class divisions and a fixed hierarchy of "high" and "low" cultures, have tended to segregate socially those who have freedom of action and can dream of "flying" from those who are compelled to obey necessity, that is, to segregate the aristocrats who can act freely from lower-class men and women who seem to be condemned to enslavement to natural necessity or—especially in the context of work in the industrialized society—to mechanical discipline. In class societies, such divisions have imposed serious constraints on the synthesis of freedom and necessity and, therefore, on the rise of voluntary instrumentalism as a universal form of political action. Class societies have tended to restrain the extension of the ideal of balancing freedom and restraint to unprivileged individual actors and to endorse a systemic balance between those who are free and those who can only obey.

Cultural and social associations of the machine with the dehumanization of work and the enslavement of workers to inexorable mechanical necessity were also made, of course, in America. Consider, for instance, Upton Sinclair's *The Jungle* (1906), about the mechanized slaughterhouses in Chicago, Morris Rosenfeld's poems on the early-twentieth-century sweatshop, Siegfried Giedion's observations in *Mechanization Takes Command* (1955), or David Nobel's notes in *America by Design* (1977). Social divisions between the realms of necessity and freedom were, of course, nourished in America by the legacy of slavery. Still, these orientations remained secondary to the dominant tendencies, particularly since the late nineteenth century, to integrate the machine and the culture of enlightened democratic politics.[20] The relative weakness of such traditions, which socially divide freedom and necessity as the respective domains of distinct classes of citizens, created more favorable conditions for the merger of the norms of freedom and necessity, of the flying machine and the clock, in the cultural domains of both technology and politics. Ideologically and culturally, the simultaneous engagement of both head and hand in the same individual agent has facilitated the integration of science and technology into a more democratic theory of action. As one American observer notes, "the combined democratic and technological revolutions made both workers of us all and aristocrats of us all."[21]

The fusion of the cultures of science and technology and the culture of liberal-democratic politics, with all their continuities and contradictions, has indeed found its most powerful expression in the modern American polity. My purpose in the following is to examine a few of the strategic links between images of technology and modern liberal-democratic politics in America, particularly from the end of the nineteenth century to the middle of the twentieth, and to distinguish them from the very different European and particularly English modes of relating technology to liberal-democratic concepts of political action.

Metaphors of Self-Regulation and Centralized Control in the American and English Democracies

Reinforced in America by the vernacular style of industrial design and by the aestheticization of the fit between function and form, machines as political metaphors came to support in America a democratic con-

cept of politics accessible to all citizens as participants or at least as
spectators. In Continental Europe machine metaphors were, by contradistinction, more typically part of the rhetoric of authoritarian
politics and hierarchical control. For the young Frederick II, for
instance, the machine metaphor did not render the principles of government transparent to the citizens but, on the contrary, justified a
claim for esoteric knowledge. "As an able mechanic is not satisfied
with looking at the outside of a watch but opens it, and examines its
springs and wheels," he wrote, "so an able politician exerts himself to
understand the permanent principles of courts, the engines of the politics of each prince, and the sources of future events . . . His trans-
cendent mind foresees the future." [22] In the service of authoritarian
rhetoric, the machine metaphor has usually been employed from the
perspective of the engineer, typically stressing the idea of an orderly
movement originating from a single source. For Johann Heinrich
Gottlieb von Justi (1717–1771), "A well constituted state must perfectly resemble a machine where all wheels and gears fit each other
with the utmost precision and the ruler must be the engineer, the first
driving spring or the soul . . . that sets every thing in motion." [23]

While, with the rise of modern party organizations, the expression
"party machine" has come to connote in American politics a kind of
blind or authoritarian political structure,[24] the earlier Anglo-American
assimilation of the machine as a political metaphor more typically
meant to suggest the principles of self-regulation, harmony between
discrete parts, and dynamic equilibrium.[25] In appropriating the
machine as a political metaphor of liberal-democratic structures of
government, machine metaphors first came to play an important role
in Anglo-American political discourse. An influential early example of
the machine as a political metaphor in the liberal tradition is, of
course, Adam Smith's idea of the market mechanism. This idea sub-
sequently furnished liberal political theory with a root metaphor
for linking its concepts of liberty, self-regulation, individualism, and
order and integrating them into a coherent theory. It was largely by
virtue of this vocabulary that early liberal ideology could rationalize
toleration, compromise, and equilibrium as principles compatible
with the values of both liberty and order.

The ideological "career" of the machine as a political metaphor,
however, followed very different paths in England and America. Again,
in English society the persistent presence of distinct class cultures and
the profound legacy of aristocratic values inhibited the use of the

machine metaphor for the promotion of democratic political values. The mechanistic images of order, which were embraced in America as, among other things, a welcomed way to dehistoricize the vocabulary of politics, were bound to be rejected in England by the powerful advocates of historical, genealogical, and organic rationales of authority. Unlike the organism as a political metaphor, the machine suggested a way of integrating parts into wholes which was more consistent with antihierarchical egalitarian values fundamental to the American, not the English, liberal-democratic polity.

One of the early expressions of the machine as a principle of decentralized yet disciplined collective action was made by Tench Coxe, a Philadelphia merchant who served as assistant to Alexander Hamilton at the U.S. Treasury. In his 1787 speech about economic production, Coxe articulated the idea that "every wheel would appear in motion that could carry forward the interests of this great body of our people and bring into action the inherent powers of the country."[26] Leo Marx suggests that in Coxe's mind "the development of steam power and the business of the constitutional convention are aspects of the same grand enterprise."[27] Benjamin Rush of Philadelphia used similar language when he referred in 1786 to the American Constitution as a system of "checks and balances."[28] Speaking at the opening ceremony of the Brooklyn Bridge about one hundred years later, in 1883, Abram Hewitt, a prominent Congressman, industrialist and philanthropist, echoed Tench Coxe's theme when he noted a direct link between the bridge and the principle of the polity as a composite of freedom and "organized intelligence."

> The structure [of the bridge] looks like a motionless mass of masonry and metal, but as a matter of fact it is instinct with motion. There is not a particle of matter in it which is at rest even for the minutest portion of time. It is an aggregation of unstable elements changing with every change in the temperature and every movement of the heavenly bodies. The problem was, out of these unstable elements, to produce absolute stability . . . If our political system were guided by organized intelligence, it would not seek to repress the free play of human interests and emotions, of human hopes and fears but would make provision for their development and exercise in accordance with the higher law of liberty and morality.[29]

Hewitt's rhetoric indicates the persistent use of mechanistic metaphors to project the polity as a system in which the ideals of self-regulation and disciplined corporate action converge. The presumed dependency of the whole, in such mechanical systems, upon the integrity of each of the parts furnishes a rhetorical glue to cement together a commitment to individualism and faith in a harmonious whole and to present such an integration as the result of "organized intelligence" or mechanistic laws rather than arbitrary force or accident. Insofar as the unity of the parts seems to evolve spontaneously from objective laws, there is no presumption of hierarchical authority. Engineering, technology, machines, and science have resonated within such a perspective as more democratic-republican than authoritarian modes of consolidating constituent parts into corporate action. Thus, while, a few years after Hewitt's remarks, James Russell Lowell compared the Constitution to a "machine that would go of itself," Justice Oliver Wendell Holmes noted that "constitutional provisions must be administered with caution. Some play must be allowed for the joints of the machine."[30] Lacking European traditions of primordial bonds and tribal genealogies which generate organic images of social bonding, Americans have tended to be more receptive to mechanistic images. "Technical unity," in the sense of connecting people by "occupational function" and "rational procedures," observes one American historian, has been the "most important single tendency in American social history" since the Civil War.[31] Notions of technical interdependence and integration are based upon relations which are "machinelike . . . impersonal, utilitarian and functionally interlocking."[32] Such relations are thought to be based on knowledge rather than on faith, morality, or personal trust.

Although critics of the machine culture in America have included prominent writers such as Nathaniel Hawthorne and Herman Melville, their criticism is less intense and encompassing than that of Europeans such as Thomas Carlyle and John Ruskin.[33] "America's affection for the machine, accompanied as it was by a cheerful submission to industrial discipline," suggests John Higham, "cannot be explained simply by economic incentives or by pointing to the prevalence of materialistic attitudes in American society."[34] The acceptance of the machine encompassed wide and diverse circles. In nineteenth-century America, "even the critics of materialism—the intellectuals who, generation after generation, assailed luxury and acquisitiveness as the deadliest national devils—rarely implicated technology in their indictment."[35] Higham points out that the role of ideology in focusing American identity outside the domain of particularistic traditional identities—what Talcott Parsons calls ascriptive traits—removed the kind of factors which inhibited the spread of machine culture in other societies. "Technical integration could thus proceed under the shelter of the American ideology without the fear of personal loss."[36] Symbolized by the evolution of national railway and telegraph networks, the growing salience of "technical unity" in the American society was indicated also by the rise of the engineering profession. Toward the close of the nineteenth century and the beginning of the twentieth, American engineers played a central role in the diffusion of technical norms of action as activists in the efficiency and conservation movements.[37]

While in England the idea of "trust between parts" has been conceived primarily in terms of metaphors of organic-hierarchic unity, in America reliance on metaphors of mechanical interdependence have appeared to support the notion of equality among the parts.[38] Conceived in mechanistic terms, such equality is therefore consistent in America more with decentralized than with centralized concepts of order. A mechanistic concept of what holds society together has also been consistent with American individualism.[39] It implies a kind of discipline which checks subjectivity, relativism, and arbitrariness without undermining the relative freedom and autonomy of the parts. It is as if the concept of "mechanical unity" has offered a way to preserve the integrity of the parts while checking the dangers of confusing the perspective of any one part with the synoptic perspective of the aggregated or the corporate whole. In addition, of course, the fusion of democratic-republican values and technological development in America has been enhanced by the widespread attitude which tied the freedom of the new nation to its economic independence and therefore to the industry and ingenuity of its people. These notions and attitudes indicate how technological progress could harmonize in the American consciousness with the deepest political aspirations.[40]

Whereas in America "technical unity," as a metaphor of social discipline, suggested social integration consistent with the values of equality, decentralization, and other nationally shared middle-class values, within the English class-conscious society, mechanistic metaphors of behavior were more commonly espoused by the middle class as ways of disciplining the working class and rendering the upper classes more practically and instrumentally oriented. While in America mechanical discipline and technical unities were generalized as norms for the entire society, in England such nineteenth-century advocates of the

diffusion of technical values had to develop different rationales for
defending the machine in distinct class cultures. From the vantage
point of this attempted synthesis, the English middle class advocated
the uses of science and technology to correct what it held to be
the excesses of short-sighted unrestrained lower-class materialism as
well as upper-class aloofness toward the concrete tests of practical
experience.[41]

While in America science and technology, perceived together as
accountable to the realms of both freedom and necessity, could have
become a strategic symbolic sphere for coping with the antinomy of
voluntarism and determinism as a general human and social problem,
in England freedoms and constraints appeared unevenly distributed
among the various classes. Hence in relation to the lower classes the
machine metaphor suggested in England not just the harmony of
parts but also controls and discipline imposed from above. Andrew
Ure, whom Karl Marx regarded as the "philosopher of the factory,"[42]
praised the mechanization of production as a way of disciplining
workers—whom the English middle and upper classes regarded as
lacking the capacity of self-discipline and delayed gratification.[43]

Consistent with characteristic liberal rationales for the deployment
of mechanical principles in the economic, social, and political contexts, Ure argues that insofar as mechanical discipline substitutes
functional for personal controls it is not only more orderly but also
more respectable. He writes about emancipating workers from "handicraft caprice" and equalizing masters and workers as subordinates of
an automatic mechanism.[44] The very machine which, according to
Marx, was depersonalizing the production process and eliminating
the worker as a purposeful agent was helping, according to Ure,
"emancipate [the human being's] animal function from brute toil."[45]

In the English class-conscious society machines did not suggest,
then, a general balance between the creative and the adaptive elements of actions relevant to all actors. They suggested, rather, a class
division between those who are expected to conform and those who
have the capacity for freedom and creativity. Educational programs
designated to use science and technology for teaching workers to conform to mechanical discipline have typically presented knowledge as
"hard, factual, solid and enduring" while educational programs prepared for the upper classes stressed the more provisional hypothetical
character of scientific knowledge.[46] Moderate liberal Victorian ideologues, such as members of the Society for the Diffusion of Useful

Knowledge and of the Mechanic Institutes, often advocated wider social and educational acceptance of the balance between the adaptive and the creative as a middle-class virtue.[47]

The idea of knowledge as a means of internalizing and making voluntary adherence to necessary external constraints was very much in line with the dualistic liberal view of technology, as a synthesis of the voluntaristic and deterministic components of action and middle-class schemes of scientific and technical education for reforming the working and upper classes. When applied to the working class, the idea of rationalized adaptation implied a strengthening of the voluntaristic component of action and thus an enhancement of the dignity of workers.[48] When applied to the upper class, it entailed an augmented respect for the deterministic component of action, the tempering of arrogant aristocratic voluntarism, and an appreciation for the requirements of realism and humility before facts. Affirming the feasibility of working-class access to a theoretical understanding of action and insisting on the relevance of empirical utilitarian considerations for the effectiveness and adequacy of voluntary, upper-class modes of action, the middle class was in effect attempting to generalize socially its own perspective on action. Middle-class liberal ideologues tended to criticize unreformed working-class styles of action as mindless and blindly materialistic and unreformed upper-class styles of action as too abstract, frivolous, and guided by fictions.[49] Science and technology furnished the English middle class with an enormously rich and flexible cultural resource for criticizing alternative class paradigms of action and generating new forms of discipline. By stressing scientific discourse as an example of responsible, disciplined use of language guided by the need to assign words to the accessible order of natural things,[50] liberal spokespeople were able to criticize upper-class educational ideologies and even to describe poetry, rhetoric, philology, and mathematics as examples of "defects of lingual discipline" and of an "unquestioning acceptance of data, axioms etc."[51] By contrast, physics was singled out as a subject more suited to representing and inculcating balance between the adaptive and the creative, the deterministic and the voluntary, components of action because of its foundations in both observation and intellect.[52] William Hodgson captured the essence of this liberal position when he stated that the "very word *order* has a double sense—*arrangement* and *command*, so natural is it for us to identify the one with the other, and to believe that arrangement or system exists only by command or law."[53] This idea about the links between "order" and "command" has been perhaps the most important basis of the integration of science into European liberal notions of discipline and authority. In the American context the imperatives of order have not been authorized so much by command as by the aesthetics and ethics of instrumental action, whose function is manifest in its form and whose agents, potentially all the citizens, balance their creativity by adaptive respectful conformism to facts.

In the long run, however, precisely because of traditional class distinctions, the association of science and technology with middle-class norms of action has also been a liability for the social diffusion of the culture of science and technology in the English polity. In a society in which the middle and even the working classes internalized versions of aristocratic codes of political action, which encourage condescending attitudes toward material needs and cultivate antimaterialistic cultural tastes, association with material gratification and adaptation to necessary external constraints tainted science and technology as sources of authoritative metaphors and norms of restrained and balanced political action. Even among the upwardly mobile lower and middle classes, moral rather than mechanical discipline, character rather than competence, have remained the predominant virtues of leadership. Despite important transformations, politics in England has retained much of its earlier character as a domain for the exercise of the aristocratic virtues of independence, voluntarism, judiciousness, and cultural scope. "The concept of the gentleman was invented by the aristocracy," observed Lord Bertrand Russell, "to keep the middle classes in order."[54] One can add that it went further than that to influence also the political norms of working-class political actors. In the conflict between the "necessary" and the "noble" in English society,[55] the machine came to be classified more with the former than with the latter. People such as Andrew Ure and Samuel Smiles, who ascribed moral purpose to industrialization as a drama of the human triumph over nature, largely failed in the long run to prevail against the liberalized and democratized versions of aristocratic codes of action and discipline.[56] The spread of such variants of aristocratic values in middle- and "upper"-working-class circles almost nationalized a degree of ambivalence toward the machine in England.

Reactions to the machine and to the values of instrumentalism by people of diverse persuasions, such as Thomas Carlyle, John Ruskin, Charles Dickens, and William Morris, as well as the criticisms leveled against the ideas of Jeremy Bentham and the Webbs, became over time an important feature of more general English attitudes. In the English class system the spread of aristocratic values has meant the diffusion of a certain contempt for utility, for the endless pursuit of material gain, for "restless stirrings,"[57] competitiveness, mechanistic efficiency, and the aesthetics of functional industrial design. From the perspective of aristocratic culture, even in its diluted popular versions, all these matters are associated with the ascription of too much value to external things. Such attitudes echo Carlyle's complaint that because of the stress on the "outward," which is cultivated through mechanical principles, the "inward" is abandoned as "it is found to yield no result."[58] Carlyle was concerned that the influence of political economics and utilitarian ideas would encourage the belief that "happiness depends on external circumstances." Concerned with what he perceived as trends toward the despiritualization of culture, Carlyle isolated signs of a rising influence of "statists, economists, and . . . merchants" and a correspondingly declining influence of "preachers and teachers." He admitted, to be sure, that the moral, religious, or spiritual dimension must be balanced by respect for outward evidence in order to check the dangers of superstition and fanaticism.[59] He recognized the value of material, visible "facts" in the epistemology and the pedagogy of tolerance. Still, he was concerned that the balance between inward and outward things had been tipped in the other direction. "Men," he noted, "have lost their belief in the invisible and believe, and hope, and work only in the visible or to speak it in other words: this is not a religious age."[60] Criticizing the spread of mechanical culture and instrumental values into the sphere of politics, Carlyle chastised his contemporaries for worshiping the "body politic" while neglecting the "soul politic."[61] Underlying much of such criticism of the effects of the working and the middle classes on the materialization of culture and politics was a concern for preserving the primacy of a less exclusive or elitist variant of the aristocratic code of high individualism. It was a concern which rested on faith in the superior quality of actions guided by inner moral judgment, prudence based on experience, the ethics of public service, and intellectual discipline over actions supposedly guided by impulse, interest, external circumstances, and the mindless application of technical skills. Like his contemporaries, Carlyle regarded the great inventors of machines, such as James Watt, as heroes.[62] He could integrate the creative act of the few who can invent machines with his appreciation of voluntary action, while criticizing what he regarded as the degrading effects of machines and machine culture on the spirit. Influential critics of the machine culture—John Ruskin, for example—carried the rejection even further by attacking the very aesthetic of the machine. Ruskin advocated a clear preference for "organic" over "mechanistic" metaphors and a return to the preindustrial pastoral society.[63] For Ruskin, as for Carlyle and Dickens, the machine stood for a deterministic and hence enslaving force, while organic qualities suggested vitality, freedom and a rich inner life.[64]

Since it was influenced by the English cultural predisposition to distinguish sharply between the realms of necessity and freedom and to regard them, respectively, as the domains of working-class life and physical labor and of upper-class life and politics, political democratization involved in England a process of socializing the lower classes into aristocratic notions of voluntary action. If in North America the absence of a comparably entrenched class culture, and the much more pronounced faith in the competence of citizens to act freely, intelligently, and responsibly, equated democratization with the extension of the norms of practical effective action from the bottom up, in England democratization meant rather the extension of the norms of free yet self-restrained action from the top down. Compared with the English, the American variant of democratization appears, therefore, more compatible with the general diffusion of scientific and technical norms of action. Within a society in which science and technology came to be associated with liberty, independence, and the "ingenuity of the people," technicalized action could appear as a more natural vehicle of increasingly active, forward-looking citizens more confident in mastering a wide arsenal of skills necessary for controlling the environment, good citizenship, and effective government action.

Because technicalized public action was likely to be perceived in England as reflecting the spread of lower-class materialistic values and lower-class forms of externally determined nonvoluntary action, the social status of science and technology was typically debated in conjunction with assessing the merits of the "materialistic" working class or middle class cultures against those of the aristocratic "high culture." It involved an encounter between scientific and classical educations, seen from an upper-class perspective as a clash between the sphere of needs, necessities, and sensual gratification and the sphere of moral discipline, internal freedom, and civic responsibility. This contrasts with the American context, where the social status of science and technology has been concerned with a general welding of freedom and competence at the basic level of the common citizen.

In mid-nineteenth-century America, the development of a universal concept of state-supported public education already reveals the commitment to the idea that the diffusion of knowledge serves the democratic political objective of participatory citizenship. Within this context, scientific and technical education is perceived not as a means of spreading imperatives of discipline and conformism to the lower classes, not as teaching industriousness and sobriety to the licentious nor "facts" to tender, upper-class minds, but as a means of enhancing the capacity of an ever-growing number of individuals for effective voluntary action. Throughout the twentieth century, liberal American ideologues have persistently advocated scientific education as a way of substituting rational voluntary action for passive acquiescence to authority and fatalistic acceptance of natural limits.[65] In England, upper-class concerns with the potential effects of extending suffrage, particularly with the dangers of permitting the "ignorant" and the "injudicious" to influence the political process, have persistently encouraged scientific and technical education of the people in order to ensure political stability.[66] By contrast, Americans have tended to stress the role of education as an indispensable instrument of popular sovereignty, the transfer of power to the people.[67]

The assumption that "reality" is both a constraint and a domain of voluntary rational action has encouraged in America an idealistic view of science and technology as universally accessible means for a shared dialogue between humanity and nature, as equalizers of participation in collective action. While in England science and technology have raised issues of relations between classes, in America an important part of their latent ideological and political function has been to define social and political issues in terms of a collective human venture of conquering nature and realizing universal human aspirations. The diffusion of knowledge was defended by people such as Thomas Jefferson, DeWitt Clinton, and Edward Everett as a necessary condition for republican institutions, a condition for resisting aristocratic claims of leadership. Since "intelligence" as well as the potential for scientific and artistic creativity was regarded by such influential American educators as Horace Mann as universally distributed among all men and women, teaching science was not perceived so much as a way to "civilize" and restrain the unruly as to facilitate the realization of that universal potential.[68] Scientific-technical education, which failed to become in England an ingredient of general culture, was boosted in America by the progressive movement and the pragmatists as an integral part of democratic education for full participation in the political process. While American moralism may ensure, as Samuel Huntington suggests, "that government will never be truly efficacious,"[69] *the impulse to reconcile the two through the moralization and aestheticization of instrumentalism has been a central theme in American political culture.*

In contrast to Victorian aesthetics and moral criticism of the machine the aestheticization of the machine and the moral sanction of the historical mission of technological progress in America have facilitated the strategic role of science and technology in coping with the antimony of freedom and restraint and the issue of generating authoritative, accountable, and disciplined public action. In the context of public affairs, the dual dimensions of scientific knowledge—as a mirror of necessary natural constraints and a tool for expanding human freedom of action to its outer limits—made instrumentalism represent both the force of amoral, that is, natural rather than social or political, constraints and the morally loaded human capacity to expand the realm of effective free action and human purposefulness into areas which were formerly regarded as belonging in the domain of inexorable natural necessities or chance. As the expression of discipline and constraint in the heart of freedom, the matrix of the lawful element in voluntary human action, science, and technology furnished in America a paradigm of action most responsive to liberal-democratic values.

In spite of periodic domestic criticisms of England's failure to modernize adequately both its private and public sectors and occasional acknowledgments of America's achievements and power, America still appears to many contemporary English critics, as it did to their Victorian predecessors, to be an example of the evil consequences of machine culture and unchecked lower-class materialism. These attitudes preserve early orientations which led representatives of the British upper classes to regard the display of plain unadorned American machines in the Crystal Palace exhibition of 1851 with such contempt.[70] American activism, "restless" competitiveness, and consumerism appear from this perspective to compare adversely with the relaxed, self-content, and leisurely manners of the English aristocracy, which became in part internalized as the ideals of the other classes.[71] As a "workshop in the wilderness," America has represented modern orientations and prospects which Europeans have regarded with both fascination and disdain. European ambivalence has manifested itself also in divergent orientations toward nature. In England, where tensions between the demands of utility and beauty were reinforced by the social distance between classes and between the occupations presumably close to the material foundations of society and those closer to its cultural and spiritual dimensions, America's attempts to aestheticize the useful and find beauty in the unity of function and form often appeared suspect.[72] In the course of the nineteenth century, English reactions to nature cultivated and improved by human endeavor increasingly reinforced the tendency to admire nature innocent of human intervention.[73]

This ambivalence, the tendency to accept the necessity of a degree of scientific and technical "modernization" of the English society and at the same time to criticize this very process as "Americanization," survived into the twentieth century. It was the process of extending scientific and technical values and their attending metaphors to the larger spheres of society and politics that writers such as Thomas Carlyle and T. S. Eliot hoped to arrest by reviving the appreciation for the "invisible" inward sphere so richly supported by a religious worldview and that thinkers such as John Ruskin and William Morris sought to check by reviving appreciation for the preindustrial culture of crafts and the force of art.

7. Social Science and the Liberal-Democratic Problem of Action

By claiming to advance an objective scientific knowledge of society, the social sciences have inevitably become the most ideologically and politically significant expression of the cognitive norms and cultural strategies of science in the modern state. Despite their respectively distinct orientations and objectives, ideology and social science share the attempt to give authoritative accounts of human conduct and social phenomena. The relations between ideology and the social sciences have been the subject of many discussions and controversies.[1] Much attention has been given to such questions as whether ethical and political problems can be reduced to scientific and technical ones, whether science can be politically or ideologically neutral, or if there is such a thing as scientific ideology. My concern in the following discussion is with yet another question: How have the social sciences come to play an important role in modern liberal-democratic ideology and in particular in fixing key terms of the political discourse about such issues as the relations between the individual and society, the nature of social action, and the place of facts and values in political life? I shall attempt to address this question while examining the latent political and ideological functions of social science in American democracy—how the social sciences have functioned in America as ideological and political resources for the construction of a particular variant of the liberal-democratic concept of action, a variant which puts a special accent on the role of the individual as the primary unit of action and which attempts to weld voluntaristic and experimental approaches to politics.

The Social Sciences as a Resource
of Liberal-Democratic Ideology

The question about the role of the social sciences in liberal-democratic ideology should not lead us to neglect the rich historical affinities between social research and nondemocratic ideologies and interests, from the absolutist monarchy to the modern totalitarian dictatorship. It was Jean-Baptiste Colbert, after all, who as early as 1667 ordered a systematic collection and publication of facts about French society. The French government continued to function as a principal initiator and sponsor of social research in France throughout the eighteenth and nineteenth centuries, particularly in connection with military needs, taxation and issues of public health. Early-seventeenth-century European social scientists like John Graunt, William Petty, and Henry Conring devised measures and collected data in order to assist and guide the actions of rulers. Petty's "political arithmetic" was pursued from the perspective of the court in order to construct a picture of the "state of the kingdom" which could inform the actions of the sovereign. He considered the task of governing as demanding skill and knowledge and drew on Bacon when he asserted that "to practice upon politick, without knowing the Symmetry, Fabrick and Proportion of it, is as casual as the practice of Old-women and Empirics."[2] Looking at society and developing knowledge of the population from the perspective of the sovereign were founded on the assumption, as Theodore Porter notes, that the members of society "are objects that could and should be manipulated at will."[3] In Germany, at about the same time, Henry Conring sought to advance knowledge of the "facts of public life" in order to help state administration cure the diseases of the social and the political body. For Conring it is the state, as the principal acting unit, which needs social knowledge to guide its operations.[4] It is noteworthy that both Petty and Conring were trained as physicians and were therefore predisposed to perceive knowledge in instrumental terms, as the means by which those who have a synoptic view of society can treat its ills. In the spirit of this approach, modern state bureaucracies have devised tools such as census surveys to facilitate their capacity to act on the social body.

Despite the nondemocratic uses of social research, the social sciences have furnished some of the most potent ideological resources for the promotion of liberal-democratic political values and practices. Perhaps one of the most intriguing aspects of the fusion of scientific knowledge and politics in the modern state is that attempts to enlist the social sciences to enhance bureaucratic controls have often increased simultaneously the role and authority of scientific and technical standards in public evaluations and criticisms of government operations. As we shall see in greater detail below, the increasing vulnerability of the executive power to authoritative public criticism of its effectiveness and competence in the modern democratic state relates to its growing predisposition toward defining its own actions in instrumental technical terms. Thus the social (as well as tne natural) sciences, although often enlisted by experts to guide and rationalize the actions of rulers, in fact also furnish an authoritative basis from which the ruled can look critically at the actions of their governors.

Social scientific perspectives on human behavior, society, and politics have served other liberal democratic values as well. They have contributed to the demystification or "disenchantment" of the political process; they have implicitly discredited—or competed with—teleological and hierarchic notions of society; they have granted normative superiority to more present-oriented, often mechanistic, factual accounts of social and political behavior over personalized and historical narratives; and they have certified abstract images of society as a self-regulating mechanism, thus furnishing a powerful, scientifically authoritative rationale for criticizing state actions as potentially disruptive of natural equilibria. Most pertinent to my concerns, certain socioscientific orientations toward political action have furnished important support for the liberal-democratic ideological need to harmonize voluntaristic and causal accounts of human conduct. It is due to such a synthesis that liberal-democratic theories of action could accommodate a commitment both to the voluntary individual as the agent of action and to the imperative that actions be sufficiently observable to permit that actors be held accountable. By casting action as something both voluntary and causal, invisible and visible, meaningful and factual, the social sciences have granted liberal-democratic ideology powerful support for separating, yet simultaneously upholding, the integrity of private agencies and public actions, of self and society. Social scientific accounts of human behavior appeared to sustain the possibility of agent's choices among alternative courses of action without denying the rational understanding of behavior as a system of knowable causal chains.

In light of the above discussion, one can see how the social deployment of the social scientific vocabularies of economics, statistics, sociology, psychology, and political science, among others, can be regarded as an important ideological development. If in nondemocratic political contexts the social sciences were enlisted primarily for the rationalization of centralized bureaucratic controls, in liberal-democratic societies like the United States they have been used also to decentralize structures of political actions and accountability. By implicitly encouraging an optimistic epistemology in the context of public affairs, the social sciences have facilitated the inclusion of political action in the sphere of attestive visual perception and defined it as a legitimate object of designative linguistic practices of the kind which have been applied to the physical world. The attempt to construct social reality as an object which can be witnessed and discussed in terms similar to those applied to physical nature has implicitly opened the way to granting the public the possibility of detached political engagement upheld by the authority to evaluate and judge what political agents say and do by reference to the common experience of certified "objective social facts." This development, which in the modern liberal-democratic state has been associated with the emergence of modern journalism as a vehicle of public political discourse, has been instrumental for the rise of the "public" or of "public opinion" as a political force reflecting a more democratic distribution of power between actors and their audiences.

The belief, or the myth, that persons can be, at least partly, transparent—like physical objects—that actions are as observable as the movements of physical bodies could, as Bentham's principle of the Panopticon indicates, support also the hierarchical surveillance of subjects.[5] But in the liberal-democratic context, the assumption about the existence of public scientific notions of the factual world was employed to "externalize" and expose government agencies and public officials as well. Instead of a privileged view from above (a view often associated with the conception of the law as a set of commands of the sovereign), it has assumed the superior validity and authority of a universal-public gaze of "public facts" of the kind liberal and democratic ideologues such as Jefferson, Paine, Priestley, and, later, Presidents Andrew Jackson and Theodore Roosevelt associated with a democratic system of government. In the early days of the American republic this position was subject to powerful objections by the antifederalists as well as by European critics like Burke and Carlyle, who, most recently joined by Oakeshott and Hayek, insisted that the locus of politics is not in the field of visual public perception but rather in the invisible interior spaces of society and culture. I have already noted Carlyle's concerns about the tendency to pay too much attention to the "body politic" while neglecting the "soul politic." Oakeshott has similar complaints about the tendency to value competence over the more elusive quality of judgment in politics.[6]

The attempts to integrate mental or spiritual and material causes in accounting for human behavior enabled the social sciences to generate authoritative strategies useful for connecting the public and the visible with the hidden aspects of politics. While social scientists have often varied in the relative weights they ascribe to the "internal" and "external" components of action, a large number of prominent social scientists share a dualistic perspective whose ideological import has been to add intellectual respectability to liberal-democratic concepts of political action. Social scientific syntheses of voluntary and causal notions of action have helped uphold the liberal-democratic emphasis on the centrality of autonomous agencies while preserving the view that their actions are objective events in a realm of observable causes and effects. The social sciences offered liberal-democratic ideology an authoritative strategy for objectifying or externalizing voluntary behavior in the public sphere of visual perception while connecting causal social accounts of these observable behavioral events with internally meaningful choices. While the externalization of trends, propensities, or choices has furnished here a basis for subjecting social and political behavior to disciplined designative language of factual descriptions and judgments,[7] the "interiorization" of externally observable acts in a world of meaningful choices has offered a way to soften the coercive and deterministic implications of such causal accounts. In addition, this dualism, by assuming logically and scientifically certifiable links between voluntary choices and causal accounts, has opened the way for accepting the relevance of scientific accounts of the conduct of political actors without appearing to discredit the common lay discourse of political behavior in terms of interests, goals, motives, and choices.

Differences in the relative weights social scientists such as Durkheim, Weber, Simmel, James, Dewey, Parsons, Merton, and Shils assign to voluntaristic and involuntary causal factors in the determination of action have, of course, significant implications for the respective ideological imports of these theories. If one examines these differences in relation to the sociopolitical and ideological ambience of the relevant social scientists they may appear in part to reflect the differences in cultural orientations toward behavior between continental Europe and the United States. Compare, for instance, the apparent American tendency to perceive social reality as secondary or derivative of the reality of individuals and the European predisposition to ascribe primary reality to society, the group, while viewing the individual as secondary or derivative.[8] The saliency of sociopsychological, economic, and statistical approaches to the study of social behavior in the American social scientific tradition, the strong preference for methodological individualism, the corresponding distrust of grand theories, and the impact of American pragmatist philosophical notions of truth, knowledge, and action[9] appear more consistent with a position which holds individual actors to be primary agents and society as derivative, or something continually constructed by the actions and interactions of voluntary actors. This feature clearly contrasts with general—although by no means exclusive—European conceptions of society as a total, all-encompassing, given, and in many respects closed system. Such differences may be related, to some extent, to the tribal gene-alogies of many European societies as well as to the monarchic notions of the existence of a privileged synoptic perspective—from the top of the social hierarchy—from which the monarch, who inherited a God's eye view of his or her subjects, has a privileged inclusive picture of the entire society. In America, a radically egalitarian refusal to grant any individual or group the claim to a privileged authoritative view of the entire society—coupled with the strong antitribal immi-grant ethos of the American society—has apparently contributed to less unified notions of society and skepticism concerning its status as a given object which can be perceived as a whole. It is perhaps due to such differences that pragmatism, as an indigenous American phi-losophy, could go so far as to reject altogether the idea of society as a unified object of the attestive gaze and advance instead a more fluid decentralized concept of society as something which diverse individ-uals encounter and experience differently in the context of action.

Within the liberal-democratic context, perhaps the most significant import of the social sciences across different social and cultural con-texts is the idea that a voluntaristic theory of action and causal accounts of behavior are reconcilable by confining the former to the level of the individual while limiting the latter to the level of collec-tives or aggregates. Adolphe Quetelet, the early nineteenth-century Belgian pioneer of statistics—who was trained as an astronomer—thought it possible to accept free will and individual differences and still discover statistical laws or regular aggregates which govern the behavior of societies.[10] This attitude was reinforced by the acceptance of indeterminism or chance in modern scientific thought, the con-straints on unique predictions of individual behavior and the sense that these constraints are nevertheless compatible with claims about the existence of statistical laws, which are revealed only at the aggregate level of social behavior. This solution to the problem of reconciling scientific accounts of social behavior, and the commitment to the notion of the human being as a voluntary agent capable of free will, was enthusiastically welcomed by such eminent scientists in other fields as the English physicist John Herschel and the Scottish physicist James Maxwell.[11] While there were those like Adolph Wagner, the German economist statistician, who insisted that periodic fluctuations in the statistics of crime, suicide, marriage, and price constitute a compelling argument against free will as a quantitative science of society,[12] statistics was generally regarded as supporting a notion of causation which does not necessarily contradict the possibility of free will or diversity at the level of individuals.

European champions of statistics such as Quetelet and Henry Buckle were aware, as Theodore Porter indicates, that although as a science, statistics contributes to the advancement of knowledge, its reception is influenced by the fact that its object is group, not individual, phenomena.[13] If statistics could render society an object of attestive-scientific observations and designative-descriptive discourse, while keeping individuals unique, diverse, unpredictable, and elusive, or at least partly invisible, it could be harmonized with the spreading liberal-democratic commitments of the age. Like other quantitative social scientific traditions in economics, sociology, and political science, statistics appeared to furnish a powerful intellectual support for the liberal-democratic claim that, to use Maxwell's words, "there is liberty which is not disorder." [14] Liberty, according to such a perspective, is the ultimate principle of order, not fear, as Hobbes thought, or privilege, as the apologists of the monarchy or the aristocracy argued.

Some European Counterparts to the American Example

Ideologically relevant features of the social scientific approaches to action in America can be clarified by comparing them with some of their principal European counterparts, such as those of the French sociologist Emile Durkheim and of the German sociologist Max Weber. Both Durkheim and Weber share a commitment to what Talcott Parsons calls a voluntaristic theory of action.[15] Both are committed to empirically oriented scientific study and causal analysis of behavior. Durkheim in his theoretical studies and in his more quantitative research shows, nevertheless, a clear propensity to "methodological collectivism," to accounting for social phenomena in terms of the properties of collectives, groups, or social forces.[16] By contrast, Max Weber tends more toward "methodological individualism," the position which explains social phenomena as resulting from the actions and interactions of individual agents.[17] Neither of these founders of modern sociology is completely consistent in his approach. Durkheim sometimes uses the language of the methodological individualist and Weber resorts to collective entities and processes in explaining social, economic, or political phenomena. Still, the differences in their methodological perspectives are sufficient to warrant significant variability in the ideological imports of their respective theories of social action.

Although according to Durkheim "collective representations," the symbolic building blocks of social life, are historically created through the complex interactions of individuals, they are in fact responses to "the conditions in which the social group in its totality is placed."[18] As such, collective representations in turn mediate and shape the behavior of the individual. While he insists that sociology should embrace both free will and determinism,[19] Durkheim in fact gives greater weight to social forces than to individual agents. "Reality," he observes, resists "modification by simple effort of the [individual] will."[20] The independence of social reality vis-à-vis the willing individual implies that "individual natures are merely the indeterminate material that the social factor molds and transforms."[21] How does Durkheim handle the apparent tension between such emphasis on the primacy of society as an entity that shapes and constrains individual behavior and his commitment to the liberal notion of autonomous individuals as social actors? How does he combine elements of sociological determinism with elements of a voluntaristic theory of action? Durkheim attempts to resolve such tensions between his individualism and methodological collectivism by conceiving individualism itself as a product of society. As Edward Tiryakian points out, for Durkheim the worship of the individual becomes a collective social end in the same way the worship of supernatural beings became an end in earlier societies.[22] Durkheim further attempts to mitigate tensions between his concept of society and the value he ascribes to the individual by advocating the normative superiority of rational-scientific orientations toward the world over mythological ones. He in fact sees a progressive historical trend in this direction consistent with Auguste Comte's sociohistorical vision. Science, according to Durkheim, is no less a collective representation, a group symbolic construct, than mythology. But unlike mythology a scientific perspective on the world enhances the autonomy of individuals and is therefore compatible with the rise of individualism as a collective representation. Whereas mythological thought unites individual minds in "a single collective mind," science serves social thought and communication without undermining the separate integrity of individual minds. It achieves this result by substituting for the unity of minds—of the kind realized in mythological thought—the unity of reality as the object of many separate minds. Guaranteeing the unity of the world as an external object outside the thinking subjects enables science to "turn minds towards impersonal truths"[23] without undermining the integrity of the individuals as discrete minds and thinking subjects. "The impersonal truth developed by science," Durkheim observes, "can leave room for everyone's individuality."[24]

Building on Cartesian dichotomies between mind and reality, Durkheim develops a kind of "liberalism of the mind" according to which the "hardness," unity, and stability of reality, as the identical object of many thinking and sensing subjects, permit freedom and diversity to various individual minds without risking chaos or disorder. By extending the concept of objective reality to the realm of society, Durkheim seeks not only to ensure the possibility of a positivistic science of society which is compatible with individualism but more broadly to ground the harmony of individualism with the kind of sharable experience which is constitutive of society. For Durkheim, therefore, the affirmation of hard factual social reality is congenial for securing the foundations of both individualism and social order, a realm of voluntary behavior and a sphere of necessities. Durkheim's methodological collectivism, his readiness to grant primacy to the reality of the group over that of the individual, therefore, limits but does not entirely undermine the liberal-democratic import of his sociology. By substituting a scientific for religious or mythological perspective on social behavior, Durkheim offers to "treat historical institutions, whatever they may be, with respect but without mystic awe."[25] Such a combination of respect without mystification is of course very much in tune with the temper of liberal orientations toward society. Ultimately the most important aspect of Durkheim's sociology for liberal-democratic ideology has been his dualistic view of behavior as something which has both private and public dimensions, which is both visible and invisible, external and internal. "Acting," he wrote, "means externalizing oneself and spreading out beyond oneself." A person cannot at the same time, according to Durkheim, be "both entirely within himself and entirely outside himself."[26] To be autonomous involves the ability to harmonize voluntarily internal states with external necessities. Such an adaptation to social reality should not challenge the dignity or autonomy of the individual because society is not just superior or exterior to us but also is "within us and is us."[27] Autonomy for the individual means "to understand the necessities he has to bow to and accept them with full knowledge of the facts."[28] As a means of discerning such necessities, of distinguishing between fact and fiction, science is, therefore, instrumental for the kind of rational adaptation to reality which preserves both the autonomy and dignity of the individual.

The tensions between conceiving scientific knowledge as a collective representation, which depends on specific forms of social organization, and viewing science as authoritative in certifying the nature of social facts run throughout Durkheim's work.[29] His constant struggle with these tensions is, however, precisely what makes his work so relevant to liberal-democratic ideological moves to appropriate science as a means of reconciling individual autonomy and the necessities of restraint and order, the desire to replace force with rational acknowledgment of restraint imposed by facts. It is largely because of his fears that radical individualism might endorse a theory of knowledge which, as in the case of pragmatism, would threaten the balance between autonomy and order that Durkheim insists on the reality of the group and on the authority of social science to represent it and make it rationally intelligible as a check on the anarchistic potential of liberalism.

Durkheim's scientific rationalism nevertheless implies elitist orientations toward public action. He advocates a special privileged role for professionals like himself in fixing standards of truth and fact and in guiding the course of public policies and state action.[30] His perspective implies the characteristic European hierarchic gaze of established authority looking at society from above, not the democratic gaze of the citizens as a public looking at the government from below. Hence, Durkheim typically asserts that the "duty of the statesman is like that of the physician: he prevents outbreak of illnesses by good hygiene and seeks to cure them when they have appeared."[31] Scientists help statesmen maintain good social and political "hygiene." Social science is here largely a resource of governmental or bureaucratic controls, a means for imposing order and discipline. Because science is not a private but an impersonal-universal reason, according to Durkheim,[32] the process of substituting knowledgeable and deliberate actions for nondeliberate and involuntary ones can be regarded as a process of democratization: it expands the sphere of autonomous voluntary action, and this means that insofar as citizens can be educated and guided to act rationally, freedom and autonomy can be induced from above.

As a means of demystifying and demythologizing the basis of social action, Durkheim's sociology has been compatible with key elements of European liberalism and its Enlightenment traditions. Still his elitist models of reform, his stress on the primacy of social reality, his derivative individualism, his concept of society, and his notions of knowledge and truth have put his scientific perspective on social action at odds with the American variant of liberal-democratic ideology.

With its special roots in European contract theories of the state, its strong natural rights tradition, its stress on the individual as the creator of the polity, and its endorsement of an experimental approach to politics, American ideology has been more hospitable to Weberian sociology.[33] The commitment to methodological individualism has made Weberian sociology more ideologically relevant to the liberal-democratic problem of action. It has furnished a way of accounting for society and the public realm which, much more than Durkheim's sociology, preserves the status of the individual as the ultimate source of action. "For sociological purposes," Weber notes, "there is no such thing as a collective personality which acts"; the state is but "a complex of social interaction of individual persons."[34] Action is social not because it derives from the properties of a given group but "insofar as its subjective meaning to the individual actor takes account of the behavior of others."[35] Weber thus combines the external observable aspect of behavior with interpretive understanding of the meanings of actions in the social context.[36] Because he starts with the individual as the ultimate agent of social action, he must show how the subjective meanings actors ascribe to their actions can be "objectified" and rationally reconstructed with the aid of reliable observations. Weber attempts to achieve this goal by viewing individual actors as purposeful agents who continually choose their actions according to their perceptions of the instrumentality of such actions to their ends. Thus the invisible internal world of subjective meanings is linked, in Weber's sociology, with the observable world of social actions which make the social order.

The discontinuities inherent in the dualism between voluntarism and determinism, meanings and causes, principles and consequences, ultimately, according to Weber, condemn political actors to life in a world burdened by profound, often unresolvable paradoxes.[37] In order to confront these paradoxes and reckon with the hard facts of any situation, political actors must have strong characters. Social science, by furnishing means by which actors can impose some structure on what is, in this ultimately skeptical view, a chaotic and uncertain world, can help enhance humanity's power to confront fate and influence the course of private and social lives. Weber's view of charisma as a creative power which can check the adverse stifling effects of bureaucratic structures suggests the potentially redeeming functions he is ready to ascribe to individual agencies vis-à-vis inexorable impersonal forces and processes. It is precisely because Weber ascribes much importance to individuals as purposeful actors who are continually threatened by irrational forces that his rational-instrumental scheme of human conduct as a deliberate adaptation of means to ends can be construed at one level as a way in which he deals with his own skepticism concerning the human capacity to reckon with the unintelligibility and moral antinomies of the world of action. At another level the means-ends scheme is, of course, a powerful social-scientific theoretical perspective from which to make sense of actions as patterned composites of normative and material elements. "We have a perfectly clear understanding," writes Weber, "of what it means when somebody employs the proposition $2 + 2 = 4$ or the Pythagorean theorem in reasoning or argument. In the same way we also understand what a person is doing when he tries to achieve certain ends by choosing appropriate means on the basis of the facts of the situation, as experience has accustomed us to interpret them."[38] Considering the significance Weber ascribes to irrational factors in social and historical process, it is not surprising that he presents many qualifications to the application of his means-ends scheme. He holds, nevertheless, that the means-ends scheme can be useful also in analyzing and understanding even "irrational affectually determined elements of behavior as factors of deviation from a conceptually pure type of rational action."[39]

The internal normative and the material causal aspects of action are thus logically inseparable in Weberian accounts. One needs to ascribe ends to actions, to establish the goals, the normative coordinates of action, in order to account for actions and to judge them as means relevant to the perceived operation of causes and effects which influence or contribute to the advancement of particular ends.[40]

In advancing his dualistic perspective on action, Weber quite explic-itly rejects "one sided spiritualistic" and "one sided materialistic" causal accounts of history.[41] His approach, therefore, accounts for political phenomena by reference to both "spiritual" and "material" causes. As a cluster of nondeterministic causal as well as teleological scripts, his sociology permits what he calls the "ethics of responsibil-ity," which assumes that knowledge of the anticipated consequences of actions can be expected to enter the choices of agents.[42] In other words, *the postulate of causation underlies the possibility of judging actors as responsible choosers among courses of action, while their values and goals in turn underlie the possibility of subjecting human behavior to causal analysis in instrumental terms.* It is when behavior is viewed neither as random phenomena nor as the expression of iron-clad laws but as interaction among free purposeful agents and recog-nizable constraints that the reconstruction of trends and regularities permits the attribution of causality as well as responsibility in the con-text of action. It is because behavior can be construed as consisting of interaction among choices, causes, effects, and contingencies that actions can be regarded simultaneously as voluntary, causally determined, observable, and meaningful, and agents can be held responsible.

From the perspective of liberal-democratic ideology Weber's soci-ology provides, then, a powerful formula for linking the observable and unobservable aspects of behavior in disciplined accounts which depend on public standards of logic and observation. Weber is quite explicit about the ideological import of social science committed to methodological individualism as well as to a voluntaristic theory of action as a challenge to idealistic, organic, and romantic conceptions of action and society. Shortly before his death he confessed that "if I have become a sociologist it is mainly in order to exorcise the spectre of collective conceptions which still linger among us. In other words, sociology itself can only proceed from the action of one or more sepa-rate individuals and must, therefore, adopt strictly individualistic methods."[43] While the aspiration to advance social science which could help discredit "collective conceptions" is not inconsistent with Durkheim's hopes of substituting scientific for mythological orien-tations, as the latter part of Weber's statement shows, he hoped to weaken "collective conceptions" by stressing methodological individu-alism. For Durkheim, by comparison, individualism itself is a deriva-tive rather than a constitutive fact, something to be upheld and protected by a scientific perspective on society which makes it possible to distance society as a unified object of separate observations.

Durkheim and Weber use different strategies for demystifying social action. Although, as I have already indicated, important sections of Weber's work are not strictly consistent with methodological individualism, his social theories, especially the view that norms can be institutionalized in social practice through social actions carried out by voluntary individual agents, have been consistent with, and supportive of, important presuppositions of liberal-democratic ideology.[44]

It has been important for the ideological relevance of Weber's theory of action that he did not regard politics as a phenomenon which results from the autonomous operation of social forces.[45] His instrumental concept of action is consistent with the ideological affirmation of the sphere of politics as a domain of free actions. Not surprisingly, therefore, an observer like Edward Tiryakian could note the special fit between Weberian sociology and key features of American culture and ideology such as "instrumental activism," the insistence on the voluntary character of action, a commitment to individualism which stresses the interaction between individuals rather than their isolation, and the notion of society as an ever-emerging, unfinished, continually constructed entity.[46] While Weber held nominalistic notions of "collective entities," American social science has shown a tendency to go considerably beyond Weber in stressing voluntaristic individualistic concepts of action, as well as indeterminate concepts of social reality. But because the significance he ascribed to factual constraints on the will of agents was the part of his sociology which was most antagonistic to romantic German notions of history and to what Leonard Kreiger calls the "German idea of freedom," it was, of course, particularly relevant to the pedagogy of liberalism in Germany.[47]

Individualism and Interactionism in American Social Theory

Partly influenced by European thinkers and partly responsive to more indigenous American intellectual and social traditions, American social theorists have developed their own variant of the dualistic approach to social action. Affinities between key elements of American ideological and political orientations toward action and authority and individualistic variants of voluntary theories of action were already discernible at the end of the last century in the context of early attempts to professionalize the social sciences. The intellectual climate in America during the last decade of the nineteenth century and the early part of the twentieth century was shaped by a combination of reactions to positivism in both its Spencerian and Marxist versions,[48] criticism of formalism, rejection of German idealism, and a growing distrust of closed-system theories of society.[49]

Challenging the foundations of Continental individualism with its stress on the discontinuities between individual and society and the predisposition to view collective action as produced from the "outside" by involuntary mechanistic or legalistic (formalistic) instruments, American social theorists showed a distinct tendency to cultivate a kind of "interactive individualism" according to which individual and society are not radically distinct or opposed. Referring to the universe of social thought in America near the turn of the century, Thomas Haskell notes how nineteenth-century American ideas of individualism and self-reliance appeared increasingly informed by an appreciation for the fluidity of social experience and the extent to which individuals are interdependent. "It was a universe," he observes, "in which the professional social scientist had a vital role to play, for it was largely through his explanatory prowess that men might learn to understand their complex situation, and largely through his predictive ability that men might cooperatively control society's future and thus get the cash value of their small measure of freedom."[50] It was such a concept of freedom, realized through action, which led American social thinkers and American liberal-democratic ideologues to accept the possibility of a synthesis between voluntarism and scientifically informed instrumentalism. The rise of the American Social Science Association near the turn of the century was apparently an expression of both an intellectual disposition to consolidate a view of social behavior as interaction among interdependent parts and the increasing ascription of sociopolitical value to science as a resource in the authoritative construction of public actions.[51] Scientific knowledge could appear in this climate as the means to prevent interdependence from degenerating either into personal or group domination or into a faceless crowd. Methodological individualism and empirical concepts of knowledge nourished by indigenous cultural and political orientations combined in American social science to produce a view of action sufficiently open-ended to allow for the stress on voluntary agency, yet sufficiently determined to permit scientific analysis and relatively objective or neutral accounts of behavior. The stress on interdependence has implied a democratic concept of reciprocal interaction among equals, a concept which rejects both the kind of radical independence which places individuals outside society and the kind of dependence which subordinates them to it.[52]

Although in his own sociological work Talcott Parsons, a central transmitter of Durkheim's ideas to America, stresses such collective aspects of social action as "normative consensus," "structural integration," and "functional" dimensions of the "social system," his theoretical orientation reveals a strong commitment to the legacy of the Weberian variant of the voluntaristic theory of action. Parsons' concern with the role of "personality" and the place of "values" as elements of social action tempers the weight he ascribes to collective systemic factors.[53] A majority of prominent American social scientists have been committed, however, to a more radical accent on the role of the individual as a maker and creator of social structures and on a reciprocal, interactionist concept of action. Parsons' concept of the "social system" has been criticized by such influential American theorists as Robert K. Merton, who discards both psychological and sociological reductionism. His stress on the individual as a chooser among socially structured alternatives makes him characteristically suspicious of the disposition of European sociologists to search for an all-embracing general theory.[54] Very much in the temper of American responses to European—especially Continental—orientations toward social phenomena, Merton, it has been suggested, "stood Durkheim on his head. Rather than having the individual confronted with ready made social norms that are external, coming down *in toto,* so to speak, for Merton individuals have to find their own orientations among multiple incompatible norms."[55]

A similar tendency to view social phenomena from the perspective of individuals as voluntary choosers and actors is discernible in a host of other social scientists such as Robert Parke, Peter Blau, and Alvin Gouldner. These inclinations have made some American social scientists particularly receptive to the influence of George Simmel, who stands out among "classical" European sociologists in his emphasis on the conception of social phenomena as processes rather than structures and in the centrality he accords to such concepts as "reciprocity," "conflict," and "exchange."[56] Other American social scientists who have stressed the primacy of individual actors over the "social system" include C. Wright Mills, who focuses on the role of social conflict, and social psychologists like Robert Bales and George Homans who stress the role of individual goals and small groups. A later generation of social scientists, including Anthony Downs, John Harsanyi, Thomas Schelling, and Robert Coleman, carries methodological individualism further by viewing behavior as a function of individual interests and strategies.[57] "Symbolic interactionists" like Herbert Mead and Erving Goffman also assume methodological-individualist perspectives in their studies of the role of individuals in shaping the meanings of social situations. A strong commitment to methodological individualism is discernible in the work of another influential American social theorist, Edward Shils, in his idea of the individual as a cultural entrepreneur.[58] Such examples seem to support the suggestion made by R. C. Hinckle and G. J. Hinckle that the outstanding persistent feature of American sociology is the assumption that the structure of any social group is "the consequence of the aggregate of its separate component individuals and that the social phenomena ultimately derive from the motivations of these knowing, feeling and willing individuals."[59] Such a stress on the individual as the ultimate unit of social action has, of course, been equally characteristic of American political science.[60] Cultural and political perspectives that stress the socio-institutional order as a continually negotiated reality appear to have furnished in America a most congenial context for the evolution of social and ideological theories of action which emphasize the efficacy of the individual as an actor.[61] In some respects, the very orientations toward politics, authority, and action which Weber hoped to cultivate in Germany were the givens that made America both receptive to his sociology and prone to develop its own, more radical individualistic variants of voluntaristic theories of action.

The stress in American sociology and political science on the role of deliberate individual actors in the production of social phenomena and the extensive commitment to methodological individualism in other fields, such as social psychology and economics, have made American social science a principal resource of liberal-democratic ideology and politics.[62] American social sciences have tended implicitly to accept the idea of freedom as a positive principle of sociopolitical construction, the notion that freedom both generates and is compatible with stable, regular patterns of political behavior and institutions. Together with the commitment to the role of rational persuasion in liberal-democratic politics, this concept of freedom has implied that the structure of the sociopolitical order can be affected by the strength of the arguments advanced in the political sphere. The characteristic ways in which American social scientists have approached the problem of explaining social phenomena have lent powerful support to the liberal-democratic attempt to base the political sphere on the objective aspects of individual actions. The continuities between the concepts of freedom underlying American ideological and social-scientific accounts of human conduct have made American liberal-democratic politics particularly receptive to social-scientific instrumentalism as a mode of describing, prescribing, justifying, and judging actions in the public sphere. Social science has helped certify and deploy scientific instrumentalism in the political rhetoric of what emerged as a particularly American variant of liberal-democratic action.

Concepts of Agency, Action, and Reality in American Pragmatism

Perhaps the most important domestic intellectual support for instrumentalism in American politics has come, since the late nineteenth century, from American pragmatism. Despite important variations of style, intellectual goals, and philosophical attitudes, thinkers such as Charles Peirce, William James, John Dewey, and Herbert Mead have generally shared the view that reality is an endless process of becoming rather than a fixed given, that the individual is the ultimate agent of action and (particularly for Peirce and Dewey) that the "republic of science" exemplifies the way in which a society of independent inquiring and experimenting individuals can generate disciplined public discourse and action.

Pragmatism constitutes, therefore, an indigenous American development of the epistemology and ethics of action as interaction. Fusing strains of individualistic-idealistic conceptions of freedom with elements of empirical theories of knowledge, the pragmatists have come to view the very ideas of truth and reality in terms of the world as a thing encountered in action rather than as an object of thought and detached observation. By presenting the philosophical problems of knowledge and reality in terms of interaction rather than contemplation or observation from a distance, pragmatism humanizes and dignifies action while concretizing and democratizing truth. Insofar as pragmatism locates truth as something which arises from a multitude of potentially incommensurable particular interactions between individual agents and experience, not as something discovered by systematic observations which progressively establish an objectively given truth, it upholds a less unified, more eclectic, and in a way more democratic concept of social reality than the one implicit in European social theories such as Durkheim's or even Weber's. By affirming the primacy of individual agencies in the cognitive construction of social facts, pragmatism risks the affirmation of radically fluid and fragmented concepts of social reality. Without a privileged perspective on reality, a variant of the earlier God's or monarch's eye view of society, without an objectively superior claim of knowledge, society loses its unity and hardness as an object. By shifting true conceptions of reality from the context of detached observers to the context of engaged individual actors pragmatism decentralizes, diversifies, and localizes the authority to fix and define social facts. Pragmatism further rejects both the rationalistic insistence on the independence of mind and reality and the traditional separation between thought and action. For the pragmatists, "truth" and "reality" are continually constructed and reconstructed in the course of interaction among actors and between actors and "experience." The experienced world contains both natural things and other persons. Reality in this view is sufficiently plastic to accommodate the actions of voluntary agents, although it is usually also sufficiently determinate to impose some constraints on the actors' wills. It is precisely such a stress on the plastic and malleable character of reality which provokes Durkheim's criticism of William James. Durkheim is concerned that the notion that the truth is made in accordance with the individual's striving to satisfy his or her needs could open the way for unrestrained subjectivism.[63]

Radical individualism, a plastic concept of reality, and a strong accent on interaction have made pragmatism most congenial for both American intellectual and political sensibilities. Consistent with wider sociopolitical trends, the rejection by both James and Dewey of the "copy" or "spectator" theory of knowledge, their more participatory epistemology, and their ethics of action accentuate the weight of the acting individual relative to the world acted upon. According to James, pragmatism converts the "absolutely empty notion" of a static relation of correspondence between our minds and reality into that of a rich and active commerce.[64] Against a view of reality as "ready made and complete for all eternity," James defends what he regards as a humanistic pragmatic view of reality as "something resisting yet malleable," something "still in the making."[65] He attacks the classical spectator view of knowledge as inconsistent with the individual's creative role in constructing the world,[66] and criticizes Herbert Spencer's positivist outlook for "so fatally lacking in . . . picturesqueness and

poetry, and [in being] so explicit, so mechanical, so flat in the pano-
rama which it gives to life."[67] A person "is not simply a mirror floating
with no foothold anywhere and passively reflecting an order that he
comes upon and finds simply existing. The knower is an actor, and
coefficient of the truth on one side whilst on the other he registers the
truth which he helps create."[68] The pragmatists reject the Cartesian
dichotomy between the world as a view and the subject as a viewer
and, as Richard Rorty points out, shift the emphasis from the vocabulary of representations to the vocabulary of practice.[69]

James's conception of reality as both made and registered is, however, more respectful of reality as a constraint on human action than
the one attributed to him by Durkheim. It corresponds with his concept of the individual as being both creative and receptive, subjective
and objective.[70] John Dewey takes a similar position. "Greek and
medieval science," he observes, "formed an art of accepting things as
they are enjoyed and suffered. Modern experimental science is an art
of control."[71] It integrates freedom and necessity into a concept of the
human being as a maker.[72] Like James, Dewey discards the old
spectator theory of knowledge and advocates a shift from "knowing as
an outside beholding" to "knowing as an active [participation] in
the drama of a moving world," knowing as something expressed in
"dealing with problems."[73]

As Morton White notes, the tendency to criticize the dichotomy
between human agency and reality and to reject apriorism, logism,
and abstract rationalism encompassed, beyond the pragmatists, other
influential American intellectuals like Oliver Wendell Holmes and
Thorstein Veblen. These intellectuals criticized the English thinkers
Jeremy Bentham, J. S. Mill, and John Austin for holding too rigid concepts of reality.[74] If for Durkheim the pragmatist's concept of reality as
constantly becoming lacks the "static aspect" necessary to warrant
the unification of individual judgments and to ground social discipline in the "liberalism of minds," the pragmatists represent an
American intellectual disposition to regard English—and even more
so Continental—positivist concepts of reality and of law as exces-
sively fixed givens.[75] These differences reflect again the effects of the
spectrum of positions—from the extremes of what one may label
European insular to interactive American individualism. For insular
individualists, reality, like law, must be fixed externally in order to
coordinate individual actions without denying the autonomy and purposefulness of agents. For interactive individualists, reality, as well as

law, is much more dynamically and continually produced and altered through interaction. It is as if for Americans even reality cannot be accepted as a finished determined "thing" without offending democratic sensibilities. Extended into the sphere of knowledge and perception, pragmatism reflects American irreverence toward authority and distrust of claims about constraints and restrictions imposed on the autonomy and the creativity of acting and interacting individuals. Such an attitude is clearly biased against a dualistic conception of reality as having both an appearance and an invisible depth. It recalls Tocqueville's observation that "in a society where citizens are placed on equal footing, they readily conclude that everything in the world may be explained, and that nothing in it transcends the limits of understanding. Thus they fall to denying what they cannot comprehend, which leaves them but little faith for what is extraordinary and almost insurmountable distaste for whatever is supernatural."[76] By comparison with the stress on vision, picturing and representing in earlier epistemological theories, pragmatist epistemology assumes that the objects of knowledge are not given but continually shaped in the context of our experience and conversation. What is trusted as real is the world encountered in experience, not the world as a distant object or a systematic intellectual construct. Reality is upheld and delineated through acting rather than through distantly observing or inferring. Such a concept of reality has been inconsistent with a concept of individualism which divides the inner (socially invisible) reality of the self from the exterior reality of the material and social worlds. The pragmatist notion that thought and action, human agency and the world, are on the same plane of phenomena, and therefore that the citizen who constructs the polity and the "real" inner person are the same, is inconsistent with characteristic European predispositions to separate more sharply between freedom of thought and the sphere of social action.

The pragmatists' belief that "reality," like "law" or "truth," is something made rather than found implies the readiness to accept the risks and uncertainties of substituting for fixed reality more dynamic terms of reference for political discourse and action. This includes, of course, also the reality or the identity of the individuals themselves, which pragmatism sees as continually evolving and changing in the course of action and interaction. The elasticity of the individual as an acting and experiencing subject corresponds to the elasticity of the world as the object experienced and acted upon. Assuming such a fluid concept of reality and its complementary concept of action as creative interaction with a plastic social—and physical—world, pragmatism is not invulnerable to criticism of the kind made by Durkheim—that its notions of reality and action have potentially anarchistic implications. The pragmatist concept of reality raises the question of whether pragmatism furnishes an epistemology which can support the theory of constraints implicit in liberal-democratic concepts of action and accountability. Does it furnish a basis for solving the liberal-democratic problem of action? Doesn't it go too far in stressing the subjective and creative aspects of individual actions for these actions to be regarded as constituents of a public order? Don't the pragmatist concepts of freedom and creativity destroy the very possibility of instrumental actions as disciplined relations between means, ends, and consequences which are open to public tests of adequacy and effectiveness?

Dewey, who is more concerned than James with reconciling pragmatism and liberal-democratic conceptions of the polity, pays more attention to the issue of how such anarchistic implications of radically plastic notions of action and reality can be tempered. For Dewey, creative individuals do not seek, as Nietzsche would have them do, to liberate themselves beyond the strictures of society and culture but, more following Weber's lead, they seek to realize their powers as voluntary actors within a web of sociocultural relations. Dewey insists on the communal aspect of individual actions, their potential public dimension. It is this very aspect of action, the objective as against the subjective, that Dewey seeks to reinforce by his references to the "scientific attitude" and his use of terms such as "cooperative" or "experimental" intelligence. While he rejects, as does James, classical liberal notions of individuality as "something ready made,"[77] he holds that once intelligence is properly integrated into actions, actions become purposeful and disciplined.[78] Advocating a shift toward a new conception of social action based on the "logic of freed intelligence as a social force,"[79] Dewey stresses the possibility of what he calls "effective liberty."[80] His conception of social action is, then, thoroughly instrumental and antianarchistic. The application of scientific methods and experimental intelligence in social and political matters is described as a way of making liberty an active and constructive force. Developing an experimental concept of political action, Dewey subscribes to the desirability of "considering social realities in terms of cause and effect and social policies in terms of means and consequences."[81]

"Democracy," he observes, is a "fighting faith . . . When its ideals are reinforced by those of scientific method and experimental intelligence, it cannot be that it is incapable of evoking discipline, ardor and organization."[82]

Dewey's social theory strives to appropriate science and technology as the basis of democratic-decentralized and yet collectively disciplined and effective instrumental actions. It presents science not so much as a means of adapation to necessity or passive contemplation of the inevitable or rational acquiescence in the tragic, nor as a justification of state demands for obedience. For Dewey, science is a bridge between individualism—conceived in the interactive mode as voluntary and creative—and collectively disciplined public choices and actions. Dewey regards experimental intelligence as the very glue which cements "freedom and authority."[83] While a neoclassical liberal like Friedrich Hayek maintains that "the only alternative to submission to the impersonal and seemingly irrational forces of the market is submission to an equally uncontrollable and therefore arbitrary power of other men,"[84] Dewey advances as a third alternative the course of active participation regimented by a scientific-experimental attitude. Intelligence integrated into a new mode of social action is an alternative both to sociological and historical determinism, which leaves no room for voluntary individual actors, and to radical individualism, whose implicit concept of freedom leaves no basis for collective discipline. Because, according to Dewey, a sharp opposition between individual and society is untenable and because individuality is shaped in the context of associations, while associations can have structure without denying the individuality of their numbers, social action can be disciplined without undercutting its basis in the integrity of voluntary individual actors.[85] Hence Dewey's analysis, although reflecting the pragmatist critique of the spectator theory of knowledge and his insistence that important aspects of experience are public, implies, perhaps inconsistently, that attestive visual orientations are relevant to the determination of public policies and public actions and assumes that there are such things as group knowledge or group intelligence.

George Herbert Mead explores the implications of the pragmatist attitude toward action that are more consistent with its commitment to individualism by fusing psychology and sociology, the science of individual behavior with the science of the structures of collective behavior. In harmony with American liberal-democratic ideology,

Mead's social psychology accepts the fundamental assumption about the continuity between the reality of the individual and the reality of society.[86] For Mead, individuals are not determined by society nor can they act without social constraints. These respective yet continuous realities evolve through a process of reciprocal interaction in the course of which control coexists with adaptation and social institutions are constructed and reformed.[87] According to Mead the individual becomes a social person by learning to employ symbolic controls of action and to enter into symbolically constructed networks of regulated roles and interactions. Mead's concepts of knowledge and action are therefore incompatible with the Durkheimian notion of an elite scientific guidance of social action from above. For Mead, the scientist's method is "the same as that of all intelligent human beings."[88] It is not an impersonal uniform method which leads to the discovery of a given inner logic of society as an independent entity but a mode of individual orientation toward action which combines the capacity to create and control with humility before the resistant elements of experience. It is through the rational discipline of the scientific approach that the individual becomes social. "The technique of the experimental method" is what, according to Mead, enables "individual perspective [to become] the perspective of the most universal community, that of thinking men."[89] Instrumentalism as an attribute of individual orientation, not of the action of corporate authority, is not a basis for rationalizing the imposition of group discipline on the individual but rather the ingredient that renders voluntary individual actions social. Instrumentalism is therefore a powerful self-legitimating rhetoric of action.

Unlike the rationalists, the pragmatists do not view the task of science as demonstrating the truth about society, which could inform and guide actors, nor as showing why, because social structures or social realities result from the intended or unintended effects of human actions, adapting, and conforming to social facts can be regarded as consistent with human freedom and dignity. Science is not employed by the pragmatists, as by Durkheim, in order to mitigate the tensions between human dignity and obedience to authority by basing the latter on voluntary rational adaptation to social facts. The pragmatist concern is primarily with "effective liberty," with effective individual actions as means of structuring collective life. In this sense it is sharply opposed to such influential views in European social science as August Comte's, according to which society is not an ever-emerging, dynamic composite of different elements but the expression of a general idea.

Durkheim's criticism of American pragmatism, especially in its Jamesian version, which became known in the French intellectual circles of his time, can further iluminate some key ideological differences between European collectivistic and American, more individualistic conceptions of social action.

One of Durkheim's first targets is the pragmatist concept of individualism. According to him a view of the individual as a voluntary actor unrestrained by "social facts" undermines social solidarity. Considering the influence of American pragmatism on some French intellectuals, he regards the threat of pragmatism not merely as an intellectual issue but as a matter of "national importance."[90] "Our whole French culture," he observed shortly before World War I, "is basically an essentially rationalistic one. The eighteenth century is a prolongation of Cartesianism. A total negation of rationalism would thus constitute a danger, for it would overthrow our whole national culture. If we had to accept the form of irrationalism represented by pragmatism, the whole French mind would have to be radically changed."[91] Durkheim believes that French society is constructed on the basis of distinct "collective representations" of knowledge and reality in relation to which pragmatism is basically antagonistic. He grants that pragmatism makes valid criticism of "traditional rationalism."[92] But he rejects the attempt to substitute truth as an aspect of action for the necessity of guaranteeing the possibility of impersonal-neutral and true judgments. He refuses to give up a "spectator" theory of truth in order to secure the primacy of "praxis." In order to substantiate the claim that truth is separated from need and thought from reality, Durkheim insists that truth can be "painful," that it often "resists us" and that it has "a certain quality of hardness."[93] James's "psychological" individualism has gone too far, in his opinion, in discarding reality as an external constraint and in attributing all social phenomena to the individual. The stress on the individual as a maker of truth and reality does not provide a satisfactory explanation for social phenomena. "Men," argues Durkheim, "have always recognized in truth something that in certain respects imposes itself on us, something that is independent of the facts of sensitivity and individual impulse."[94] Pragmatism fails to recognize, then, according to this approach, that there are things which do not result from "individual experiences" but have "an extra-individual origin."[95]

This encounter between pragmatism (especially in its Jamesian version) and French Durkheimian rationalism illuminates the correspondences between different responses to the social scientific problem of explanation and distinct liberal-democratic responses to the problem of action. Attempting to establish sociology as a rationalist paradigm for integrating the dignity of individuals and the requirements of social order, Durkheim sees pragmatism as a disruptive alternative. "Both sociology and pragmatism," he argues, "take the position that man is a product of history and hence is in a state of constant becoming; there is nothing in him that is given or defined in advance . . . But if sociology poses the problem in the same way as pragmatism does, it is in a better position to solve it. The latter, in fact, claims to explain truth psychologically and subjectively. However, the nature of the individual is too limited to explain all things human . . . sociology provides us with broader explanations."[96] Sociology, implies Durkheim, is also more consistent with French rationalism as a constituent of national culture. There is in his fear of the loss of reality as a constraint on individual will an element analogous to the fear of earlier centuries that the loss of the belief in hell may lead to chaos.[97] A belief in reality as an inflexible given is for Durkheim a prerequisite for the availability of mechanisms of social control based on rationalistic premises and the authority of science. As evidenced by his comments on the relations between James and Bergson,[98] his criticism of pragmatism, and his defense of French notions of the individual and society against American concepts of action as reciprocal interaction, his entire sociological enterprise appears as part of an ideological struggle over the character of the sociopolitical order in late-nineteenth-century and early-twentieth-century France.

Durkheim's criticism of pragmatism is also a reaction against a conception of reality which puts everything, including thought and action, individual and society, on the same epistemological-ontological plane. He objects to the notion that "things as they appear to us are the surface, [that] that is what we live on, and what reality is; [that] there is no reason to look beneath appearances; [and that] we must deal only with the world as it appears to us . . . Pragmatism," notes Durkheim, "does not really leave [the phenomenal] world."[99]

What is objectionable to Durkheim is precisely the readiness to dispense with external, distant, objective reality without which there is, in his opinion, no basis for true judgments, no grounds for a science of society as a substitute for religion or myth and therefore no basis

for autonomous individuals who can maintain their dignity as independent thinking selves in the context of social action.[100] Without an
external objective reality beyond the context of the human encounter
with the world of appearances, a reality which forces individuals to
discipline their engagement by a measure of detached respect for
facts, Durkheim does not see how science can turn minds toward
impersonal truths and enhance social consensus.[101]

It is, however, precisely that voluntaristic instrumentalism which
presupposes a pragmatist conception of reality without separation
between "internal" and "external," without the discrepancies between
appearance and the layers beneath appearance, which in a society
committed to interactive individualism constitutes an effective response
to the liberal-democratic problem of action. It is because pragmatism
sees the private person and the public citizen as united in the same
plane of experience that the problem of constructing a public order
from the voluntary actions of individual actors appears solvable.

Although both Dewey and Durkheim were concerned with social
reconstruction and both regarded education—particularly when it is
scientifically informed—as a principal means to advance this objective, they held very different notions of the educational process. For
Durkheim, education is fundamentally a process of socialization. "It
is society," he observes in his essays on education, "that draws for us
the portrait of the kind of man we should be, and in this portrait all
the peculiarities of its organization come to be reflected . . . In sum,
education, far from having as its unique or principal object the individual and his interests, is above all the means by which society per-
petually recreates the conditions of its very existence." [102] For Dewey,
education is, by contrast, primarily a means to facilitate "self-realization." [103] Although, like Durkheim, he is concerned with inculcating
self-discipline, his purpose is to ensure that "individuality, moral and
intellectual, shall not be swamped by a disproportionate amount of
the experience of others." [104] For Durkheim, the primary concern is to
protect social solidarity and discipline from overly self-centered individualism. "Education," he observes, "answers above all to external,
that is social, necessities." [105] The only power which Durkheim believes
can moderate and check individual egotism is the power of the group.
This approach reflects his distinction between the reality of the group
and the reality of the individual and his readiness to ascribe to the
former both ontological and moral primacy over the latter. Such an
approach allows Durkheim to claim that adherence to external neces-

sities assumes moral significance for the individual as doing "one's duty." [106] If for pragmatists like Peirce and Dewey science and intelligence are the means by which individuals transcend private beliefs and introduce a public social dimension into their own thoughts and attitudes, for Durkheim private beliefs are checked from the outside by the state in order to prevent social disintegration. Durkheim's centralized ethical instrumentalism leads to the conclusion that "it is . . . up to the state to remind the teacher constantly of the ideas, the sentiments that must be impressed upon the child to adjust him to the milieu in which he must live." [107]

In Dewey's social theory, as in Durkheim's, instrumentalism converges with social ethics. But their differences illustrate the distinct theoretical foundations of decentralized and centralized variants of ethical instrumentalism. "Effective liberty," to use Dewey's term, is a combined choice of that which is practically rational and that which is morally right. But, consistent with the general spirit of American social theory and with the American political creed, the focus as well as the agent of the synthesis is the individual.

Like the pragmatists, several leading American social theorists have been very explicit in their views about the special continuities between the norms and practices of science and the American variant of liberal-democratic politics. As such, they have consistently articulated some of the key themes of voluntaristic individual instrumentalism as a liberal-democratic doctrine of action. Robert K. Merton is again a pertinent example. In an essay entitled "Science and Technology in a Democratic Order," Merton observes that a comparative study of scientific institutions supports the assumption that "science is afforded opportunity for developing in a democratic order which is integrated with the ethos of science." [108] In another context, Merton notes that central norms of democratic politics such as distrust of hierarchical authorities and commitment to publicity have close affinities to the "normative structure of science." [109] Both democratic politics and scientific practice are based on the notion of the individual as a free agent and as an autonomous judge of the utternaces and actions of others. The assumption that key elements of the normative structures of science and democratic politics converge implies not only that political democratization can aid the development of scientific activity and its institutionalization but also that—as Dewey claims—to render civic discourse scientifically informed and to instrumentalize civic actions is to democratize politics.

Talcott Parsons and Gerald Platt observe, along similar lines, that as an institutionalized body of scientific-academic norms, the American university is a powerful agent of democratization. If "the older ascriptive bases of society are attenuated," they note, and "the particularistic solidarities of religion, ethnicity, localism and class have been eroding as bases of status and even of relationship, the spread of higher education has contributed to that erosion. Thus modern society has become increasingly pluralistic on bases of functional differentiation." [110]

The emancipation of social action from ascriptive and traditional bonds implies, according to Parsons and Platt, "high average levels of responsibility for personal action and thus a greater need for knowledge, competence and intelligence to guide action." [111] The academic community which generates and imparts knowledge and competence represents, therefore, a "culture" of actions based on functional rather than on ascriptive considerations. To render action or speech more "scientifically" acceptable is, in this view, to make it also less dependent upon traditional, hierarchic, religious, and other nondemocratic authorities. The influence of the norms and structures of scientific and academic communities in the larger society is associated with the decline of traditional authority and a progressive process of democratization.

Parsons and Platt maintain then that academic education encourages democratic political orientations. The rules of the academic community, they observe, protect undergraduates who are the most vulnerable part of the academic community "against dogma, propaganda and sectarianism. [They permit them] to develop voluntarily their packages of differential commitments and participations." [112]

Individuals who are, or formerly were, students are consequently expected to be better, more democratically oriented citizens. The sensibilities they acquire in academic settings supposedly make them less vulnerable to the influence of traditional orientations as well as to the forces of mass enthusiasm and propaganda. [113] Integrating scientific and technical norms of persuasion and action in political practice is, then, a factor in the cultivation of modern democratic virtues. The view that the values and ethos of science and democratic politics converge, at least partially, also encompasses the attitude that "political science is a democratic science of politics. Where democracy is strong political science is strong, where democracy is weak political science is weak." [114]

I have suggested that on the one hand making political decisions and actions more acceptable by standards of empirical validation, logical consistency, experimental results, and other such impersonal technical criteria ideologically implies, in the liberal-democratic polity, that those actions are also more consistent with the dignity of individuals and with the accountability of actors. On the other hand, politicizing science, mixing science with politics, is regarded from this perspective as a negative process of undermining the institutional and cultural foundations of objectivity, impersonality, and rationality in our society, and as opening the door for the "corruptive" effects of unrestrained partisanship, subjectivism, and unbridled passion.[115]

Toward the end of the twentieth century, however, this asymmetry between the positive value ascribed to science in liberal-democratic politics and the negative value ascribed to politics as a factor in scientific activity has been partly reversed. The extension of "the scientific attitude" or "the scientific method" to the political sphere has not seemed to realize earlier hopes of democratization, progress, and rationalization while the aim of making science and technology more politically responsive has in fact become a more widely shared objective.[116]

8. Persons, Facts, Rules, and the Production of Public Action in Liberal-Democratic America

Decentralized group interaction and centrally directed action are two distinct contexts for the ideological and political uses of science in the modern American democracy. As two alternative modes of public action, decentralized interaction and centralized direction present different kinds of difficulties for converting the actions of individual agents into democratically authoritative public actions. Whereas in the case of decentralized interaction the principal problem is to secure interpersonal authoritative standards that allow a multitude of independent individuals to generate collective actions, in the case of centrally directed action the principal problem is one of balancing a nondemocratic unequal distribution of the power to act, the claim of only a few actors to be the agents of public actions, with liberal-democratic values. In the former the issue is how inclusive participation can be reconciled with discipline, order, and coordination; in the latter it is how centralized nonparticipatory modes of action can be made democratically accountable.

Individualism, Empirical Knowledge, and the Participatory Concept of Public Action

While liberal-democratic ideology grants to individual agents the ultimate power and authority to act, not all variants of individualism uphold liberal-democratic theories of action. Some of the basic metaphors of selfhood, metaphors which underlie the perceptions and the vocabularies invoked to describe the individual as well as the concomitant notions of how separate individuals can come together in a collective action, are antagonistic to liberal-democratic ideology. There is also, of course, a considerable diversity of notions of the individual and of collective action within the very bounds of liberal-democratic ideology and theories of action.[1]

Of the concepts of the individual which are compatible with the liberal-democratic theory of action, I shall refer to two principal ones as *atomistic* and *social* individualism. Atomistic individualism is associated with images or metaphors of the individual as a socially insulated entity which largely eludes the knowledge of others. Social individualism depends, by contrast, on images of the self which allow for reciprocal interaction, mutual knowledge, and social cooperation among individuals.

These differences between atomistic and social individualism are connected with distinct ideas of how a multitude of autonomous agents can generate public actions, of how a commitment to individualism can be reconciled with the demands of a public order. Atomistic individualism, which implicitly rejects the possibility of purposeful reciprocal interaction, has tended to be associated with forms of public action that depend upon nonreciprocal interaction or involuntary coordination induced by external mechanisms, such as the invisible hand of the market, the bureaucracy, and the judicial system. In nondemocratic ideological or political contexts, reliance on a third party to coordinate and consolidate the actions of insulated individuals has often been connected, of course, with the endorsement of a charismatic leader. Social individualism which, by contrast, does not reject or discard face-to-face interaction as a threat to individual autonomy tends to belittle the need for externally induced coordination and to stress instead the capacity of free, purposeful agents to generate public action through decentralized interaction. While as a component of liberal-democratic ideology social individualism does not negate the important role of laws and bureaucratic organizations in upholding the public realm, the stress on participatory citizenry leads to the elevation of politics as the primary means for generating authoritative public actions. It is, I would like to suggest, precisely because of this emphasis on open face-to-face political interaction and citizen activism that the flexible, open-ended, and dynamic authority of scientifically certified empirical knowledge—and its more popular social versions—can be such a significant resource for coordinating, depersonalizing, and legitimating public actions.

I would like to suggest further that while atomistic individualism, and its concomitant reliance on external regulatory and mediative instruments, has been characteristic of Continental variants of liberal-democratic notions of public action, social individualism, with its stress on the primacy of open, face-to-face methods of political negotiation to generate collective actions, has been a characteristic of the American liberal-democratic tradition.

I shall not try to trace here the roots of such variants of liberal-democratic ideology in the American and European political traditions. For our present purposes it will suffice to note the particular significance of European traditions and doctrines such as absolute monarchy, indivisible sovereignty, aristocratic privilege, hierarchical church structures, theological notions of God as a superagency, and nationalistic notions of the primordial givenness of the group or the tribe in downgrading the creative political function of voluntary individuals relative to external agencies or processes. By contrast, distinct features of the American experience, which emerged largely in opposition to these European ideas and practices—such as the concept of divisible sovereignty, decentralized state and church structures, and the primacy of the individual citizen—have been most congenial for upholding voluntaristic-interactive individualism.

Students of French culture, society, and politics note the connection between the importance accorded centralized bureaucratic coordination in the French polity and the French predisposition for avoiding face-to-face interactions due to the perceived risk of losing individual autonomy and dignity. It has been suggested that the tendency to depersonalize individual action by subordinating it to rules has been a characteristic French response to the problem of generating collective actions in a society conceived as an association of strangers.[2] It has been further noted that in the French society there is a polarity between "aesthetic individualistic" orientations and "doctrinaire hierarchical" ones, which corresponds to a dichotomy between the personal and the impersonal, the individual and the social.[3] Around the pole of the individual lies the domain of aesthetic values where actions are characteristically singular, unique, and unrepeatable. Inasmuch as in France such actions are conceived as the expressions of the unique in the individual, they are antithetical to rule-governed behavior and are typically articulated in spheres of behavior which, as in the case of artistic achievement and military heroism, normally escape the direct regulatory control of the bureaucracy or the courts. In France, in those social contexts where aesthetic individualistic notions of action prevail, the personal component is apparently too important to allow individual agents to be self-validated with reference to standardized external norms. In America, however, where Puritan values have been so central, "self validation [can] be achieved through pragmatic success that is objectively measured."[4] While from the perspective of aesthetic French individualism pragmatic success is often too dependent on considerations of objective facts to be compatible with the value granted to personal autonomy, in America pragmatic success allows public or social measures of individual performance which, like scientific and technical standards of effective action, do not necessarily undermine individuality and autonomy.[5] It has been suggested further that in France rules are devised not so much in order to produce certain results as to prevent arbitrary intrusions into the sphere of the self. There is a clear preference, in this view, for the protection of individual autonomy even at the cost of realism.[6] Yet in America social or interactive individualism permits and even encourages realism and the utilization of scientific and technical standards as impersonal public measures of individual competence and success. Hence specialization, division of labor, and teamwork are conceived in America as aspects of public actions which are perfectly compatible with the principles of liberal-democratic individualism.

Tensions between individualism and realism in France and their relative absence in America may reflect differences between the respective French and American sociocultural definitions of the place of the real in relation to the individual and the social, that is, the different implications of atomistic and social individualisms. Laurence Wylie discerns a characteristically French "dual concept of reality according to which there is, on the one hand, a 'reality' which resides in the deeper self where it is hidden, mysterious and inaccessible to rational reconstruction and on the other a social 'reality' which resides in the intersubjective domain where there are rules, laws and practical needs, which is public and rationally accessible reality."[7] Between these two realities Wylie, like Crozier, sees constant strains. It is a French tendency, notes another observer in the same vein, to "disassociate the 'real' inner private life from the facade of official life."[8] The perceptions of such tensions, between the space of the solitary individual and the group, tensions which are implicit in the attempts to integrate the premises of atomistic individualism and a liberal-democratic order, are recurrently expressed in French social and political thought.[9] The theatrical—in the sense Rousseau conceived as hypocritical—character of behavior in the social space, where the individual is supposedly observed by the others, the sense that exposure in social space threatens the authentic expression of the true self, has been a central theme in French culture, especially in the spheres of art and politics.[10] At the institutional level this theme is manifest in the polarization between the respective domains and styles of collective and individual action. In France the principles of command and consent are not blended within each governmental institution but rather become "fully embodied in different and ultimately antagonistic institutions."[11]

The ideal of a true untheatrical self, purified by nature from the distortions and corruptions of society, has had, to be sure, profound resonance in America as well.[12] In the American context, however, it is an ideal which has characteristically, although by no means exclusively, been interpreted as consistent with a definition of the individual as a citizen whose autonomy is not only preserved but indeed even enhanced in the context of social interaction. In contradistinction to French orientations which presume a bifurcation between a largely inaccessible private—inner—self and an external, rationally organized, and largely hierarchical social world, in America the individual and social realms—including the state—coexist and partly converge in the cultural space of the same experience.

"The usual American point of view," notes Wylie in juxtaposing French and American orientations toward reality, is "that there should be only one level of reality."[13] Such a unified conception of reality in which the spheres of private and public actions are continuous is, of course, more congenial for permitting science and technology to integrate individual and public actions. Contrary to the dualistic conception which divides private and public realities, the epistemological commitments underlying American conceptions of individualism, politics, and public action, and particularly the belief that both the individual and the group are objects of knowledge accessible through observation and interaction, have encouraged in the context of American liberal democracy the sense that instrumental rationality is an acceptable strategy for making individual actions cohere as collective actions.

The sense of continuity between the individual and the social planes has for a long time been reinforced in America by what Sacvan Bercovitch, elaborating on Emerson, calls "representative selfhood,"[14] the idea that the life of every individual is in some respects a microcosm of the life of the community, that individual biography can be a version of the collective history of America. This idea has made the American concept of subjectivity less threatening to the social order.

According to this view, introspection does not lead one into a progressively internal world of a socially inaccessible self. It is a method through which the individual may discern the essence and the sensibilities of the entire society. The idea of the "American self as the embodiment of a prophetic universal design"[15] furnishes a metaphoric foundation and a pedagogic justification for the transparency of the self.[16]

Contrary to the Continental aristocratic or romantic variant of the insular self, the uniqueness of the democratic self in America is not celebrated here in the denunciation of the others. "Emerson's hero, like Mathers' Winthrop," observes Bercovitch, "derives his great man from the enterprise he represents. Despite his distaste for and fear of the mass of actual Americans, he did not need to disassociate himself from America because he already disassociated the mass from the American idea. Carlyle's hero [by contrast] gathers strength precisely in proportion to his alienation. He stands sufficient in himself, a titan born to master the multitude."[17] Self-reliance does not deny community in America. "It is the consummate expression of a culture which places an immense premium on independence while denouncing all forms of eccentricity and elitism."[18] Whereas "elsewhere, to be independent was to challenge society, in the United States, it was to be a model of consensus. . . . Ideals of community wholly supported the goals of free enterprise . . . representative selfhood bound the rights of personal assent to the rites of social assent."[19]

Although this trust in the continuity between self and community has important roots in American Puritanism, it could also, of course, accommodate nonreligious modes of integrating the individual into a larger collective enterprise. Such an attitude must have contributed to the special American receptivity to the ideological uses of science and technology and the political functions of instrumental paradigms of action as means for the universalization and externalization of individual actions as elements of a collective American mission of progress. Where moral virtues could not be considered sufficiently reliable to realize Rousseau's dream that "exterior appearance [would be] a reflection of the heart's dispositions,"[20] technicalization of individual actions could at least ensure that some actions be "exteriorized" and made publicly accessible as relations between means and ends. Actions whose forms manifestly fit their functions, or whose adequacy as means can be demonstrated by their consequences, could appear to testify to the absence of arbitrariness, to the capacity to avoid self-deception, and therefore to exemplify the virtue of honest realism which, as Judith Shklar reminds us, was praised by Machiavelli as the ability to see "things as they are."[21] The special relations between the "faithful eye" and the "sincere hand," to use Robert Hooke's language, between disciplined observations and actions constrained by factual reality, invested technical action with the special moral power of manifest sincerity.[22] Contrary to the norms of "aesthetic individualism," representative selves are not expressed or confirmed through the uniqueness of unrepeatable acts. Authenticity does not reside in singularity but in an individual expression of universal human possibilities.[23] For the most part the impulse against elitist-romantic claims of inaccessible uniqueness has facilitated the fusion of individualism and discipline in America without resorting to hierarchical authority. An idea of "reality" shared by all selves, both as private persons and as citizens participating in a public enterprise, substantiated in America an epistemological justification for the authority of scientific and technical standards in commensurating individual and collective actions. The authority of science, which was socially represented and reinforced by the compelling success of machines and techniques that visibly work, offered a mode of welding individual and collective actions in ways that precluded the tensions and the conflicts inherent in religious or moral paradigms of public action. The American self could celebrate heroes like Thomas Edison, a prototype of the American as technologist, as the individual whose small step toward the conquest of nature could become a "giant step for mankind."[24] Just as individual Americans could discover within themselves, or in nature, the threads that connect them with a universal enterprise so, as we have seen above, could private business firms and "economic men" be transformed by the use of science and technology into agents of public actions and national missions.[25]

The ideological functions of science in the rationalization of modern American concepts of politics and public action stand out more sharply against the background of earlier American concepts of politics as a domain of passions, conspiracies, and personal conflicts, an enterprise of agents corrupted by power.[26] Gordon Wood observes that, during the eighteenth century, conspiracy theories of politics and a "paranoid style" were familiar to more than a few Americans and in fact constituted dominant features of American politics. They reflected a tendency to explain political events by reference to hidden motives, designs, deceits, and subversions. The conspiratorial view of politics, which "presumes a world of autonomous, feeling, acting individuals who are capable of directly and deliberately bringing about events through their decisions and actions,"[27] is of course very much rooted in individualist theories of society and politics, which have been fundamental to liberal-democratic images of order. But insofar as the conspiratorial view is connected with distrust among agents, it tends to be closer to the atomistic than to the social variant of liberal-democratic individualism. Within this earlier paradigm of politics Americans tended to distrust the possession and exercise of political power as the reflection of personal desires and partisan interests. James S. Young notes the prevalence of such antipower attitudes and conspiracy theories of politics well into the first decades of the nineteenth century.[28] He also notes their inhibitory effects on the development of assertive political leadership in the American polity.[29]

Such conspiracy theories of politics and the attribution of hidden motives to political actors were later tempered by the authorization of partially impersonal, causal accounts of political behavior, which were facilitated by the cultural diffusion of the modern vocabularies of the natural and the social sciences.[30] This development opened the way for tempering personalistic accounts of political behavior by authoritative references to impersonal mechanisms, processes, and causes.[31]

Ideas such as those developed by Bernard Mandeville (1670–1733) and Adam Smith (1723–1790) furnished conceptual means with which causal links between actions and their consequences could substitute for, or moderate, accounts based on the presumed moral links between motives and the perceived results of actions.[32] Through subordinating the imputation of motives to the analysis of certain public and objective aspects of the actions, rather than to personal traits of the agents, scientific perspectives on politics became a central resource in a new liberal-democratic rhetoric of political action and accountability. While in the context of earlier liberal-democratic paradigms of politics the inevitable gaps between the manifest motives, or intentions, of political actors and the perceived consequences of their actions were bridged by conspiracy theories of behavior, Gordon Wood has shown that social scientific perspectives on behavior made it possible to bridge or explain such gaps without attributing them to hidden motives. This was achieved in part by establishing that motives are not in themselves causes but elements in complex systems of interacting factors that include external forces, mechanisms, and processes over which actors have but little influence. The authority of amoral accounts of political behavior was reinforced further by the view that not all the uncertainties confronted by actors can be overcome by the acquisition of knowledge and that in some respects all actions have unanticipated consequences. The social sciences further contributed to mitigating the influence of conspiracy theories of political action by requiring that valid accounts of the motives and goals of actors be grounded in the manifest observable aspects of human conduct.

As I have already indicated, social scientific accounts of political behavior contributed to the liberal-democratic ideological move to externalize political behavior and construct it culturally as a view in a public space of perception. This development has been associated with a shift from the early perception of the federal government as a government "at a distance and out of sight"[33] to the modern perception of the government as a principal performer in an ongoing public spectacle. At the level of "horizontal" voluntary political interaction among the citizens, the shifts, encouraged by the social sciences, from focusing on the words of political actors to focusing on their actions, from stressing character or personality to stressing the public features of performance, that is, from moral to instrumental orientations toward action, were congenial for lowering the temperature of politics. Social scientific views of political behavior also provided considerably more humble notions of what individual actors could do than those found in conspiracy theories of behavior. Underplaying the power of insulated individuals to control the course of politics, viewing the political world as a complex, partly impersonal system of forces, supported social nonatomistic individualism and the corresponding notions of political action. By comparison with insular asocial individualism, this view of public actions as the products of complex interactions among voluntary individuals implies that the respective weights given to *agency* vis-à-vis *situation,* or *actors* vis-à-vis objective *circumstances,* are equally balanced in the determination of the course and effects of political actions.

The sociocultural changes which increased the importance of social, interactive individualism and the role of impersonal causes and processes in modern liberal-democratic American orientations toward public action have facilitated the diffusion of social trust in politics as a principal mode of public action. It is in this context that one should analyse the special role of science and technology in the modern American liberal-democratic response to the issue of honesty or sincerity in politics. Whereas in France political behavior has been typically perceived as necessarily alienated from the inner self or personality of the actor,[34] in America presumed continuities between the private person and the public actor have encouraged the emergence of honesty as a political virtue—indeed an imperative—in the field of action. Science and its socially relevant practices and authorities have provided here the means with which sincerity (or insincerity) can be attributed to individual actors by reference to external and hence accountable and supposedly decidable, factual aspects of action.[35]

The view that it is an American cultural trait to maintain that the "real" individual can be transparent, that the private person is also the social person, is supported by Lionel Trilling. He notes that the American, unlike the European, tends to develop a concept of a self which is not typically alienated from the social world and that basic continuities between self and society are a fundamental cultural presupposition in America.[36] Benjamin Franklin's autobiography is in many ways an instructive early prototype of this notion of the American self insofar as it discards, as Judith Shklar shows, the existence of a private inner self which is truer than the one socially articulated as "the sum of his actions."[37] Emerson, whose private journals actually reveal such a private, hidden, inner self, nevertheless articulated an American cultural norm when he stated that "genuine action will explain itself"[38] or when he observed that "an action is the perfection and publication of thought."[39]

The idea that thoughts can be manifest in actions, that action is like a mirror which renders thought socially visible, was reinforced by available authoritative scientific methods of connecting voluntaristic and causal, spiritual and material, invisible and visible aspects of action. The belief that reliable methods of inferring motives and values from the observable aspects of behavior facilitated the draining off of many of the passions and tensions inherent in personalist, moralist, and dramaturgic conceptions of politics as a struggle, or a clash of agencies, in a largely invisible space. The related institutionalization of politics as a view within attestive visual culture has been, of course, congenial for this process of restraining political passions by shifting the focus of discourse and action to the visual space of public facts and public acts.

The more socially individualistic, interactive, and public view of liberal-democratic politics that evolved in modern America contrasts sharply with European aristocratic notions of political actions as the product of the character, intentions, and wills of heroic individuals. These characteristics of American orientations toward personality, society, and politics, which, as I have shown above, stand out by comparison with French orientations, can be still further clarified by comparing them with other European counterparts. As one observer has noted, in America "each individual is a more public fact than is the individual Englishman whose personal definition depends on a more effectually plural social world."[40] The American liberal-democratic ideological synthesis between social, interactive individualism and scientific instrumentalism contrasts particularly sharply with German orientations. Like the French, the Germans also have tended to regard the social and the political worlds as "external to the individual."[41] Because to move away from the private domain of the inward self has been typically construed in Germany as wandering away from the sphere of real freedom,[42] the German idea of freedom appears to support an apolitical individualism and a form of personalized corporatism.[43] Such orientations have been associated in Germany with the tendency to regard science and technology as belonging in the "materialistic" sphere of "Zivilization," which the Germans regard as inferior to the sphere of "Kultur," understood as the domain of literature, speculative thought, and metaphysics.[44] Thus, while an American thinker such as John Dewey could regard the scientific method as a tool for bonding individual contributions in collective democratic action, in Germany a preference for authority which cannot be challenged from below by references to "facts," a preference for speculative thought and understanding over empirical and experimental knowledge, has been linked with nondemocratic concepts of political action as something produced by superagencies.[45] Hence in the German context, at least until the end of World War II, science, technology, liberal individualism, and liberal-democratic concepts of authority and accountability did not converge to form a paradigm of decentralized public action.

Juxtaposition of American and European orientations toward individualism and knowledge can illuminate, then, the distinct features of American conceptions of political action. The pervasiveness of attitudes corresponding to many elements of insular individualism has encouraged in both France and Germany a variety of nonreciprocal interaction and nonparticipatory modes of collective action, such as bureaucratic centralism, legalism, and charismatic personal leadership. The European failure to evolve a nonelitist liberal-democratic variant of instrumental political action reflects the fact that, as Walter Benjamin so aptly observed, "the average European has not succeeded in uniting his life with technology, because he has clung to the fetish of creative existence."[46] In England, a strong parliamentary tradition has articulated a significant commitment to interactive individualism which had been nourished by the influence of British empiricism but tempered by aristocratic codes of elite leadership.[47] These factors have tended to encourage in England a very moderate form of instrumentalism and only a limited ideological role for science, a role which is constrained by legalism, deference to elites, and the notion that public action must be largely entrusted to worthy "generalists."

In America, the influence of the British political tradition, unconstrained by the legacy of feudalism and aristocratic values, has allowed for the development of a much more radical form of interactive individualism. Further reinforced by strong commitments to egalitarianism, by Protestant conceptions of the self, and by the challenge of conquering the newly discovered continent and achieving economic independence, the American political tradition has given rise to instrumentalism, with its stress on scientific and technological orientations toward action, as one of the most characteristic forms of modern American "national" political style. Instrumentalism in politics has emerged as one of the principal strategies with which Americans have sought to cope with the problem of generating public actions without destroying their source in voluntary individual actors.[48]

Science, Facts, and Rules in the American Legal Context

Along with authoritative facts, authoritative rules have constituted a principal means of coordinating, regulating, and depersonalizing, social interaction without apparent recourse to the arbitrary and coercive exercise of power by hierarchical authority. Like factual referents, legal referents have been extensively employed by the modern state in order to discipline the actions of free individual agents and thereby secure order. Compared, however, with the English and Continental theories of democracy, American constitutional and legal theories have gone considerably further in protecting the integrity of decentralized political interaction against the interventions of hierarchical authorities. The principal strategy used to resist hierarchical authority structures in the American legal context has been to grant "public facts," including open contests about what constitutes a fact in any particular case, a central role in determining both the adequacy of legal rules and their applications in the judicial process. Inasmuch as the law is the domain *par excellence* of rule-governed behavior, of actions whose legitimacy is judged with reference to their adequacy in regard to established rules, any indication that even judicial decisions about rules and their applications are partly subordinate, in the American case, to decisions about facts and their relevance should give us clues about the special significance of scientific and expert authority not only in the legal context but also beyond it in the larger context of American society and politics.

What distinguishes the place of "facts" in the American, as compared to European, legal context is not simply the special authority of factual referents or experts but the ways in which this authority is fixed and integrated into legislative and judicial decisions. In this regard it is instructive to note some relevant differences between the American and European legal cultures, particularly between the American and English systems. Perhaps the most important difference between these two legal traditions concerns their respective theories of sovereignty. In England—as in other European states—sovereign authority is final and indivisible, while in America it is neither. Lacking the monarchic legacy of its European counterparts, the American polity evolved as a system of concurrent jurisdictions and "of many coequal sovereignties."[49] "Separation of powers," notes the American historian Gordon Wood, "whether describing executive, legislative and judicial separation or bicameral division of the legislature, was simply a partitioning of political power, the creation of a plurality of discrete governmental elements, all detached from yet responsible to and controlled by the people, checking and balancing each other, preventing any one power from asserting itself too far."[50] In another study comparing the American and English legal cultures, P. S. Atiyah and Robert S. Summers similarly distinguish the American "multi-jurisdictional legal system," which consists of fifty states and a federal system, from the English system of "single jurisdiction."[51]

Such differences relate to the observation I made earlier that in the American constitutional tradition, in contradistinction to its European counterparts, no privileged perspective on the entire polity is granted to any individual or institution to the exclusion of the others. In the legal context this assumption is articulated by the fact that while in England legal and political theory defines the laws as commands of the sovereign laid down from above, in America the laws are presumed to come "from grass roots origins—from the people."[52] Atiyah and Summers suggest along these lines that while English legal reasoning stresses source-oriented standards of validity and is characteristically positivistic and formalistic, American legal reasoning stresses content-oriented standards of validity and is characteristically substantive and antiformalistic.[53] Atiyah and Summers note further that while the English positivistic legal tradition, which has treated the law as something posited by a superior authoritative agency, has stressed the place of certain and fixed procedural norms in legal reasoning, in the American system a tradition which relied heavily on natural law and natural rights theories has settled on a more fluid, open-ended, less certain concept of the law (and of justice) as something which is continually generated from substantive legal contests.[54] This American propensity to reject finality and certainty in the legislative and judicial contexts is linked, of course, with key features of the American political system including the rejection of mechanical majority rule and the special consideration given to the minority as well as the individual as coparticipants in the political process.

These and other differences between American and European—including, on the whole, the English—legal cultures have significant implications for the place of factual assertions and scientific-technical expertise in the legitimation of judicial decisions. The principal point is, perhaps, that the more pluralistic, decentralized, substantive, and contest-oriented American judicial system lends facts and expertise a greater role in legitimating decisions. Don K. Price notes that in America the "unwillingness to take the answers from established authority leads to a tremendous use of research as a basis of decisions at all levels."[57] This tendency contrasts with the English practice, where the legacy of the monarchy has generated much higher tolerance for the practice of secrecy and discretion by high officials.[58] Moreover, whereas in the English system it is assumed that the court, the law, or the sovereign represents a given united, synoptic, and neutral perspective on the contests among various actors or factions, in the American system such a nonpartisan, relatively neutral perspective is not presumed as given but as something which must be continually negotiated and established from below. It is a perspective that is not represented by a single privileged decision-maker but that emerges from a fair competitive contest in which all parties have equal opportunity to present evidence and participate in controlling the proceedings. It is precisely because the status of legal rules is not unambiguously given, and because their interpretation is not subordinate to plain or literal standards of meaning, that certifiable facts and expert authority can, and actually do, play such a central role in deciding legal contests.[59] The American answer to the question What is the law? is not a definitive reference to something written in books of law but is a much less certain and more context-dependent answer which gives greater weight to the facts of the relevant situation. The importance of factual arguments in the American judicial context is reinforced further by an antiauthority predisposition to demystify legal rules (what Jerome Frank calls "rule-skepticism"[60]) and by the need to fix publicly acceptable standards for deciding the case at hand on a nonarbitrary, nonpartisan basis. Such factors encourage in America the role of factual referents and expert authority in checking the power of discretion, in addition to the limits imposed on it by reference to rules. These inclinations of the American system have many manifestations, the most important of which include the centrality of legal instrumentalism in American legal theory and of the jury in the judicial process.

Unlike legal formalism, legal instrumentalism ties the acceptability of legal and judicial decisions to their perceived effectiveness as means for handling specified problems or situations. It has been noted that an emphasis on legal instrumentalism is an indigenous characteristic of American legal theory.[61] Among the most influential thinkers who contributed to American legal instrumentalism between the end of the nineteenth century and the middle of the twentieth century are John Chipman Gray, Oliver Wendell Holmes, Walter Wheeler Cook, Joseph Walter Bingham, Herman Oliphant, Jerome Frank, Karl N. Llewellyn, Felix S. Cohen, and John Dewey.[62] These theorists shared both a distrust of legal formalism and the propensity to support legal interventionism. The language of American legal instrumentalism has been characteristically replete with metaphors taken from the cultures of science and technology. Laws and governmental agencies are commonly compared in their discourse to "instruments," "tools," and "machines," especially engines. The law is conceived as a kind of technology and legal experts as "social engineers."[63] Holmes referred to the uses of law as "experiments" and to society as a "legal laboratory."[64] "The significance of [any] particular rule in the [legal context]," wrote Llewellyn, "will appear only after the investigation of that vital, factual phenomenon: the behavior."[65] Such legal instrumentalism has encouraged the employment of social scientific expertise, including statistical techniques, in the legal context.[66]

The persistent force of the tendency to appeal to scientific analysis of facts as a partial substitute for the reliance on a hierarchy of legal rules and authorities is indicated by the upsurge of a body of literature on the economic approach to legal action during the 1970s. The instrumental orientation toward legal action produced influential works such as Guido Calabresi's *Costs of Accidents* (1970) and Richard Posner's *Economic Analysis of Law* (1972).[67] Economic analysis of actions has apparently provided one of the most attractive ways to get around legal principles or sacred rules without making arbitrary judgments. It has provided a powerful tool for the legal instrumentalist objective of commensurating, and then comparing, the relative costs and benefits of alternative rules. As a generalized science of human interaction, economics has appeared to promise a fusion of the commitment to the idea that the free individual is the ultimate unit of action and the need to find empirically determinate, and hence public, criteria for judging and evaluating actions without relying on subjective evaluations or on authorities outside the context of social interaction. Although such an approach was bound to provoke the reaction of exponents of the more purely moralistic or legalistic approach to the law,[68] legal theorists like Calabresi and Posner have had considerable influence in their efforts to enlist economics in legal decision making as a way to "predict the effects of legal rules and arrangements"[69] and to ground instrumentally conceived legal decisions. An instrumental perspective on rules as a means of solving specific problems rather than as imperatives to which conduct must conform facilitates the special role of research and academic legal knowledge in the American legal culture. The notion that the law is "made" rather than "found," that it needs to be adjusted to changing circumstances and goals rather than represent the capacity of normative rules to endure in diverse times and contexts, is reflected, for instance, in one of Holmes's most quoted statements: "the life of the law has not been logic, it has been experience."[70]

An American legal instrumentalist tendency to stress the importance of the facts of the relevant situations in the determination and evaluation of legislative or judicial decisions has implied an appeal to a more decentralized, more democratic authority than is implied by European legal positivism. To subject the authority of legal and judicial agencies to the open-ended tests of experience suggests an American commitment to a more inclusive participatory distribution of the power to make and apply laws. This has been connected, among other things, with the fact that "most civil actions in America are tried by juries while in England they are decided by judges."[71] Moreover, in England experts are assimilated in a judicial (and political) process in which public officials show a degree of didactic paternalism and distrust toward the governed; in the United States experts are integrated instead into a system in which laypersons are much more trusted as a source of authoritative decisions and actions.[72] Since the authority to legislate and judge is not vested in institutions which sharply separate the governors and the governed, U.S. citizens can feel more keenly than the citizens of most other democracies that they belong on both sides of the fence. Americans have rarely opposed the state as such, writes the American historian Alan Trachtenberg, "for to do so . . . was to place themselves perilously outside the nation, to declare themselves antagonists to the corporate entity of America itself. Constituted in the name of 'the people' the republican state seemed one with the nation, society, the culture."[73]

One must recognize, however, that the weight given to factual referents in the legal context and that the links between this tendency and the attempt to check hierarchical structures by decentralized interactive modes of resolving conflicts in the American legal (and also political) context may in fact be thoroughly incongenial for trusting and preserving the integrity of scientific and technical standards or procedures.[74] A European court, where the experts are selected by the judges and expected to give the judge an unbiased professional opinion, often accords more respect to the norms of scientific reasoning than an American court, where a client-oriented adversarial system expects the experts to advance the best cases for their respective paying clients. This state of affairs, however, suggests an interesting paradox. Because the adversarial system cannot rely, for its coordination and discipline, upon a neutral third-party authority, it requires trust in the possibility of general agreement on the facts of the relevant situations. In order to produce socially authoritative decisions, nonhierarchical decentralized legal structures are dependent upon faith in the possibility of objectively determinate facts, which are sufficiently self-evident or compelling to resolve conflicts of opinion. Nevertheless, adversarial procedures may in fact encourage a practice that subordinates the fixing of facts to norms of fairness which are likely to distort scientifically or technically professional standards. The equal distribution of the opportunity to present evidence and control decision-making procedures may be more important in such cases than some more professionally adequate yet esoteric criteria for establishing certain aspects of experience as facts. Such discrepancies between legal or political and scientifically certified constructions of facts are connected with the importance of science as a resource of legitimation rather than as a body of instrumentally useful knowledge. The rhetoric or myth of objectively determinate facts is often significantly more important to the legitimation of legal and political actions in America than the actual practice of scientific and technical experts. What makes a fact a fact in the legal or political context is not so much the satisfaction of rigorous scientific or technical requirements as the satisfaction of moral and ideological requirements, which ensure the contending parties equality in the opportunity to present and contest assertions of fact and to participate in the definition of the situation. Moral and ideological norms seem more important to the acceptance of certain "facts" as binding upon the behavior of a social group than technically accurate or relevant considerations.[75]

Recognizing that the status of factual referents and their authority to depersonalize, decentralize, and unify actions and decisions in the American political and legal contexts may be inconsistent with scientific and technical standards means that the distinction between substantive American and formalistic English legal reasoning need not be as sharp as Atiyah and Summers suggest. In America substantive, including factually oriented, decisions are often subordinate to what may be called democratic formalism. In other words, whereas in England source theory of the law validates decisions with reference to the authority to issue commands from above, in America what may be called a democratic source theory of the law specifies how decisions can be validated from the bottom up, that is, with respect for equal participation and access. In both cases, substantive factual statements are very often generated by procedures of fact fixing which adhere more to primary moral, political, or legal norms than to scientific and technical ones. Significant differences between the American and the English systems nevertheless remain because, as I have already argued, the American liberal-democratic creed has accorded a more central position to the myth or rhetoric of public facts and public knowledge in the construction (and legitimation) of the exercise of political power than have its European counterparts. This no doubt relates to the impression that whereas English legal reasoning tends to be formalistic, American legal culture supports substantive legal reasoning. It links also with the centrality of what I have called attestive visual cultural norms in American politics, the assumption that reality, including political reality, is inscribed, as it were, on the visible surface of the situation, that testimonies are more authoritative than inferences or interpretations, and that lay witnesses are, in the final analysis, more authoritative than privileged—including expert— authorities. Again there is no gap, in this view, between the facts of the reality of common sense experience and the facts to which scientists refer. The American democratic ideology—and practice—of popular education serves to buttress this view, which is, of course, intellectually indefensible.[76]

In this cultural and intellectual climate the attempt, to use Holmes's own language, to "constantly translate words into the facts for which they stand [in order] to keep the real and the true"[77] can be seen as a strategy for commensurating, coordinating, and checking the arbitrariness of decisions in the context of a politically decentralized system of interaction. In light of these comments it should not be surprising to find that science—which is widely regarded as being in itself a democratic enterprise—can be seen in the American polity as a means of generating trust in legislative and judicial decisions.[78] The American legal context reveals then a dimension of a nontechnocratic democratic variant of instrumentalism as a political strategy of legitimation according to which the authority, and to a lesser extent the actual standards, of science and technology are assimilated into a decentralized, nonhierarchical system that generates politically authoritative public actions.

At the deeper ideological level, instrumental legal theory has furnished an attractive response to the liberal-democratic problem of action. It has suggested a way to balance a liberal-democratic commitment to a voluntary theory of action and a recognition of the necessity of situational constraints, to weld Roman legal concepts of the law as the expression of a sovereign will and natural law concepts of universal limits that are imposed on all actors.[79] It is in this nexus that American legal instrumentalism has appeared to incorporate elements of the cultures of science and technology into a voluntary theory of action in which the idea of lawful factual reality that is accessible to both laypersons and experts is enlisted to ensure that free action does not degenerate into arbitrary action and that the harmony between freedom and order does not require the intervention of external authorities. It is largely due to these ideological functions of science in the legal and political contexts of action that instrumentalism could have played such an important role not only in complementing but often in substituting for the law, the market, the moral code, or the bureaucracy as a rationale of legitimate public action in America.

9. Science and the Legitimation of Centralized Political Powers in American Democracy

The liberal-democratic state has been constantly threatened by the anarchistic potential inherent in its commitment to freedom and, perhaps even more, by the periodic antidemocratic overreactions, such as the impulse to centralize power, which the fear of anarchism has tended to provoke. Although the liberal-democratic state is, on the whole, sufficiently committed to the diffusion of power to tolerate its adverse consequences for the coherence and effectiveness of governmental actions, the reactive pull toward centralization has been an integral part of the modern liberal-democratic experience. The pressures to recentralize government, to impose some restrictions on participatory politics in order to enhance the effectiveness and efficiency of government operations, have characteristically increased in the modern democratic state at times of national military, diplomatic, economic, or social crisis. Liberal-democratic moral and political criticism of the unequal distributive effects of decentralized modes of political, public action or of free economic competition have furnished, however, an additional and, as the defense of Franklin D. Roosevelt's New Deal programs illustrate, powerful support for recentralizing the exercise of political power. Samuel Huntington notes that the American political experience is in some respects a series of repeated attempts to overcome the gaps between the ideals of democratic polity and the institutional structures and practices of political life, which never fully succeed in realizing these ideals.[1] The gap between the commitment to participatory politics and the realities of an unequal distribution of power is illustrative. Whereas in dictatorial regimes tensions between political ideals of order and political practice are handled by repressive methods, in the democratic polity a policy of centralization must reckon with the pressures of a dominant democratic creed and its institutional expressions.

The Partial Depoliticization of Executive Action

In America the interplay between pressures to decentralize and those to centralize political power has often taken the form of a competition between congressional and executive powers. Already during the time of Thomas Jefferson a democratic ethos hostile toward the very concept of leadership and followership, per se, "inhibited the desire of presidents to lead."[2] In due course such ambivalence toward presidential leadership did not prevent the "swelling of the presidency"[3] and the growth of the executive branch.[4] It is therefore interesting to ask, in the face of such powerful democratic institutions and ethos, how presidential powers could acquire their modern proportions. A part of the answer, of course, can be found in the evolving public expectation that the government assume an active role in matters of general concern and pursue the advancement of goals such as full employment, public health, economic growth, education, and defense.[5] I would like to suggest a complementary explanation that has to do with the utilization of science and technology as political and ideological resources for casting and presenting the actions of the chief executive as impersonal, nonarbitrary, and publicly accountable measures to enhance the public good. It is precisely because the presidency, compared with the other institutions of the American government, allows for and augments the role of personality in politics that science and technology can become important ideological and political resources for checking the corruption of presidential power by over-personalization and arbitrariness. The fact that the modern presidency has become such a powerful political agency, that modern American publics have been willing to move from the earlier view of the government as a passive guardian of the free play of social and economic forces to a view of the executive branch as an active and reformative agency, suggests that the attempts to project executive powers as impersonal, representative, and publicly accountable have been, at least temporarily, spectacularly successful.

This success, the liberal-democratic endorsement of assertive executive power, has been made possible to a considerable extent by the readiness to view political leaders not only as personalities but also as professional technicians who, like physicians, can represent and serve their "patients" with a detached application of knowledge and skills. Even in political contexts where the appeal to the authority of scientific and technical experts does not in fact save the instrumental effectiveness of public actions but constitutes just a part of a political ritual of legitimation, such appeal helps shift the terms of the involved actors' accountability from their personalities, intentions, or integrity to the overt instrumental adequacy of their actions. In a society in which scientific and professional authorities are established, the acts of tracing and judging the relations between agents, actions, and their consequences can be more intellectually disciplined and moral and political evaluations will then appear, by comparison, less objective, neutral, and authoritative. Such conditions have clearly enhanced the political value of professional standards in the American polity by projecting executive actions, and legitimating them, as apolitical instrumental measures.

A key component of such a shift from moral-political to instrumental-professional vocabularies of action has been, as I suggested above, the assumption that the grounds of action, and the causal connections between the agent's actions and their effects, are observable and amenable to detached analysis and evaluation. Such a shift, therefore, has profound implications for the accountability of political actors. Insofar as "power observed is power diminished,"[6] the visibility and transparency of centralized power, that is, the decentralization of accountability, could mitigate the antidemocratic implications of centralization.

Wider Sociocultural and Intellectual Rationales of Centralization

There is perhaps no modern liberal-democratic state in which science has exerted more extensive influence on the evolution of specifically liberal-democratic rationales for centralized structures of action and decision making than the United States. In other liberal democracies, the periodic need to justify recourse to centralization and hierarchy usually relies upon the residue of doctrines and structures of non-democratic centralism that the process of democratization has not completely eradicated. In England, for instance, pressures to recentralize political power have always been facilitated by the traditional deference to elites and the persistent influence of aristocratic styles of political leadership, even in the face of decline in aristocratic political power. In France, historical and political circumstances have permitted centralized structures of action to be perpetuated as an all-powerful national bureaucracy. In the United States, however, the special importance ascribed to science and technical expertise in facili-

tating periodic efforts to discipline the decentralization of political
power and furnish instrumental justifications for centralized modes of
executive action stems precisely from the absence of such traditions
and from a powerful ideological and political resistance to elitist and
centralized bureaucratic principles of public action. Even in social
spheres, where bureaucratic structures play a major role, American
bureaucratic culture is much more pluralistic and antihierarchical
than its European counterparts.[7] The particular attractiveness of science as a rationale for political centralization in America has derived
from the fact that, unlike elitist or bureaucratic principles of action,
science is perceived in itself as an inherently decentralized activity
which is strongly committed to the values of publicity and criticism.
As such, science can appear as furnishing a basis of action which constitutes an alternative to, rather than a component of, elitist, bureaucratic, or other hierarhical structures of action.

In addition to its structural traits, the special place of science as an
ideological and political factor in the legitimation of modern instrumental styles of public action in America stems, of course, from its
sociohistorical role in the evolution of modern American values, identities, and institutions. There is an impressive body of research of the
many direct and indirect links between science and technology and
the rise of moderately centralized "styles of action" in the social,
economic, and political spheres of modern America, especially from
the closing decades of the nineteenth century to the first half of the
twentieth.

Robert H. Wiebe, for example, indicates that between the late 1870s
and the 1920s the United States of America was transformed from a
nation of numerous loosely connected social "islands," largely autonomous and insulated local communities, into a nation unified, in the
main, by an urban, impersonal middle-class professional culture.[8]
This process was accelerated in his view by the expanding networks
of railroads and communications which consolidated the temporal
and spatial incorporation of American society. The expanding geo-
graphical and temporal dimensions of social mobility and interaction
rendered local codes of personal trust and morality less and less relevant for mediating social commitments and actions. Along similar
lines, Daniel Calhoun notes that the development of America from a
group of provinces into a nation was accompanied by the replacement
of local and particularistic orientations by more generalized ones. As
one of the key features of this change he notes the shift from reliance

upon personal informal judgments of people and events to reliance on impersonal, analytical, and calculative techniques. In the recruitment of employees for shipbuilding or bridge construction, for instance, criteria of competence and generalized indicators of professional knowledge have increasingly come to replace personal reliability based on local reputations.[9] John Higham argues similarly that the cultural and institutional integration of America after the Civil War was induced by the spread of technical-functional values as well as by the spread of large bureaucratic organizations.[10] David F. Nobel shows that between 1880 and 1930 modern technology and engineering became instrumental for the rise of corporate capitalism. He also indicates the extent to which the rise of functional-instrumental rationales for deliberate corporate actions led to the legitimation of centralization and hierarchy at the heart of the business sector, which for classical liberals was the sanctuary of individualism.[11] Edward A. Purcell notes the intellectual trends which led influential American thinkers such as Charles S. Peirce, John Dewey, and Lester Ward to criticize fatalistic determinism of the kind associated with Darwinian and Spencerian ideas of evolution induced by open competition and to endorse instead a purposeful deliberate activism guided by knowledge and intelligence.[12] To be sure, Purcell registers as problematic the wider tensions created in the period from 1910 to 1935 between the growing confidence in scientific accounts of behavior and politics and the key presuppositions of democratic government.[13]

Samuel Haber explores the close relations between the progressive movement in America (1890–1920), the increasing popularity of scientific management, and the ideal of efficiency in the sociopolitical sphere.[14] Samuel P. Hays indicates how during this period the ideology of the progressives and the "gospel of efficiency" combined to boost the conservation movement.[15] Thomas L. Haskell advances the thesis that the emergence of professional social science in late-nineteenth-century America was a response to the "abandonment of the ethics of self-reliance" and the increasing urge to redefine authority and action in terms of interdependence rather than former concepts of atomistic individualism. For Haskell, the evolution of professional social science is linked with the breakdown of traditional values and authorities and the need to evolve a concept of society in which voluntary human action is a legitimate as well as effective mode of shaping collective life.[16]

Alan Trachtenberg writes about the "incorporation of America" from another perspective; he stresses the spread of professionalism and bureaucracy as a response to the threat of chaos created by the "massification" of modern politics.[17] He notes also the trend to aestheticize functional principles of corporate action and authority in the monumental architecture of public space and the glorification of the "great city."[18] Ronald C. Tobey examines the historical links between political, economic, and cultural incorporation in America during the third decade of the twentieth century and the aspiration for a national scientific enterprise which could safely lead democracy through the march of progress and civilization.[19] While the progressives had great faith in the "scientific method" as a basis of social and political action, and science played, as we shall see below, a major role in rationalizing the centralization of political action during the first half of the twentieth century, as Tobey shows, attempts to centralize science itself as a nationally directed enterprise failed. Tobey regards it as ironic that by the 1930s the scientist-advocates of national science, in order to check corrupt government and "make democracy work," became servants of industrial capitalism.[20] Although, following World War II, such moves to incorporate science were met with greater success in some areas, the fact that, in comparison with the spread of corporate forms of action in the political and economic spheres, the incorporation of scientific research was much more restrained illuminates the special character and place of science in the liberal-democratic polity.[21]

I believe that, contrary to Tobey's interpretation, there is no deep conflict between the integration of science into corporate political and economic structures and the resistance to the extension of the principle of incorporation to the organization of science. It was precisely because scientific knowledge was perceived as a product of voluntary, decentralized interaction among peers, not as a product of a centralized, hierarchical enterprise, that it could constitute a democratically acceptable basis for corporate public action.[22] It is the integrity of science as a decentralized collegial enterprise that is vital—as Michael Polanyi and Robert Merton have shown—for the very credibility of scientific conceptions of objectivity and impartiality.[23] It is this feature which accounts for the central role of science and instrumental norms in the justification of centralized forms of action in the liberal-democratic state and their acceptability as at least partial alternatives to spontaneous self-regulation.

Important aspects of the role of science and technical knowledge in supporting democratic ideological rationales for centralized political action in modern America are revealed in the rhetoric of American political and social thinkers during the first half of the twentieth century. Herbert Croly, Charles Merriam, and John Dewey are perhaps among the most prominent. Croly observed in *The Promise of American Life* (1909)[24] that "at present our administration is organized chiefly upon the principle that the executive shall not be permitted to do much good, for fear that he will do harm."[25] He hoped, however, that a spread of the spirit of professionalism and of the respect for professional standards would have the effect of replacing the fear of an arbitrary and harmful executive by trust in his, and the government's, capacity to do good.[26] Croley's hopes were supported by his faith in the unproblematic givenness of public goals[27] and in the potential of that society in which "personal action is dictated by disinterested motives" to achieve "harmony between private and public interests."[28] Joined in later years by other liberals, such as Walter Lippmann who became affiliated with *The New Republic* which Croly founded and edited, Croly continued to defend the idea that professional ethics can be a key component of civic ethics. Croly espoused social reform which would be carried out by an elite whose integrity and commitment to public service are secured by technical competence and professional discipline.[29] Inasmuch as the American liberal-democratic creed was perceived as defining some goals as self-evident, social and policy problems could appear to be amenable to technical treatment while scientific-professional standards could be presented as means for replacing partisan political modes of action with "superior" apolitical ones. Insofar as liberals like Croly and Lippman have associated scientific expertise and professionalism with apolitical, nonpartisan, and truly public action, they have supported the view that what is scientific or technical is trustworthy whereas what is political—political motives, goals, or styles of action—is suspect. Efficiency elevated to the level of an ethical imperative for both individual and collective actions has come to reflect an increasing tendency to enlist expertise as a means of securing the "hygiene" and honesty of depoliticized civic actions.[30] Scientific-technical, expert standards are advanced here as a means of furthering the integrity of public actions along with, although at times also as an alternative to, legal and bureaucratic standards of action.[31] The belief that the integration of professional expertise reinforces the integrity and the civic morality of public action appears to help in mitigating the tensions between the elitism inherent in the progressives' respect for scholarly intelligence and the value they ascribe to popular sovereignty.[32] Constant shifts between trusting and distrusting experts, between relying upon or discarding the capacity of an "enlightened" public for self-government, and the inconsistencies inherent in alternatively believing in both, have been characteristic of American liberal-democratic advocates of instrumentalism in public affairs, especially throughout the first six decades of the twentieth century. The fusion of instrumental and democratic values was facilitated in this context by the fact that the belief that "truth" can command the assent of most rationally disposed individuals could be easily transformed into the claim that rational action is, if not explicitly, at least implicitly supported by consensus or assent of the majority. This claim has rested on the assumption that the majority is likely to be right, because rationality, truth, and knowledge are, as Condorcet held, inherently public and nonpartisan.[33] It is as if the status of being scientifically certified carried with it an implicit endorsement by an ideal, universally enlightened public.

In the 1920s and the 1930s, a growing number of American liberals tended to subscribe to similar views, trusting science as the basis of a centrally guided public action which is nevertheless compatible with liberal values. Charles E. Merriam provides an instructive illustation. A political scientist from the University of Chicago, a progressive reformer, a senior adviser of American presidents, and a leader in the professionalization of American political science, Merriam, like Condorcet, was a great believer in the role of civic enlightenment and public education as means of reconciling scientifically informed state actions and liberal-democratic values. Merriam, as his biographer notes, was confident that "the American voting public could be persuaded to want what it needed."[34] His faith in the existence of discernible and teachable truths in public affairs encouraged him to espouse what may be called "paternal instrumentalism," the special mission of scientists (especially social scientists) to guide state and society in choosing the objectives as well as the means of public action and in educating the public to understand and endorse these objectives and means. Like his European predecessors, Merriam insisted that modern trends are making politics both more democratic and more scientific.[35] "Generally speaking," he wrote in 1925, "in education and in organization we have long since ceased to rely on force, fear, magic or routine, and in proportion as we have been able to

replace these factors by scientific analysis and reorganization, progress has been made."[36] He urged a massive use of psychology, statistics, biology, public administration, and other fields of knowledge in
order to make government more scientific or at least to advance the
level of its political prudence.[37] "Politics as the art of the traditional,"
he observed, is transformed into "politics as the science of constructive,
intelligent social control."[38] Like many of his fellow social scientists,
Merriam was a great believer in "fact collection" as a way of facilitating the influence of scientific considerations on public choices.

Franklin D. Roosevelt's New Deal policy was regarded as a reflection of such an attitude, combining a commitment to participatory
democracy with an activist executive branch that is "rationalized" by
a professional-technical approach to public policy making.[39] Insofar
as the very actions of government were based on rational considerations, political science, so Merriam thought, could serve a vital
function. Instead of basing civic education on Bible reading, flag cere-
monies, and pledges of allegiance, he wanted schools to teach children
how their government works.[40] Like John Dewey and other advocates
of instrumentalism in political affairs, Merriam believed that analyzing political problems scientifically would have the beneficial effect
of at least partially depoliticizing the handling of public problems and
encouraging the application of analytical as well as managerial and
administrative techniques.

This view was reinforced at the time by Frank J. Goodnow's influential idea about the separation of politics and administration and its
wide appeal as a way of distinguishing the handling of goals and
values from the consideration of facts and means.[41] By delineating
what appeared as safe boundaries between facts and values and
ensuring a peaceful coexistence between expertise and politics, this
approach seemed to secure the harmony of instrumentalism and
democracy. Charles Merriam was sufficiently optimistic about such
developments to note that in a "new world made over by modern science . . . the new politics is likely to be scientific and constructive,
forward looking rather than traditional, authoritative and retrospec-
tive." By scientific and constructive he means here, among other
things, a "conscious direction of future evolution."[42] Strengthened by
the establishment and the consolidation of social science associations
during that period,[43] Charles Merriam and his fellow social scientists
tried to further this process practically by involving themselves in the
establishment and operation of such bodies as the National Planning

Board, the Public Administration Clearing House, and the Social Science Research Council.

In 1933, when he became associated with Roosevelt's New Deal and its attempts to introduce national planning, Merriam found it necessary to distinguish between democratic and nondemocratic planning, between American planning, which is experimental, evolutionary, and accepting of decentralization and the absence of regimentation, and Russian or French planning, which is much more centrally controlled and logically disciplined.[44] His concept of planning reflects the intellectual strategies of democratic instrumentalism during the first half of the twentieth century as well as its inherent difficulties and contradictions.

In England, similar attempts to mesh moderate scientific instrumental and liberal-democratic values were articulated by influential thinkers such as E. G. Catlin[45] and Karl Popper.[46] Catlin insisted that the task of the legislature is more like that of the physician than the evangelist.[47] Popper, while recognizing the limits of knowledge, insisted on a piecemeal experimental approach to policy and public action. Both defended versions of a democratic instrumentalism against nondemocratic planning as well as against attacks by such critics as Friedrich Hayek who argued, for instance, that the collectives of statistics are not wholes and that there is no knowledge of the causal relations between human actions and their consequences which would warrant faith in the possibility of rationally planned public actions.[48]

A particularly instructive illustration of the function of science in the rationalization of centrally directed executive action in modern democratic America is the role of economics, as a social science discipline and as a cadre of professional experts. Economics as a cluster of theories, models, analytical techniques, and vocabulary applicable to a wide range of social problems has constituted, perhaps, the most important intellectual resource for justifying the use of centralized executive and administrative powers in postwar liberal-democratic politics. On the face of it, the metaphor of a self-regulating mechanism, which was enlisted by classical economic and liberal political thought to conceptualize and rationalize the limits imposed by "natural" market regularities on the actions of the state, appears diametrically opposed to the ideas of managed economy, economic policy, and the interventionist state.

Nevertheless, the same scientifically certified regularities, which in the earlier variant of economic liberalism were used to ensure that liberal action—conceived as the product of spontaneous aggregations of individual acts—have a public impersonal dimension, became in later liberalism the basis for the double process of diagnosis and prognosis that rationalizes selective, technically controlled interventions. The scientific ideas and metaphors which are used in the classical liberal paradigm of collective action to guarantee that an "invisble" hand naturally adjusts individual acts and produces public benefits are, with some modifications, used in later welfare liberalism to ensure that the artificial operations of the visible hand of the interventionist state be equally impersonal, apolitical, and publicly beneficial, and hence acceptable.

The climate of opinion from World War I through the mid-1960s was sympathetic to this legitimation of centralized structures of action in the democratic state. Faced with the need to prove that democracy can be strong and effective in the face of the challenge of both fascism and communism, a majority of Americans were ready to endorse a host of national goals, including strengthening national defense, boosting economic growth, developing advanced technology, and enhancing general public welfare.[49] These attitudes, at least temporarily, fostered the depoliticization of vast areas of public affairs and the acceptance of the authority of scientific and technical standards in the making and implementing of public policy.[50]

In this atmosphere, post–laissez-faire economic theories could be more readily adopted as means of guiding and rationalizing the instrumental handling of social problems. Some of the principal intellectual innovations in modern economic theory such as aggregate econometric models,[51] national income and expenditure estimates,[52] welfare economic theories,[53] input-output analysis,[54] and Keynesian fiscal and monetary remedies for massive unemployment[55] appeared to furnish respectable intellectual support for the notion that the economy (and by implication often other social phenomena) displays the properties of a partly predictable and manipulable system.

Keynesian economics played a particularly strategic role in adding to the earlier role of economics, as a source of rationales for the minimal state, a new, and often opposed, role in the justification of the interventionist liberal-democratic state. As in the case of Condorcet, Keynes's ideas show how the liberal-democratic starting point—the notion of collective behavior as an aggregate individual behaviors—can generate rationales for moderate, state-induced social engineering. Although

Keynes does not trust the market to correct imbalances without deliberate state policies, he must assume the logic and the relative stability of the market-mechanism in order to pinpoint the specific kind of interventions that are the technically or functionally adequate remedies for the situation. Keynes was thus able to prescribe state interventions as actions prestructured by the constraints and opportunities inherent in the regularities of economic phenomena.[56] Keynesianism expresses the special character of liberal-democratic instrumentalism in which *the power to manipulate reality is predicated on the assurance that reality is sufficiently regular to reward (usually visibly) rational actors and penalize arbitrary ones.* The confidence that deliberate human actions can carry out human aspirations, beyond those that could be accomplished if the world were left alone, does not serve here as a decisive substitute for the confidence in spontaneous, mechanical, natural self-regulation. The flying machine, to use our metaphor for instrumentally creative voluntary action, is not substituted for but rather superimposed on the clock as a metaphor of mechanical synchronization with necessary regularities. The market mechanism— the clock—functions as a crucial check on utopian or arbitrary social engineering.

During the early decades of the twentieth century, effective criticism of the possibility of self-corrective natural equilibrium, as well as of the likelihood of securing justice and general welfare by the spontaneous interplay of social forces, created in America a favorable climate for increasing government intervention. This mood inspired, among other things, the massive instrumental programs expressed in a series of laws enacted between the mid-1930s and the mid-1940s. They include such landmark welfare legislation as the Act for the Relief of Unemployment (March 1933), the National Industrial Recovery Act (June 1933), the Vocational Education Act (May 1934), the National Housing Act (June 1934), the Social Security Act (August 1935), the Unemployment Compensation Payments Act (August 1932), the Fair Labor Standards Act (June 1938), the Public Health Service Act (November 1943), and the Employment Act (1946), which established the President's Council of Economic Advisers. "The establishment of the Council in 1946," writes one observer, "epitomized the evolution of 'big government' and its contribution to the nation's economic well being. The organization and operations of the Council reflect the attempt to achieve rational direction of diverse and complex federal activities through the application of a body of knowledge . . . Above all, the life and times of the Council symbolize the phenomena of presidential leadership . . . [and the president's] newest role as 'manager of the prosperity.'"[57]

On the practical side, there is perhaps no field of public policy where rationales for governmental application of technically prescribed remedies for market failures illustrate more clearly the attractiveness of economic instrumentalism than the field of welfare economics. Based on the contributions of theorists such as A. C. Pigou (1920), Vilfredo Pareto (1892–1896), and John Maynard Keynes (1936), welfare economics extended the authority of the technical vocabularies of economic theory to particularly sensitive issues of distributive justice. Although professional welfare economists have rarely lost sight of the normative political aspects of their models, the desire to base public policy on a formula like the "Pareto optimum" (which signifies a form of joint action that is admissible because all alternate courses of action would improve the condition of some individuals only by worsening that of others) had the great attraction of a technical fix that could finally end complicated ethical and political disputes and substitute calculation for judgment.

Of the wide spectrum of noneconomic public policy areas into which economic models and techniques were extended, the field of defense is particularly instructive. It is perhaps the best illustration of how effectively economic techniques for the instrumentalization of policy making and the depoliticization of government actions are integrated in areas outside the specific field of the economy where and when national goals are presumed clear and uncontroversial. Policy goals such as winning a war or developing a credible deterrence, for example, have proven very effective in justifying the application of economic techniques and centralized managerial structures.

The Economics of Defense in the Nuclear Age, written by Charles J. Hitch and Roland N. McKean in 1960, is an example of an influential attempt to conceptualize and rationalize the extension of economic methods beyond the field of economic policy in postwar America.[58] The main theme of the book is that defense policy making is basically a technical task which requires the application of economic and other "scientific" techniques. The editors insist that policy decisions ought to be treated as rational choices among well constructed alternatives. "In our view," they write, "the problem of combining limited quantities of missiles, crews, bases and maintenance facilities to 'produce' a strategic air force that will maximize deterrence of enemy attack is just as much a problem of economics (although in some respects a harder one) as the problem of combining limited quantities of coal, iron, ore, scrap, blast-furnaces and mill facilities to produce steel in such a way as to maximize profits. In both cases there is an objective, there are budgetary and other resource constraints and there is a challenge to economize."[59]

In an essay on the influence of economics and other sciences on strategic planning in America, Bernard Brodie acknowledges some of the limitations inherent in the application of scientific methods to policy making. He insists, however, that it still remains the best available approach "to bring some order into the vast chaotic mass of technological, economic and political facts and predictions which form the universe of data in which reasonable military decisions have to be made."[60] In another essay, Robert C. Wood notes the growing influence of scientists on government operations and attributes this development to their special authority as an "apolitical elite."[61]

Democratic variants of instrumental centralism gave Western democracies both the experience and the rhetorical resources to prescribe centralized managerial strategies for developing countries as well. Despite the differences between Western preoccupation with mass unemployment and inflation and Third World focus on poverty, the concerns appeared sufficiently noncontroversial in their respective political contexts to encourage hope for centrally induced, apolitical, functional solutions. "Given what seems their overwhelming problem of poverty," writes Albert Hirschman, "the underdeveloped countries were expected to perform like wind-up toys and to 'lumber through' the various stages of development single-mindedly."[62] This expectation is reflected in the optimism of postwar liberal-democratic concepts of modernization, which tended to assume that "all good things go together,"[63] that economic and technical modernization, social welfare, political democratization, and cultural growth are mutually reinforcing. This view of modernization tended to assume close affinities between instrumental attitudes toward the physical environment and toward society, between seeing the human being as a master of scientific techniques for manipulating nature and as a creator and maker of political institutions.[64]

Characteristic expressions of liberal-democratic instrumentalism, such as David Apter's idea of modernization as the replacement of coercion with information, have had affinities to the postwar "end-of-ideology" ideology.[65] A composite of Enlightenment rationalist optimism, scientism, and the aspiration of scientific intellectuals to influence the course of public affairs, the end-of-ideology ideology came, during the 1950s and the 1960s, to be shared by wide social and intellectual circles. In essence, the end-of-ideology idea proclaimed a progressive depoliticization of the handling of public affairs, which corresponds to an increasing tendency to define and treat social problems in functional-instrumental terms.[66] As such, like the idea of technically induced modernization, it constituted an intellectual rationale of the postwar liberal-democratic welfare-defense state, with its emphasis on the role of reformative legislation and assertive executive leadership.

The Public Space of Administrative-Democratic Centralism

I have suggested that the politically and ideologically most important feature of administrative-democratic centralism is the use of functional-instrumental terms not only to rationalize and depersonalize the centralization of power but also, ostensibly, to expose it to observable external tests of performance consistent with liberal-democratic principles of accountability. Just as the language of rational scientific analysis presumably explicates and "externalizes" the grounds of policy choices, so the focus on the technical features of action deliberately or nondeliberately implies that performance is transparent to external beholding which would check the nondemocratic implications of centralization.

The evolution of a public space within which political action in the democratic polity becomes visualized depends on a complex of political and legal principles which have developed in the liberal-democratic state over a long time, and, as I suggested earlier, on a relatively recent convergence of a host of cultural and social factors. These latter factors include the rise, since the second half of the nineteenth century, of national communications systems which, among other things, had a profound impact on the consolidation of a national press;[67] the growing role of photography in generating standardized pictures and visual representations of principal political actors and events; and the complex cultural processes which have made observable "facts" and "operations" authoritative referents for claims and counterclaims in the political sphere.[68]

The new opportunities which technology created for authorizing claims and actions through visual referents in the sphere of public appearances were not exploited right away. As Philip Fisher suggests in his study of social space in late-nineteenth-century literature and culture in America, "the new materials of personality and action suitable to be made conspicuous were only slowly discovered in different realms of culture."[69] Illustrations of this process can be found in the great international exhibition in the Crystal Palace of London in 1851 or in the centennial exhibition of 1876 in New York, which demonstrated the rhetorical powers that can be generated by the display of machines and instruments and their use in enhancing social faith in progress. In the sphere of democratic politics, one of the principal innovators was Theodore Roosevelt, who was called in his time "the most famous man in the world." In what was the first large-scale modern political use of mass communications to project national leadership in America, Roosevelt explored, tested, and demonstrated the new materials and strategies which could convert the presidency into an ongoing effective performance before a national audience.[70] Alan Trachtenberg shows how the cultural reception and interpretations of photography in America between the 1840s and World War II were mediated by the belief in the existence of objective, visually accessible reality and the presumed links between public seeing and public knowing.[71]

Fisher traces similar shifts in the definition and employment of visual experience in other fields, such as the "theatricalization of Christmas" in John Wanamaker's store, which set the pattern for the use of socially carved visual space for commercial purposes in America; the paintings of Thomas Eakins, such as "The Gross Clinic" which visually explicates surgery as the performance of a skilled master; the novels of Theodore Dreiser which are written in a naturalistic-realistic mode and employ the "concept of performance . . . for a social account of personality"; and the muckraking journalism of Lincoln Steffens uncovering the "real facts" behind politically contrived misrepresentations and presenting them before the gaze of the public.[72]

I have already attempted to show that because democratic political performers lack control over strategic factors which determine the success of their public performances, the actors who enter the visual space of democratic politics inevitably run the risk of exposed failure before skeptical spectators. The political fate of American presidents in the twentieth century, such as Lyndon B. Johnson, Richard Nixon, and Jimmy Carter, as well as of leaders of other Western democracies, illustrates this point. The democratic theater of action often furnishes a stage for a series of tragic heroes. Rising to the status of stars, they are—with few exceptions—destined to fall or at least lose their heroic luster as the discrepancy between their claims and the records of their actions becomes apparent.[73]

Considering these factors, the pessimistic assessment of liberal-democratic thinkers, such as Walter Lippmann, that the policy-making process or the actual uses of political power are in fact not sufficiently transparent to the public to sustain liberal-democratic political principles may overstate the threat.[74] As a public spectacle, to be sure, liberal-democratic political action falls short of maximalist ideals of participatory democracy. But neither is it an authoritarian spectacle where performers control the representation of action as well as the public indicators of their success (see Chapter 4). Although, as spectators, citizens do not act in the political theater of liberal-democracies, they do have sufficiently independent influence over the reputation of performers to secure that visibility is not risk-free.

In addition to the political fate of democratic leaders, the public arena of the modern liberal-democratic polity continually tests and decides the acceptability and credibility of alternative scripts for the drama of instrumental political action. It has tested, for instance, Keynesianism as a credible political drama of how to combat massive unemployment. It has politically tested the beliefs and trust of democratic audiences in the epic called "building the welfare state," which is a story of how equality, justice, and welfare can be achieved without undermining affluence and economic growth. It has tested variations of America's role in the world, such as "isolationism," "interventionism," and "detente." The public arena has also generated a series of scripts on the role of public actors in the drama of humanity's struggle against nature, including "saving" the environment, exploring space, and conquering disease such as polio, cancer, and AIDS. The "New Deal," the "Great Society," and the "Cold War" encode the central themes of such political dramas during different administrations. Again, I should stress that these are not tests in the strict technical, laboratory-like sense that Dewey, for example, called for in his experimental concept of politics, but tests in the wider sense which is primarily political-ideological. Insofar as a political drama relies on the authority of science and technology, however, it lends political value to apparent or perceived technical effectiveness.

In the theater of liberal-democratic political action, such large public dramas usually consist of multiple sideshows, each of which subjects a more specific and concrete aspect of the general narrative to clearer and more focused tests. Thus, welfare state dramas like the New Deal or the Great Society have become less attractive over time as a result of the apparent—although not always substantive—failure of a series of separate programs and actions to sustain the credibility of the script of the grand drama.[75] The financing of defense and welfare in the modern democratic state has come to prove an impossible burden on available resources, at least at the level of aspirations which guided post–World War II expectations and legislative reforms. In addition, the Great Society suffered from the political discrediting of a series of such smaller stories as the "war on poverty," "community control," "urban renewal," "low-cost medical services to the poor," and the gift of a "head start" to disadvantaged children through special compensatory educational programs.[76] The last project, for example, collapsed into a controversy when the premise of the entire effort—the idea that unequal scholastic achievements result from relative "environmental deprivation"—came under the attack of advocates of a competing "hereditary" account of these inequalities. A series of programs in the field of education subjected these approaches to many tests whose results were inconclusive and ambiguous enough to discredit or at least weaken large-scale future attempts to ameliorate the situation.

The political power of visible indicators of "performance" to determine the reputations of both performers and their approaches presupposes the very complex cultural-institutional apparatus which totalitarian states such as pre-Gorbachev USSR or pre-1989 East Germany have repressed. This is why a false scientific claim such as Lysenko's environmentalism could control agricultural policy in the Soviet Union for several decades despite its manifestly disastrous impact on agricultural production.[77] In a state like the Soviet Union it took much longer for an instrumentally functional approach to prove its credentials and defeat a competing alternative through a compelling superior performance. Until the reforms of 1989, communist East Germany furnished another illustration of a system where, in the absence of the appropriate cultural-institutional support system, "performance" lacked the power to decentralize the accountability of actors and subject them and their actions to public tests of legitimation. The regime waged a systematic war against the very tendencies and institutions which could authorize nongovernmental agents as judges and subject public actors to politically uncontrollable, instru-mental tests of adequacy. Centralism was not tempered by the scru-tiny of the public eye and performers were not uniformly vulnerable to the risks of exposed failures. East German students who were suspected of having too much independence were characteristically accused of "petty bourgeois skepticism" and of the arrogance of an "intelligentsia elite" toward workers and peasants.[78] The recruitment of officials to the government bureaucracy was controlled by prefer-ence for "red experts" who, along with their technical skills, could demonstrate satisfactory political socialization into the dominant ide-ology.[79] Not being integrated into decentralized and politically autono-mous rituals of legitimation, instrumentalism was clearly subservient in this system to strict political controls and indoctrination.

Not surprisingly, among the first signs of the breakdown of such totalitarian regimes is the declining ability of the government to continue to control fully the use of the television network for the cele-bratory representations of its own authority and actions. The revolu-tionary transformations in East Germany and Romania during the closing weeks of 1989 are illustrative. The moment when the popular opposition gained control over the television network was also a moment of dramatic shift from celebratory to inquisitive-attestive gaze at the government as the camera's lens, now functioning as the public eye, was directed against the old regime, taking the viewers into the sanctuaries of the demoted communist leaders and thereby exposing the corruption of their royally luxurious private lives.

At the same time, the new leadership was driven to employ the tele-vision cameras to relay celebratory pictures of mass popular demon-strations, thus symbolically establishing the emergence of the "people" as the principal actor in the public realm. In the postrevolutionary phase of a well-established liberal-democratic order such one-sided exclusive employment of either celebratory or attestive strategies of representing political authority diminishes. Established authority, although inherently predisposed to celebratory self-presentation even in a democracy, lacks the power to prevent the relatively autonomous institutions of mass communications from subjecting the government to the inquisitive-attestive gaze which is rationalized in terms of the public's right to know and hold the government accountable.

In contemporary democracies, the autonomy of the institutions that generate and diffuse critical-attestive orientations toward political authority is not sufficient to ensure a democratic culture of discourse and visual communications which can uphold a decentralized system of accountabilities. As we shall see, the authority of the *public view* or of the *public eye*, as a spontaneous aggregate of a multitude of autonomous testimonies, is not vulnerable so much to an arbitrary monopolization of the official eye by a political elite, which would then repress the freedom of autonomous citizens or win the people over by the effective use of aesthetic engagement or other affective and evocative strategies of mobilization. The public's authority is endangered much more by the subtle but pernicious implications of a spreading belief in the primacy of the subjective point of view, a growing distrust in the possibility of objective, documentary pictures of reality, and by the values of late-twentieth-century variants of insular individualism, which undermine citizens' faith in the very possibility that individual witnesses can agree on what they see or that individual testimonies tend to converge in producing the same version of the world.[80]

Part III

The Privatization of Science in Late-Twentieth-Century American Democracy

10. From the Politics of Meliorism to the Politics of Equilibrium

Any attempt to discern or explain general trends in the relations between science, technology, liberal-democratic ideology, and politics in late-twentieth-century America must remain for the time being largely speculative. Combined with the inherent complexity of the subject, the absence of an historical perspective limits our ability to interpret recent experience and distinguish significant from marginal developments. Bearing such constraints in mind, I would like to suggest that a wide range of developments in recent American culture and politics seems to indicate that the Icarian dream of flying on the wings of science and technology toward a more perfect society, toward a "knowledgeable society"[1] in which ideology and politics are replaced by technically rational choices approved by an informed public, may have lost its earlier hold upon the political imagination.

The Transformation of "America" as a Cultural Symbol of the Partnership of Science and Democracy

"America," as Sacvan Berkovitch observes, is "the most compelling cultural symbol of the modern era nationally and internationally."[2] A fundamental aspect of "America" as a modern cultural symbol concerns the perception of America as a great democracy, as a world capital of modern science, and as a spectacular embodiment of the technological revolution in the twentieth century. A shift in the apparent partnership between democratic politics, science, and technology in modern America is bound, therefore, to be significant not only in the context of American ideology and politics but also for the meaning and implications of "America" as an internationally powerful symbol.

It is therefore most instructive to note that, in the closing decades of the twentieth century, spectacular scientific and technological developments coexist with a distinct sense of the declining relevance of science for political rhetoric and action, with an "anticonstructionist" mood, and with a deepening sense of the constraints imposed on deliberate radical attempts to bridge the gaps between the ideal and the real. Instead of the earlier preoccupation with discovering and trying out new solutions for persisting social problems, such as inequality, poverty, disease, crime, and economic well-being, the motive for deliberate political and social reconstruction is being tempered by a growing recognition of the limits of comprehensive social or economic planning, the limits of public management, the limits of knowledge, the limits of economic and industrial growth, the limits of technology, and the constraints upon deliberate, comprehensive, and rationally controlled change in complex social, economic, and political systems.[3] The underlying tone of late-twentieth-century advocates of the "new economics" and the "new politics" is not that of a hopeful prospect for reaching new heights but of a more sober, more conservative and "realistic" assessment of what can be known or done by public agencies. Instead of the vigorous instrumental activism of the earlier decades, the new mood reflects a new appreciation for the potential role of private agencies and resilient partisan political forces in shaping public life. There is a deeper and wider recognition of the intellectual and practical difficulties of replacing political judgments by techniques and of the constraints on significantly enhancing the coherence or effectiveness of public policy.[4] The demonstrable technological success of science coexists with perhaps unprecedented distrust in the uses of science and technology to depoliticize and instrumentalize the handling of public affairs. Since the mid-1960s, a growing appreciation for the fact that the problems which experts are trying to handle are often extremely complex and unique, and that the situations in which they operate are uncertain, unstable, and ridden with value conflicts, has led many professionals to substitute a more reflective, open-ended, and improvised approach to action for the earlier "rationally applied knowledge" approach.[5] In this climate, it is no longer politically costly, and perhaps it has at times become even politically expedient, for political leaders to announce their doubts about whether, by comparison with various private voluntary entrepreneurs, the government can do much good at all. In 1980 and in 1984, for instance, the president of the United States received massive electoral mandates to dismantle large parts of the welfare state, diminish the influence of the federal government on domestic policy, and "restore powers to the people."

The record of American politics and especially the political success of presidential candidates who, following the Kennedy and Johnson administrations, criticize the massive programs of the politics of meliorism, reveal the diminishing political force of enlightenment visions of progress and political engineering in America. Changes both in late-twentieth-century liberal-democratic conceptions of politics and in social perceptions of science and technology indicate loss of faith in the kind of radical solutions to social and economic problems which made science and technology such valuable ideological and political resources in earlier times. It has apparently become much more difficult to defend, as effectively as before, the expectations that a community of free individuals can progressively perfect itself through the assimilation of knowledge into unforced, decentralized public choices, that scientific knowledge and technical competence can depersonalize and deideologize the handling of public affairs, that nonpartisan apolitical professionals can fix objective-neutral standards for directing and judging public actions without privileging any particular ideological or political perspective, and finally that public agents can be regarded as dispassionate functional representatives of the citizens just as doctors are expected to be in relation to their patients or lawyers in relation to their clients. In twentieth-century America political actors have increasingly come to discover that scientific and technical competence in the sphere of public affairs is less important for the legitimation of their claims and actions than before and that accountability is not as dependent upon the appearance of instrumentally adequate performance.

These developments are connected with the declining role of science and technology in upholding the epistemological and cultural premises of late-twentieth-century liberal-democratic American politics. This is indicated by, among other things, the signs of the weakening influence of attestive visual cultural norms in mediating the interaction of American political actors and their publics, of a decreasing willingness to assume the existence or the possibility of an informed public gaze which can penetrate behind the theatrics of public action and resist aesthetic or moral responses to the principal personalities on the public stage.[6] An important aspect of this indicated decline in the authority of attestive visual norms in controlling the display and perception of political actions has been the diminishing role of the machine as a political metaphor. In a universe of political discourse in which the vocabularies of the social sciences and the language of instrumental tinkering have been increasingly overtaken by the vocabularies of moral and aesthetic politics, mechanistic images of the polity and technical paradigms of action are bound to lose their force.

The decline in the power of the "machine" as a political metaphor in late-twentieth-century American political rhetoric relates, no doubt, also to dramatic social events in which the machine has reappeared as the villain. Incidents such as those involving failing nuclear reactors at Three Mile Island or Chernobyl made it increasingly difficult to continue to employ the machine as a metaphor of liberal-democratic political principles such as self-regulation, equilibrium, and checks and balances. The publicly perceived role of the machine in the context of the modern war, the disruption of ecological balance, and the depersonalization of social interaction in large organizations have in fact transformed the machine into an icon of social excess, not of discipline and equilibrium, of blind powers running wild rather than knowledge voluntarily transformed into rational control. Since the early 1970s, one indication of these shifting attitudes toward technology has been a drastic rise in the public preoccupation with, and the growth of the scientific study of, risks associated with the new technologies. While, as Mary Douglas and Aaron Wildavsky note, some of the causes of this development may be traceable to independent social and cultural processes, it is nonetheless an important aspect of a partial disenchantment with the role of technology in the rationalization of public as well as private actions.[7]

In light of the historical role of the machine in culturally upholding the notion that science is a form of public knowledge that helps the modern person defy the anxieties of being lost in a universe of invisible forces, it is ironic, of course, that environmental pollution and failing nuclear reactors have come to dramatize the lethal power of invisible forces such as radiation. If the diffusion of scientific and technical values in earlier times encouraged the attempt to overcome external constraints and boosted faith in the power of technology, conceived as visible knowledge, to control and translate action into a visual public drama, in late-twentieth-century America "big machines" have come to suggest the return of invisible dangers, the threatening operation of insidious forces unleashed by humanity, of the machine itself.[8]

This development has encouraged a shift from the perception of the machine as the embodiment of rational laws, a sort of humanly contrived extension of nature, to a view of machines as extensions of human ambition and impulse. This development has been accompanied by a massive process of moral and political reassessment of technology in America, a new public focus on the machine not as the embodiment of uncontroversial instrumental intelligence but rather as an expression of often indefensible ethical, political, and aesthetic choices.[9]

This loss of the machine as a rhetorical resource for culturally validating rationality and objectivity has relaxed earlier inhibitions on moral and aesthetic responses to objects and events which formerly appeared to belong in the jurisdiction of the scientific intellect and attestive visual norms.[10] There is perhaps no more symbolically suggestive illustration for the power of aesthetic visual orientations to supersede attestive visual norms in modern America, an illustration that is equally indicative of the trends toward the privatization of technology, than the appropriation by art of the mechanical eye of the camera. While the former authority of the camera as a machine for the objective—mechanistic—documentation of the world was associated with the urge "to overcome subjectivity by automation, by removing the human agent from the task of reproduction,"[11] in the late twentieth century it has been increasingly engaged, like the painter's brush, as a tool for the construction of authentic subjective visions in art, in journalism, and in other spheres.[12] This development represents the triumph of an approach developed by a few early photographers who, like Alfred Stieglitz, already at the beginning of the century, treated photographs not as windows onto the external world but rather as mirrors of the artist's eye.[13] The privatization of the photographic eye reveals the force with which the role of science and technology as cultural foundations of modern realism, and the belief in the existence of a world external to us yet manifest in the surface appearance of things, have been discredited by late-twentieth-century sensibilities. The appropriation of the camera for aesthetic persuasion is just one aspect of a much wider cultural-economic and institutional trend to enlist technology in the enhancement of private rather than public values.[14]

The decline of science and technology as sources of symbols and metaphors that culturally uphold public norms of perception, discourse, and action has been manifested during the second half of this century also in the progressive erosion of the influence of the social sciences on both the ideological and the intellectual conceptions of society as a causally discernible and manipulatable mechanistic system. Linked with the decline of the machine as a political metaphor, and reinforced by the predisposition of journalism to mobilize public attention by stressing the dramatic and personal aspects of social and political events, this development reflects a trend to imagine society more in terms of narratives about persons, feelings, and values than in terms of causal processes, material bonds, or interests, a tendency to reemphasize "agencies" relative to causes, personalities relative to regularities or processes, and to think of politics as dealing with symbols, meaning, beliefs, and even illusions rather than, although by no means to the complete exclusion of, the material physical aspects of collective existence.[15] Furthermore, toward the end of the 1970s, the formerly normative conception of policy making as a process of rational or informed problem solving, became widely discredited on the grounds that it represented a version of utopian rationalism that ignored both the complex symbolic and normative aspects of collective choices and the fundamentally political logic of public policy making involving negotiations, compromises, and control.[16]

Within the social sciences themselves, observers have seen a complementary shift. Clifford Geertz notes a "turn taken by an important segment of social scientists" away "from physical process analogies to symbolic form ones," a turn which "has introduced a fundamental debate into the social science community concerning not just its methods but its aims . . . the social technologists' notion of what a social scientist is, is brought into question by all this concern with sense and signification."[17] Richard Rorty has recognized this development as a tendency "to get rid of traditional notions of 'objectivity' and scientific method" while admitting the extent to which, by constructing narratives and interpreting people's behavior, the social sciences and literature can be located on a continuum.[18] The links between changing social and cultural perspectives on scientific knowledge and the declining faith in the feasibility of monumental political engineering in late-twentieth-century American democracy—and other democracies as well—recall the role of secularization, and particularly, the declining faith in hell and paradise, in undermining the cultural foundations of the seventeenth-century politics of sin and punishment. Fears of the political and social implications of a declining trust in the value of knowledge and rationality in our culture are comparable in some respects to the anxieties expressed by seventeenth-century thinkers, that without fearing eternal punishment most people would behave "without any moral restraint whatever," a state in which "society would collapse in an anarchical orgy."[20]

The anti-instrumentalist mood of late-twentieth-century America is also reflected in the works of contemporary political theorists. In a field which has historically generated comprehensive blueprints of just, equal, free, or in any other way ideal political universes, the recent upsurge of skepticism toward generalized ideas of the polity or toward political instrumentalism is very suggestive. "As a practical political matter," notes John Rawls, "no general moral conception can provide a publicly recognized basis for a conception of justice in a modern democratic state."[21] Rawls prefers a loose concept of justice as fairness, as something politically negotiated among individuals and groups who share a commitment to democratic procedure.[22] "What would succeed," observes J. G. A. Pocock, "is hard to imagine— the indications of the present point inconclusively toward various kinds of conservative anarchism—and the end does not seem to have arrived."[23] "To think small in politics," writes another political theorist, is to admit that "the older . . . supporting myths of politics— providence, nature and history, have been challenged and defeated."[24]

The decline of the myth of enlightened scientifically guided rational politics has been a part of this process. The language employed by one commentator on the decline of utopian city planning in modern society is a particularly apt expression of the anti-instrumentalist sensibilities which have undermined the value of the ideological and political uses of science and technology in rationalizing meliorist public action.

Architects, notes Robert Hughes, cannot create working utopias because

> cities are more complex than that, and the needs of those who live in them less readily quantifiable. What seems obvious now was rank heresy to the modern movement: the fact that societies cannot be architecturally "purified" without a thousand grating invasions of freedom; that the architect's moral charter, as it were, includes the duty to work with the real world and its inherited content . . . It is better to recycle what exists, to avoid mortgaging a working past to a non-existent Future, and to think small. In the life of cities, only conservatism is sanity.[25]

The Democratization of Uniqueness and the Fragmentation of Comprehensive Political Mandates of Action

The single most salient change in the temper of established as distinguished from newly created liberal-democratic states in the course of the twentieth century is, then, a decisive decline in the meliorist reformative spirit which fueled liberal-democratic instrumentalism, a tendency to discredit deliberate large-scale schemes of social improvement. I am suggesting that what seems to have replaced the politics of guided progress in these countries is the politics of pluralistic equilibrium.[26] What currently legitimates political leadership in America, as well as in some other liberal democracies, is no longer the "New Deal" type programs of massive social reconstruction, no more dreams of a "Great Society" in which knowledgeable governors and administrators control poverty, crime, and inflation and promote welfare and equality. It is, rather, a more modest conservative posture, more skeptical with regard to the powers of government to centrally generate and direct coherent programs designed to solve large social problems radically. What is emphasized and even celebrated is the value of tolerance for diversity, freedom for local initiatives and local self-government, and, most of all, a more limited role for the government as merely a facilitator of the pursuit of individual well being, not its principal responsible agent. Public authority seems to project a commitment to maintaining and enlarging diverse possibilities rather than to realizing a coherent idea of social justice and happiness; it seems more concerned with projecting responsiveness to the need of symbolic equilibrium among diverse sociocultural and political commitments than to a single overriding commitment or a comprehensive ideology which endorses a consistent set of principles and actions.

The new conservative political orientation is not in itself, of course, devoid of some ideological coherence. If it rests on a degree of consensus on matters of domestic public policy, however, it is a consensus on the absence of mandates for massive social and economic reforms, on the necessity of diminishing the size of the government and the extent of its intervention in the economic and social spheres. It is, in other words, a political position whose core value is anti-instrumentalist, the negation of the very idea of the government as an agent for the sculpting of society or for the radical correction of socioeconomic ills, a negation of the state's assertive role in promoting a comprehensive idea of collective well-being.

While it is neither linear nor wholly irreversible, this development, which has profound implications for the place of science and technology in the late-twentieth-century liberal-democratic state, corresponds to a host of changes in ideology and political practice. Shifting attitudes toward the problem of ordering the goals of the polity—

toward the very definition of these goals, the nature of pluralism, the adequacy of representation, the function of political participation, and the temporal dimensions of the political process—can be construed in part as responses to the perceived inadequacies of the political instrumentalism of meliorist democracy and the widely shared perception of its failures.

Such changes have, no doubt, been affected by erosion in the self-confidence and sense of prowess that democratic states enjoyed immediately following World War II. The earlier assertiveness in domestic affairs was boosted by preoccupation with postwar reconstruction and by the patriotic spirit induced in democratic states by the ideological and military challenges of European dictatorships.[27] During the 1960s, however, these liberal-democratic states became more introspective and more troubled by their own domestic problems and contradictions.

It is important to note, however, that the devaluation of science and technology as cultural-ideological materials for the rationalization of the public realm and the legitimation of public actions has not necessarily implied a decline in the authority and impact of science in other social and cultural spheres. On the contrary, as David Dickson for example shows, the earlier focus on the partnership between science, technology, and public agencies in the advancement of public goals has been largely replaced during the 1980s by a growing partnership between science, technology, and business firms in the pursuit of private values.[28] In some respects this change is a late-twentieth-century instance of the periodic American tendency to shift public trust from government to private actors as promoters of the public good.[29]

With respect to the new politics of American science, this development has been connected with a tendency to justify basic research on private economic grounds, not public cultural ones, a change which is reflected in, among other things, the pressure exerted on university laboratories to treat knowledge as a private, not a public, good.[30] Republican administrations during the 1980s actually encouraged this trend by setting as a national priority the goal of enhancing America's competitiveness on the international market.[31] This policy in fact provided a public justification for viewing science and technology as means of enhancing the profitability of private firms and of strengthening the corporate sector. The move to deregulate whole areas of science-based industrial technology illustrates the readiness to relax public controls over potentially adverse spill-over effects of technological and industrial growth in order to reduce production costs and increase profitability.[32] Government officials and private businesspeople who cooperated in cutting down the scope and severity of regulations have in fact employed the authority of science in rationalizing deregulation and checking the power of trade unions, neighborhood associations, and other such affected groups to increase production costs by forcing them to accept high risk estimates.[33] While, especially following World War II, government contracts for the promotion of defense, space, and welfare programs reflected the extent to which private business firms could be trusted in America to serve public goals, in the late twentieth century the accent has been on the role of science and technology in the promotion of private values, on a sort of privatization of science including its symbolic disengagement from its earlier role in directly upholding public values. The shift from the instrumental politics of meliorism to the responsive politics of symbolic equilibrium, from the social perception of science as a public cultural enterprise to the view of science as a more privatized resource for the advancement of diverse particular values, is connected with deep cultural and ideological developments which have made the modern American polity less hospitable to instrumental concepts of politics and to the authority of science and technology.

Perhaps the most important of these changes relates to the conception of the individual in the closing decades of twentieth century America. Orientations and attitudes toward the individual during this period seem to suggest a marked trend toward what I would call the "democratization of uniqueness," the view of each individual as a singular entity, as a particular being different from all others, as having the property of uniqueness not by virtue of a privileged birth, an extraordinary talent, a special education, or a remarkable achievement, but by virtue of the elementary fact of being a person. Richard Rorty suggests likewise that contemporary conceptions of the individual, which he partly attributes to influences such as Freud's, tend to stress creative consciousness as a universal capacity which in each case generates a unique self. Each person is seen as composing from the large contingent materials of experience—birth, family, work, environment, and so forth—a particular life form which is just as distinct from all others as each poem, as a unique composition of words, sentences, and meanings, is distinct from other poems.[34]

A view of the individual which stresses uniqueness, radical autonomy, and self-creation is, to be sure, deeply rooted in the American variant of liberal individualism. Yet an accent on the aspects of the self as a unique self-creation also represents a break with those other elements of the American conception of the self which underlie the assumption that individuals are sufficiently alike to be mutually transparent and knowable as well as to coordinate their behaviors voluntarily in the pursuit of shared social and political goals—that is, a break from the view that a multiplicity of free and autonomous individuals can agree on common conceptions of justice and fact, that in some ultimate sense all individuals live in the same moral and factual universe, and that each American is sufficiently like all others to render even introspection a respectable way to understand other Americans, and perhaps even America itself as a collective enterprise.[35]

The view of the individual as a particular instance, a representative, of a general idea of the American person has been associated with American "civic individualism,"[36] with the possibilities of social and political cooperation and responsibility, the voluntary association of autonomous individuals to enjoy and exploit the world in the pursuit of shared ends.[37] It is this tradition of "civic individualism" that late-twentieth-century variants of radical individualism seem to have challenged. While the notion of each individual as a unique, authentic reality had formerly been confined mainly to artists and intellectuals, it has now penetrated into wider social circles, weakening the foundations of earlier civic structures of interaction and association.[38] The contemporary focus on uniqueness, originality, creativity, and radical autonomy as the potential attributes of any individual life have discouraged the belief that the public realm is created and sustained by free individuals who, despite some differences, can agree on common standards. The democratization of uniqueness has shaken the conventional, cultural, and epistemological presuppositions of the American theory of democratic citizenship and the concomitant idea of politics as the enterprise of public-regarding individuals.

It has been partly in reaction to the corrosive effects of modern radical individualism on the foundations of liberal-democratic politics that communitarian social and political theorists have attempted to advance more social definitions of the individual as a contextually bounded self, which could constitute a more solid basis for reinvoking the classical virtues of direct participatory democracy and the citizen's engagement in shaping and directing the common life.[39] Accommodating both late-twentieth-century skepticism toward grand meliorist political engineering and moral conceptions of the relations between the self and the political community, advocates of participatory democratic politics have often tended to localize and deinstrumentalize their conception of public acts.[40] Benjamin Barber observes that the democratic nostalgia for the town meeting and the commitment to local participatory communal politics partly converge with a conservative stress on family values and the local community.[41] These neoclassical notions of direct participatory democracy and modern individualism have provided a powerful basis for attacking the idea and the institutions of instrumental politics at the level of the larger society, including the acceptability of functional representation and professional-like accountability by public agents. This line of criticism has been supported further by the attempts to extend the claim of uniqueness from the level of the individual to the level of the group. Women, ethnic minorities, and homosexuals, for example, have demanded to share power with established groups, arguing their claims not so much on the grounds that they are "like" all others but rather that they are "different," that they internally share unique ungeneralizable traits and preferences not represented in the political system.

This accent on the heterogeneity of individuals and groups has been partly manifested and reinforced during the closing decades of the twentieth century by what some observers have characterized as the increasing saliency of nonmaterial symbolic issues in American politics—and for that matter in other Western democracies as well. It has been suggested that, although attention to material rewards and physical security has persisted in the orientations of democratic citizens toward their government, there are signs of a growing concern for a host of nonmaterial, symbolic issues relating to individual and group identities, cultural status, and quality of life.[42] Students of Western democracies suggest that this development has been significantly affected by the fact that a large part of the citizenry comprises people whose formative years, following World War II, were free of the traumas and upheavals which had encouraged materialistic and security concerns in earlier generations.

Of particular interest to us are the effects of the democratization of the claims for individual and group uniqueness, as well as the spread of nonmaterialist and noninstrumental orientations, on the decline of professional authority and the autonomy of professional standards in America and in other liberal democracies. The aspect of professional authority most vulnerable to these effects has been the assumption that professionals have a mandate to maximize given values such as health, welfare, efficiency, and economic growth, which are both self-evident and universally shared. Like many other American professional establishments, medicine for example suffered a significant loss of confidence in the 1970s.[43] The legal creation of the institution of "informed consent," which requires doctors to provide their patients with relevant medical information to facilitate the exercise of the latter's right to agree or disagree to a proposed treatment, expresses the realization that "health" is not a socially uniform fixed value but something that can have a multitude of uniquely distinct meanings and therefore must be negotiated anew in each particular case. It is as if each treatment required a separate contract reflecting the contextualization of professional service in a particular order of values and preferences. The balance between such values as the length and the quality of life is no longer left to considerations of professional economy and authority. Conventional professional codes of ethics are no longer sufficient to regulate treatments and services which require responsiveness to diverse individualized balances of competing personal values. The relations between doctors and patients have consequently come increasingly to depend on less standardized arrangements.[44] This differentiation in the interaction between patients and doctors has been further enhanced by a progressive commercialization of medical services, a response to the need to diversify the supply of medical treatment. The heterogeneity of transactions between patients and doctors at the level of the individual has also extended to the level of the group, as is indicated by the pressures, for instance, by women's groups to provide medical services which are responsive to unique needs and preferences of women.[45]

The breakdown of the tacit social contract which granted medical professionals their traditional autonomy illustrates a wider process which has touched and partially transformed expert authority in other fields of knowledge and technology including engineering, architecture, physics, chemistry, biology, economics, and sociology. The point I am advancing here is that these developments have contributed to undermining the very basis of instrumental paradigms of public action. These effects have been produced, first, by forcing scientific and technical professionals to share with laypersons the power to define the problems and to decide upon the acceptable strategies and means of handling them. Second, normative fragmentation and heterogeneity at both the individual and the group levels have diminished the capacity, and often also the incentive, of public agents to present their actions as instrumentally conceived means of achieving given general ends. It has become less acceptable and less politically expedient for political actors in the public arena to claim the authority and competence of nonpartisan experts on the issues at hand.

The fragmentation of public goals has been institutionally articulated in America in the weakening of political parties as instruments for aggregating particular interests and generating comprehensive mandates of political action, especially in domestic affairs.[46] An important symptom of this change has been the saliency of "single issue politics" which, unlike the more ideologically comprehensive and more stable party-based politics of earlier decades, depends upon more ad hoc, "fluid," or transitory political coalitions built around very narrow interests.[47] "We have constructed for ourselves a system that articulates interests superbly," observes Morris Fiorina, "but aggregates them poorly."[48] This development clearly signifies a radical setback for the instrumental conception of government action. The fragmentation of public goals reflects a kind of privatization of norms which at the level of the larger polity is more compatible with the pursuit of equilibrium than with instrumentally conceived amelioration.[49] When political participation is not directed at achieving collective public values the stress is on registering desires rather than on satisfying them.[50] Just as a political speaker who tries to persuade a heterogeneous audience may discover the virtues of equivocation and ambiguity in political speech, so political actors are likely to discover in such situations both the risks of strictly effective actions and the political merits of eclectic and ambiguous ones.[51] In such a context, both political speakers and political actors reveal the superior weight of the equilibrium of symbolic gestures and multiple—sometimes even incompatible—signaling over coherent and unambiguously focused instrumental programs of amelioration.

Deinstrumentalization of the policy-making process as a diminishing emphasis on the value of "government for the people" is still consistent with emphasis on the values of government "of the people" and "by the people," on the moral, political, and psychological values of participation.[52] The increase in the saliency of nonmaterial values obviously encourages noninstrumental forms and rationales of political participation. Issues of social equality, identity, self-realization, and minority rights seem to stimulate direct action and protest rather than the negotiation and compromise which are typical to materialist, party-mediated politics.[53] One of the most instructive expressions of this trend is a section from the "Port Huron Statement" of the Students for a Democratic Society (1962) which called for individual political participation, stressing that the purpose of participation "is not to have one's way so much as it is to have a way that is one's own."[54] Such political orientations and their corresponding style of action are thoroughly inhospitable to the uses of scientific knowledge and technical skills in rationalizing, judging, and legitimating public actions. The focus on the intrinsic value of acting rather than on its outcome, on the relation between actions and actors rather than on the relations of actions and their effects or the status of actions as means, is incongenial for entrusting actions to representatives and regarding experts who act so as to instrumentally or functionally enhance the goals of the people they purport to serve as, in some sense, representatives of the latter. Personalizing and moralizing political-participation diminish the relevance of science or technology in depoliticizing the grounds of collective action and in furnishing authoritative, seemingly extrapolitical means for facilitating the achievement of consensus, cooperation, and compromise.[55] A new emphasis on non-materialist participatory politics, on acting as an aspect of realizing identities or affirming commitments rather than on acting "for" the advancement of certain material goals, tends, furthermore, to localize rather than generalize or equalize political participation across social and normative boundaries. "Conflicts based on individual value priorities are relatively difficult to bargain over, for they do not have the incremental nature of economic issues," says Ronald Inglehart; "like religious conflicts, they tend to take on a moralistic tone."[56]

The fragmentation of public goals and the difficulties of aggregating individual preferences have been further accentuated in late-twentieth-century American democracy by the realization that the unintended and unanticipated effects of measures taken to enhance widely shared goals and the resources committed for this purpose are in fact a serious constraint on the ability to enhance other, often equally cherished, goals. "The attempt to enforce equality of income," notes Arthur Okun, "would [often require that] society . . . forgo any opportunity to use material rewards as incentives to production. [Because] it would lead to inefficiencies that would be harmful to the welfare of the majority . . . any insistence on carving the pie into equal slices would shrink the size of the pie."[57] Particularly since the

1960s a growing gap between the goals of the "welfare-defense" state, the political aspirations for instant prosperity and security, and the scarcity of the resources available for pursuing these ideals have constituted a compelling check on postwar American meliorist instrumentalism in public affairs. This disaffection with instrumental approaches to public actions has been further reinforced by a widening recognition of the organizational difficulties entailed in the attempts to provide effective technical solutions to social problems. The political strength of the conservative reaction to the policies of the welfare-defense state in late-twentieth-century America suggests that the more trusted way to handle the gap has been not by committing more resources, or trying even harder to effectively implement general goals, but by lowering public expectations. This kind of response has been in harmony not only with the fragmentation of public goals but also, as we shall see below, with changing styles of political action and leadership, or, more fundamentally, with the transformation of the temporal and spatial parameters of political action.

The Normative Superiority of the Present and the Rhetorical Superiority of Instantly Visible Gestures

"We hold our politicians individually accountable for the proposals they advocate," observes the American political scientist Morris Fiorina, "but less for the adoption of those proposals and the evaluation of their results. In contemporary America officials do not govern, they merely posture."[58] The deinstrumentalization of political action in a system which "articulates interests superbly but aggregates them poorly" shifts the emphasis from the aggregation of interests to the aggregation of commitments, from instrumentally conceived actions to solve social problems to symbolic responses to the grievances of individuals and groups whose problems are largely insoluble. The result is a change from a politics focused primarily upon actions designated to ameliorate material, social, and economic conditions to a politics focused more on gestures designated to generate emotional and aesthetic majorities and to maintain symbolic political equilibrium.

A fundamental aspect of this trend has been a drastic shortening of the temporal dimension of political discourse, action, and accountability, a growing tendency to subscribe to what Jacob Burckhardt called "the normative superiority of the present,"[59] an attitude which attributes greater value and meaning to the present than to both the past and the future.[60] Such a change in the temporal dimensions of politics had already occurred, of course, during the early modern era in connection with the secularization of the political domain. The separation of church and state, which was reinforced further by the rise of liberal-democratic ideology, led to the historicization of politics as a human enterprise directed to influence the world of the living. The process of secularization implied the disengagement of politics from the issues of redemption, from reward and punishment in eschatological time. It was accompanied by a process of epistemological materialization of politics as something observable and analyzable, as an object of knowledge. As part of the cultural revolution involving the elevation of objects of sense perception to their status as sources of knowledge, in defiance of the referents of religious knowledge in the transcendental or invisible domain, the rise of modern science reinforced the perception of politics as a this-worldly historical, not other-worldly, enterprise.

By stressing the accountability of political authority to the living, liberal-democratic political values contributed even further to shortening the temporal dimension of politics. Such considerations had led Jefferson to suggest that every generation should have the right to create its own laws and that the validity of no laws should extend beyond the time span of a generation. "No society," he wrote to James Madison, "can make a perpetual constitution or even a perpetual law. The earth belongs always to the living generation."[61] While secularization and democratization were connected with the historicization of politics, the modern political experience, especially in America, reveals the extent to which liberal ideology contained even more radical possibilities in the same direction—the replacement of the longtime perspective of the historian by the much more immediate time frame of the journalist. The increasing status of the person both as an individual and as a source of political values has made the time perspective of the individual in late-twentieth-century democracy more politically binding than that of the "immortal society" or the nation;[62] it has elevated the political importance of personal narratives, of biographical over historical time frames, of stories about individuals over epic dramas about the rise and fall of collectives or historical accounts of long-term processes. The political importance of journalism in the modern liberal-democratic state is intimately connected with the political trend to accord normative superiority to instant, largely personalized accountabilities over accountabilities which temporally extend to decades and generations.

Since the late 1940s an important aspect of the contraction of the time frame of political action in the modern democracy concerns the growing influence of public opinion polls. The early pollsters defended the public opinion poll as a means of speeding up the democratic process.[63] "The speed with which sampling references can be completed for the entire nation," noted George Gallup in 1948, "is such that public opinion on any given issue can be reported within forty-eight hours if the occasion warrants. Thus the goal has nearly been reached when public opinion can be ascertainable at all times."[64] Whether, as Lord Bryce asked, "the counting of heads [is] the same as public opinion" is of course still a sticky question.[65] An ongoing, inconclusive, debate on what constitutes reliable measurement and representation of "true" public opinion limits the authority of such polls to challenge the authority of official elections.[66] In the absence of definitive quantitative or qualitative formulas for defining the true state of public opinion, the electoral procedure has at least the legal-political authority to declare the results of elections binding, an authority which the pollster's survey and computational statistical techniques lack. Still, a continual polling of democratic publics, instant mirroring of their shifting attitudes, and the wide publicity accorded to the results have had the effect of disintegrating the coherence and shortening the life expectancy of official political mandates. Within weeks or months following an election, the political efficacy of an electoral mandate can seriously erode as a result of public opinion polls indicating a sharp decline in former levels of support. Even if the results of public opinion polls are neither authoritative nor necessarily accurate, their effects are considerable. Measuring changing public attitudes toward policy issues and political actors, public opinion polls, like mass media news reporting, are commonly regarded by political actors as very important indicators of how well they are doing and what they need to do next in order to keep or enhance their political support. The instant "reflections" of actions taken, or not taken, in the polls or the news lend journalism, or the "judgment of the press," the authority formerly granted to the "judgment of history."

In the United States, the pressures to shorten the time span of political mandates of action have been partly formalized by the requirement of annual congressional authorizations. "Before 1960," notes Arthur Maass,

> programs were authorized generally without limits of time, so that Congress relied principally on appropriation procedures to control

them. Since then Congress has been intent on authorizing programs for short periods, so that today a very large portion of the expenditures proposed in the President's annual budget for controllable programs (that is, excluding entitlements and other fixed expenditures like interest on the national debt) cannot be approved in appropriation bills until Congress has passed and the President has signed legislation authorizing these expenditures for the one year or in some cases for several years.[67]

The requirement of annual authorization has forced enterprises which need much longer time spans to demonstrate their usefulness over short time spans. As Maass points out, this development has had adverse effects on the coherence and efficiency of public policy.[68]

The extension of annual authorization to cover also such institutions as the National Science Foundation (NSF), which was established following World War II as a channel of public support for basic research, is instructive.[69] As long as basic research, like art, is regarded as having intrinsic cultural value regardless of its usefulness, its support, however limited, is relatively free from direct political and economic pressures.[70] But the increasing demand to justify basic research in terms of its payoffs, a development which has opened up the possibilities of greater public support for science, has also increased the pressures to hold the scientific enterprise accountable in terms of short-term tests of political acceptability. In such a climate, an agency like the NSF has found it necessary to protect the base of its political-public support by redefining "basic research" broadly enough to include also categories of applied research and, in particular, research directed at helping to solve practical economic and social problems.[71]

The shortened political time perspective which has forced the scientific community to demonstrate the tangible payoffs of investing in research has weakened the authority of internal scientific-professional standards at other levels as well. Consider, for instance, the increasing pressures on medical scientists to disengage the goal of advancing medical knowledge from the context of treatment in order to protect the integrity of the latter from long-term objectives of the former.[72]

Pressures to favor research responsive to immediate needs over exploratory research, pressures felt in the field of medicine, are also applied in other fields such as biology, physics, chemistry, and the social sciences.[73] Guidelines and procedures fixed by such bodies as the National Institute of Health (NIH) and the Psychological and the Anthropological Associations to protect the rights of human subjects from potential abuse and violation in the course of research reveal another kind of pressure that limits the capacity of scientists to maximize long-term research goals.[74] Such strictures imposed on research by the increasing weight of moral, psychological, social, economic, and legal considerations have changed the environment of research in late-twentieth-century democracy. The professional roles of many scientists and engineers "become inextricably intertwined with those of lawyers, legislatures and regulators. Increasing numbers of scientists and engineers . . . become professionally involved in legal, legislative and regulatory affairs."[75]

The need to validate and justify science before democratic audiences in a pluralistic polity has affected American science in ways that recall Tocqueville's observations on the impact of democracy on Christianity. It has encouraged a tendency inherent in the culture of democratic politics to stress short-term success at the expense of a larger and longer view of the course of human affairs.

As I have indicated above, the changes in the temporal dimensions of political actions and events have involved changes also in their spatial dimensions. "Contemporarization," which gives rhetorical advantages to the instantly communicable over that which is communicated only in the course of the longer time span, renders potentially more politically significant the gestures which convey an agent's commitments than the actions directed to carry out that agent's goals. While gestures can communicate instantly, actions, whose results may at best be manifest in months or years, can uphold merely long-term accountabilities. The political conduct of agents who act within the temporal parameters of the present gives a political advantage to actions which are guided, to use Max Weber's vocabulary, by the "ethics of conviction" over actions guided by the "ethics of responsibility," to actions designed to fit given principles over actions designed to bring about certain consequences. Modern American tendencies to stress instant accountabilities simply do not allow for the time perspectives necessary to capture the links between causes and effects in the field of action. Consequently journalism and the contemporarization of the political arena tend to some extent to reverse an earlier trend and restore the primacy of agency over action, of responses to the personality and the theatrics of action over responses to its technical-instrumental efficacy. Whereas enlightened democratic political experimentalism replaced the "I" of the king, the ubiquity of personal judgment, with the "we" of socially shared choices and of knowledge as a cooperative enterprise,[76] in the late twentieth century there is a reversal. It is, however, not a complete reversal. The repersonalization of politics does not constitute a return to a superior singular "I" like the king's but to the unique autonomous "I" of the democratic citizen. In some respects it is therefore another "we," not of a collective homogeneous public but of an eclectic assortment of a multitude of discrete "I's."

Alexis de Tocqueville anticipated the force of democratic individualism to contemporize or dehistoricize the perception of politics when he wrote that democracy not only "makes every man forget his ancestors, but it hides his descendants and separates his contemporaries from him. It throws him back forever upon himself alone and threatens in the end to confine him entirely within the solitude of his own heart."[77] In this connection, Tocqueville also noted the corrosive effects of democratic sensibilities on religious conceptions of time. He noted that it is difficult to ascertain from the discourses of American preachers "whether the principal object of religion is to procure felicity in the other world or prosperity in this."[78] A twentieth-century Catholic theologian, Jacques Maritain, criticized such "present-orientedness" as a form of individual egotism. "Immediate success is success for a man . . . not for a State or a nation according to the duration proper to state vicissitudes."[79]

American present-orientedness has been perceived also as a reason for not respecting or appreciating the enterprise of the historian and the political significance of historical memory. European critics have often associated what they perceived as an American lack of historical consciousness with American materialism.[80] Hannah Arendt was concerned that in a polity where "both life and the world [are] perishable, mortal, and futile" actors lose their incentive to become immortalized through noble deeds which can stand as "imperishable monuments."[81] Present-orientedness has been linked as well with the various forms of modern skepticism. In a skeptical world, notes one writer, "there is no past and no guaranteed future, [there is only] a present instant . . . there is no time but only sensation."[82]

It is precisely this shift from action to gesture, from an accent on logic, which unfolds in the course of time, to instant gratification, which reinstates stagecraft as the primary art of statecraft. Such a shift permits aesthetic and moral responses to politics as a view to become dominant while attestive visual orientations toward politics as an instrumental enterprise in the "real" world are weakened. The contemporarization of political performance, the democratization of uniqueness, and the strength of symbolic rather than material orientations toward the political domain have converged to encourage the aestheticization of liberal-democratic politics. The instant symbolic and aesthetic gratifications of "live" audiences enhance the importance of the theatrical experience of politics as an enterprise based on the suspension of disbelief. It is different, however, from the suspension of disbelief demanded by a dictatorship. While the latter employs stagecraft in order to glorify and protect centralized political authority, the former responds to the more autonomous demands of spectators and tends to focus on liberal-democratic themes. Dictatorial regimes cannot afford to dehistoricize the public domain radically because they cannot accept or legitimate the authority of live audiences to judge political performers and because they need faith in future progress in order to rationalize the great sacrifices they extract from their citizens in the present. The Soviet writer Leo Bobrov, for instance, insists on the importance of optimism and the long historical view in order to understand present actions as "laying new roads to the future." [83]

It was largely against such claims, which assume knowledge of the distant future and an understanding of how actions taken at any given time can be linked to desirable and probable future states, that liberal-democratic critics of totalitarianism, such as Karl Popper, directed their attempts at discrediting "historicism." [84] While Popper criticized the idea of central comprehensive planning as a totalitarian approach to public affairs, his criticism of the intellectual foundations of "historicism" and of massive future-oriented reforms implicitly undermines the premises of meliorist democratic politics as well. In the absence of sufficient knowledge with which to evaluate the relations between our actions and the advancement of our shared goals the instantly visible gesture becomes, as I have already indicated, more politically persuasive than any lengthier and more complicated instrumental action. An effective communication of a commitment to a widely held concept of justice is more politically compelling in such a universe than the attempts to realize that concept.

There is perhaps no more distinct expression in modern American politics of the shift from instrumental to symbolic modes of public action, from the role of political leaders as agents of competent action to their role as a source of effective political gestures, than the Reagan presidency. [85] If an instrumental concept of action and leadership presupposes the attestive visual norms that control the definition and judgment of actions as technically rational means of advancing specific ends, the political universe of Reaganism rested on celebratory visual orientations toward politics as a field of instant theatrical, aesthetic, and emotional gratifications. While instrumental paradigms of politics are based on the imperative of facing and witnessing even the harshest facts of public life, in Reagan's democratic variant of celebratory politics reality is selectively aestheticized and moralized for the purpose of edifying, uplifting, or comforting a willingly credulous public. In Reagan's political style the choreography of candor, the production and the diffusion of fictitious evidence of sincerity and competence, replaces both public tests of instrumental efficacy and the exposure of the political leader to the critical gaze of a merciless public. In this convergence of Washington and Hollywood,[86] political authority is produced and legitimated through what Edmund Burke called "pleasing illusions." These, however, are not the kind of pleasing illusions which have been devised to legitimate monarchic authority or spread garlands on the chains that enslave the subjects of a dictatorship. The Reagan presidency was not directed at soothing a public devoid of basic freedoms or without access to the powerful instruments of criticism. It was, rather, a uniquely democratic variant of political spectacles, a coproduction of leaders and followers who conspired, as it were, in imagining into existence a world that celebrates the "unintimidating Everyman as hero,"[87] a world in which the ordinary is aestheticized and idealized, in which the harsh facts of scarcity, uncertainty, and risks are not permitted to spoil the ability of citizens to feel good about themselves and the world. It was a political show in which free citizens elected gifted actors willing to cooperate with their desire to fuse fantasy and politics in realizing a radical interpretation of the right to pursue happiness as the right to defy collectively the pains of skepticism and realism and live in an imagined world, in which the present is an ongoing celebration of human potential and hopes neither humbled nor interrupted by human failings. The fact that modern democratic citizens need not assemble in the public arena in order to observe their leaders, that modern mass visual communication permits citizens to gaze at their leaders through numerous discrete acts of seeing in private spaces and private times, is, of course, crucial. Such a democratic public is less vulnerable to the evocative instruments of aesthetic politics, less likely to be turned from a public conceived as an aggregate of independent individuals into the threatening mob of the "politics of enthusiasm." It is in such a context that the demystification, even the inauthentic familiarization, of the leader as "Everyman" can become the optimal strategy of democratic political stagecraft.[88]

The role of Disney Studios in designing Reagan's inauguration as California governor anticipates the culmination of a political variant of national politics as the artful production of the democratic political personality, of gestures focusing on democratic themes, of healing symbols and visions gratifying to an audience that willingly suspends its capacity for disbelief, an audience inclined to reject criticism as the irritating disruption of a good show.[89] "Reaganland" was a political universe in which acting in the theatrical sense subordinates acting in the instrumental sense, in which stage presence is the supreme political virtue of a leader and competence in decision making and management are only secondary. These developments in modern American politics confirm Fiorina's observation that in contemporary America "officials do not govern, they merely posture."[90] It is an observation which applies not only to executives but also to legislatures whose dependence on heterogeneous and shifting publics enhances the political costs of unambiguous decisions and actions.

Contrary to Fiorina's observation, however, "posturing" is not a substitute for but a style or a technique of governing. As symbolic gestures public actions are designed primarily as rhetorical devices to persuade the public that political authorities deserve their support not because their actions solve substantive problems but because they articulate balanced commitments to a spectrum of distinct, and sometimes competing, values. American leadership styles during the 1980s reveal a tendency to focus "Americans' attention on how they feel, not what they think their country should do."[91] While instrumental paradigms of public action still persist in significant areas of public affairs, the political efficacy of Reagan's stagecraft demonstrates the resiliency and the force in modern American politics of the alternative paradigm of public actions as gestural symbolic acts. A polity where posturing is a working technique of political mobilization, where political gestures can be more effective in galvanizing political support than actions designed to achieve instrumental goals, where instrumental standards often impose politically costly constraints on the politically optimal rhetoric of actions as gestures, is a polity in which science and technology are devalued as cultural resources for the legitimation of political authority.

11. Science and the Decline of Public Culture

Although, as Bertrand Russell's *Icarus* (1924) illustrates, expressions of skepticism and doubt with regard to Icarian political objectives accompanied the attempts to fuse science and democratic politics earlier in the twentieth century, it is only against the record of unprecedented massive attempts to bring science and technology to bear upon the handling of public affairs following World War I that late-twentieth-century reactions to the politics of meliorist instrumentalism can be fully appreciated. An important aspect of this development concerns the intellectual criticism of the conceptions of knowledge which underlay earlier democratic reformism.

The Erosion of Scientific Rationales for Meliorist Public Policies

Since the early 1960s, one of the most important aspects of the declining role of science in the rationalization and legitimation of public actions is a steady moderation of the expectations that the social sciences can enable us to subject public policies and public programs to rational controls. An important part of this process is indicated by a series of intellectual attempts to redefine "rationality" as an attribute of public policy decisions and actions so that it can accommodate the newly appreciated complexities of their inherent political components. The central theme of scholarly discussions on the character of public action since the late 1960s is no longer how to use scientific knowledge and techniques to rationalize public policy and check the irrational aspects of politics.[1] It is, rather, how to effect a balance between the need to save politics from the illusions of utopian rationalism and the desire to protect a moderate pragmatic rationalism from the skepticism which tends to follow the exposure of the futility of these rationalist illusions. And it is how not to fall from

The Privatization of Science

discarded faith in the availability of best solutions to public problems into self-paralyzing relativism which fatalistically accepts the position that "anything goes."[2]

The intellectual shift in this direction was anticipated as early as 1958, when James G. March and Herbert A. Simon criticized "classical" organization theory for failing, like classical economic theory, to explicate the "subjective and relative character of rationality."[3] "Most human decision making," they noted, "whether individual or organizational, is concerned with the discovery and selection of *satisfactory* alternatives. Only in exceptional cases is it concerned with the discovery and selection of *optimal* alternatives."[4] This emphasis on "satisfying" rather than "maximizing" (or even just optimizing) signified an important break with Simon's own earlier radical instrumentalist optimism in his *Administrative Behavior* (1947).[5] Another such early anticipation of what would become a more pronounced trend toward the middle and late 1960s was Charles E. Lindblom's criticism of comprehensive rational models of decision making. In an article entitled "The Science of Muddling Through" (1959), Lindblom suggested that the "rational-comprehensive" approach to decisions and actions be replaced by an approach relying on "successive limited comparisons."[6] The rational-comprehensive approach was discarded on the grounds that it rested on a host of inadequate premises and practices: that the values and objectives of public policy must be clarified before alternative policies are properly evaluated, that policy making is formulated within a framework of means-ends analysis, that such a framework presupposes the feasibility of separating ends and means, and finally that a policy is good when the best and most effective means to achieve given ends are identified and applied. By contrast, Lindblom insisted that one cannot separate considerations of values and ends from the choice of the measures of action, that means and ends are largely indistinguishable, that analysis of means and ends of action is always subject to constraints, and that a comprehensive approach to policy making is not practical.[7] As against common instrumental rationalism, Lindblom held that decision making is not so much a context for the application of theory to action as it is a context for pragmatic "muddling through." In a later publication with David Braybrook (1963),[8] Lindblom further elaborated on this theme, admitting the influence of Herbert Simon's retreat from "maximizing" to "satisfying" as standards of decision making and of Karl Popper's criticism of large-scale utopian social engineering.[9] The authors acknowledge that Simon and March's satisfying model of decision making is an adaptation to the "limited cognitive faculties and costliness of search, just as Popper's . . . 'piecemeal engineering' is an adaptation to the discrepancy between the complexity of the problem and the capacity of the human mind."[10] They criticize the "problem-solving" approach for ignoring the limits of human cognitive capability, for its failure to recognize the inadequacies of the information available to actors, its lack of appreciation for inherent conflicts of values, and the impossibility of a sharp separation between facts and values.[11] In the same vein, social psychologists and cognitive scientists such as Daniel Kahneman, Amos Tversky, and Irving Janis have pointed to the limits of individual as well as group decision-makers as rational information processors and judges of situations.[12]

One of the most important intellectual influences on the movement to moderate the problem-solving approach in the context of public affairs, and to adapt the instrumental orientation to a new recognition of the limits and complexities imposed on any solution to the problem of collective choices, is Kenneth Arrow's analysis of the difficulties of constructing a welfare function from diverse individual preferences.[13] Despite the limited practical relevance of Arrow's theorem, the widely shared view that it undermines confidence in the existence of rules or techniques, which can construct a majority group preference from a multitude of individual preferences, was consistent with the growing skepticism about technical algorithmic procedures for guiding social choices without denying liberal-democratic individualism.

The intellectual doubts about progressing from rational individual choices to rational collective ones touches a most sensitive premise of liberal-democratic politics. If such a transition is analytically problematic, public policy cannot be instrumentalized in a way that is consistent with liberal-democratic presuppositions. Abram Bergson noted as early as 1954 that the Arrow theorem "apparently contributes to welfare economics—conceived as the science of 'collective' decisions taken by a public official to implement the values of other citizens—the negative finding that no consistent social ordering of preferences could be found to serve as a criterion of social welfare in the counselling of the official in question."[14] Arrow himself suggested sometime later that the inability to agree on a course of action could lead to "democratic paralysis."[15] In 1973 he added that the "incommensurability and incomplete communicability of human wants and values," the possibility that attempts "to aggregate individual expressed preferences . . . [will] lead to a paradox," suggests that there cannot be a completely consistent meaning to "collective rationality."[16]

The effects of these doubts concerning the feasibility of a computational-instrumental approach to public policy making or public administration were further compounded by an increasing concern with the unanticipated social and political consequences of even technically unproblematic choices. Robert Heilbroner noted in 1970 that the application of economic analysis in the context of public policy is restricted by the fact that neither economists nor anyone else can predict with any degree of certainty the social or political effects of economic change.[17] To make economic analysis more practically relevant, he recommends that economists learn to integrate economic and political analysis of public policy alternatives.

A very instructive statement on the irreducible political dimensions of public policy was made in 1964 by Aaron Wildavsky in his influential book *The Politics of the Budgetary Process*.[18] Wildavsky's basic contention is that a close observation of the budgetary process in the United States reveals the operation of a political logic of continual multiple adjustments and compromises among contending interests rather than a functional-technical logic based on rational analysis and calculation. During the 1960s, it became increasingly recognized that "negotiation rather than seeking to reach an unequivocally 'best' solution is invariably involved in policymaking"; that policy emerges from interaction rather than from a rational analysis of alternatives.[19] As public decision making came to be perceived more as a form of "pluralistic accommodation" than of rationally directed and managed process, scientific research lost much of its earlier aura and policy relevance. The bargaining model of government decision making and the perception of bureaucratic agencies as complex political systems, which handle internal conflicts as well as policy issues through compromises and concessions, have gained wide acceptance since the 1960s and have altered the prevailing view of the role of research in the context of policy making.[20]

In *Usable Knowledge: Social Science and Social Problem Solving* (1979), David Cohen and Charles Lindblom consolidated many of the elements of the new approach into a coherent statement which recommends replacing analytical approaches with an approach that views the expert not as a "problem solver" but as a facilitator in a complex interaction between policymakers and their social, political, and organizational environments. Critical of the "hyper-rationalism" implied in common strategies of problem solving such as "policy analysis," "system analysis," "cost-benefit analysis," and "program budgeting," the authors prefer the flexibility and versatility of "practical judgments." To be sure, they do not suggest that analytical problem solving be completely discarded but rather that it be supplemented and corrected by an interactive mode of approaching and tackling problems.[21] Renewed appreciation for the inherent political aspects of the policy-making process has also encouraged the development of novel strategies of scientific advice and research for policy making, such as "evaluative research," which are more compatible with the view of policy as the continually changing outcome of an interplay between competing interests.[22]

That a systematic selection of best alternatives by a rational agency is not a tenable or feasible approach to policy making, that the kind of problems raised in the context of public affairs cannot be completely solved but at best settled, was known, of course, to acute observers all along.[23] Still, following the optimistic instrumentalism of the postwar years, the record of accumulating failures and disappointments was bound to reinforce a mood of conservative skepticism.[24] The kind of measures that social scientists tend to recommend are likely to be politically unfeasible, wrote Edward Banfield in 1968, while the government seems to have a "perverse tendency" to choose measures which, in the light of social scientific analysis, are likely to be functionally indefensible.[25] Banfield recognized, however, that "what stands in the way of dealing effectively with . . . [many] problems is mainly the virtues of the American political system and of the American character."[26] If earlier liberal criticism of governmental interventions in public affairs was based primarily on arguments of constitutionality and citizens' rights, toward the closing decades of the twentieth century, arguments against massive government intervention have been supported by a profound intellectual reassessment of the limits of the social sciences and their capacity to generate apolitical instrumental standards of public actions.

Some of these new orientations toward domestic problems and policies were bound to extend also to attitudes about America's mission in bringing freedom and prosperity to the rest of the world. By the 1970s more and more Americans came to recognize that it is necessary to "learn to live with a world of diversity" and overcome the tendency to absolutize the particular American variant of the liberal-democratic tradition.[27] Rationality and political freedom have increas-

ingly come to be perceived as depending on variable sociocultural conditions, and technical and economic progress on implicit moral and
political choices, which Americans can neither justify on scientific and
technical grounds nor authoritatively espouse on any grounds outside
their cultural regions.[28]

The recognition of the complex moral and political consequences of
scientific-technical interventions in foreign or domestic systems of
behavior and institutions and the limits of the power of science and
technology to depoliticize and rationalize social problems undermined, of course, the end-of-ideology idea. Although already in the
1960s there were those who recognized that the "end of ideology"
was itself an ideology, one particularly self-serving for sociologists,[29]
this view became dominant only toward the mid-1970s. Raymond
Aron, one of the influential supporters of the end-of-ideology thesis in
the 1950s, noted about twenty years later that he was wrong to distinguish between ideological and nonideological positions on the
principal issues.[30] Such a misjudgment, he thought, is less likely to
be repeated because ideological discussions have become considerably richer since the Cold War. "Today," he observed in 1977, "the
very foundations of contemporary society are subject to debate."[31]
Although versions of the end-of-ideology idea were revived in 1989 in
light of the decline of East European communist regimes, I believe
there is no reason to revise Aron's criticism of the distinction between
ideological and nonideological positions nor his observation about an
ongoing inherently inconclusive debate between competing views of
the social and political orders. Compounded by the new humility
of the social sciences, the growing recognition that no nonideological
positions on public issues are possible has been undermining the earlier image of the social scientist as a trusted, dispassionate seeker of
truth, an outside representative of objective considerations.

Reflecting late-twentieth-century skepticism toward earlier dreams
of politics guided and improved by science, Don K. Price, the most
important American scholar in the field of science and politics and a
former optimist about the possible integration of scientific knowledge
in the governmental process, admits that "we had come to distrust not
only our earlier prescriptions for political reform and our confidence
in presidential leadership, but also our faith in a rational scientific
method for dealing with public issues."[32] This mood has found an
institutional expression in the declining power of scientific advisers in
the American government.[33]

Although modern political history of the West reveals a record of both periodic anti-instrumentalist, antirationalist attacks on the idea of scientifically controlled public policy and regular attempts to subordinate government decisions to scientific and technical considerations, the scope and depth of late-twentieth-century criticism of the uses of science and technology in public affairs suggest, at least to me, the possibility of a less reversible trend. In this instance, the "repoliticization" of public policy making seems to be connected with developments in the very fabric of scientific notions of rationality and of liberal-democratic politics, developments which may indicate the possibility of a turning point rather than a pendulum movement.

Modern Science and the Disestablishment of the Spectator

I would like to suggest that, like the privatization of art or religion in earlier centuries, towards the end of the twentieth century the interaction between developments internal to the culture and practice of science and developments in its external sociopolitical environment have been encouraging the privatization of science. While some of the developments I discussed above, such as the rise in the normative superiority of the present as a term of reference for political action or the fragmentation of coherent normative and ideological bases of collective action, have influenced the place of science in democratic politics independently of developments within the practice and culture of science itself, some of the latter have had equally significant implications for the declining role of science in the cultural support system of meliorist democratic politics. Although it is still too early to reconstruct and assess the scope of the relevant changes in the practice, ethos, and social perceptions of science, particularly since the middle of the twentieth century, it is possible to note some of the most salient transformations. They include a decline in the belief that science confirms that the "world" is an observable object and that seeing is a public act of knowing, that scientific knowledge mirrors objective reality uninfluenced by the interests, theories, and instruments that the scientists "bring with them," or, to put it differently, that there is—or could be—such a thing as determinate, objective, ultimately true representations of the world.[34] There are also signs of a growing distrust in the idea that science develops, clarifies, and refines the "truth" within the bounds of common sense knowledge and is normative in relation to common discourse and action.

Such beliefs, to be sure, had not gone unchallenged in the Western tradition before the twentieth century. Their force was sufficiently persistent, however, to encourage the partially successful construction of a political order in which, consistent with some of the most cherished ideas of the Enlightenment, autonomous individuals were regarded as generating public discourse and public actions, which are supposedly checked by nonsubjective, apolitical, scientifically certifiable natural or social facts.

Modern social scientific theorists, such as Durkheim and Weber, especially since the latter part of the nineteenth century, sought to reinforce further the role of scientific norms in upholding the cultural space of the public realm in the modern liberal-democratic state by extending the standards of scientific discourse from nature to society. For Durkheim the idea of the social world as a scientifically observable object is fundamental, as I indicated above, to warrant the reconciliation of individual autonomy with an order conceived in liberal-democratic terms. Influenced by August Comte's positivism, Durkheim devotes much of his intellectual energy to modeling a science of society after physics as a science of objective facts, which would substitute knowledge based on dispassionate observations for myth as a basis of social action.[35]

Since the early decades of the twentieth century, however, it is physics, the most enduring socially authoritative expression of the norms of scientific knowledge as knowledge of the physical world, as a detached yet observable object, that defies key classical notions of the authority of sight or observation in validating claims of knowledge. Physics, which has culturally validated the belief that seeing is knowing, that observation can confirm or prove wrong assertions about what is real and what is true, has increasingly come to undermine confidence in the power of the attestive gaze to ground or check claims of knowledge. "Physical theories," notes Werner Heisenberg, "can have a structure differing from classical physics only when their aims are no longer those of immediate sense perception, i.e., only when they leave the field of common experience dominated by classical physics."[36] "We must admit," he observes, "that a blind man may learn and understand the whole of optics and yet he will have not the faintest knowledge of real light."[37] The ironic possibility of knowing light without vision already suggests the changes that in the course of the twentieth century have rendered Enlightenment metaphors of knowledge anachronistic. In some respects the progress of science

has always involved sacrifices of "the possibility of making the phenomena of nature immediately and directly comprehensible to our
way of thought."[38] Goethe, Heisenberg recalls, fought for saving a
sensual conception of color theory against Newtonian physics.[39] But
until some of the philosophical and cultural implications of modern
physics—as well as the other modern sciences—became sufficiently
evident to begin exposing the futility of the idea that progressive
refinement of systematic observations leads to comprehensive and certain knowledge of the universe, this idea substantiated a wide-ranging
faith in the role of science in grounding and perfecting commonsense
realism as a reliable everyday mode of knowing the world and acting
upon it as an object. Science was thought of as demonstrating the
possibility of cementing many independent individual sense experiences of the world into a public sense experience, which can then
function as an authoritative constraint on the validity of claims made
by speakers and actors in the social sphere. This authority of science
in the larger social context was, of course, reinforced by deliberate
or undeliberate blurring of the discontinuities between the scientific
notion of "public knowledge" as the kind of knowledge which rests
on intellectually detached application of rigorous intellectual norms
of describing experience and reasoning and the more ordinary popular
notion of "public knowledge" as widely shared information.

Considering the central role of modern science in culturally—if
not philosophically—validating the power of witnessing and the
authority of the attestive eye to know a world conceived as a view, any
doubts expressed by the scientists themselves concerning the status
of observing as a source of knowledge, any decline in the status of
attestive visual norms, was bound to have wide-ranging implications
in different cultural domains. A world which accepts the resubjec-
tivization of vision, which endorses the notion that any act of seeing is
not prior to, or autonomous in relation to, interpretation but essentially and inescapably an interpretative act, could no longer support
Diderot's claim that an observation of how one egg develops into a
creature can overthrow all the schools of theology and the temples of
religion.[40] Such a world could no longer generate trust in Emile Zola's
ideal of the modern novelist as a dispassionate, objective observer who
follows the scientific-experimental method, as it has been developed
and exemplified by scientists such as Claude Bernard, and extends
it to the field of art. It would discard Zola's view that, concerning
the role of observation, "it is only a question of gradation on the

same scale from chemistry to physiology and then from physiology to anthropology and sociology. The experimental novel comes at the end"; that is, the novelist-observer "ought to be the photographer of phenomena."[41] In such a world no special trust is granted to the literature of "the scientific age," to the elevation of observation over production, and to conveying "truth through art," as Balzac, Stendhal, and Flaubert maintained, nor to the ideals of painters such as Courbet, Manet, and Degas who used photographs in order to extend attestive, documentary visual norms to the art of painting.[42] This subjectified understanding of vision would cast doubts on the notion cultivated by writers, Lincoln Steffens, for instance, that muckraking is a way to expose illusions, to be "on the track of a truth," to provide a basis for "a science of politics."[43] It would also repudiate the claims made by critics such as C. K. Ogden and I. A. Richards and the publicist Stuart Chase, who shared a faith in the power of direct observation of an objective world undistorted by fantasies and fictions to discipline the use of language and enhance responsible discourse.[44]

Toward the end of the twentieth century, the increasingly visible rift between scientific and common sense knowledge, between professional and lay concepts of evidence and proof, has inevitably devalued science as a cultural resource for promoting, in the wider social context, respect for the superiority of factual reports and "objective" observations as requirements of valid claims about the world. "Our experiments are not nature itself," notes Heisenberg, "but nature changed and transformed by our activity in the course of research."[45] The dichotomy implied by classical physics between objective and subjective experience can no longer be sustained as it becomes evident that the "objective world" which science constructs "is a product of our active intervention,"[46] and that seeing itself is not an act of automatic mechanical mirroring but a way of "making the world." From this new perspective, the force of sight as a metaphor of public knowledge is thoroughly discredited, as is the notion of the world as a given object of our observation which imposes uniform constraints on what can be persuasively asserted and what can be sensibly or practically done. "In science," Heisenberg concludes, "we realize more and more that our understanding of nature cannot begin with some definite cognition, that it cannot be built on such a rock-like foundation, but that all cognition is, so to speak, suspended over an unfathomable depth."[47]

Revising earlier conceptions of scientific experiments as direct contact with nature as a given, toward the end of the twentieth century historians and sociologists of science have been giving greater attention to the role of complex theoretical, epistemological, linguistic, rhetorical, and technological considerations in structuring experiments.[48] Albert Einstein, for instance, criticized the belief in the existence of some definite cognition as a "rock-like foundation" for scientific understanding when he insisted that "we must make up our mind to accept the fact that the logical basis [of physical theory] departs more and more from the facts of experience" and that we are often deluded by the failure to distinguish between what is "seen" and what is "happening."[49] The notion that nature as we know it is not an independent object but a product of the interaction between what is "inside" and what is "outside" us also found its way into Dewey's assertion about historically changing modes of knowing, from knowing as an "outside beholding" to knowing as "an active participation in the drama of an on-moving world."[50]

Reflecting upon this shift from the more general historical perspective, Stephen Toulmin notes that "during the twentieth century scientific developments on many fronts have challenged any assumption that scientists can constantly adopt a fully detached attitude, even for their own scientific purposes; and as a result we are now moving into a phase of scientific thinking that differs from the science of the eighteenth and nineteenth centuries quite as significantly as the 'new philosophy' of the seventeenth century differed from the scholastic science of pre-Renaissance Europe."[51] But why should we think that such a shift in the thinking and understanding of limited intellectual circles, which Toulmin, like Dewey, describes as the decline of the spectator concept of knowledge, has any implications for the "privatization" of science in the larger social context? Are not modern physical theories at least as rigorous and universalistic as earlier ones? Don't we know that although the extent of the dependence of seeing on modes of thinking and observing has not been sufficiently appreciated until recently—when it became more manifest in the context of modern physics—there has never been such a thing as scientific practice based on completely neutral and detached observations unguided by concepts, selective cognitive capacities, and interests?

The point, however, is that even if the recent decline of the spectator theory of knowledge does not undermine the internal grounds of science and its practice, even if the implications of this development are understood mainly by a relatively small group of practicing scientists, philosophers, and historians of science, it has indirect cultural and social ramifications, a wider resonance which weakens the authority of the very images and metaphors that mediated the earlier ideological and political import of science in the liberal-democratic polity. Thus questions raised by modern physicists about the adequacy of the belief in a sharp distinction between the observer and an objective world as a view have weakened the cultural and rhetorical force of the construction of "the world" as an object outside us, as something which can be known and visualized from a distant and detached point of view, as a premise of discourse and action on the physical universe and other "objects."[52]

When the practice of science, the orientations of scientists and philosophical or historical conceptions of scientific knowledge, no longer seem to support the belief that the world is an independent object which can be known through observation, when the dynamic and theoretically conditioned scientific conceptions of the real are construed by laypeople as raising doubts about the capacity of science to assure the firmness of the facts of common sense experience, it becomes more difficult to deploy and sustain the metaphor of reality as a physical object and the complementary authority of attestive visual orientations in certifying the existence of such an objective reality in the sociopolitical sphere. If the status of the attestive gaze is questioned as a source of knowledge of even the physical universe it becomes all the more vulnerable as an authoritative source of knowledge of society and politics.

Such developments question not only the earlier notions of scientific knowledge as a mirror of an objective world of observable facts but also the more fundamental traditional commitments and presuppositions of Western culture such as the sharp distinction between myth and reality or fiction and truth and the concepts of discourse, action, and historical change which came to depend upon such distinctions. It is the strategic, cultural, and political functions of the belief that science confirms these basic distinctions that renders any change in the social understanding of science so loaded with implications in the wider sociocultural spheres, including politics. It is largely due to the assumption that science confirms the distinction between myth and reality and embodies the norms of rational discourse about reality, as distinct from orientations guided by myth and fantasy, that scientists could function in our culture as sages and critics. And it is because of the new doubts about these earlier claims that the cultural authority of scientists has been devalued in the course of the twentieth century. If scientists were formerly in a position to criticize religion, myth, ideology, and poetry in the name of an objective knowledge of the "real" world, or on the grounds that systematic observations can "give" us a true picture of the universe, the attacks on the unity, universality, and autonomy of the reality of the world have hurt their claims to represent neutral and generalized standards of discourse and action which are sharply distinguishable from the particular domains of myth and ideology. No wonder internal debates among scientists concerning the nature of matter and knowledge, such as the debate about the interpretations of quantum mechanics, have been socially perceived as having important general implications for culture, society, and politics. It is only natural, therefore, that scientists who have become aware of the shifts in the scientific perspective on the world and the growing gap between public expectations and what the practice of science can warrant are anxious about their wider sociocultural implications. Already in the early 1950s James Conant, for example, thought it necessary to help the public face the disillusionment which comes with the recognition that scientific theories are not like "pictures" of the world.[53] This was also Heisenberg's and Einstein's concern. Heisenberg's particular concern was the potential loss of the instinct for distinguishing illusion from reality and, therefore, the danger of nihilism.[54] Einstein was concerned that the very detachment of language from "the background of impressions," which allows language to be more freely abstract and hence a more potent "instrument of reasoning," is also what "turns language into a dangerous source of error and deceptions."[55]

Although science remains a public intellectual enterprise, in the sense of being impersonal and dependent upon universal conventions of describing, explaining, and reasoning, the loss of its supposed links to shared and vigorously disciplined visual sense experience contributes to its decline as a public enterprise in the cultural sense, as well as to its growing weakness in supporting "observing" and "being observed" as self-evident constituents of the public realm in the modern liberal-democratic state. Such science is, of course, also much more rhetorically vulnerable to the charge of being a form of esoteric knowledge, an epistemologically privatized enterprise. The deauthorization of science as the normative model of a purely attestive-analytical vision, of a form of knowledge which employs the eye as a neutral recorder of objective external facts, corresponds to, and reinforces, the privatization of the eye of the democratic citizen. The spreading awareness that seeing is a form of interpreting and constructing, not simply of mirroring, the world, supports and reinforces a growing appreciation for the creative and interpretive character of seeing in the wider context of politics and modern mass visual communication.

Some of the main features of this link between the changing place of science and the shifts in key features of the visual culture of modern liberal-democratic politics can be further clarified if we compare the implications of the decline of the spectator in modern science with the changing place of the spectator in modern art. Figurative or representational art has generally implied the beholder's authority to judge artistic works in terms of the adequacy of their correspondence to observable facts. The accuracy and realism of representation, of course, have not necessarily been criteria of aesthetic worth in themselves. They have, however, been central to the rhetoric of art, that is, to the persuasiveness of art works in the larger society. Realist, representational, or figurative art appears to leave the spectator some clues for evaluating art works. He or she can attest to the accuracy of Gustave Courbet's depiction of French peasants or check whether the potatoes or apples in Cezanne's paintings resemble "real" apples and potatoes. The rhetoric of representational art implies that the observer has visual experiences in "real" life which are relevant for the judgment of pictures.

In the most general sense, scientific realism assumes that scientific theories are stories about what really is, that science discovers rather than invents, and that, like pictures, theories can be judged in some respects as true or false representations. When a Heisenberg or an Einstein discards the authority of the eye in judging scientific theories or in understanding the world, he does not deny that scientific theories are objective rather than arbitrary.[56] It is not that their claims are understood as subjective or relativistic, only that the "objectivity" of scientific claims about the world is not granted or denied with reference to its visual properties. What is denied is not the possibility of rigorous scientific knowledge but the established authority of visual witnessing. The fact that the considerations which are relevant to the confirmation or disconfirmation of scientific claims are usually inaccessible to the larger public does not necessarily create intellectual problems for the practice of science, but it has enormous implications for the rhetoric of science and its normative status in relation to political discourse and action.

The implications of the shift from representational to nonrepresentational art are quite different. First, unlike nonrepresentational science, nonrepresentational art is not necessarily committed to the norm of objectivity. On the contrary, the romantic strain and the experimental spirit in avant-garde art celebrate the cultivation and the exploration of the subjective and the unrepresentable.[57] While still committed to the value of representing the world, the Impressionists already emphasized the individual perspective of the painter. In the works of Van Gogh, for example, representations of the world are shaped by uniquely subjective emotional lenses.[58] There is in modern art an increasing shift from stressing the value of "truth to nature" to stressing the expression of inward individual worlds.[59] "Art," notes E. G. Gombrich, "seems the only haven where capriciousness and personal quirks are still permitted and even treasured."[60] Meyer Schapiro says, in a similar vein, that "art grants a greater value to what refers to the artists than to the world of external things."[61] The primacy ascribed to the inward reality of the artist permits in the domain of art what would be inconceivable in the context of science, a state of affairs where "communication seems to be deliberately prevented."

But the same liberal-democratic society which has granted modern art the autonomy to articulate the values of individual freedom, subjectivity, uniqueness, and creativity has granted autonomy to science largely for the more restricted purpose of realizing transsubjective, transindividual values such as the advancement of knowledge, rationality, and objectivity. While art in the liberal-democratic society enjoys the mandate to express and symbolize the integrity of the sphere of the private self, science has a mandate to symbolize the integrity of knowledge, rationality, and objectivity, which have been among the key cultural building blocks of the public realm. While the artist who is unaccountable to the public still confirms the status of art as the enterprise of the individual, the publicly unaccountable scientist is perceived as a deviant, an abuser of science who violates the terms of science's claim for autonomy in the liberal-democratic society, the explicit or implicit commitment to promote public values.[62]

What I referred to above as the privatization of science is, then, *not* comparable to the privatization of art or religion in earlier centuries in the sense that matters of faith or beauty have become privatized, respectively, as matters of personal conviction or taste. The status of scientific theories is not left to the individual discretion of the private person in the sense in which aesthetic or religious claims are. The privatization of science is comparable to the earlier privatization of art and religion, not as subjectivization in the sense of rendering knowledge, like taste or faith, a matter of personal judgment, but only in the more restricted sense of its decline as an important cultural and normative foundation of the public realm, as a source or a model of generally compelling standards of public discourse and action. The decline of the spectator and the "reproblematization" of seeing as an act of knowing in the context of science has contributed to the privatization of science in the cultural-ideological sense what the commercialization of basic research as a part of private business firms has contributed to the privatization of science as an activity in the institutional sense.

Thus, while science has not been subjectivized as an enterprise of the solitary individual in the domain of the private self, it has been disestablished as a principal cultural building block in the construction of the democratic public realm. The growing tendency in late-twentieth-century democracies to regard science more as a resource in competitive ventures, such as economic and industrial growth or military conflict, and less as an intrinsically valuable universalistic cultural activity reflects this decline of Enlightenment models of public political discourse and action. Inasmuch as the politics of symbolic equilibrium requires, as I suggested above, that collective actions not offend a diverse and profoundly heterogeneous audience, action as a carefully contrived bundle of gestures tends to be more adequate than instrumentally functional actions directed at solving specific problems. In such a setting, there are no longer neutral or objective spectators or witnesses who judge the effectiveness of transparent performers. The focus of politics as a performance is no longer the encounter between agents and reality before a community of critical spectators—citizens who can be both detached and engaged. It is rather a more direct interaction between performers and spectators unmediated by actions directed toward factual reality, an interaction in the course of which performers and spectators both face each other and switch places. Both leaders and citizens utilize in this process the mass media as a means of sharing the construction of the symbolic equilibrium that fixes the boundaries of politically effective actions as public gestures.[63]

When, as in Tom Stoppard's plays, spectators of the political spectacle are metamorphosed into actors, the nature of politics as a spectacle is profoundly transformed.[64] In such a situation, the perspective of the actor often tends to eclipse, and overlap, the perspective of the observer. While instrumental action divides the polity into a few competent performers and a multitude of spectators or witnesses, action as the articulation of symbolic equilibriums in the modern democracy tends to blur the distinction by democratizing both access and participation. Such actions fit, therefore, a kind of political spectacle in which spectators are more reflexive and more aware of their powers and influence over the theatrics of public actions, more mindful of the limits imposed on the claims of the principal performers, and more assertively engaged in approving or disapproving their behavior on the public stage. This process diminishes the power and incentive of the principal actors to legitimate their actions in instrumental-technical terms. By comparison with the "heroic" political performers of earlier liberal-democratic spectacles, where public action was designated for such monumental historical missions as the conquest of space, disease, or poverty, or for the defeat of an enemy like fascism, the actors of late-twentieth-century liberal-democracies often look like minor characters. But this is not so much because gifted leaders have become extinct as because the parameters of legitimate public actions have been profoundly altered. By contrast with their potent predecessors, late-twentieth-century democratic leaders often resemble Samuel Beckett characters: icons of the dissolution of coherent universes of action and discourse, of the fragmentation of the modern individual as a purposeful actor. What we are observing, however, is a new kind of political action which cannot be adequately judged by the standards of earlier times.

The retreat of science and technology from the cultural space of the public realm of the liberal-democratic polity is connected with the erosion of the belief in an objective reality manifest in the visible surface of the observable world, which can discipline both discourse and action. It indicates a decline in the power of reality as a readily and universally available standard for the impersonal distribution of social trust among competing claims and actions. While democratic politics is still culturally dependent upon the premise that politics is essentially transparent and visible, and that political discourse and action are checked by external public facts, the visual culture of the late-twentieth-century American democracy is no longer as firmly upheld as before by reality as a cultural construct of the world as a visually ascertainable object. While visual experience is still invested in our culture with the extraordinary powers of giving viewers the sense of having witnessed or contacted the real and the true, moral, emotional, and aesthetic responses to what is visually experienced seem less constrained by what can be asserted about the world as a bundle of facts, causes, and effects.

The lay public, to be sure, lacks the basic knowledge or skills to appreciate such a shift directly. But once it becomes intellectually established that knowledge is not simply a mirror of objective reality but rather a product of interaction through which both subjects and objects reciprocally shape and "edit" each other,[65] scientists cannot— without appearing hypocritical or ignorant—invoke the rhetorical powers of the image of science as a transhistorical, transsocial mirror of reality in order to depersonalize, depoliticize, or dehistoricize utterances and actions effectively in the sociopolitical context. Once the interpretive function appears intrinsic to any scientific claim, science's authority to check or criticize as "unscientific" strategies of interpretation in the wider sociocultural arena becomes seriously curtailed. The scientific intelligentsia of the late twentieth century cannot defend eighteenth- and nineteenth- or even early-twentieth-century notions of "objectivity," "rationality," and "truth" without discarding respectable philosophical and historical views which have cast serious doubts on the validity of the very notion of knowledge as a neutral mirror of the world and which have enhanced our appreciation of such limits of scientific knowledge as its historicity.[66]

There have certainly been some serious attempts to argue that a shared language of commonsense reporting or describing the "facts" of the world can remain sufficiently autonomous vis-à-vis more particular theoretical or evaluative commitments of diverse observers to warrant the possibility of a scientific discourse in the social sciences.[67] Even if this position can be substantiated, however, it is not sufficient to counterbalance the effects of the trends to relativize socially and culturally the claims of science. Moreover, even if the recognition that science evolves within specific sociohistorical contexts does not undermine the strictly intellectual claims of science, the stress on the connection between science and context seems to impoverish its rhetorical powers to rationalize and validate transpersonal and transpolitical norms of public discourse and action. In addition, the theoretical pluralism and the intellectual humility which have come to be accepted as legitimate features of the modern scientific enterprise impose serious internal intellectual constraints on the rhetorical force with which scientists can present, in the context of social or political discourse, a uniform concept of reality as superior to all competing concepts.[68] Although working scientists and philosophers of science may live comfortably with a state of affairs in which there is no decisive choice among several—often alternative—theories, and although they may simultaneously employ distinct metaphors to describe, create, and work with different versions of the world,[69] such situations make it more difficult for scholars and experts to authorize scientific and technical criteria in the social context. Ultimately, without the external contextual and intellectual elements which secure an apolitical public "space" within which all political claims and actions in the liberal-democratic polity are tested against a self-evident "objective world of facts," no political authority can be reinforced by whatever extrapolitical sanctions science can still impose, nor can a scientific authority effectively set limits on politics and ideology.

Once seeing is conceived as a way not so much to discover or to contact the world of objects but rather to construct or produce it, once the passive observer who documents or records a world exposed to his or her gaze is replaced, in the "visual culture" of late-twentieth-century science and liberal-democratic politics, by the active, creative, and reflexive observer, the earlier boundaries between facts and fictions, or between what is "found" and what is "made," cannot be sustained.[70] Reflexive observers are guided by interactive rather than analytical notions of vision. They tend to be more keenly aware of the gestural, symbolic, and theatrical character of political actions and of the powers of political actors—including themselves as citizens—to shape the political universe. Reflexive observers seem increasingly aware that the theatrical aspect of politics is not just a deplorable deviance from political reality but constitutive of the very reality of politics. From this new cultural perspective, "truth," "facts," and "knowledge" are appreciated by democratic political performers mostly for their rhetorical value in strategies and in rituals of legitimation than for their instrumental value in improving substantive performance. Late-twentieth-century reflexive citizens may commonly attribute the gestural character of political action to a variety of different causes, such as the influence of the mass media, the styles of particular political leaders, and the character of politics. But by taking this feature of politics for granted they only help, of course, to institutionalize it as a sociopolitical fact.

From the perspective of liberal-democratic ideology, such a disengagement of politics from intellectual standards of "objective" truth and "facticity" is perhaps the ultimate move toward the autonomy of politics in our culture. Emancipated earlier from the grip of invisible religious agents, democratic politics seems now well on its way to being emancipated also from a compelling secular concept of uniform, factual, publicly visible reality.

Although politics, in which the theatrical is free from constraints imposed in the name of the "factual" and the "real," has been associated in the twentieth century with the antidemocratic politics of totalitarian systems like fascism,[71] neither the record of such political systems nor recent trends in liberal-democratic states suggest that carrying the autonomy of politics beyond such limits should necessarily be antagonistic to democratic values. A rejection of factual and technical constraints, which in one context encourages arbitrary speech and action or enhances totalitarian politics, may in another context be perfectly consistent with a radical democratic rejection of the limits on the freedom and autonomy of the individual. The question remains, however, what kind of life there will be for democracy after the decline of instrumental politics. What kind of democratic politics can emerge in a society where radical heterogeneous individualism is no longer tempered by the norms of an authoritative public culture, where science and technology no longer carry their earlier weight in constraining what can be legitimately asserted or done, where politics as observable facts is significantly eclipsed by politics as a subject of moral sentiments, emotional experiences, and aesthetic responses, and, finally, where the private self is not balanced by the public citizen but rather reinforced by respectable modern versions of cultural relativism and intellectual skepticism?

12. Postmodern Science and Postmodern Politics

The decline of instrumental paradigms of public action, the devaluation of mechanistic metaphors in political discourse, and the shift from the politics of meliorism to the politics of symbolic equilibrium signify a change in the relevance of coherence as an attribute of public actions. When what legitimates public actions is instant responsiveness to the expectations and interests of heterogeneous publics, the gestural-symbolic aspect of actions becomes more significant as these actions become instrumentally and functionally less consistent and coherent.

But at the end of the twentieth century the specific feature of liberal-democratic politics is not so much the actual decline of coherent structures of public action as the decline of coherence as a norm or an ideal of public action. In the context of late-twentieth-century liberal-democratic politics, inconsistencies are neither unexpected nor unacceptable. Considering the presuppositions of contemporary liberal-democratic politics, coherence at the level of public action may even be suspect, as it is incoherence or eclecticism that would indicate the existence of appropriate respect for the values of freedom and equality in the culturally and socially heterogeneous context of action. Within earlier contexts of liberal-democratic action, coherence at the level of public action was construed either as a sign of an invisible hand at work, a spontaneous harmony of numerous individual acts, or as a sign of the operation of a nonarbitrary rational agency. In any case, perceived coherence served as an indicator of the existence of "objective" constraints on the discretion and arbitrariness of public actors. It was the belief in the universality and neutrality of factual reality, in the existence of a "neutral cosmos,"[1] which in the liberal-democratic polity made such constraints appear politically unproblematic. Toward the latter decades of the twentieth century, it is incoherence and inconsistency instead which indicate the absence of large-scale arbitrary action. In a society deeply affected by ethical relativism and cognitive skepticism, coherence tends to stand for pretense, untenable claims of knowledge and authority, and the unacceptable exercise of power. Incoherence, by contrast, seems to indicate humility, a refusal to suppress subjectivity and diversity, the toleration of numerous notions of purpose, causation, and reality. In a society in which the incoherence or the inconsistency of public actions indicates the desirable absence of a directing mind or a guiding hand, where the shape of the public realm is more like an eclectic pile of discrete structures than a unified comprehensive structure,[2] coherence in public actions would tend to suggest numerous invasions of freedom. As a feature of public actions and policies, eclectic pluralism is therefore more compatible with contemporary liberal-democratic sensibilities than coherent pluralism; it indicates the existence of freedom from the domination of any particular idea, logic, or agency in the sphere of political action. It is one of the main features of the postmodern condition that grand narratives, the collective superstories which provide a sense of direction and meaning to history and society, lose their credibility and legitimating power. There is in the new climate no privileged time, no privileged space, no privileged language, no privileged list of "great books," and no privileged vision. Of course in our pluralistic culture, fundamentalists, millenarians, and some "neoconservatives" are still committed to total social and even cosmic narratives. Such a view is resistant to postmodern cultural orientations. Postmodern sensibilities do not encourage the notion that individuals are participating in, or witnessing, an epic drama such as the progressive conquest of freedom, the realization of an idea of justice, the advancement of knowledge, the march of civilization, or any other religious or secular plan of salvation. The architectural vision suggested by late-twentieth-century American democracy is not that of the perfectly coherent city planned according to shared ideals of freedom, justice, and beauty. It is rather like a gigantic condominium, a hodgepodge of diverse individual worlds.[3]

This eclectic pluralism is both a negation of the idea that rational collective actions result from spontaneous aggregates of individual choices and a reaction against the notion that they can result from calculations made by a centralized authority with privileged access to the relevant knowledge, including knowledge of the preferences of the citizens. It undermines, therefore, both coherent pluralism and justifications for democratic executive centralism: the idea that decentral-

ized interaction is compatible with collectively rational actions and
the idea that centralism can be democratized by subordinating political
actors to instrumental rational controls which secure nonarbitrariness,
functional adequacy, and publicly visible tests of effectiveness.

If, in the context of executive-democratic centralism, the technical
or instrumental definition of actions helps balance the centralization
of power by the decentralization of accountability, in the context of
eclectic pluralism, power is checked by both the decentralization of
power and the fragmentation of intellectual and political mandates for
pragmatic and instrumental uses of power on a large scale. While in the
context of executive-democratic centralization accountability has been
characteristically secured by the limitations that irreducible uncertainties and the visibility of failures and errors impose on the freedom
of the principal agents to deceive the public and to "play it safe," in
the context of eclectic pluralism the uncertainty in the field of action
goes far enough to foreclose the possibility of playing it at all, of
defending the taking of any decisive public actions even by those
who are willing to take high risks. While in the case of executive-
democratic centralism actors are subordinated to public tests of
competent performance over which they have but little control, in
late-twentieth-century eclectic pluralism, democratic controls are
exercised by drastically reducing the capacity to act. The fragmentation and the short-term "life-expectancy" of political mandates of
action ensure that actors cannot do too much damage or, for that
matter, too much good. In essence, the temper of contemporary
liberal-democracy is indeed anti-instrumentalist "conservative anarchism."[4] Freedom is manifest not in a realized idea of order but in a
benign disorder. Unlike earlier variants of anarchism, "conservative
anarchism" does not reject meliorist instrumentalism because of its
own faith in spontaneous harmonies or progress induced through
enlightened cooperation. It is "anarchism" fed not by faith in the
capacity of freedom to generate a coherent order but by skepticism, not by trust in self-evident ethical principles but by ethical pluralism, not by relying on certain knowledge but by acknowledging
irreducible uncertainties and accepting the inescapable presence of
the contingent. No wonder, then, that such attitudes rarely generate
utopian visions of society. During the second half of the twentieth
century the prime subject of utopian visions of the perfect life rarely
encompasses the larger society. The main focus is, rather, the life of
the individual or of the small group.[5] The dominant genre of uto-

pianism is the micro- not macro-utopia. In its ideal form, the larger society is regarded not so much as the actual or potential embodiment of a single overriding idea of the desirable order as a federation of local micro-utopias.[6]

This development is connected with a host of changes to which I have alluded above. They include the shift from the politics of meliorism to the politics of symbolic equilibrium, the privatization of science, the spread of "bohemian individualism" or what I have called the democratization of uniqueness, a growing recognition of the constraints on aggregating individual preferences into collective social choices, the trends to contemporize the referents of political action and substitute instant emotional, symbolic, and aesthetic gratifications for the pursuit of instrumentally effective public actions, the move to increase political discourse on nonmaterial issues, and the trends to subject science, technology, and the exercise of expert authority to closer critical, ethical, and political scrutiny.

A particularly neglected aspect of the deinstrumentalization of public actions has been the transformation of political action as a public spectacle.[7] While as agents of instrumental actions public actors characteristically have been held accountable within the framework of attestive visual culture in which actions are treated as observable factual events, as causes which have discernible consequences in a public space of perception, deinstrumentalized public actions involve different definitions of the relations between actors, actions, and spectators. Once the notion that the political order can be sculpted by deliberate actions has lost its power, instrumental actions can no longer be self-legitimating. When the stress shifts to the gestural-symbolic aspects of actions, publicly observable facts can no longer be relevant in the same sense. Sight can no longer constitute the means through which actions, events, or objects are expected to become knowable to subjects; the "democratic" eye can no longer be the powerful instrument with which skeptical yet discerning citizens presume to witness the actions of political agents and hold them accountable. The sense of sight in such a universe is transformed from its attestive documentary function into a means through which both leaders and citizens participate in the symbolic construction of public actions. As I have suggested above, within such a political universe the former distinctions between performers and spectators are blurred as the two groups are joined in an ongoing process of symbolic interaction. Once attestive-analytical visual orientations toward actions, although not fully suppressed, are widely superseded by "reflexive" visual orientations, the viewers, who are more aware than their predecessors of the creative-constructive nature of seeing, become more inclined to discard both the claims that photographic-attestive vision represents a neutral picture of objective reality and the complementary notion that the world is an observable object, a view.[8]

The wider anticipated cultural-political implications of the erosion in the status of attestive visual orientations in mediating the accountability of public actors and the presentation of their actions have been a source of great anxiety. Liberal democrats, who were sensitized by ideology and practice to regard "objective public facts" as a necessary basis for distinguishing between "political reality" and "political fictions," statesmen and demagogues, rational persuasion and propaganda, responsible and irresponsible actors, and democratic and nondemocratic journalism, cannot easily compromise what appears to be the very foundation of their political universe. The sensibilities of late-twentieth-century liberal-democracy nevertheless encourage skepticism toward any insistence that something is a compelling fact while something else is a mere fiction. The cherished dichotomy between myth and reality seems more difficult to defend in a climate where perspectivist and constructivist notions of reality are respectable. It is also politically costly to insist on the constraints imposed by facts where the principles of freedom and equality and the right to the pursuit of happiness have been extended to encompass—beyond the advancement and distribution of things such as health and wealth—the right to treat certain edifying fantasies as unshakable truths invincible to rational or factual criticisms, and the right to live within certain belief systems even when they are deemed unwarranted by rational orientations toward experience. Ironically, unclear demarcations between "facts" and "opinions" can be construed as an aspect of democratizing discourse and political participation in the modern liberal-democratic polity. If the Enlightenment program of democratization founded decentralization on equal access to knowledge and truth, late-twentieth-century democratization is founded on irreducible uncertainties that weaken the claims of knowledge and authority on the part of all competing spokespeople and actors. The factor that levels political authority in this cultural climate is not so much shared knowledge as the acknowledgement of shared ignorance, not so much faith in epistemologically accessible objective reality but in the declining authority of such an idea of reality to constrain the political employment of the imagination to create and recreate emotionally and aesthetically gratifying worlds. Whereas the Enlightenment ideal of politics rested on faith in the power of public knowledge to both discipline and democratize the uses of political power and authority, in the context of contemporary liberal democracy the decentralization of political power and the checks on public authority seem to be anchored in a spreading sense of the limits of knowledge. It is in the name of irremediable ignorance of which conditions and factors warrant confidence in the prospects of large-scale programs and reforms, and because of the irreducibly ambiguous public interest, that the legitimacy of massive public actions is called into question by late-twentieth-century publics.

The ignorance which currently discredits instrumental public actions is not the kind of ignorance that is corrected with knowledge. It is rather a kind of "rational ignorance" or "informed ignorance" which, according to Socrates, is enhanced not reversed by further knowledge.[9]

Although such rational ignorance has been gradually replacing or tempering earlier confidence in knowledge as a basis for maintaining order while decentralizing political power, it has simultaneously been corroding the very basis of liberal-democratic instrumentalism. If in the Enlightenment vision reality, as a unified determinate object of public knowledge, "guarantees" the harmony between commitments to government by consent, widespread sharing of political power, and a stable yet peacefully changeable political order, today's rational ignorance and informed skepticism induce a conflict between liberal-democratic political principles and the possibilities of creative political action. Late-twentieth-century liberal-democratic concepts of restraint and accountability not only question the very existence of intellectual and moral grounds for taking public actions to improve the common life but also discredit the cultural and epistemological premises underlying political actions as performances or events which can be the objects of public perceptions and judgments.

It is precisely such disengagement of democratic politics from the norms of instrumental action and the conditions of critical attestive orientations toward political action which encourages also the reauthorization of invisible and nonmaterialist aspects of political action. The resurgence of religious fundamentalist, moralist, and aesthetic—as opposed to materialist, rationalistic, and instrumentalist— orientations toward political discourse and action is one of the most important expressions of the current change in the cultural foundations of the American liberal-democratic polity.

In earlier encounters between the culture of enlightened politics and antimaterialist and celebratory conceptions of authority and politics, liberal-democratic spokespersons could rely on the social authority of attestive visual orientations and scientific realism in defending rational, experimental instrumentalism against religious-moralist and aesthetic concepts of politics. During the closing decades of the twentieth century, however, reflexive visual orientations, supported by pessimistic theories of knowledge and reinforced by an accent on normative pluralism, seem to undermine what was formerly an effective line of defense of classical liberal-democratic political values. While it would be unwarranted to interpret such developments as a sharp radical shift from instrumental to noninstrumental conceptions of politics, they surely demonstrate the resiliency of noninstrumental paradigms of politics in the liberal-democratic tradition.

Still, it is too early to assess the implications of this latest encounter between instrumentalist and anti-instrumentalist orientations toward politics. Does the descent to Icarus lead toward a return to fatalistic submission to necessity or perhaps to a new, more extensive and deeper sense of freedom? Does it reestablish the tyranny of "pleasing illusions" or lead rather to recognizing the inevitability of the contingent and the uncertain, to a public less likely to be misled by the illusive grand schemes of instrumental politics? Is this just another passing reaction to the effort to tame politics by reason or indeed the final blow to the program of the Enlightenment? Although the contemporary trend against instrumental politics reflects a retreat from earlier commitments to the values of rationality and objectivity, as well as from the earlier trust in the long-standing dichotomies between reality and myth—truth and fiction in liberal-democratic politics—it does not seem to indicate a retreat from the principles of liberal-democratic political order.

As long as the rejection of the values and practices of Enlightenment meliorist rationalism stems from a more radical interpretation of liberal-democratic values, it is not likely to encourage the re-enchantment of political authority, the mystification of a corporate will, or the development of mass political enthusiasm. The American political experience reveals with impressive consistency the power of a liberal-democratic creed to transform, and enlist the rhetoric and practices of religion, science, and art, which were employed as cultural resources of authoritarian governments in Europe and elsewhere. Alexis de Tocqueville observed how America evolved a unique synthesis between democratic values and religion. My study attempts to show how the American political experience evolved an equally unique synthesis between science, technology, and democratic politics. Now that this partnership is apparently declining, America may go even further to challenge the notion that, as Walter Benjamin suggested, the aestheticization of politics is the particular trait of fascism. As an alternative to the use of art and the exploitation of aesthetic sensibilities to repress democratic political values and to celebrate authoritarian leadership, America may yet produce a uniquely liberal-democratic variant of aesthetic politics, of politics in which the sense of the beautiful serves democratic ends.

The cultural foundations of liberal-democratic ideology and politics are, to be sure, manifestly heterogeneous and dynamic. Shifts such as those between religion, science, and art, as the primary cultural resources of liberal-democratic political rhetoric and practice in America, are never decisive or wholly irreversible. These shifts may nevertheless indicate profound transformations in the fabric of politics. It is significant, therefore, that in postmodern American politics it is not science or technology but art in the wider sense, including the popular arts and kitsch, which increasingly seems to provide the vocabulary, the metaphors, and some of the norms that govern political discourse and action. Again, major economic, military, or social crises are likely to revive the rhetoric of realism, the criticism of "pleasing illusions," and the appeals to science and technology. For the time being, however, where stagecraft as the art of eloquent, edifying, and politically effective gestures is the supreme technique of statecraft, and as long as political sensibilities are controlled by commitments to the democratization of uniqueness, instant accountability, inclusive political participation, eclectic pluralism, and symbolic equilibrium, it is not science, technology, and instrumental rationality but the theater, the plastic arts, and the arts of the camera that guide the construction of political actions and the legitimation of political power.

Ultimately the delegitimation of grand social and political engineering and the decline of instrumental rationality in the context of public affairs may lead not so much away from the idea of a liberal-democratic order as toward a novel interpretation and perhaps a deeper realization of the Enlightenment vision of freedom. The descent of Icarus does not necessarily represent a return to darkness. By forcing postmodern politics and postmodern science to face their own respective limits it may in fact bring us closer to the light.

Notes

Index

Notes

Introduction

1. Edmund Burke, "A Letter to a Noble Lord," in *The Works of Edmund Burke*, vol. V (London: George Bell & Sons, 1906), p. 141.

2. Ibid., p. 142. On Priestley's use of mice in scientific experiments, see John A. Passmore, ed., *Priestley's Writings on Philosophy, Science and Politics* (New York: Collier, 1965), pp. 136–138, 147, 148. On Priestley's experimental approach to politics, see, for instance, pp. 179, 192, 219, 251.

3. Niccolo Machiavelli, *The Prince and the Discourses* (New York: Modern Library, 1950), p. 3.

4. Ibid., p. 102. See also Quentin Skinner, *The Foundations of Modern Political Thought*, vol. I, *The Renaissance* (London: Cambridge University Press, 1978), pp. 180–186.

5. J. B. S. Haldane, *Daedalus, or, Science and the Future* (New York: E. P. Dutton & Co., 1924), pp. 81–82.

6. Bertrand Russell, *Icarus, or, the Future of Science* (New York: E. P. Dutton & Co., 1924), p. 5.

7. Ibid., pp. 5, 6, 55, 62, 63.

8. John Dewey, "Science and the Future of Society," in *Intelligence in the Modern World: John Dewey's Philosophy*, ed. Joseph Ratner (New York: Modern Library, 1939), p. 360.

1. The Balance between Free Agency and Causation in the Liberal-Democratic Theory of Action

1. Clifford Geertz, *The Interpretation of Cultures* (New York: Basic Books, 1973), p. 216.

2. Ann Swidler, "Culture in Action: Symbols and Strategies," *American Sociological Review* 51 (April 1986), 273–286.

3. G. Almond and S. Verba, eds., *The Civic Culture Revisited* (Boston: Little, Brown, 1980).

4. This perspective implicitly stresses the relevance of the institutional features and the social norms of science as well as its ethos and its perceived practices. Among the studies which have illuminated such aspects of science, note

Robert K. Merton, "Science and the Social Order" and "The Normative Structure of Science," in *The Sociology of Science*, ed. Norman Storer (Chicago: University of Chicago Press, 1973), pp. 254–278; Michael Polanyi, *Personal Knowledge* (Chicago: University of Chicago Press, 1968); Talcott Parsons and Gerold M. Platt, *The American University* (Cambridge, Mass.: Harvard University Press, 1973).

5. Paul Feyerabend, "Democracy, Elitism and Scientific Method," *Inquiry* 23 (March 1980), 3–18; Richard Rorty, "Science and Solidarity," an unpublished paper sent to me by the author on August 27, 1985.

6. Roger Hahn, *The Anatomy of a Scientific Institution: The Paris Academy of Sciences, 1666–1803* (Berkeley: University of California Press, 1971).

7. David Layton, *Science for the People: The Origins of the School Science Curriculum in England* (London: George Allen & Unwin, 1973); Robert H. Kargon, *Science in Victorian Manchester* (Baltimore: Johns Hopkins University Press, 1978); Jack Morrell and Arnold Thackrey, *Gentlemen of Science* (Oxford: Clarendon Press, 1968); Steven Shapin and Barry Barnes, "Science, Nature and Control: Interpreting Mechanics Institutes," *Social Studies of Science* 7 (1977), 31–74.

8. Paul Forman, *The Environment and Practice of Atomic Physics in Weimar Germany* (Ann Arbor: University of Michigan Microfilms, 1970); Alan D. Beyerchen, *Scientists under Hitler* (New Haven: Yale University Press, 1977); Joseph Haberer, *Politics and the Community of Science* (New York: Van Nostrand Reinhold Co., 1969).

9. George H. Daniels, *American Science in the Age of Jackson* (New York: Columbia University Press, 1968); A. Hunter Dupree, *Science in the Federal Government* (Cambridge, Mass.: Belknap Press of Harvard University Press, 1957); Ronald C. Tobey, *The American Ideology of National Science, 1919–1930* (Pittsburgh: University of Pittsburgh Press, 1971); Don K. Price, *The Scientific Estate* (Cambridge, Mass.: Belknap Press of Harvard University Press, 1965).

10. David Joravsky, *Soviet Marxism and Natural Sciences, 1917–1932* (New York: Columbia University Press, 1961); Loren R. Graham, *Science and Philosophy in the Soviet Union* (New York: Alfred A. Knopf, 1972).

11. D. P. Walker, *The Decline of Hell: Seventeenth-Century Discussions of Eternal Torment* (Chicago: University of Chicago Press, 1964), pp. 3–4.

12. Michel de Montaigne, *Selected Essays*, trans. and intro. D. M. Frame (New York: Walker J. Black, 1943), p. 117.

13. For an instructive discussion of approaches to this problem in seventeenth-century England, see John A. W. Gunn, *Politics and the Public Interest in the Seventeenth Century* (London: Routledge and Kegan Paul, 1969).

14. Montaigne, *Selected Essays*, p. 125.

15. See, for instance, the discussion of Max Weber's approach in Chapter 7.

16. Galileo, "Letter to the Grand Duchess of Tuscany," cited in A. C. Crombie, *Medieval and Early Modern Science*, vol. II (Garden City: Doubleday Company, 1959), p. 202.

17. Frank E. Manuel and Fritzie P. Manuel, *Utopian Thought in the Western World* (Cambridge, Mass.: Belknap Press of Harvard University Press, 1979).

18. Charles Edward Merriam, *New Aspects of Politics* (Chicago: University

of Chicago Press, 1925, 1931); Herbert Simon, *Administrative Behaviour* (New York: Free Press, 1957).

19. Jacques Ellul, *The Technological Society* (New York: Vintage Books, 1964); Herbert Marcuse, *One Dimensional Man* (Boston: Beacon Press, 1964); Lewis Mumford, *Technics and Civilization* (New York: Harcourt, Brace and World, 1963).

20. Price, *The Scientific Estate.*

21. Edmund Burke, *Reflections on the Revolution in France* (1790), ed. and intro. Conor Cruise O'Brien (Harmondsworth: Penguin, 1976), p. 161.

22. See, for instance, Judith N. Shklar, *Montesquieu* (Oxford: Oxford University Press, 1987).

23. Bernard de Mandeville, *Fable of the Bees* (1723) (New York: Penguin Classics, 1970); Adam Smith, *An Inquiry into the Nature and Causes of the Wealth of Nations* (1776), ed. E. Cannan (New York: Modern Library, 1937).

24. Smith, *The Wealth of Nations,* p. 423.

25. Friedrich A. Hayek, *The Road to Serfdom* (Chicago: University of Chicago Press, 1944, 1969), p. 203.

26. Friedrich A. Hayek, *The Counter Revolution of Science* (Glencoe: Free Press, 1952), p. 83.

27. Ibid., p. 84; Hayek, *The Road to Serfdom,* p. 57.

28. Hayek, *The Counter Revolution of Science,* p. 93. Important variants of the idea that decentralized interaction can serve the collective good without relying on the purposeful cooperation of enlightened individuals are associated with the ideas of Montesquieu, Madison, and Spencer. For different reasons, none of these held that enlightened, public-regarding citizens are a necessary condition of good liberal government.

29. The idea that society is governed by statistical laws led, for example, mid-nineteenth-century laissez-faire British liberals to argue for limiting the role of government. See Theodore M. Porter, *The Rise of Statistical Thinking, 1820−1900* (Princeton: Princeton University Press, 1986), p. 57.

30. Smith, *The Wealth of Nations.* See also Amos Funkenstein, *Theology and the Scientific Imagination from the Middle Ages to the Seventeenth Century* (Princeton: Princeton University Press, 1986), esp. pp. 317, 323−324. On the role of the clock metaphor in conveying the notion of "system [as] an integrated assembly of numerous dynamically interacting parts," see Otto Mayr, *Authority, Liberty, and Automatic Machinery in Early Modern Europe* (Baltimore: Johns Hopkins University Press, 1986), esp. p. 119.

31. Michael Polanyi, "The Republic of Science: Its Political and Economic Theory," *Minerva* 1 (Autumn 1962), 54−73.

32. John Ziman, *Public Knowledge: The Social Dimension of Science* (Cambridge: Cambridge University Press, 1968).

33. On the early Soviet image of science see, for instance, *Science at the Cross Roads,* papers presented to the International Congress of the History of Science and Technology, London, June 29−July 3, 1931, fore. J. Needham and intro. P. G. Wersky (London: Frank Cass, 1971). On liberal criticism see, for instance, Michael Polanyi, *Personal Knowledge* (New York: Harper Torchbooks, 1982), pp. 222−245.

34. On science as an expression of the democratic value of free individual creativity, see Karl Mannheim, "The Democratization of Culture," in his *Essays on the Sociology of Culture* (London: Routledge and Kegan Paul, 1956), esp. pp. 188–199.

35. In its less democratic version, this position rationalizes centralized action. In the case of Galton's eugenics, for instance, the idea of controlled breeding is not guided by revealed individual preferences but by a certain "scientific" notion of a collective good. Francis Galton, "Hereditary Improvement," *Fraser Magazine* n.s. 7 (1873), 116–130. See also Porter, *The Rise of Statistical Thinking*, pp. 128–146.

36. In the Western tradition the notion that a free will can be embodied in lawful and necessary actions had already been developed by medieval theologians who attempted to reconcile God's omnipotence with order and the laws of nature. The medieval distinction between *potentia Dei absoluta* and *potentia Dei ordinata* later developed into a principal rationalization for the claim that science is compatible with the theological idea of a divine free will. See William J. Courtenay, *Covenant and Causality in Medieval Thought* (London: Variorum Reprints, 1984); Funkenstein, *Theology and the Scientific Imagination*.

37. Consider, for example, Newton's role as Master of the Mint. See Frank E. Manuel, *A Portrait of Isaac Newton* (Cambridge: Belknap Press of Harvard University Press, 1968), pp. 229–244.

38. Samuel P. Huntington, *American Politics: The Promise of Disharmony* (Cambridge, Mass.: Belknap Press of Harvard University Press, 1981), p. 75. On the cultural foundations of reciprocal transparency as a feature of modern democratic politics, see Chapters 3 and 4.

39. See the development of this argument in Chapters 3 and 4.

40. On the periodic shifts between centralized instrumentally oriented and morally conceived decentralized styles of liberal-democratic politics, see Huntington, *The Promise of Disharmony*.

41. Giovanni Sartori, *Democratic Theory* (Detroit: Wayne State University Press, 1962), p. 408.

42. On the history of the modern transition from personal to impersonal bases of political authority, see O. Skinner, *The Foundations of Modern Political Thought*, vols. I, II (Cambridge: Cambridge University Press, 1978). See also, Ernst H. Kantorowicz, *The King's Two Bodies: A Study in Medieval Political Theology* (Princeton: Princeton University Press, 1957).

43. Walter Ullmann, *Medieval Foundations of Renaissance Humanism* (London: Paul Elek, 1977), p. 181. On the contribution of Machiavelli and Hobbes to the ideas and ideals of impersonal political power, see Harvey C. Mansfield, Jr., "On the Impersonality of the Modern State: A Comment on Machiavelli's Use of State," *American Political Science Review* 77 (1983), 849–857; Harvey C. Mansfield, Jr., "Hobbes and the Science of Indirect Government," *American Political Science Review* 65 (1971), 97–110.

44. A. P. D'Entrèves, *Natural Law* (New York: Harper Torchbooks, 1965); Shklar, *Montesquieu*; Robert S. Summers, *Instrumentalism and American Legal Theory* (Ithaca, N.Y.: Cornell University Press, 1982).

45. Theodore M. Porter, *The Rise of Statistical Thinking, 1820–1900* (Princeton: Princeton University Press, 1986).

46. Karl Marx and Friedrich Engels, *The German Ideology* (New York: International Publishers, 1963).

47. See, for instance, Tom Settle, "The Rationality of Science versus the Rationality of Magic," *Philosophy of the Social Sciences* 1 (1971), 173–194.

48. Gordon Wood notes that during the eighteenth century Anglo-Americans tended to regard political events as the consequences of plots and conspiracies. This tendency waned, he indicates, toward the end of the century when, under the influence of Scottish theorists like Ferguson and Smith, political events came to be increasingly attributed to impersonal causes and processes rather than to individual agents and their motives. See Gordon Wood, "Conspiracy and Paranoid Style: Causality and Deceit in the Eighteenth Century," *William and Mary Quarterly* 39 (July 1982), 401–441.

49. See Chapter 9.

50. The existence of such a neutral-apolitical space of perception, of course, in itself depends to a large extent upon the socioculturally established boundaries between the political and the nonpolitical spheres.

51. See, for illustration, the case of East Germany in Thomas A. Baylis, *The Technical Intelligentsia and the East German Elite* (Berkeley: University of California Press, 1979).

52. David M. Schneider and Raymond T. Smith, *Class Differences and Sex Roles in American Kinship and Family Structure* (Englewood Cliffs, N.J.: Prentice-Hall, 1973), pp. 19, 20.

53. On the role of scientific standards in mediating the negotiation of political interests, see Yaron Ezrahi, "The Political Contexts of Science Indicators," in *Toward a Metric of Science,* eds. Y. Elkana, J. Lederberg, Robert K. Merton, A. Thackray, and H. Zuckerman (New York: John Wiley and Sons, 1978), pp. 285–327.

54. Consider, for instance, the case of a doctor prescribing for his patient a medicine which is more expensive and demonstrably less adequate than some other alternative treatments. An impartial judge may have to choose between regarding the doctor as incompetent or attributing to him tacit, covert motives such as profit rather than the stated end of healing.

55. An early illustration of such reliance on science for imputing and judging actors' motives is the involvement of the British physicist Michael Faraday in the investigation of the Haswell Colliery explosion in September 1844. Morris Berman, *Social Change and Scientific Organization: The Royal Institution, 1799–1844* (London: Heinemann, 1978), pp. 177–186.

The explosion occurred against a climate of crisis induced by strikes and mounting tensions between the miners and the owners of the company. Faraday was authorized to investigate the explosion and determine its causes. There were conflicting attitudes ranging from those who defined the explosion as an accident that could not be foreseen or controlled to those who described it as a consequence of the owners' deliberate negligence, of their readiness to sacrifice workers' safety for reduced production costs. Knowledge sufficient to decidedly "externalize" the owners' motives and unambiguously blame or exonerate them was apparently lacking (ibid., pp. 178, 180). The very relevance of available scientific knowledge to Faraday's investigation was largely questionable. Still, the authority of science as an instrumental framework for attributing causality and responsibility was enlisted in the effort to solve the problem. Faraday's report determined that "the catastrophe was purely accidental" (ibid., p. 181, citing *The Civil Engineer and Architect's Journal* 8 [1845], 115). Neither incompetence nor selfish economic motives could be clearly attributed to the Colliery's owners.

This case indicates the main features of instrumental definitions of actions as a basis for attributing motives and competence and holding actors accountable. It illustrates an approach which has come to dominate the attributions of responsibility and competence in vast areas of the public sphere of the modern liberal-democratic state. A contemporary illustration is *The Report of the President's Commission on the Space Shuttle Challenger Accident* (Washington, D.C., June 9, 1986).

56. On the integration of instrumental-performance evaluation standards and political attitudes toward governments see, for example, Douglas A. Hibbs, Jr., *The Political Economy of Industrial Democracies* (Cambridge, Mass.: Harvard University Press, 1987).

2. Science and the Making of Representative Actions and Accountable Actors

1. Irvin Stewart, *Organizing Scientific Research for War* (Boston: Little, Brown, 1948).

2. The drawing depicts the sovereign as a gigantic figure whose body consists of numerous little figures joined together. See its reproduction in Thomas Hobbes, *Leviathan* (New York: Penguin, 1982).

3. Don K. Price, *The Scientific Estate* (Cambridge, Mass.: Belknap Press of Harvard University Press), pp. 57–81.

4. Ibid., p. 75.

5. This is very different from the symbolic role of technology in the Nazi state as the embodiment of a collective spirit and will. See, for example, Jeffrey Herf, *Reactionary Modernism, Technology, Culture, and Politics in Weimar and the Third Reich* (Cambridge: Cambridge University Press, 1984).

6. These are precisely objectivity and rationality as the scientific components of technology and their restraining effects on the creative will, which were rejected in the context of German "reactionary modernism" and which permitted technology, like art, to be identified with the free expression of spiritual values (ibid.).

7. Walter Benjamin, "The Work of Art in the Age of Mechanical Reproduction," in *Illuminations*, ed. Hannah Arendt (New York: Schocken Books, 1969), p. 220.

8. Michael Oakeshott, *Rationalism in Politics and Other Essays* (London: Methuen, 1977), pp. 1–36, 197–247.

9. By contrast, some nationalist conservative notions of leadership permit the incorporation of the unique, subjective traits of the individual personality of the leader, conceived as a representative yet idealized embodiment of the traits of the group or its members.

10. Michael Foucault, *Language, Counter Memory and Practice* (Ithaca, N.Y.: Cornell University Press, 1977), p. 106n67.

11. The value ascribed to an aristocratic conception of action which stresses the centrality of the agent may, at least partly, account for the negative image of engineers in England. See, for instance, J. E. Gerstl and S. P. Hutten, *Engineers: The Anatomy of a Profession* (London: Tavistock, 1966), esp. p. 12; and, for a wider sociocultural background, Eric Ashby, *Technology and the Academics* (London: Macmillan, 1958).

12. See, for instance, Andrew Ure's observations in his *The Philosophy of Manufacturers* (1835) (London: Frank Cass and Co., 1967), p. 8.

13. Octavio Paz, "Eroticism and Gastrosophy," in "How Others See the United States," *Daedalus* 101 (Fall 1972), 77.

14. J. S. Coleman, E. Katz, and H. Manzel, *Medical Innovation: A Diffusion Study* (Indianapolis: Bobbs-Merrill Co., 1966).

15. Daniel J. Boorstin, *The Americans* (New York: Vintage Books, 1974), pp. 165–246.

16. Recent revisionist history and sociology of science criticize this view and develop instead a more local-contextual concept of the historical growth of knowledge. See, for instance, Karin Knorr-Cetina and Michael Mulkay, eds., *Science Observed: Perspective on the Social Study of Science* (London: Sage, 1983); Martin Rudwick, *The Great Devonian Controversy: The Shaping of Scientific Knowledge among Gentlemanly Specialists* (Chicago: University of Chicago Press, 1985); Clifford Geertz, *Local Knowledge* (New York: Basic Books, 1983).

17. Harold F. Gosnell, *Democracy the Threshold of Freedom* (New York: Ronald Press Co., 1948), p. 146.

18. Ibid.

19. Ibid., p. 130.

20. Hannah Pitkin, *The Concept of Representation* (Berkeley: University of California Press, 1967), p. 140.

21. Ibid., p. 142.

22. Ibid., p. 211.

23. Ibid., pp. 190–191. See also John A. W. Gunn, *Politics and the Public Interest in the Seventeenth Century* (London: Routledge and Kegan Paul, 1969), pp. 112–115.

24. It is on such a premise, for instance, that government responsibility for "the state of the economy" has come to take such an important place in public attitudes toward, and judgments of, government actions in such Western democracies as the United States, France, England, and West Germany. Douglas A. Hibbs, Jr., *The Political Economy of Industrial Democracies* (Cambridge, Mass.: Harvard University Press, 1987).

25. On the complex relations between the cognitive and normative parameters of public actions, see Yaron Ezrahi, "Utopian and Pragmatic Rationalism: The Political Context of Scientific Advice," *Minerva* 18 (Spring 1980), 111–131.

26. "Politics refers to 'unsolvable problems': that is situations where no effective computational procedure (or algorithm) is available by means of which a solution can be found which dissolves the problem, carrying irresistible conviction." Bertrand de Jouvenel, *The Pure Theory of Politics* (Cambridge: Cambridge University Press, 1963), pp. 189, 204–213.

27. Jean-Jacques Rousseau, *The First and Second Discourses*, ed. R. D. Masters (New York: St. Martin's Press, 1964), pp. 56–58.

28. Hannah Arendt, *Between Past and Future* (Cleveland: Meridian, 1961); Bernard Crick, *In Defense of Politics* (Harmondsworth: Penguin, 1964); Moses F. Finley, *Democracy Ancient and Modern* (London: Chatto and Windus, 1973); Hans Eulau, *Technology and Civility* (Stanford, Calif.: Hoover Institution Press, 1977).

29. On the idea of tracing accountabilities, see Mary Douglas, *Evans Pritchard* (Glasgow: Fontana Paperbacks, 1980), pp. 57–58; Mary Douglas, "Passive Voice Theories in Religious Sociology," *Review of Religious Research* 21 (Fall 1979), 51–61.

30. Douglas, *Evans Pritchard*, pp. 57–58.

31. Yaron Ezrahi, "The Jensen Controversy: A Study in the Ethics and Politics of Knowledge in Democracy," and Lee Cronbach, "Five Decades of Public Controversy Over Mental Testing," in *Controversies and Decisions: The Social Sciences and Public Policy*, ed. Charles Frankel (New York: Russell Sage Foundation, 1976), pp. 123–170.

32. H. L. A. Hart and A. M. Honoré, *Causation in the Law* (Oxford: Clarendon Press, 1973), p. 85n2. See also ibid., pp. 4, 84–89, 92, 96–102, 104–105, 124–125, 126, 172; Frank D. Fincham and Jos. Jaspers, "Attribution of Responsibility: From Man the Scientist to Man as Lawyer," in *Advances in Experimental Social Psychology*, ed. L. Berkowitz, vol. XIII (New York: Academic Press, 1980), p. 19.

33. John Ziman, *Public Knowledge* (Cambridge: Cambridge University Press, 1968).

34. Keith Thomas, *Religion and the Decline of Magic: Studies in Popular Beliefs in Sixteenth- and Seventeenth-Century England* (Harmondsworth: Penguin Books, 1971), p. 771.

35. Quentin Skinner, *The Foundations of Modern Political Thought*, vol. I, *The Renaissance* (Cambridge: Cambridge University Press, 1978), p. 107.

36. G. Vico, *Opere*, ed. F. Nicolini (Milan, 1953), pp. 293–307, cited in Paolo Rossi, *Philosophy, Technology and the Arts in the Early Modern Era* (New York: Harper and Row, 1970), p. 145.

37. Ibid.

38. On science, actions, and examples as rhetorical devices, see, for instance, Lisa Jardin, *Francis Bacon: Discovery and the Art of Discourse* (Cambridge: Cambridge University Press, 1979); Paolo Rossi, *Francis Bacon* (London: Routledge & Kegan Paul, 1968); and, for a modern example, David Gooding, "In Nature's School: Faraday as an Experimentalist," in *Faraday Rediscovered*, eds. P. Gooding and A. J. L. James (Basingstoke: Stockston Press, 1985), pp. 105–135.

39. Rossi, *Philosophy, Technology and the Arts*, p. 59.

40. On Alberti and Palladio, see Rudolf Wittkower, *Architectural Principles of Humanism* (New York: Norton, 1971).

41. Benjamin Farrington, *The Philosophy of Francis Bacon*, Phoenix ed. (Chicago: University of Chicago Press, 1964), p. 73.

42. Owen Hannaway, *The Chemists and the Word: The Didactic Origins of Chemistry* (Baltimore: Johns Hopkins University Press, 1975); Owen Hannaway, "Laboratory Designs and the Aim of Science: Andreas Libavius versus Tycho Brahe," *Isis* 77 (1986), 585–610.

43. Francis Bacon, *De Augmentis*, bk. 6, ch. 2, *The Works of Francis Bacon,* vol. IV, eds. J. Spedding, R. C. Ellis, and D. D. Heath (London, 1875), p. 449. See also Jardin, *Francis Bacon*, p. 15.

44. Cited in Rossi, *Philosophy, Technology and the Arts*, p. 163.

45. Steven Shapin, "The House of Experiment in Seventeenth-Century England," *Isis* 79 (1988).

46. See Chapters 3 and 4.

47. Robert Darnton, *Mesmerism and the End of the Enlightenment in France* (Cambridge, Mass.: Harvard University Press, 1968), pp. 18—24.

48. Niccolo Machiavelli, *The Prince and the Discourses* (New York: Modern Library, 1950), p. 94. Also Skinner, *Foundations*, I, 137.

49. Machiavelli, *The Prince*, p. 102.

50. John Locke, *Letter on Toleration* (Indianapolis: Bobbs-Merrill Co., 1955), pp. 17, 18, 19, 56—59. Also see Chapter 4. The goal of substituting, at the foundations of the state, human and horizontal for other-worldly and vertical accountabilities also guided Thomas Hobbes in his attempts to demystify political authority and discredit religious doctrines that stressed the possibility of eternal life and of rewards and punishments in the afterlife. Hobbes was concerned that such doctrines were lessening the dependence of subjects on sovereign power. See the discussion of this issue in David Johnson, *The Rhetoric of Leviathan* (Princeton: Princeton University Press, 1986).

51. On the role of experiments and demonstrations in substantiating claims of knowledge in early modern science, see David Gooding, Trevor Pinch, and Simon Schaffer, eds., *The Uses of Experiment* (New Rochelle, N.Y.: Cambridge University Press, 1989).

52. Michael Walzer, *Obligations: Essays on Disobedience, War, and Citizenship* (Cambridge, Mass.: Harvard University Press, 1970), pp. 126, 131.

53. Ibid., p. 132.

54. Benjamin, "Art in the Age of Mechanical Reproduction"; Walter Benjamin, "Karl Kraus," in *Reflections* (New York: Harcourt Brace Jovanovich, 1978), pp. 239—273; Edward Timms, *Karl Kraus Apocalyptic Satirist* (New Haven: Yale University Press, 1986).

55. Anne-Robert-Jacques Turgot, "Discourses sur les progrès successifs de l'esprit humain," in *Oeuvres*, I, 214—215, cited in Peter Gay, *The Enlightenment: An Interpretation*, vol. II (London: Weidenfeld and Nicholson, 1969), p. 124.

56. An artist like Chiberty works like a scientist not only to evoke aesthetic admiration or to please but also in order to exemplify methods for solving problems shared by his fellow artists. E. H. Gombrich, *Norm and Form Studies in the Art of Renaissance*, vol. I (London: Phaidon, 1978), pp. 1—10. Renaissance architects like Filippo Brunelleschi, Leon Batista Alberti, and Andrea Palladio thought of architecture as a mathematical-geometrical science of celestial archetypes. The subjective pole of the artist's individuality is balanced in Renaissance aesthetics by the objective pole of the cosmic order. In the late eighteenth century the hold of this objective pole is broken. The recognition of the infinite possibilities of constructing or representing the world in art led modern aesthetic theorists like John Ruskin to stress the inspiration and the inventiveness, rather than the scientific-like, technical fidelity of the artist. See discussion in Rudolf Witt-

kower, *Architectural Principles in the Age of Humanism* (New York: W. W. Norton, 1971), pp. 117–118, 154; Walter John Hipple, Jr., *The Beautiful, the Sublime and the Picturesque in Eighteenth-Century British Aesthetic Theory* (Carbondale: Southern Illinois University Press, 1957).

57. On the humanistic notion of the human being as a "maker" and "molder," see Giovanni Pico della Mirandola, *Oration on the Dignity of Man*, in *The Renaissance Philosophy of Man*, eds. E. Cassirer, P. O. Kristeller, and J. H. Randall (Chicago: University of Chicago Press, 1948), pp. 223–254.

58. Skinner, *Foundations*, I.

59. Amos Funkenstein, *Theology and the Scientific Imagination: From the Middle Ages to the Seventeenth Century* (Princeton: Princeton University Press, 1986), pp. 336–337. Again, the notion of free action as action which freely applies natural causality in the construction of order perpetuates earlier medieval notions of a nonarbitrary divine will operating through the laws of nature. This is the divine power which is celebrated in Psalm 19:2, "The heavens declare the glory of God." On the issue of agency and contingency in Greek culture, see Martha C. Nussbaum, *The Fragility of Goodness, Luck and Ethics in Greek Tragedy and Philosophy* (Cambridge: Cambridge University Press, 1986).

60. Novum Organum I, cited in Rossi, *Philosophy, Technology and the Arts*, p. 186.

61. Roger Hahn, *The Anatomy of a Scientific Institution: The Paris Academy of Sciences, 1666–1803* (Berkeley: University of California Press, 1971), pp. 141–144, 147.

62. Machiavelli, *The Prince*, p. 91.

63. Ibid.

3. Science and the Visual Culture of Liberal-Democratic Politics

1. See, for instance, John Dewey's distinction between "old"—Spencerian—and "new" liberalism in his *Liberalism and Social Action* (New York: Perigee Books, 1980). See also the concept of social action developed by Karl R. Popper in his *The Poverty of Historicism* (London: Routledge and Kegan Paul, 1963).

2. See, for instance, "The Federalist no. 10," *The Federalist*, from the original text of Alexander Hamilton, John Jay, and James Madison, intro. Edward Mead Earle (New York: Modern Library, 1937) pp. 53–62.

3. Cited in Eric Foner, *Tom Paine and Revolutionary America* (London: Oxford University Press, 1976), p. 85.

4. See in this connection the discussions of Dewey's theory of action in Stuart Hampshire, *Thought and Action* (London: Chatto and Windus, 1959), and Richard J. Bernstein, *Praxis and Action* (Philadelphia: University of Pennsylvania Press, 1971), pp. 165–229.

5. Jefferson's "Letter to James Madison," Dec. 1794, in *Thomas Jefferson*, ed. Merrill D. Peterson (New York: Viking Press, 1975).

6. Note again Walter Benjamin's observation that fascism aestheticizes politics, "The Work of Art in the Age of Mechanical Reproductions," in *Illuminations*, ed. and intro. Hannah Arendt (New York: Schocken Books, 1969), p. 242.

7. This expression appears in Jane Wagner's script for Lily Tomlin's one-

woman show, *The Search for Signs of Intelligent Life in the Universe* (New York: Harper and Row, 1987), p. 18: "I got the kind of madness Socrates talked about, a divine release of the soul from the yoke of custom and convention! I refuse to be intimidated by reality anymore. After all, what is reality anyway? Nothin' but a collective hunch. My space chums think reality was once a primitive method of crowd control that got out of hand . . . reality is the leading cause of stress amongst those in touch with it. I can take it in small doses, but as a lifestyle I found it too confining."

8. Clifford Geertz, *Negara: The Theatre State in Nineteenth-Century Bali* (Princeton: Princeton University Press, 1980), p. 136.

9. Ibid., p. 13.

10. Ibid., p. 104.

11. Ibid., p. 123.

12. Hans Speier, *Social Order and the Risks of War* (New York: G. W. Stewart Policy Sciences Books, 1952), pp. 327–335; Keith M. Baker, "Politics and Public Opinion under the Old Regime: Some Reflections," in *Press and Politics in Pre-Revolutionary France*, eds. J. R. Censer and J. D. Popkin (Berkeley: University of California Press, 1987), pp. 204–246.

13. Geertz, *Negara: The Theatre State*, p. 109.

14. S. Orgel, *The Illusion of Power: Political Theatre in the English Renaissance* (Berkeley: University of California Press, 1975); S. Orgel and R. Strong, *Inigo Jones: The Theatre of the Stuart Court* (London: Sotheby Parke Bernet, 1973); D. J. Gordon, *The Renaissance Imagination*, vol. I, coll. and ed. S. Orgel (Berkeley: University of California Press, 1975); J. D. Redwine, Jr., ed., *Ben Jonson's Literary Criticism* (Lincoln: University of Nebraska Press, 1970).

15. Orgel, *The Illusion of Power*, p. 52. On the use of plays and pageantry to mystify and promote the power of the Spanish kingship during the reign of Philip IV, see Jonathan Brown and J. H. Elliott, *A Palace for a King: The Buen Retiro and the Court of Philip IV* (New Haven: Yale University Press, 1980). On early-seventeenth-century court culture see also R. J. W. Evans, *Rudolf II and His World: A Study in Intellectual History, 1576–1612* (Oxford: Clarendon Press, 1984); A. M. Nagler, *Theatre Festivals of the Medici, 1539–1637* (New Haven: Yale University Press, 1969).

16. Orgel, *The Illusion of Power*, pp. 10–11, 14, 16.

17. Orgel and Strong, *Inigo Jones*, p. 25, and Orgel, *The Illusion of Power*, p. 43.

19. Niccolo Machiavelli, *The Prince and the Discourses* (New York: Modern Library, 1950), p. 4.

20. I am indebted to Michael Heyd for instructing me on this point. On the alliance between the Anglo-Catholics, the court, Puritans, and moderate Anglicans in political opposition to Charles I, see Perez Zagorin, *The Court and the Country: The Beginning of the English Revolution* (New York: Atheneum, 1970), esp. pp. 190–191.

21. W. V. Quine, "Two Dogmas of Empiricism," in *From a Logical Point of View*, 2nd ed. (New York: Harper Torchbooks, 1961), p. 49.

22. See, for instance, Thomas Burnet, *Sacred Theory of Earth* (1681–1689), William Derham's *Physico-Theology, or, a Demonstration of the Being and At-*

tributes of God from His Works of Creation (1713), and William Paley's *Natural Theology, or, Evidence of the Existence and Attributes of the Deity Collected from the Appearances of Nature* (1802). See also the discussion by C. C. Gillispie, *Genesis and Geology: A Study in the Relations of Scientific Thought, Natural Theology, and the Social Opinion in Great Britain, 1790–1850* (Cambridge, Mass.: Harvard University Press, 1951).

23. Thomas Sprat, *History of the Royal Society* (1667) (St. Louis: Washington University Studies, 1958); Thomas Birch, ed., *The Works of the Honourable Robert Boyle*, 2nd ed., 6 vols. (London: J. & F. Rivington, 1772); Robert Hooke, *Micrographia* (1665), reprinted as vol. XIII, *The Life and Work of Robert Hooke*, in R. T. Gunther, *Early Science in Oxford* (1938; London: Dawsons, 1968); Robert Hooke, *Philosophical Experiments and Observations*, ed. William Derham (London, 1726); Steven Shapin and Simon Schaffer, *Leviathan and the Air-Pump: Hobbes, Boyle, and the Experimental Life* (Princeton: Princeton University Press, 1985); Owen Hannaway, "Laboratory Designs and the Aim of Science: Andreas Libavius versus Tycho Brahe," *Isis* 77 (1986), 585–610; David Gooding, "In Nature's School: Faraday as an Experimentalist," in *Faraday Rediscovered: Essays on the Life and Work of Michael Faraday, 1791–1867*, eds. David Gooding and Frank A. L. James (Basingstoke, N.Y.: Stockton Press, 1985), pp. 105–135.

24. Sprat, *History of the Royal Society*, p. 73.

25. Hooke, *Micrographia*, cited in S. Alpers, *The Art of Describing: Dutch Art and the Seventeenth Century* (Chicago: University of Chicago Press, 1983), p. 73.

26. Sprat, *History of the Royal Society*, p. 371.

27. W. E. Knowles Middleton, *The Experimenters: A Study of the Accademia del Cimento* (Baltimore: Johns Hopkins University Press, 1971), p. 260.

28. Raymond Phineas Stearns, *Science in the British Colonies of America* (Urbana: University of Illinois Press, 1970), pp. 413–414.

29. Ibid., p. 425.

30. Shapin and Schaffer, *Leviathan and the Air-Pump*, p. 20.

31. Ibid., p. 25.

32. Ibid., p. 39.

33. Steven Shapin, "The House of Experiment in Seventeenth-Century England," *Isis* 79 (1988), 390.

34. As we shall see below, once "collective witnessing" as a model of decentralized participation in constituting authority and in holding actors accountable was appropriated by the liberal-democratic state, it provided a strategy for balancing the concentration of the power to act by forcing on the actors the risks and uncertainties of universal exposure. Decentralized accountability through various forms of public witnessing has become perhaps the principal method for the democratic legitimation of centralized power. See my further discussion in Chapter 9.

35. Shapin and Schaffer, *Leviathan and the Air-Pump*, pp. 64, 69; Shapin, "The House of Experiment," p. 22.

36. Simon Schaffer, "Priestley's Questions: An Historiographic Survey," *History of Science* 22 (1984), pp. 151–183; Gooding, "In Nature's School."

37. Shapin and Schaffer, *Leviathan and the Air-Pump*, p. 186.

38. See, for instance, Hobbes's observation on witnessing as "knowing together" in *Leviathan*, ed. M. Oakeshott, intro. Richard S. Peters (New York: Collier Books, 1962), p. 57.

39. Shapin and Schaffer, *Leviathan and the Air-Pump*, p. 129.

40. For a different interpretation, which links Hobbes's materialism with the objective of subordinating politics to public judgments in a public space of perception, see David Johnston, *The Rhetoric of Leviathan* (Princeton: Princeton University Press, 1986).

41. Shapin and Schaffer, *Leviathan and the Air-Pump*, p. 341.

42. Robert Boyle, "The Christian Virtuoso," in *Works of Robert Boyle*, eds. Thomas Birch and George Olms (Hildesheim: Verlagsbuchhandlung Anollung, 1966), p. 513.

43. Ibid., p. 514.

44. Shapin and Schaffer, *Leviathan and the Air-Pump*, p. 336.

45. Shapin, "The House of Experiment," pp. 395–404.

46. Ibid., p. 395.

47. For a twentieth-century discussion of the "massification" of politics, see George L. Mosse, "Political Style and Political Theory—Totalitarian Democracy Revisited," in *Totalitarian Democracy and After*, International Colloquium in Memory of Jacob L. Talmon (Jerusalem: Israel Academy of Sciences and Humanities, 1984), pp. 167–176. On Edmund Burke's criticism of visual as opposed to verbal persuasion, see W. J. T. Mitchel, *Iconology* (Chicago: University of Chicago Press, 1986).

48. Michael Heyd, "The New Experimental Philosophy: A Manifestation of 'Enthusiasm' or an Antidote," in *Minerva* 25, no. 4, 432–433.

49. Simon Schaffer, "Natural Philosophy and Public Spectacle in the Eighteenth Century," *History of Science* 21 (1983), 1–43.

50. Raymond Phineas Stearns, *Science in the British Colonies of America* (Urbana: University of Illinois Press, 1970), pp. 506–514.

51. Ibid.; J. A. Leo Lemay, *Ebenezer Kinnersley: Franklin's Friend* (Philadelphia: University of Pennsylvania Press, 1964).

52. Lemay, *Ebenezer Kinnersley*, pp. 66, 77.

53. See Margaret C. Jacob, *The Cultural Meaning of the Scientific Revolution*, (New York: Alfred A. Knopf, 1988), pp. 142–151.

54. Lemay, *Ebenezer Kinnersley*, pp. 20–21.

55. William M. Ivins, Jr., *Prints and Visual Communication* (Cambridge, Mass.: MIT Press, 1953).

56. Ibid., pp. 161, 162, 116.

57. Denis Diderot, ed., *A Diderot Pictorial Encyclopedia of Trades and Industry*, intro. and notes Charles Coulston Gillispie (New York: Dover Publications, 1959).

58. On the deaestheticization of attestive pictorial reports of scientific experiments and on the practices of the Accademia del Cimento, see Middleton, *The Experimenters*.

59. Using the "light" metaphor to signify a democratized concept of knowledge involved a shift of Christian notions of divine or inner illumination, which refer to extrasensible light, to an understanding of light as an experience dependent upon the engagement of the external senses. On some early antecedents of

this distinction see, for example, David C. Lindberg, "The Genesis of Kepler's Theory of Light: Light Metaphysics from Plotinus to Kepler," *Osiris*, 2d ser., 2 (1986), 5–42.

60. Cited in Keith M. Baker, *Condorcet: From Natural Philosophy to Social Mathematics* (Chicago: University of Chicago Press, 1975), pp. 75, 79.

61. See, for instance, Rush Welter, *Popular Education and Democratic Thought in America* (New York: Columbia University Press, 1962), and Merle Curti, *The Growth of American Thought* (New York: Harper & Brothers, 1943).

62. Kate Silber, *Pestalozzi: The Man and His Work* (London: Routledge and Kegan Paul, 1973); *Pestalozzi's Educational Writings*, eds. J. A. Green and F. A. Collie (New York: Longmans, Green Co., 1912).

63. Ruth Miller Elson, *Guardians of Tradition: American Schoolbooks of the Nineteenth Century* (Lincoln: University of Nebraska Press, 1964), p. 19.

64. Ibid., pp. 19–20 and the discussions on pp. 15–40, 221–242.

65. Referring to the balloon flights, Robert Darnton observes that "the flights reached audiences full of men who could not read the *Journal de Physique* . . . [The enthusiasm for science] spread beyond the scientific bodies of Paris, beyond the limits of literacy and, as far as literacy matters went, beyond the boundaries of prose." See Robert Darnton, *Mesmerism and the End of the Enlightenment in France* (Cambridge, Mass.: Harvard University Press, 1968), p. 22.

66. Alma S. Wittlin, *Museums: In Search of Usable Future* (Cambridge, Mass.: MIT Press, 1970). See also Donald Horne, *The Great Museum: The Representation of History* (London: Pluto Press, 1984).

67. Perry Miller, *Life of the Mind in America* (New York: Harcourt, Brace and World, Inc., 1965), p. 297.

68. Francis Bacon, *The New Organon*, ed. and intro. Fulton H. Anderson (Indianapolis: Bobbs-Merrill Co., 1960), p. 116.

69. Walter J. Ong, *Ramus, Method and the Decay of Dialogue* (New York: Octagon Books, 1974), pp. 151, 251.

70. "Among the greater part of the lay public, it would seem that the authority of science rests rather heavily on the technological achievements which it ultimately made possible. The increasing comforts and conveniences deriving from technology invite the social support of scientific research and promote generally favorable though grotesquely distorted images of the physical scientist . . . [A]bstract and difficult theories which cannot be understood or evaluated by the facts are presumably 'proved' in a fashion which can be understood by all through their technological applications." Robert K. Merton and Paul K. Hatt, "Election Polling Forecasts and Public Images of Social Science," *The Public Opinion Quarterly* 13 (Summer 1949), 187–188.

71. Michael Heyd, "The Reaction to Enthusiasm in the Seventeenth Century: Towards an Integrative Approach," *Journal of Modern History* 53 (June 1981), 258–280.

72. Gooding and James, eds., *Faraday Rediscovered*; Carl Bode, *The American Lyceum* (Carbondale: Southern Illinois University Press, 1968); Steven Shapin and Barry Barnes, "Science, Nature and Control: Interpreting Mechanics Institutes," *Social Studies of Science* 7 (1977), 31–74; David Layton, *Science for the People* (London: Allen Unwin, 1973).

73. Gooding, "In Nature's School," pp. 105–135.

74. Ibid., pp. 106–108.

75. Ibid., p. 107.

76. For another illuminating discussion of the complex theoretical and practical basis of Faraday's seemingly self-evident facts, see Ryan D. Tweney, "Faraday's Discovery of Induction: A Cognitive Approach," in *Faraday Rediscovered,* eds. Gooding and James, pp. 189–209.

77. Robert P. Multhauf, "A Museum Case History," *Technology and Culture* 6 (Winter 1965), 56.

78. On the inferior visual articulation of the social compared with the natural sciences, see, for instance, *The Behavioral and Social Sciences: Outlook and Needs,* a report by the Behavioral and Social Sciences Survey Committee, the Committee on Science and Public Policy, National Academy of Sciences, and the Committee on Problems and Policy, Social Science Research Council (Washington D.C.: National Academy of Sciences, 1969), p. 5. See also Merton and Hatt, "Election Polling, Forecasts and Public Images of Social Science," pp. 187–188.

79. See Chapter 7.

80. Martin Heidegger, "The Age of the World View," *Measure,* a critical journal, 2 (Summer 1951), pp. 277–279, 282.

81. There were, of course, alternative concepts of the public as a liberal-democratic agency which were less compatible with both individualism and the intellectually disciplined gaze of the governors. Compared with the traditional theater, which was typically stratified horizontally by balconies in an amphitheater, some designs, for instance those by architects who identified with the French Revolution, intended that the people would be visible to each other. While this development reflects the rise of the public as a political-ideological category, that is, the emergence of citizens as both actors and spectators, such a conception of the public is more closely associated with the view of the public as an emotionally unified group than with the view of the public as an association of discrete, partly detached and partly engaged individuals. See the instructive observations by James A. Leith, "Desacralization, Resacralization and Architectural Planning during the French Revolution," *Eighteenth Century Life* 7 (May 1982), 74–84.

82. Boyle, "The Christian Virtuoso," p. 514.

83. James Engell, *The Creative Imagination: Enlightenment to Romanticism* (Cambridge, Mass.: Harvard University Press, 1981), pp. 248–258.

84. See, for instance, Michael Schudson, *Discovering the News: A Social History of American Newspapers* (New York: Basic Books, 1973).

85. On the probabilistic conception of empirical knowledge in seventeenth-century England, see Barbara J. Shapiro, *Probability and Certainty in Seventeenth-Century England* (Princeton: Princeton University Press, 1983); on the cultural and political implications of the differences between mathematical and empirical concepts of knowledge, see also Yaron Ezrahi, "Science and the Problem of Authority in Democracy," in *Science and Social Structure,* a Festschrift for Robert Merton, ed. T. F. Gieryn, Transactions of the New York Academy of Sciences (1980), pp. 43–60.

86. For a classical treatment of the limits imposed on the capacity of actors to

predict the effects of their own actions, see Robert K. Merton, "The Unantici- pated Consequences of Purposive Social Action," *American Sociological Review* 1 (1936), 894–904.

87. See Mosse, "Political Style and Political Theory," and Yaron Ezrahi, "Comments on Mosse's Paper," in *Totalitarian Democracy and After,* Inter- national Colloquium in memory of Jacob L. Talmon, pp. 167–182. See also William Kornhauser, *The Politics of Mass Society* (New York: Free Press, 1959); George L. Mosse, *The Nationalization of the Masses: Political Symbolism and Mass Movements in Germany from the Napoleonic War through the Third Reich* (New York: H. Fertig, 1975).

88. Walter Lippmann, *The Phantom Public* (New York: Harcourt, Brace and Co., 1925); Joseph Schumpeter, *Capitalism, Socialism, and Democracy* (New York: Harper & Bros., 1947); Harold D. Lasswell, *The Political Writings of H. D. Lasswell* (Glencoe, Ill.: Free Press, 1951).

89. Shapin and Schaffer, *Leviathan and the Air-Pump,* pp. 65–69.

90. See a more detailed discussion of this point in Chapter 10.

91. L. Bobrov, *Grounds for Optimism,* trans. H. C. Creighton (Moscow: Mir Publishers, 1974), p. 35.

92. J. L. Talmon, *The Origins of Totalitarian Democracy* (London: Mercury Publishers, 1961); Berthold Hinz, *Art in the Third Reich* (New York: Pantheon Books, 1979).

93. Orgel, *The Illusion of Power.*

94. Marc Bloch, *Feudal Society,* trans. L. A. Maynon (Chicago: Chicago University Press, 1964), p. 83.

95. Shapin and Schaffer, *Leviathan and the Air-Pump,* p. 344.

96. Late 1980s Russian and Polish politics may serve as illustrations.

97. Any attempt to resolve this dilemma, therefore, only diminishes or under- mines the democratic character of politics.

4. Science, Experimental Politics, and the Culture of Democratization

1. Pierre Duhem, *The Aims and Structure of Physical Theory,* trans. Philip P. Wiener (Princeton: Princeton University Press, 1954), pp. 65–67.

2. J. B. Bernal, *The Social Function of Science* (Cambridge, Mass.: MIT Press, 1964), p. 42.

3. Peter Dear, "Miracles, Experiments and the Ordinary Course of Nature," unpublished paper presented at the conference on Fifty Years to the Merton The- sis, Jerusalem, May 1988.

4. Cecil O. Smith, Jr., "Material for Colloquium on French Engineers," unpublished paper presented in Philadelphia, March 26, 1974. I am indebted to Dr. Smith for the permission to use this material. See also W. J. T. Mitchell, *Icon- ology, Image, Text Ideology* (Chicago: University of Chicago Press, 1986), pp. 116–149, for the view that there are differences in the propensity to rely on visual versus verbal modes of persuasion between the French and the English.

5. Svetlana Alpers, *The Art of Describing* (Chicago: University of Chicago Press, 1983), p. xxvii. On a different cultural attitude in France, see Michael Fried, *Absorption and Theatricality* (Berkeley: University of California Press, 1980).

6. Alpers, *The Art of Describing*, p. 51.
7. Ibid., p. 82; John B. Knipping, *Iconography of the Counter Reformation in the Netherlands* (Leiden: B. de Graaf-Nieuwkoop, W. A. Sigthoff, 1974).
8. Fried, *Absorption and Theatricality*.
9. Fred Licht, *Goya: The Origins of the Modern Temper in Art* (New York: Universe Books, 1979), see esp. pp. 67–82. On the relations between Goya and the themes of the Enlightenment, see also A. E. Pénez Sánchez and E. A. Sayre, codirectors of the exhibition, *Goya and the Spirit of the Enlightenment,* catalogue (Boston: Museum of Fine Arts, 1989).
10. See further discussion in this chapter and in Chapter 5.
11. William Blake, *Complete Writings,* ed. Geoffrey Keynes (Oxford: Oxford University Press, 1976); Jean H. Hagstrum, *William Blake—Poet and Painter* (Chicago: University of Chicago Press, 1964). For a study of Blake's attack on the visual strategies of science, see Donald D. Ault, *Visionary Physics: Blake's Response to Newton* (Chicago: University of Chicago Press, 1974).
12. James Engell, *The Creative Imagination: Enlightenment to Romanticism* (Cambridge, Mass.: Harvard University Press), pp. 197–214, 188.
13. Alan Trachtenberg, *Reading American Photographs: Images as History, Mathew Brady to Walker Evans* (New York: Hill and Wang, 1989).
14. Ibid., p. 20.
15. Michael Fried, *Realism, Writing, Disfiguration: On Thomas Eakins and Stephen Crane* (Chicago: University of Chicago Press, 1987); Alan Trachtenberg, *Brooklyn Bridge: Fact and Symbol* (Chicago: University of Chicago Press, 1979).
16. William S. Heckscher, *Rembrandt's Anatomy of Dr. Nicholaas Tulp* (New York: New York University Press, 1958).
17. Philip Fisher, "Appearing and Disappearing in Public: Social Space in Late Nineteenth Century Literature and Culture," in *Reconstructing American Literary History,* ed. S. Bercovitch (Cambridge, Mass.: Harvard University Press, 1986), p. 158.
18. Ibid., p. 157.
19. Ibid., p. 159.
20. Ibid., p. 161.
21. Daniel Calhoun, *The Intelligence of a People* (Princeton: Princeton University Press, 1973).
22. Fisher, "Appearing and Disappearing in Public," p. 169.
23. Fried, *Realism, Writing, Disfiguration*, p. 21.
24. Cited in Robert H. Kargon, *The Rise of Robert Millikan* (Ithaca, N.Y.: Cornell University Press, 1982), p. 32.
25. Ibid.
26. Ibid., p. 162.
27. In *The Portable Thomas Jefferson,* ed. and intro. Merrill D. Peterson (New York: Viking Press, 1975).
28. Ibid., p. 162.
29. Ibid., p. 211.
30. "The Declaration of Independence," ibid., p. 236.
31. "Second Inaugural Address," ibid., p. 320.
32. Ibid. (my emphasis).
33. Ibid.

34. "To Elias Shipman and Others," ibid., p. 296.

35. "To Thomas Jefferson Randolph," ibid., p. 514.

36. "To Roger C. Weightman," ibid., p. 589.

37. Judith N. Shklar, *Montesquieu* (Oxford: Oxford University Press, 1987), p. 120.

38. Ibid., p. 122.

39. Cited in Austin Ranny, "The Divine Science: Political Engineering in American Culture," *American Political Science Review* 70 (1976), 141.

40. From *The Federalist Papers,* cited in ibid., p. 145.

41. Cited in Adrienne Koch, *Power, Morals and the Founding Fathers* (Ithaca, N.Y.: Cornell University Press, 1961), p. 128. Also cited in Ranney, "The Divine Science," p. 147.

42. G. A. Peek, ed. and intro., *The Political Writings of John Adams* (New York: Liberal Arts Press, 1954), pp. 117–118.

43. Ibid., p. 117.

44. "A Letter of Luther Martin to the Citizens of Maryland," (1788) in *The Antifederalists,* ed. Cecelia M. Kenyon (Indianapolis: Bobbs-Merrill Co., 1966), p. 171.

45. George H. Daniels, *American Science in the Age of Jackson* (New York: Columbia University Press, 1968).

46. *Hans Christian Andersen's Fairy Tales,* trans. R. Spink (London: J. M. Dent, 1958), pp. 79–81.

47. Thomas Paine, *Rights of Man: An Answer to Mr. Burke's Attack on the French Revolution* (London: Carlile, 1819), p. 36.

48. The sensitivity of the monarch to any perspective that undermines the seeming solemnity of the monarchy is indicated by an incident in 1633 when William Prynne's comment that "women actors are notorious whores" was interpreted as an attack on the queen and the court theatricals and led to the severe punishment of the offender. See S. Orgel, *The Illusion of Power: Political Theatre in English Renaissance* (Berkeley: University of California Press, 1975), pp. 39–40, 43–44, 79–80, 88.

49. *The Works of William Makepeace Thackeray,* Kensington Edition, vol. XVII, *The Paris Sketch Book of Mr. M. A. Titmarsh,* with the author's illustrations (New York: Charles Scribner's Sons, 1904), p. 404. The drawing appears opposite p. 404.

50. Niccolo Machiavelli, *The Prince and the Discourses* (New York: Modern Library, 1950), pp. 85, 67.

51. Edmund Burke, *Reflections on the Revolution in France* (1790), ed. and intro. C. C. O'Brien (Harmondsworth: Penguin, 1976), p. 169.

52. Edmund Burke, "Three Letters on a Regicide Peace," in *The Works of E. Burke,* vol. V (London: George Bell & Sons, 1906), pp. 391–392.

53. Burke, *Reflections,* p. 171.

54. Ibid.

55. Ibid.

56. Ibid.

57. Eric Foner, *Tom Paine and Revolutionary America* (London: Oxford University Press, 1976), p. 204.

58. Paine, *The Rights of Man,* cited and discussed by W. J. T. Mitchell, *Iconology: Image, Text, Ideology* (Chicago: University of Chicago Press, 1986), pp. 141–142.

59. Paine, *Rights of Man,* pp. 36–37.

60. Foner, *Tom Paine,* pp. 6–7, 38, 120.

61. Paine, *Rights of Man,* p. 36.

62. *The Rights of Man,* cited in Mitchell, *Iconology,* p. 147.

63. Joseph Priestley, "Letters to the Right Honourable Edmund Burke" (3rd ed., 1791), third letter in *Priestley's Writings on Philosophy, Science and Politics,* ed. and intro. J. A. Passmore (New York: Collier, 1965), p. 246.

64. Ibid., pp. 246–247.

65. From Priestley's "Lectures on History and General Policy" (4th ed., 1826), in ibid., p. 188.

66. Ibid.

67. *Priestley's Letters to E. Burke* (3rd ed.) (Birmingham: T. Pearson, 1791), p. 27.

68. Ibid., p. 8; and *Priestley's Writings,* ed. Passmore, pp. 303–304.

69. Alexis de Tocqueville, *Democracy in America,* vol. II, ed. Phillips Bradley (New York: Vintage Books, 1945), pp. 4–5.

70. Ibid., p. 42.

71. Ibid., pp. 84–85.

72. Ibid., p. 4.

73. J. Bentham, *Panopticon,* postscript pts. I and II (1843), in his *Collected Works,* vol. IV, ed. J. Browning (New York: Russell & Russell, 1962).

74. Ibid., p. 23.

75. Ibid., pts. I and II.

76. Ibid., p. 28.

77. A most instructive early-twentieth-century attempt to enlist attestive visual orientation to the rationalization of the behavior of subordinates can be found in F. W. Taylor, *Scientific Management* (1911) (New York: Harper, 1947).

78. Bentham, *Panopticon.*

79. Michel Foucault, *Discipline and Punish: The Birth of the Prison,* trans. A. Sheridan (New York: Pantheon Books, 1977), pp. 195–228, esp. p. 205.

80. Ibid., p. 222.

81. Consider, for instance, the powerful political impact of televised public Congressional investigations in the Watergate and Iran-Contra scandals. Exposing discrepancies between the public presentations and the covered features of government actions has become one of the key means of delegitimating and shattering political authority in modern democratic states.

82. George Orwell, *Nineteen Eighty-Four* (Harmondsworth: Penguin, 1954).

83. See, for instance, *Freedom of Information Act and Amendments of 1974* (P.L. 93-502), Committee of Government Operations, U.S. House of Representatives Committee on the Judiciary, U.S. Senate (Washington, D.C.: U.S. Government Printing Office, 1975).

84. Bentham, *Panopticon,* p. 24.

85. Ibid., postscript pt. II table.

86. *Priestley's Writings,* ed. Passmore, p. 319.

87. Burke, "A Letter to a Noble Lord," in *The Works of E. Burke*, vol. V, p. 144.

88. Ibid., p. 120.

89. Ibid., p. 141.

90. Ibid., p. 143.

91. Burke, *Reflections*, p. 172.

92. Burke, "Regicide Peace," p. 397.

93. Burke, "Letter to a Noble Lord," pp. 140, 148.

94. Burke, *Reflections*, p. 281.

95. Ibid., p. 182.

96. Ibid., p. 158.

97. Burke, "Regicide Peace," p. 153.

98. Burke, *Reflections*, p. 152.

99. Ibid., p. 194.

100. *Priestley's Letters to E. Burke*, p. 4.

101. Ibid., p. 1. This preference of "events" over "treaties" corresponds to the preference of "works" over "words" in the early expressions of the ethos of experimental philosophy in Bacon as well as in Bishop Sprat's *History of the Royal Society* (1667).

102. From Priestley's "Lectures on History and General Policy" (1826) in *Priestley's Writings*, ed. Passmore, p. 179.

103. Ibid., pp. 187–188.

104. Ibid., p. 192.

105. Joseph Priestley, "An Essay on the First Principles of Government" (2nd ed., 1771), in *Priestley's Writings*, ed. Passmore, p. 219.

106. Priestley, "Letters to Burke," in *Priestley's Writings*, ed. Passmore, p. 254.

107. Simon Schaffer, "Priestley's Questions: An Historiographic Survey," *History of Science* 22 (1984), 151–157.

108. *Priestley's Writings*, ed. Passmore, p. 180.

109. Schaffer, "Priestley's Questions," pp. 174–175.

110. Hilary Putnam, *Reason, Truth and History* (Cambridge: Cambridge University Press, 1981), p. 179.

111. For a modern illustration of the discrepancy between scientific and lay attributions of causality and responsibility and its consequences see R. A. Howard, J. E. Mathesn, and D. W. North, "The Decision to Seed the Hurricanes," *Science* 176 (June 1972), 1191–1202.

112. See, for instance, Michael Schudson, *Advertising: The Uneasy Persuasion* (New York: Basic Books, 1986), esp. pp. 44–89. The difficulties of generating adequate information about, and anticipating, consumers' responses to different stimuli undermine, of course, also Benthamite utilitarian rationales for centralized structures of decision making.

113. David Johnston, *The Rhetoric of Leviathan* (Princeton, N.J.: Princeton University Press, 1986).

114. J. Locke, *Letter Concerning Toleration* (Indianapolis: Bobbs-Merrill, 1955), pp. 17, 18, 19, 56–59.

115. See, for example, James Farr, "Political Science and the Enlightenment of Enthusiasm," *American Political Science Review* 82 (March 1988), 51–69.

116. John Stuart Mill, *On Liberty,* in *The Utilitarians* (Garden City: Anchor Books, 1973), p. 51.

117. This assertion does not mean, of course, to ignore the significant presence of the credulous, nonskeptical observers of the kind who are devoted to the programs of television evangelists.

5. The Aesthetic and Rhetoric of the Machine and Its Role as a Political Metaphor

1. William Paley, *Natural Theology, or, Evidences and Attributes of the Deity Collected from the Appearances of Nature* (London: J. Foulder 1809).

2. See John A. Kouwenhoven, *The Arts in Modern American Civilization* (New York: Norton Library, 1967), p. 16.

3. B. P. Johnson, *Great Exhibition of the Industry of All Nations, 1851,* a report (Albany: C. Van Benthuysen, public printer, 1852), pp. 14–15.

4. Ibid.

5. Ibid.; and Kouwenhoven, *Arts in Modern American Civilization,* p. 17. See also Cecelia Tichi, *Shifting Gears: Technology, Literature, and Culture in Modern America* (Chapel Hill: University of North Carolina Press, 1987).

6. Kouwenhoven, *Arts in Modern American Civilization,* p. 17.

7. Ibid., p. 90.

8. Ralph Waldo Emerson, *The Conduct of Life* (1860), cited in ibid., p. 94.

9. Alan Trachtenberg, *The Incorporation of America: Culture and Society in the Gilded Age* (New York: Hill and Wang, 1982), p. 215.

10. Ibid., p. 226. See also John Szarkowski, *The Idea of Louis Sullivan* (Minneapolis: University of Minnesota Press, 1965).

11. Kouwenhoven, *Arts in Modern American Civilization,* pp. 76, 197–224.

12. Ibid., pp. 203–204.

13. Nikolaus Pevsner, *Pioneers of Modern Design from William Morris to Walter Gropius* (Harmondsworth: Penguin, 1975).

14. See, for instance, Keith Thomas, *Man and the Natural World: A History of the Modern Sensibility* (New York: Pantheon Books, 1983), pp. 254–300.

15. Kouwenhoven, *Arts in Modern American Civilization,* p. 13.

16. "The great split between man and nature, the dualism that scarred so much European thought, simply was not a large factor in America before 1820 or 1830, and so the imagination was not required to stitch it up." James Engell, *The Creative Imagination: Enlightenment to Romanticism* (Cambridge, Mass.: Harvard University Press, 1981), p. 190.

17. Kouwenhoven, *Arts in Modern American Civilization,* p. 83.

18. See, for instance, M. Fisher, "The Iconology of Industrialism, 1830–1860," *American Quarterly* 13 (Fall 1961), 347–364.

19. Alan Trachtenberg, *Brooklyn Bridge: Fact and Symbol* (Chicago: University of Chicago Press, 1979), p. 60.

20. Perry Miller, *The Life of Mind in America* (New York: Harcourt, Brace and World, 1965), pp. 277, 278, 290.

21. Ibid., p. 293.

22. Thomas H. Johnson, ed., *Final Harvest: Emily Dickinson's Poems* (Bos-

ton: Little, Brown, 1962), p. 149. Reprinted by permission of the publishers and the Trustees of Amherst College from *The Poems of Emily Dickinson*, Thomas H. Johnson, ed., Cambridge, Mass.: Belknap Press of Harvard University Press, Copyright 1951, © 1955, 1979, 1983 by the President and Fellows of Harvard College.

23. See Preface to "Milton," *Blake: Complete Writings*, ed. G. Keynes (London: Oxford University Press, 1972), p. 481.

24. Raymond Williams, *The Country and the City* (New York: Oxford University Press, 1973).

25. See Herbert L. Sussman, *Victorians and the Machine: The Literary Response to Technology* (Cambridge, Mass.: Harvard University Press, 1968), pp. 56–57; Tichi, *Shifting Gears*, pp. 117–132.

26. John F. Kasson, *Civilizing the Machine: Technology and Republican Values in America, 1776–1900* (Harmondsworth: Penguin, 1976), pp. 55–106.

27. Leo Marx, *The Machine in the Garden: Technology and the Pastoral Ideal in America* (New York: Oxford University Press, 1967).

28. Martin J. Wiener, *English Culture and the Decline of the Industrial Spirit, 1850–1880* (Cambridge: Cambridge University Press, 1981).

29. Miller, *The Life of Mind in America*, p. 304; L. Marx, "American Literary Culture and the Fatalistic View of Technology," *Alternative Futures* 3 (Spring 1980), 52.

30. Marx, *The Machine in the Garden*, p. 115.

31. Ralph Waldo Emerson, *Complete Works*, vol. I (Boston: Contemporary Edition, 1964), pp. 361–395; and Marx, *The Machine in the Garden*, pp. 226–228.

32. Kasson, *Civilizing the Machine*, p. 99.

33. R. Wittkower, *Architectural Principles in the Age of Humanism* (New York: W. W. Norton, 1971).

34. Trachtenberg, *Brooklyn Bridge*, p. 60.

35. Ibid., p. 92.

36. Oscar Wilde, *Impressions of America*, ed. Stuart Mason (Sunderland, 1906), cited in Kouwenhoven, *Arts in Modern American Civilization*, p. 173.

37. Sussman, *Victorians and the Machine* (Cambridge, Mass.: Harvard University Press, 1968), pp. 41–75. See also Wiener, *English Culture and the Decline of the Industrial Spirit*, pp. 88–89.

38. On the image of industrializing America, see M. Fisher, *Workshops in the Wilderness, 1830–1860* (New York: Oxford University Press, 1967); and Raymond Williams, *The Country and the City*.

39. *Fifty Years of Public Work of Sir Henry Cole, K.C.B., Accounted for in His Deeds, Speeches and Writings*, vol. II (London: George Bell and Sons, 1884), pp. 178–179.

40. Ibid., p. 368.

41. Neil Harris, *The Artist in American Society* (Chicago: University of Chicago Press, 1982), pp. 183, 311–315.

42. Daniel Walker Howe, ed., "Victorian Culture in America," *American Quarterly*, Special Issue, 27 (December 1975); J. S. Larson, *The Rise of Professionalism* (Berkeley: University of California Press, 1977), pp. 80–135; Thomas

L. Haskell, *The Emergence of Professional Social Science—The American Social Science Association and the Nineteenth Crisis of Authority* (Urbana: University of Illinois Press, 1977).

43. See V. L. Parrington, *Main Currents in American Thought,* vol. III (New York: Harvest, 1930); Rush Welter, *Popular Education and Democratic Thought in America* (New York: Columbia University Press, 1962); and "Mass Culture and Mass Media," *Daedalus* 89 (Spring 1960).

44. Barbara Novak, *American Painting of the Nineteenth Century: Realism, Idealism and the American Experience* (New York: Praeger, 1969), p. 9; and Harris, *The Artist in American Society,* p. 173.

45. J. J. Jarves, *The Art Idea* (1864), ed. B. Rowland, Jr. (Cambridge, Mass.: Belknap Press of Harvard University Press, 1960), p. 86, cited in Novak, *American Painting of the Nineteenth Century,* p. 23.

46. Johnson, *Great Exhibition,* p. 13.

47. Thomas Ewbank, "Artists of the Ideal and the Real, or, Poets and Inventors—Revival of an Old Mode of Carving," *Scientific American* 4 (December 23, 1848); Kasson, *Civilizing the Machine,* p. 149.

48. See also Alexis de Tocqueville, *Democracy in America,* vol. II, ed. Phillips Bradley (New York: Vintage Books, 1945), pp. 42–47.

49. Herbert L. Sussman, *Fact into Figure: Technology in Carlyle, Ruskin and the Pre-Raphaelite Brotherhood* (Columbus: Ohio State University, 1977).

50. Ibid., p. 8.

51. Cited in Kasson, *Civilizing the Machine,* p. 117.

52. Edward Shils, *The Torment of Secrecy* (Glencoe, Ill.: Free Press, 1956).

53. On engineering as a visual display of intelligence and competence in America, see Daniel Calhoun, *The Intelligence of a People* (Princeton: Princeton University Press, 1973).

54. *Nature* 286 (August 7, 1980), 545.

55. Michael Oakeshott, *Rationalism in Politics* (London: Methuen, 1981), pp. 23, 29, 31–36.

56. Ibid.

57. For a study of negative American images of politics as the domain of power and partisan interests, see Sterling Young, *The Washingtonian Community, 1800–1828* (New York: Columbia University Press, 1966).

58. See Chapter 8.

59. Judith Shklar, *Ordinary Vices* (Cambridge, Mass.: Belknap Press of Harvard University Press, 1984), p. 242.

60. Henry Adams, *The Education of Henry Adams: An Autobiography* (London: Constable & Co., 1918), pp. 421–422.

61. Monte A. Clavert, *The Mechanical Engineer in America* (Baltimore: Johns Hopkins University Press, 1962), p. 265.

62. Cited in A. C. Crombie, *Medieval and Early Modern Science,* vol. II (Garden City: Doubleday, 1959), p. 203. See also Stillman Drake, *Discoveries and Opinions of Galileo* (Garden City: Doubleday, 1957).

63. Clavert, *The Mechanical Engineer in America,* p. 266.

64. Tichi, *Shifting Gears,* pp. 117–132.

65. Clavert, *The Mechanical Engineer in America,* p. 266.

66. See Chapters 8 and 9.

67. See Chapters 3 and 4.

68. Lionel Trilling, *Sincerity and Authenticity* (Cambridge, Mass.: Harvard University Press, 1972).

69. On science and styles of political action, see Yaron Ezrahi, "Political Style and Political Theory—Totalitarian Democracy Revisited," comments on G. L. Mosse paper in *Totalitarian Democracy and After*, International Colloquium in memory of J. L. Talmon (Jerusalem: Magnes Press, 1984), pp. 177–182.

70. Calhoun, *The Intelligence of a People* (Princeton, N.J.: Princeton University Press, 1973), pp. 118, 334. In this connection see also Emile Durkheim's criticism of the American pragmatists for not sufficiently distinguishing between the "surface" and the "substance" of things, in his *Pragmatism and Sociology* (Cambridge: Cambridge University Press, 1983), pp. 3–4.

71. See Chapters 4 and 5.

72. A relevant example is the practice of citing research as a rationale of policies and actions in order to generate public trust. Elements of attestive visual culture and its normative presuppositions are thus employed to present established political authority in a favorable light.

73. This fact has led some observers to suggest that what I characterize as the demands of the theatrics of liberal-democratic political legitimation be deliberately used as an incentive for political actors to increase their reliance on knowledge. See, for instance, Donald T. Campbell, "Reforms and Experiments" in *Evaluating Action Programs*, ed. Carol H. Weiss (Boston: Allyn and Bacon, 1972), p. 197.

74. Wiener, *English Culture and the Decline of the Industrial Spirit*, pp. 132–145.

6. Machines and Images of Order

1. John Passmore notes the early cultural expressions of special affinities between a tragic view of humanity's place in nature and science. He cites Epicurus' assertion that "it would be better to follow the myths about the gods than to become a slave to the physicist's destiny. Myths tell us that we can hope to soften gods' hearts by worshiping them, whereas destiny involves an implacable necessity." He cites further A. N. Whitehead's observation that the ancient Greek's vision of remorseless and indifferent fate "is the vision possessed by science. Fate in Greek tragedy becomes the order of nature in modern thought." See John Passmore, *Science and Its Critics* (London: Duckworth, 1978), pp. 29–30. For an illuminating discussion of the story of the flight of Daedalus and Icarus and the problem of the antithesis between nature and art, see Molly Myerowitz, *Ovid's Games of Love* (Detroit: Wayne State University Press, 1985), pp. 150–167.

2. See Laurence Goldstein, *The Flying Machine and Modern Literature* (Houndsmill: Macmillan, 1986).

3. Lynn White, "The Iconography of Temperantia and the Virtuousness of Technology," in *Action and Conviction in Early Modern Europe*, eds. T. K. Rabb and J. Feigel (Princeton: Princeton University Press, 1969), p. 202.

4. Ibid., pp. 207–209.

5. Ibid., pp. 211–219.

6. Otto Mayr, *The Origin of Feedback Control* (Cambridge, Mass.: MIT Press, 1970), and his *Authority, Liberty and Automatic Machinery in Early Modern Europe* (Baltimore: Johns Hopkins University Press, 1986).

7. Goldstein, *The Flying Machine and Modern Literature*.

8. Francis Bacon, "Novum Organum," *The Works of Francis Bacon*, vol. I, eds. R. L. Ellis, J. Spedding, and D. D. Heath (London, 1857–1874), p. i.

9. One can trace Western ambivalence about the idea of limitless power and will to medieval Christian theology. William Courtenay notes that "western Christian theology was suspicious of a power dependent exclusively on the will of God and unchecked by any other attribute or agency . . . It may be that western theologians shaped some aspects of their idea of God on the basis of their experience with the misuse of power . . . Power without responsibility, without conformity to accepted standards of justice and truth was a clear invitation to evil and perversity." See William J. Courtenay, *Covenant and Causality in Medieval Thought*, vol. I (London: Variorum Reprints, 1984), p. 64.

10. Jeffrey Herf, *Reactionary Modernism: Technology, Culture and Politics in Weimar and the Third Reich* (Cambridge: Cambridge University Press, 1984).

11. Ibid., pp. 71, 85; Goldstein, *The Flying Machine*, pp. 8, 22, 33, 36, 37, 40, 132; R. W. Flint, ed., *Marinetti: Selected Writings* (New York: Farrar, Straus & Giroux, 1972).

12. Herf, *Reactionary Modernism*, p. 71.

13. Ibid., p. 173; and Goldstein, *The Flying Machine*, pp. 14–40.

14. Herf, *Reactionary Modernism*, p. 16.

15. Ibid., pp. 42, 163, 174.

16. J. F. Kasson, *Civilizing the Machine: Technology and Republican Values in America, 1776–1900* (Harmondsworth: Penguin, 1976), pp. 152–153.

17. Samuel P. Huntington, *American Politics—The Promise of Disharmony* (Cambridge, Mass.: Belknap Press of Harvard University Press, 1981).

18. Ibid., p. 11.

19. On the interplay between the themes of conquering and conserving nature in America, see Joseph L. Sax, *Mountains without Handrails* (Ann Arbor: University of Michigan Press, 1980).

20. Upton Sinclair, *The Jungle* (1906) (New York: New American Library, 1980); I. Howe and S. Greenberg, eds., *A Treasury of Yiddish Poetry* (New York: Holt, Rinehart and Winston, 1969), p. 78; Siegfried Giedion, *Mechanization Takes Command* (New York: Oxford University Press, 1955); David F. Noble, *America by Design* (New York: Oxford University Press, 1977).

21. See Lynn White, *Machina ex Deo: Essays in the Dynamism of Western Culture* (Cambridge, Mass.: MIT Press, 1968), esp. p. 79. There is perhaps no more powerful expression of the democratic spirit of voluntary instrumentalism in America than that offered by James Madison when he referred to America as the "Workshop of Liberty [to] the Civilized World." Cited in Adrienne Koch, *Power, Morals and the Founding Fathers: Essays in the Interpretation of the American Enlightenment* (Ithaca, N.Y.: Great Seal Books, Cornell University Press, 1961), p. 128.

22. Cited in Mayr, *Authority, Liberty and Automatic Machinery*, p. 108.

23. Ibid., p. 111.

24. The negative authoritarian use of the machine metaphor to suggest, for

instance, the "party machine" of former Mayor Richard Daley of Chicago shows clear affinities to the nonliberal uses of the machine metaphor in Europe. In his *Reflections on the Revolution in France,* for example, Edmund Burke talks about an executive officer as "a machine, without any sort of deliberative discretion" (p. 317). The machine as a metaphor of authoritarian social or political structures has been as much a possibility as the liberal-democratic appropriation of the term. On the Chicago "party machine," see Edward C. Banfield, *Political Influence* (New York: Free Press, 1961), pp. 237–238.

25. Mayr, *Authority, Liberty and Automatic Machinery,* pp. 139–163.

26. Leo Marx, *The Machine in the Garden: Technology and the Pastoral Ideal in America* (New York: Oxford University Press, 1967), pp. 159–160.

27. Ibid., pp. 164–165.

28. Kassan, *Civilizing the Machine,* pp. 32–33; and Marx, *The Machine in the Garden,* p. 165.

29. Cited in A. Trachtenberg, *Brooklyn Bridge: Fact and Symbol* (Chicago: University of Chicago Press, 1979), p. 123.

30. Cited in Michael Kammen, *A Machine That Would Go of Itself* (New York: Alfred A. Knopf, 1986), pp. 18, 125. On countertendencies to view the constitution or the polity in terms of the organic metaphor, see ibid., pp. 18–23, 189.

31. John Higham, "Hanging Together: Divergent Unities in American History," *The Journal of American History* 61 (June 1974), 19.

32. Ibid.

33. Ibid.

34. On European perplexity concerning American acceptance of the machine, see ibid. See also Hugo Meier, "Technology and Democracy, 1800–1860," *Mississippi Valley History Review* 43 (1957), 631.

35. Higham, "Hanging Together," pp. 19–20.

36. Ibid.

37. Monte A. Clavert, *The Mechanical Engineer in America,* (Baltimore: Johns Hopkins University Press, 1962), p. 226; Higham, "Hanging Together," p. 21; Samuel P. Hays, *Conservation and the Gospel of Efficiency, 1890–1920* (Cambridge, Mass.: Harvard University Press, 1959); Samuel Haber, *Efficiency and Uplift: Scientific Management in the Progressive Era, 1890–1920* (Chicago: University of Chicago Press, 1969); Cecilia Tichi, *Shifting Gears: Technology, Literature, and Culture in Modern America* (Chapel Hill: University of North Carolina Press, 1987), pp. 97–170.

38. Patrick S. Atiyah and Robert S. Summers, *Form and Substance in Anglo-American Law* (Oxford: Clarendon Press, 1987).

39. See Chapter 8.

40. See Kasson, *Civilizing the Machine;* and Marx, *The Machine in the Garden.*

41. See Brian Simon, ed., *The Radical Tradition in Education in Britain* (London: Lawrence and Wishart, 1972). See also Simon's *Studies in the History of Education: Education and the Labour Movement, 1870–1920* (London: Lawrence and Wishart, 1965); Steven Shapin and Barry Barnes, "Science, Nature and Control: Interpreting Mechanics Institutes," *Social Studies of Science* 7 (1977), 31–74.

42. Karl Marx, *Capital,* vol. I (1867), ed. F. Engels (New York: International Publishers, 1967), p. 299.

43. Andrew Ure, *The Philosophy of Manufacture* (1835; London: F. Cass, 1967), p. 423. For Spencer, scientific education and scientific disciplines constituted the means of checking "disastrous meddling" by both the masses and the state. J. Tyndall et al., eds., *The Culture Demanded by Modern Life* (Akron: Werner Company, 1862), pp. 303, 306.

44. Ure, *The Philosophy of Manufacture,* p. 8.

45. Ibid., p. 370. For Karl Marx's opposing view, see his *Grundrisse* (Harmondsworth: Penguin, 1981), p. 705.

46. Shapin and Barnes, "Science, Nature and Control," pp. 49–50.

47. Steven Shapin and Barry Barnes, "Head and Hand," *Oxford Review of Education,* special issue on the history of education (n.d.), 17.

48. The young were supposed to be educated so that they could avoid the degradation of mindless labour and, through becoming familiar with the laws of nature, hold in their "hand one link of a chain which led to God." David Layton, *Science for the People* (London: George Allen, 1973), p. 87.

49. See Richard P. Altick, *The English Common Reader* (Chicago: University of Chicago Press, 1957), pp. 133, 198.

50. Tyndall et al., eds., *The Culture Demanded by Modern Life,* p. 5.

51. Ibid., p. 11.

52. Professor John Tyndall (1862) noted, for instance, that scientific education was valuable precisely because it combined training in both inductive and deductive methods of reasoning. The dualistic liberal appropriation of science as a synthesis of freedom and respect for necessary external constraints is expressed in his recommendation that science be used to inculcate "honest receptivity" and "humble . . . acceptance of what nature reveals" as well as to "penetrate nature's secrets" and "master its law." Tyndall held that a science properly balanced between its links to material culture and to the world of high ideas can both elevate and teach humanity to surrender and be loyal to nature (ibid., pp. 72–79, 85). For William Whewell it is the empirical dimension of science which makes it superior to law as a means of teaching the mind to "escape from illusion." It is because science stresses "inductive reasoning," he thought, that it constitutes the appropriate means to inculcate "mental discipline." See his lecture "On the Scientific History of Education," in ibid., pp. 240–247.

53. Cited in ibid., p. 258.

54. Cited in Martin J. Wiener, *English Culture and the Decline of the Industrial Spirit, 1850–1880* (Cambridge: Cambridge University Press, 1981), p. 13.

55. Ibid., p. 31.

56. Ibid., p. 130.

57. Cited in ibid., p. 39.

58. T. Carlyle, "Signs of the Times" (1829), in his *Critical and Miscellaneous Essays,* vol. II (London: Chapman and Hall, 1905). It was precisely the notion that politics should be limited to "outward things" and should leave the inward domain to the private self that the liberal tradition has advanced at least since John Locke and which science and technology have appeared to support.

59. Ibid., p. 73.

60. Ibid., p. 74.

61. Ibid., p. 67.

62. Herbert L. Sussman, *Victorians and the Machine: Literary Responses to Technology* (Cambridge, Mass.: Harvard University Press, 1968), pp. 27, 132.

63. Ibid., pp. 33, 76–103.

64. Ibid., pp. 88–94. See also Raymond Williams, *The Country and the City* (New York: Oxford University Press, 1975). The scope of nineteenth-century English criticism of machines and machine culture is most instructively illustrated in the person of William Morris, who fused elements from both conservative and socialist criticism of industrialization and machine culture. Morris ascribes great value to the creative faculty and celebrates the cultural superiority of handicraft and art over mechanization. Sussman, *Victorians and the Machine*, pp. 104–134; and Williams, *The Country and the City*, pp. 268, 272–274. Opposed to machine discipline, which he sees as imposing docility and obedience on the "people," Morris endorses folk art as a means of universalizing the norms of "creative action," that is, allowing actors to fulfill and express themselves in their products. Morris represents the attitude which extends elements of the aristocratic ideal of action as "voluntarism," "individuality," "playfulness," appreciation for the beautiful, and "creativity" into the domain of labor, of work through art and craft. His approach represents, therefore, a view of democratization as in some sense the spread of aristocratic values to the lower classes of the English society. On Morris' complex and often contradictory ideas, see also Peter Stansky, *Redesigning the World: William Morris, the 1880's and the Arts and Crafts* (Princeton, N.J.: Princeton University Press, 1985).

65. Arthur Bestor, *The Restoration of Learning* (New York: Alfred A. Knopf, 1955), pp. 34–35.

66. Rush Welter, ed., *American Writings on Popular Education: The Nineteenth Century* (Indianapolis: Bobbs-Merrill, 1971), pp. xx, xxxi, lix.

67. Ibid., pp. lvi–lvii. Hence scientific and technical education have more characteristically been justified in America as a way to enhance active citizen participation, rather than to discipline or control the disruptive potential of the lower classes. American "Victorians," who were concerned, like their English counterparts, with potential disorders caused by "masses" of uneducated and supposedly materialistic citizens, were eventually eclipsed by those who confronted the call for cultivated cultural education and high standards with a powerful defense of native "American" virtues, such as intelligence, activism, plainness, preference for austere vernacular aesthetics, self-reliance, and democratic participation in cultural and political life. Americans who held an elitist conception of leadership, based on pessimism toward the potential competence of the people, were generally a small and, for a long time, defeated minority (ibid., p. lix). Thus, while in England sociocultural features of democratization as the socialization of the lower class into a watered-down version of the aristocratic code has not encouraged the diffusion of science and technology, in America a method of democratization by social diffusion of the capacity for competent, self-disciplined political participation, informed judgment, and effective voluntary action has encouraged the integration of technical knowledge and political values. While in England the status of science and technology has focused attention on issues of freedom and discipline within a hierarchic class structure and on the tensions between the sup-

posedly socially discrete domains of "low" and "high" cultures, impulse and reason, or determinism and voluntarism, in America science and technology have appeared to furnish resources for a universal fusion of freedom and discipline within an antihierarchic and progressively more democratic society.

68. Bestor, *The Restoration of Learning*, pp. 91–92; Merle Curti, *The Social Ideas of American Educators* (Totowa, N.J.: Littlefield, Adams & Co., 1959), pp. 101–138.

69. Huntington, *American Politics*.

70. See Chapter 5.

71. Wiener, *English Culture and the Decline of the Industrial Spirit*, pp. 88–90.

72. Ibid., p. 282.

73. Ibid., p. 287. On attitudes toward nature in English society, see also Keith Thomas, *Man and the Natural World: A History of the Modern Sensibility* (New York: Pantheon Books, 1983), esp. pp. 242–303; Raymond Williams, *The Country and the City* (New York: Oxford University Press, 1975).

74. On the tensions between English traditional conceptions of politics and action and the culture of science and technical modernization, see S. H. Beer, *Modern British Politics* (New York: W. W. Norton, 1982). Similar European-like criticisms of American materialism as a threat to spiritual values and "poetic awareness" have characterized some Latin American intellectuals. See, for instance, Jose Enrique Rodo, *Ariel* (Cambridge: Cambridge University Press, 1967).

7. Social Science and the Liberal-Democratic Problem of Action

1. See, for example, Max Weber, *Max Weber on the Methodology of the Social Sciences*, trans. and intro. E. Shils and H. A. Finch (New York: Free Press, 1949); Seymour Martin Lipset, ed., *Politics and the Social Sciences* (New York: Oxford University Press, 1969); Gunnar Myrdal, *The Political Element in the Development of Economic Theory*, trans. Paul Streeten (New York: Simon and Schuster, 1969); H. Stuart Hughes, *Consciousness and Society: The Reorientation of European Social Thought, 1890–1930* (New York: Vintage Press, 1958); Alvin W. Gouldner, *The Coming Crisis of Western Sociology* (New York: Avon Books, 1970); Charles Frankel, ed., *Controversies and Decisions: The Social Sciences* (New York: Russell Sage Foundation, 1976); Chaim I. Waxman, *The End of Ideology Debate* (New York: Funk & Wagnalls, 1968); A. L. Caplan, ed., *The Sociobiology Debate* (New York: Harper & Row, 1978).

2. William Petty, "The Political Anatomy of Ireland" (1691) in *Economic Writings* 1 (1899), 129. See also the instructive discussion in Theodore M. Porter, *The Rise of Statistical Thinking, 1820–1900* (Princeton, N.J.: Princeton University Press, 1986), p. 19.

3. Porter, *The Rise of Statistical Thinking*, p. 19.

4. Paul F. Lazarsfeld, "Notes on the History of Quantification in Sociology—Trends, Sources and Problems," *Isis* 52 (1961), 270–289, 290, 331. On a different variant of the elitist instrumental view of social knowledge in the case of Leplay, the French pioneer of social empirical research, see esp. pp. 311–332.

5. A theory about the inaccessibility of the real self, about the discrepancy

between the private and the social person, served in France to mitigate the powers of hierarchical authority to control the individual. On Rousseau's struggle with the issue of the transparency of the self, see Jean Starobinski, *J. J. Rousseau: Transparency and Obstruction* (Chicago: University of Chicago Press, 1988).

6. Michael Oakeshott, *Rationalism in Politics and Other Essays* (London: Methuen, 1967), pp. 1–36. A view which separates the authentic and the social person is, of course, not necessarily a feature of conservative political ideology. As I show in Chapter 8, it is characteristic also of atomistic individualism which can support both conservative and liberal modes of collective action. Ralf Dahrendorf, for example, has attempted to integrate the view that "society is the alienated persona of the individual" and that the social man is but "a shadow that has escaped the man to return as his master" with a liberal-democratic conception of order. See Ralf Dahrendorf, *Homo Sociologicus* (London: Routledge & Kegan Paul, 1968), p. 26, for the above citations, and the rest of the book for his nonconservative view of society and politics.

7. For instructive comments on Quetelet's attempts to connect the invisible interior aspects of behavior with its visually manifest aspect, see Lazarsfeld, "Notes on the History of Quantification in Society," 305–309.

8. On the differences between American and European conceptions of self and society, see Geoffrey Hawthorn, *Enlightenment and Despair: A History of Social Theory* (Cambridge: Cambridge University Press, 1987); and Steven Lukes, *Individualism* (Oxford: Basil Blackwell, 1989).

9. See discussion below.

10. Porter, *The Rise of Statistical Thinking*, pp. 149–192.

11. Ibid., pp. 120, 196.

12. Ibid., p. 169.

13. Cited in ibid., p. 163.

14. Ibid., p. 196.

15. See Talcott Parsons, *The Structure of Social Action*, vols. I, II (New York: Free Press, 1937).

16. See, for example, Emile Durkheim, *The Elementary Forms of the Religious Life* (New York: Free Press, 1968); and Emile Durkheim, *Le Suicide: étude de sociologie* (Paris: Alcan, 1951).

17. Max Weber, *Economy and Society*, eds. Guenther Roth and Claus Wittich (New York: Bedminster Press, 1968); and Weber, *Max Weber on the Methodology of the Social Sciences*.

18. Emile Durkheim, *The Rules of Sociological Method* (1885) (New York: Free Press, 1964), p. 106.

19. Ibid., p. 141.

20. Ibid., p. 28.

21. Ibid., p. 106.

22. See Edward Tiryakian, *Sociologism and Existentialism* (Englewood Cliffs, N.J.: Prentice-Hall, 1962), pp. 54–60. On Durkheim's idea of the individual as a product of the state, see also Emile Durkheim, *Professional Ethics and Civic Morals*, trans. Cornelia Brookfield (London: Routledge & Kegan Paul, 1957), pp. 55–64.

23. Emile Durkheim, *Pragmatism and Sociology*, trans. J. C. Whitehouse, ed.

J. B. Allcock (Cambridge: Cambridge University Press, 1983) (oral delivery 1913–14), esp. pp. 86–98.

24. Ibid., pp. 88–91; Emile Durkheim, *Sociology and Philosophy,* trans. D. F. Pocock (Glencoe: Free Press, 1953), pp. 96–97.

25. Durkheim, *The Rules of Sociological Method,* p. 143.

26. Durkheim, *Pragmatism and Sociology,* p. 80.

27. Durkheim, *Sociology and Philosophy,* p. 57.

28. Durkheim, *Professional Ethics and Civic Morals,* p. 91.

29. Timothy V. Kaufman-Osborn, "Modernity's Myth of Facts: Emile Durkheim and the Politics of Knowledge," *Theory and Society* 17 (1988), 121–147.

30. Durkheim, *Professional Ethics and Civic Morals,* pp. 98–109.

31. Ibid., p. 75.

32. Durkheim, *Sociology and Philosophy,* p. 65.

33. On the closeness between aspects of Weberian sociology and American liberal-democratic values, see Edward Tiryakian, "Neither Marx nor Durkheim . . . Perhaps Weber," *American Journal of Sociology* 81 (1975), 1–33.

34. Weber, *Economy and Society,* vol. I, p. 14.

35. Ibid., p. 4.

36. Ibid., p. 15.

37. Max Weber, "Politics as a Vocation," in *From Max Weber Essays in Sociology,* eds. H. H. Gerth and C. Wright Mills (New York: Oxford University Press, 1958), pp. 77–128.

38. Weber, *Economy and Society,* vol. I, p. 5.

39. Ibid., p. 6.

40. On some of the key weaknesses of rational choice accounts of human behavior from a modern perspective, see Jon Elster, "The Nature and Scope of Rational Choice Explanation," *Science in Reflection,* The Israel Colloquium: Studies in History, Philosophy and Sociology of Science, vol. 3, ed. E. Ullmann-Margalit (Dordrecht: Kluwer, 1988), pp. 51–65.

41. See Max Weber, "Objectivity in Social Science and Social Policy," in *Max Weber on the Methodology of the Social Sciences;* and Max Weber, *The Protestant Ethic and the Spirit of Capitalism,* trans. T. Parsons, intro. A. Giddens (New York: Charles Scribner & Son, 1978), p. 183.

42. Weber, "Politics as a Vocation," esp. pp. 118–128.

43. Quoted in W. Mommsen, "Max Weber's Political Sociology and His Philosophy of World History," *International Social Science Journal* 17 (1965), 25.

44. See Jurgen Habermas' pertinent discussion in his *The Theory of Communicative Action,* vol. I, trans. T. McCarthy (Boston: Beacon Press, 1981), pp. 243–271.

45. Dennis Wrong, "Max Weber and Contemporary Sociology," in *Max Weber's Political Sociology,* eds. R. M. Glassman and V. Murvar (Westport, Conn.: Greenwood Press, 1984), p. 76.

46. Tiryakian, "Neither Marx nor Durkheim," 1–33.

47. Leonard Krieger, *The German Idea of Freedom* (Chicago: University of Chicago Press, 1972); and Ralf Dahrendorf, *Society and Democracy in Germany* (Garden City, N.Y.: Doubleday, 1969). The contemporary liberal-democratic

ideological import of Weberian attempts to conceptualize social action in terms of voluntary individual actions are particularly evident when his view is juxtaposed with the kind of dichotomies between self and society one can find in the works of German thinkers such as Wilhelm Von Humboldt, Goethe, Shopenhauer, Nietzsche, and Thomas Mann. See W. H. Bruford, *The German Tradition of Self-Cultivation: "Bildung" from Humboldt to Thomas Mann* (Cambridge: Cambridge University Press, 1975); and Thomas Mann, *Reflections of a Nonpolitical Man,* trans. and intro. Walter Morris (New York: Frederick Ungar Publishing Co., 1983).

48. See Morton G. White, *Social Thought in America: The Revolt against Formalism* (Boston: Beacon Press, 1952); Parsons, *The Structure of Social Action;* and H. Stuart Hughes, *Consciousness and Society.*

49. Thomas L. Haskell, *The Emergence of Professional Social Science: The American Social Science Association and the Nineteenth-Century Crisis of Authority* (Urbana: University of Illinois Press, 1977), p. 9; Hawthorn, *Enlightenment and Despair,* pp. 191–216.

50. Haskell, *The Emergence of Professional Social Science,* p. 14.

51. Ibid., pp. 24–47.

52. Such categories of social action did not always apply equally to all Americans. See, for instance, Gunnar Myrdal, *An American Dilemma: The Negro Problem and Modern Democracy* (1944; New York: Harper and Row, 1969).

53. S. N. Eisenstadt with M. Curelaru, *The Form of Sociology: Paradigms and Crises* (New York: John Wiley and Sons, 1976), p. 105; Parsons, *The Structure of Social Action,* vol. II, p. 18; T. Parsons, "Unity and Diversity in Modern Intellectual Disciplines," *Daedalus* 94 (1965), 39–65.

54. L. A. Coser, "Merton's Uses of the European Sociological Tradition," in *The Idea of Social Structure,* ed. L. A. Coser (New York: Harcourt Brace Jovanovich, 1975), p. 98.

55. Rose Laub Coser, "The Complexity of Roles as a Seedbed of Individual Autonomy," in ibid., p. 239.

56. D. N. Levine, E. B. Carter, and E. M. Gorman, "Simmel's Influence on American Sociology I," *American Journal of Sociology* 81 (January 1976), 813–845, and "II," *American Journal of Sociology* 81 (March 1976), 1112–32. See also Donald N. Levine, *Simmel and Parsons* (1952; New York: Arno Press NYT, 1980).

57. T. C. Schelling, *The Strategy of Conflict* (Cambridge: Harvard University Press, 1960); T. S. Coleman, *Power and the Structure of Society* (New York: W. W. Norton, 1974); A. Downs, *An Economic Theory of Democracy* (New York: Harper, 1957); J. C. Harsanyi, "A Simplified Bargaining Model for the n-Person Cooperative Game," *International Economic Review* 4 (1963), 194–220.

58. S. N. Eisenstadt, *The Form of Sociology* (New York: J. Wiley, 1976), pp. 194–276.

59. Cited in Haskell, *The Emergence of Professional Social Science,* p. 251.

60. See David Truman, *The Government Process* (New York: Knopf, 1958); Robert A. Dahl, *Pluralist Democracy in the United States* (Chicago: Rand McNally & Co., 1967); H. Simon, "Political Research: The Decision Making Framework," in *Varieties of Political Theory,* ed. David Easton (Englewood

Cliffs, N.J.: Prentice-Hall, 1966); Herbert A. Simon, "Human Nature in Politics: The Dialogue of Psychology with Political Science," *American Political Science Review* 79 (1985), 293–304; Anthony Downs, *An Economic Theory of Democracy* (New York: Harper and Row, 1957); and, for some historical observations, Donald Moon, "The Logic of Political Inquiry," in *Handbook of Political Science*, vol. I, eds. Fred I. Greenstein and Nelson W. Polsky (Reading, Mass.: Addison-Wesley, 1975), pp. 131–228.

61. I had useful conversations on this point with Ed Tiryakian in 1985. See also the discussion of "citizen competence" and citizen's influence in the formation of general policy in Gabriel Almond and Sidney Verba, *Civic Culture Political Attitudes and Democracy in Five Nations* (Princeton: Princeton University Press, 1963), pp. 168–207.

62. Bernard Crick, *The American Science of Politics* (Berkeley: University of California Press, 1959).

63. Durkheim, *Pragmatism and Sociology*, p. 48.

64. See William James, *Pragmatism* (New York: New American Library, 1974), p. 55; and R. J. Bernstein, *Praxis and Action* (Philadelphia: University of Pennsylvania Press, 1971), pp. 181–190.

65. James, *Pragmatism*, p. 162.

66. Ibid., p. 243; and William James, *Principles of Psychology*, vol. I (Cambridge, Mass.: Harvard University Press, 1981), p. 350.

67. James on Spencer, cited in Richard Hofstadter, *Social Darwinism in American Social Thought* (1903; Boston: Beacon Press, 1955), pp. 128–129.

68. William James, *Collected Essays and Reviews* (New York: Longmans, Green, 1920), p. 26.

69. Richard Rorty, *Consequences of Pragmatism* (Minneapolis: University of Minnesota Press, 1982), p. 162.

70. James, *Principles of Psychology*, vol. I, p. 350. For a very different English perspective, see John Tyndall, "On the Study of Physics," in J. Tyndall et al., *The Culture Demanded by Modern Life*, intro. E. L. Youmans (Akron: Werner Company, 1862), pp. 22–24. See also Steven Shapin and Barry Barnes, "Head and Hand: Rhetorical Resources in British Pedagogical Writings, 1850," *Oxford Review of Education*, ed. C. Webster (undated reprint).

71. *John Dewey's Philosophy*, ed. Joseph Ratner (New York: Modern Library, 1939), p. 327.

72. Rorty, *Consequences of Pragmatism*, pp. 82, 86–87.

73. John Dewey, *The Quest for Certainty* (1929; New York: Putnam's and Sons, 1960), pp. 204, 211, 215.

74. White, *The Revolt against Formalism*, pp. 44–62.

75. On these differences see P. S. Atiyah and Robert S. Summers, *Form and Substance in Anglo-American Law: A Comparative Study of Legal Reasoning, Legal Theory, and Legal Institutions* (Oxford: Clarendon Press, 1987).

76. Alexis de Tocqueville, *Democracy in America*, vol. II (New York: Vintage, 1955), p. 4.

77. John Dewey, *Liberalism and Social Action* (1935; New York: Perigee Books, 1980), p. 39.

78. Ibid., pp. 44–47.

326 Notes to Pages 188–195

79. Ibid., p. 55.

80. Ibid., p. 57.

81. Ibid., p. 73.

82. Ibid., pp. 91–92.

83. Ratner, *John Dewey's Philosophy*, p. 360.

84. Fredrich Hayek, *The Road to Serfdom* (1944; Chicago: University of Chicago Press, 1956), pp. 205–206.

85. Dewey, *Liberalism and Social Action*, pp. 41–42.

86. George Herbert Mead, *On Social Psychology*, ed. A. Strauss (Chicago: University of Chicago Press, 1964), pp. 216–228, 263–264.

87. Ibid., pp. 31, 234–235, 280–281.

88. Ibid., p. 32.

89. Ibid., pp. 346–347.

90. Durkheim, *Pragmatism and Sociology*, p. 2.

91. Ibid., p. 1.

92. Ibid.

93. Ibid., p. 74.

94. Ibid., p. 68.

95. Ibid., pp. 68, 75, 76.

96. Ibid., p. 67.

97. D. P. Walker, *The Decline of Hell: Seventeenth-Century Discussions of Eternal Torment* (Chicago: University of Chicago Press, 1964).

98. Durkheim, *Pragmatism and Sociology*, pp. 9, 27, 32, 102.

99. Ibid., pp. 3–4. It is instructive to note how from Durkheim's perspective pragmatism appears to endanger the spectator's theory of knowledge and the concommitant commitment to attestive visual orientations toward the social world.

100. Ibid., pp. 25–26.

101. Ibid., p. 88.

102. Emile Durkheim, *Education and Sociology*, trans. and intro. S. D. Fox (1911; Glencoe, Ill.: Free Press, 1956), p. 123.

103. John Dewey, *The Child and the Curriculum, and School and Society*, intro. L. Carmichael (1900; Chicago: University of Chicago Press, 1956), p. 9.

104. Ibid., pp. 112–113.

105. Durkheim, *Education and Sociology*, p. 127.

106. Ibid., pp. 89–90.

107. Ibid., p. 79.

108. Robert K. Merton, *The Sociology of Science*, ed. N. W. Storer (1942; Chicago: University of Chicago Press, 1973), p. 269.

109. Ibid., pp. 222–223.

110. Talcott Parsons and Gerald Platt, *The American University* (Cambridge, Mass.: Harvard University Press, 1973), p. 188.

111. Ibid., p. 166.

112. Ibid., p. 199.

113. Parsons and Platt believe that survey data indeed confirm that college educated citizens show greater disposition for democratic orientations as distrust of hierarchical authority (ibid., pp. 209–210).

114. Samuel P. Huntington, "One Soul at a Time: Political Science and Political Reform," *American Political Science Review* 82 (March 1988), 6–7. On the claim about the historical affinities between the rise of modern political science and the diffusion of liberal-democratic political values, such as moderation, public enlightenment, public opinion, liberty, and tolerance, see James Farr, "Political Science and the Enlightenment of Enthusiasm," ibid., 51–69.

115. On the perceived role of science in checking irrational social forces, see Joseph Ben-David, *The Scientist's Role in Society* (Englewood Cliffs, N.J.: Prentice-Hall, 1971); and A. O. Hirschman, *The Passions and the Interests: Political Argument for Capitalism before Its Triumph* (Princeton, N.J.: Princeton University Press, 1977).

116. For a very instructive illustration of the shift from the early hopes to the later skepticism with regard to the reformative functions of science in the democratic state, compare Don K. Price's *The Scientific Estate* (Cambridge, Mass.: Harvard University Press, 1965) with his *America's Unwritten Constitution* (Baton Rouge: Louisiana State University, 1983).

8. Persons, Facts, Rules, and the Production of Public Action in Liberal-Democratic America

1. M. Brewster Smith, "The Metaphorical Basis of Selfhood," in *Culture and Self: Asian and Western Perspectives*, eds. Anthony J. Marsella, George Devos, and Francis L. K. Hsu (New York: Tavistock Publications, 1985), pp. 56–88.

2. J. R. Pitts, "Continuity and Change in Bourgeois France," in *In Search of France*, eds. Stanley Hoffmann et al. (Cambridge, Mass.: Harvard University Press, 1963), pp. 239–243. Pitts traces French formalism, the authority of deductive chains of reasoning, the insistence on the power of the center, the acceptability of hierarchy, and the view of individuality as one's position in the hierarchy to the influences of French Catholicism. See also Michel Crozier, *The Bureaucratic Phenomenon* (Chicago: University of Chicago Press, 1964); W. R. Schonfeld, *Obedience and Revolt: French Behavior toward Authority* (Beverly Hills: Sage Publications, 1976), pp. 176–182.

3. Pitts, "Continuity and Change," pp. 239–243.

4. Ibid., p. 242.

5. It is instructive to note in this connection a characteristic French tendency to interpret the mechanization of production as a sign of a loss of human will, a development often associated with the "corruptive" effects of American influences on European and particularly French society. Laurence Wylie, "Social Change at Grass Roots," in *In Search of France*, eds. Hoffmann et al., p. 207.

6. Crozier, *The Bureaucratic Phenomenon*, p. 187.

7. Wylie, "Social Change at Grass Roots," pp. 202–203.

8. Stanley Hoffmann, "The French Political Community," in *In Search of France*, eds. Hoffmann et al., p. 9.

9. Such tensions are the context of Rousseau's dilemma of reconciling freedom and authority without resorting to intermediate bodies between the individual citizen and the state; they also inform his theory of education which enlists nature to the task of preparing the young to resist the deauthenticating influences

328 **Notes to Pages 200–203**

of society once they enter social relations; they underlie the discrepancies between legalism and individualism in the thought of Montesquieu, are at the root of the differences between Emile Durkheim and Louis Tard, and are very much discernible in the problematic attempts of a modern French thinker like Sartre to integrate existentialism, with its stress on the exposed solitary individual, and Marxist ideas of the moral community.

10. M. Fried, *Absorption and Theatricality* (Berkeley: University of California Press, 1980); Jean Starobinski, *J. J. Rousseau: Transparency and Obstruction* (Chicago: University of Chicago Press, 1988).

11. N. Wahl, "The French System," in *Patterns of Government,* eds. S. Beer and Adam Ulam (New York: Random House, 1962), pp. 278–279.

12. Joseph L. Sax, *Mountains without Handrails: Reflections on the National Parks* (Ann Arbor: University of Michigan Press, 1980).

13. Wylie, "Social Change at Grass Roots," p. 204.

14. Sacvan Bercovitch, "Rites of Assent: Rhetoric, Ritual, and the Ideology of the American Consensus," in *The American Self,* ed. Sam B. Girgus (Albuquerque: University of New Mexico Press, 1981), p. 9.

15. Sacvan Bercovitch, *The Puritan Origins of the American Self* (New Haven, Conn.: Yale University Press, 1972), p. 136.

16. Ralph Waldo Emerson, *Representative Man* (Boston: Houghton Mifflin, 1903).

17. Bercovitch, *Puritan Origins,* pp. 174–175.

18. Ibid., p. 176.

19. Bercovitch, "Rites of Assent," pp. 11, 13, 32.

20. J.-J. Rousseau, "The First Discourse," in *The First and Second Discourses,* ed. Roger D. Master (New York: St. Martin's Press, 1964), pp. 37–38.

21. Judith Shklar, *Ordinary Vices* (Cambridge, Mass.: Belknap Press of Harvard University Press, 1984), p. 85.

22. S. Alpers, *The Art of Describing* (Chicago: University of Chicago Press, 1983), pp. 72–74.

23. Commenting on America, Octavio Paz suggests that there is something in the "overlapping between science and Puritan morality [which] permits without recourse to direct coercion, the imposition of rules that condemn all singularities." Octavio Paz, "Eroticism and Gastrosophy," *Daedalus* 101 (Fall 1972), 77. I shall argue later that in late-twentieth-century America this predisposition has taken the peculiar and somewhat self-contradictory form of a trend toward the "democratization of uniqueness." Yaron Ezrahi, "Science and Utopia in Late 20th Century Puralist Democracy," in *Nineteen Eighty-Four: Science between Utopia and Dystopia: Sociology of the Sciences,* eds. E. Mendelsohn and H. Nowotny, vol. VIII (Dordrecht: D. Reidel, 1984), pp. 273–290, 283.

24. In the same light, Joseph Priestley was celebrated as an example of an amateur who effortlessly discovers great things. See S. Schaffer, "Priestley's Questions: An Historiographic Survey," *History of Science* 22 (1984), 151–183.

25. See my discussion in Chapters 2 and 10; and Don K. Price, *The Scientific Estate* (Cambridge, Mass.: Belknap Press of Harvard University Press, 1965), pp. 71–79.

26. Gordon S. Wood, "Conspiracy and the Paranoid Style: Causality and

Deceit in the Eighteenth Century," *The William and Mary Quarterly*, 3rd ser., 39 (July 1982), 401–441.

27. Ibid., p. 409.

28. James Sterling Young, *The Washington Community, 1800–1828* (New York: Columbia University Press, 1966), p. 59.

29. Ibid., pp. 63, 113, 207.

30. Wood, "Conspiracy and the Paranoid Style," 409–413.

31. Ibid., 413–415.

32. Ibid., 418.

33. A quote from Alexander Hamilton (*Federalist* 27) adopted by James Sterling Young in his description of the government throughout the Jeffersonian era, in Young, *The Washington Community*, p. 33.

34. As Judith Shklar notes, according to Montesquieu it was impossible to think "that the good man and the good citizen should ever be the same." See Shklar, *Ordinary Vices*, p. 33.

35. Ralph Nader turned such analysis of the evident factual aspects of the behavior of business firms into a potent technique of exposing the discrepancies between their manifest objectives and their actual operations. See Ralph Nader, *Unsafe at Any Speed* (New York: Simon and Schuster, 1966).

36. For his comparative notes on American and European concepts of authenticity and sincerity, see Lionel Trilling, *On Authenticity* (Cambridge, Mass.: Harvard University Press, 1972), esp. pp. 64–65, 113.

37. Benjamin Franklin, "Autobiography," in *A Benjamin Franklin Reader*, ed. Nathan G. Goodman (New York: Thomas Crowell Co., 1921); Shklar, *Ordinary Vices*, p. 24.

38. Ralph Waldo Emerson, "Self Reliance," in *The Collected Works of Ralph Waldo Emerson*, vol. II, *Essays*, 1st ser. (Cambridge, Mass.: Belknap Press of Harvard University Press, 1979), p. 34.

39. Ralph Waldo Emerson, "Nature," in *Selections from Ralph Waldo Emerson*, ed. S. E. Whicher (Boston: Houghton Mifflin, 1957), p. 41.

40. Quentin Anderson, "John Dewey's American Democrat," *Daedalus* 108 (Summer 1979), 146.

41. See W. H. Bruford, *The German Tradition of Self-Cultivation: "Bildung" from Humboldt to Thomas Mann* (Cambridge: Cambridge University Press, 1975); Ralf Dahrendorf, *Society and Democracy in Germany* (Garden City: Doubleday, 1969), p. 302. Oswald Spengler observed, in reference to the British Parliament, "with us [the Germans] Parliamentarism will always be a conglomeration of externalities." See Oswald Spengler, *Selected Essays*, trans. D. O. White (Chicago: Henry Regmers, 1967), pp. 12, 83.

42. Dahrendorf, *Society and Democracy*, p. 343; and L. Dumont, *Essays on Individualism* (Chicago: University of Chicago Press, 1986), pp. 134, 139, 146, 153.

43. Leonard Krieger, *The German Idea of Freedom* (Chicago: University of Chicago Press, 1972), pp. 125, 133, 177, 188. See also Thomas Mann, *Reflections of a Nonpolitical Man* (1918) trans. and intro. Walter Morris (New York: Frederick Unger, 1983).

44. Dahrendorf, *Society and Democracy*, p. 127.

45. Ibid., pp. 156–57. On freedom as an aesthetic idea in Schiller's thought, see also the essay by Patrick Gardiner, "Freedom as an Aesthetic Idea," in *The Idea of Freedom*, Essays in Honour of Isaiah Berlin, ed. Alan Ryan (Oxford: Oxford University Press, 1979), pp. 27–39. While the modernization of Western societies like England, France, and the United States rested upon, among other things, the disenchantment of the world as an objective external constraint on human aspirations, in Germany a myth of an external reality that can resist the will was not as strong and culturally available to counter the myth of a free will that can triumph over matter without assuming the discipline imposed by empirical scientific knowledge.

46. Walter Benjamin, "Karl Kraus," in *Reflections*, ed. P. Demetz (New York: Harcourt Brace Jovanovich, 1978), p. 272.

47. On the persistence of aristocratic codes of elite leadership, see Samuel H. Beer, *Modern British Politics* (New York: Norton, 1982), pp. 414–415.

48. A misunderstanding of the unique integration of technology and liberal-democratic political values in America has led observers such as Jacques Ellul to misinterpret the place and the effects of science and technology in the American polity as well as, more generally, in the modern liberal-democratic state. In order to be understood, American political instrumentalism must be regarded as reflecting more than the influence of materialistic values and the impact of science and technology on American politics. First and foremost it is a central American ideological-political response to the liberal-democratic problem of action and the need to reconcile individualism, voluntaristic theories of action, and the imperatives of public order. In America, therefore, the instrumentalization of public action has not emerged so much as a strategy of centralizing power, a threat to liberal-democratic principles, as to serve a liberal-democratic commitment to the nonarbitrary and accountable exercise of power.

49. Gordon S. Wood, *The Creation of the American Republic, 1776–1787* (New York: W. W. Norton, 1972), p. 529.

50. Ibid., p. 604.

51. P. S. Atiyah and Robert S. Summers, *Form and Substance in Anglo-American Law: A Comparative Study of Legal Reasoning, Legal Theory, and Legal Institutions* (Oxford: Clarendon Press, 1987), p. 67.

52. Ibid., p. 38.

53. Ibid., pp. 1, 15, 42, 148, 233, 251.

54. Ibid., pp. 223–226, 148.

55. John W. Thibaut and Laurens Walker, eds., *Procedural Justice: A Psychological Analysis* (New York: John Wiley and Sons, 1975), pp. 22–27, 28–40.

56. Ibid., p. 77.

57. Price, *The Scientific Estate*, p. 27.

58. Edward A. Shils, *The Torment of Secrecy* (Glencoe, Ill.: Free Press, 1956), pp. 37–57.

59. Atiyah and Summers, *Form and Substance in Anglo-American Law*, pp. 96–101.

60. Jerome Frank, *Law and the Modern Mind* (Garden City, N.Y.: Anchor Books, 1963), p. x.

61. Robert S. Summers, *Instrumentalism and American Legal Theory* (Ithaca, N.Y.: Cornell University Press, 1982), p. 19.

62. Ibid., p. 23.

63. Ibid., pp. 193–208.

64. Cited in ibid., p. 91.

65. Cited in Edward A. Purcell, *The Crisis of Democratic Theory: Scientific Naturalism and the Problem of Value* (Lexington: University Press of Kentucky, 1973), p. 82. The importance of legal instrumentalism has been linked also with the growing volume and weight of statutes devised as means of solving social problems and responding to changing circumstances. Guido Calabresi, *A Common Law for the Age of Statutes* (Cambridge, Mass.: Harvard University Press, 1982), pp. 1–15.

66. Purcell, *The Crisis of Democratic Theory*, p. 82.

67. Guido Calabresi, *Costs of Accidents* (New Haven, Conn.: Yale University Press, 1970); Richard A. Posner, *Economic Analysis of Law* (Boston: Little, Brown, 1972).

68. See Arthur Allen Leff, "Economic Analysis of Law: Some Realism," *Virginia Law Review* 60 (March 1976), 451.

69. Posner, *Economic Analysis of Law*, pp. 4–5.

70. Oliver Wendell Holmes, *Collected Legal Papers* (New York: Harcourt, Brace, 1921), p. 139.

71. Atiyah and Summers, *Form and Substance in Anglo-American Law*, p. 4.

72. In other professional contexts such as medicine, for example, one finds similar differences. English doctors enjoy a degree of authority in the exercise of professional judgment which their American counterparts do not share. Guido Calabresi, *Tragic Choices* (New York: W. W. Norton, 1978), pp. 184–186. See also Paul Starr's comparison of English and American physicians and his distinction between "status profession" and "occupational profession" in his *The Social Transformation of American Medicine* (New York: Basic Books, 1982), pp. 37–47.

73. Alan Trachtenberg, *The Incorporation of America: Culture and Society in the Gilded Age* (New York: Hill and Wang, 1982), p. 180.

74. I decided to develop this point in response to an astute comment by an anonymous reader of the manuscript who noted the tensions between the open adversarial testing of facts and the authority of science in American judicial and political contexts. I am grateful to him or her for raising this important question.

75. On the concept of evidence implied in the American jury system, see H. Kalven and H. Zeisel, *The American Jury* (Chicago: University of Chicago Press, 1966), esp. pp. 121–190. See also Calabresi, *Tragic Choices; Technical Information for Congress*, Report to the Subcommittee on Science, Research and Development of the House Committee on Science and Astronautics, 92nd Cong. (Washington: U.S. Government Printing Office, 1971).

76. Rush Welter, *Popular Education and Democratic Thought in America* (New York: Columbia University Press, 1964). See also Y. Ezrahi, "The Authority of Science in Politics," in *Science and Values*, eds. A. Thackray and E. Mendelsohn (New York: Humanities Press, 1974), pp. 215–251.

77. Holmes, *Collected Legal Papers,* p. 238.

78. Lawrence Friedman, *The Legal System: A Social Science Perspective* (New York: Russell Sage Foundation, 1975), pp. 215–216.

79. On the pertinent characteristics of Roman and natural law, see A. P. D'Entrèves, *Natural Law* (New York: Harper Torchbooks, 1965), p. 71; and Judith Shklar, *Legalism: Law, Morals, and Political Trials* (Cambridge, Mass.: Harvard University Press, 1986), pp. 38, 63, 65.

9. Science and the Legitimation of Centralized Political Powers in American Democracy

1. Samuel P. Huntington, *American Politics: The Promise of Disharmony* (Cambridge, Mass.: Belknap Press of Harvard University Press, 1981).

2. James Sterling Young, *The Washington Community, 1800–1828* (New York: Columbia University Press, 1966), p. 207.

3. Thomas E. Cronin, "The Swelling of the Presidency," in *Classic Readings in American Politics,* eds. P. S. Nivola and D. H. Rosenbloom (New York: St. Martin's Press, 1986), pp. 413–426.

4. James Q. Wilson, "The Rise of the Bureaucratic State," in ibid., pp. 427–447.

5. Edward S. Corwin, *The President: Office and Powers, 1787–1957* (New York: New York University Press, 1957), pp. 294.

6. Huntington, *The Promise of Disharmony,* p. 75.

7. Michel Crozier, *The Bureaucratic Phenomenon* (Chicago: University of Chicago Press, 1964).

8. Robert H. Wiebe, *The Search for Order, 1877–1920* (New York: Hill and Wang, 1962).

9. Daniel Calhoun, *The Intelligence of a People* (Princeton, N.J.: Princeton University Press, 1923), pp. 241–255, 283–322.

10. John Higham, "Hanging Together: Divergent Unities in American History," *The Journal of American History* 61 (June 1924), 19–26.

11. David F. Nobel, *America by Design: Science, Technology and the Rise of Corporate Capitalism* (Oxford: Oxford University Press, 1977).

12. Edward A. Purcell, *The Crisis of Democratic Theory: Scientific Naturalism and the Problem of Value* (Lexington: University of Kentucky Press, 1973), p. 10.

13. Purcell, *The Crisis of Democratic Theory,* pp. 11–16.

14. Samuel Haber, *Efficiency and Uplift: Scientific Management in the Progressive Era, 1890–1920* (Chicago: University of Chicago Press, 1964).

15. Samuel P. Hays, *Conservation and the Gospel of Efficiency, 1890–1920* (Cambridge, Mass.: Harvard University Press, 1959).

16. Thomas L. Haskell, *The Emergence of Professional Social Science* (Urbana: University of Illinois Press, 1922), pp. 121–123.

17. Alan Trachtenberg, *The Incorporation of America: Culture and Society in the Gilded Age* (New York: Hill and Wang, 1982), pp. 101–139.

18. See my Chapter 5 and ibid., pp. 208–234.

19. Ronald C. Tobey, *The American Ideology of National Science, 1919–1930* (Pittsburgh: University of Pittsburgh Press, 1971).

20. Ibid., pp. 1–20, 199–232.

21. See Don K. Price, *The Scientific Estate* (Cambridge, Mass.: Harvard University Press, 1965); and Daniel Greenberg, *The Politics of American Science* (Harmondsworth: Penguin, 1969).

22. On this conception of the socio-organizational character of science, see Michael Polanyi, "The Republic of Science," *Minerva* 1 (Autumn 1962), 54–73.

23. See Robert K. Merton, *The Sociology of Science*, ed. and intro. Norman W. Storer (Chicago: University of Chicago Press, 1973), pp. 228–342.

24. Herbert D. Croly, *The Promise of American Life* (New York: Macmillan, 1909). See also David W. Levy, *Herbert Croly of the "New Republic": The Life and Thought of an American Progressive* (Princeton, N.J.: Princeton University Press, 1985).

25. Croly, *The Promise of American Life*, p. 207.

26. Ibid., p. 418.

27. Ibid., pp. 417, 418, 431.

28. Ibid., p. 418.

29. See R. Steel, *Walter Lippmann and the American Century* (New York: Vintage Books, 1980), p. 29. See also W. Lippmann, *Drift and Mastery* (New York: N. Kennerley, 1914). On the liberal consensus and the notion that in America a sense of "an irreversible ethics made all problems technical," see Louis Hartz, *The Liberal Tradition in America* (New York: Harcourt, Brace & World, 1955), pp. 221–222.

30. Haber, *Efficiency and Uplift*, pp. 52–93.

31. Hays, *Conservation and the Gospel of Efficiency*, p. 136.

32. On this tension and its mitigation, see Rush Welter, *Education and Democracy in America* (New York: Columbia University Press, 1964), pp. 258–259.

33. Keith M. Baker, *Condorcet: From Natural Philosophy to Social Mathematics* (Chicago: University of Chicago Press, 1975); Charles C. Gillispie, "Probability and Politics: Laplace, Condorcet and Turgot," *Proceedings of the American Philosophical Society* 116 (February 1972), 1–20; Bernard Cazes, "Condorcet's True Paradox or the Liberal Transformed into Social Engineer," *Daedalus* 105 (Winter 1976), 47–58.

34. Barry D. Karl, *Charles E. Merriam and the Study of Politics* (Chicago: University of Chicago Press, 1974), p. 255.

35. Charles E. Merriam, *New Aspects of Politics*, 2nd ed. (Chicago: University of Chicago Press, 1931), p. 242.

36. Ibid., p. viii.

37. Ibid., p. xxx.

38. Ibid., pp. 17–18.

39. Karl, *Charles E. Merriam*, p. 36.

40. Ibid., p. 121.

41. Haber, *Efficiency and Uplift*, pp. 103–104. See also Frank J. Goodnow, *Politics and Administration: A Study in Government* (New York: Macmillan, 1900).

42. Merriam, *New Aspects of Politics*, pp. 22–23.

43. Albert A. Somit and Joseph Tonnenhous, *American Political Science: A Profile of a Discipline* (New York: Atherton Press, 1964); and Haskell, *The Emergence of Professional Social Science*.

44. Karl, *Charles E. Merriam*, pp. 235–243; Harold Orlans, "Academic Social Scientists and the Presidency: From Wilson to Nixon," *Minerva* 24 (Summer-Autumn 1986), 172–204.

45. E. G. Catlin, *The Science and Method of Politics* (New York: Alfred Knopf, 1927).

46. Karl Popper, *The Poverty of Historicism* (1944; London: Routledge & Kegan Paul, 1963); and Karl Popper, *The Open Society and Its Enemies*, vols. I, II (1945; London: Routledge & Kegan Paul, 1966).

47. Catlin, *The Science and Method of Politics*, p. 295.

48. F. Hayek, *The Counter Revolution of Science* (Glencoe: Free Press, 1952), p. 52.

49. Purcell, *The Crisis of Democratic Theory*, pp. 117–158.

50. Louis Hartz, *The Liberal Tradition in America* (New York: Harcourt, Brace, 1955).

51. Jan Tinbergen, *Statistical Testing of Business Cycle Theories* (Geneva: League of Nations Economic Intelligence Service, 1939).

52. Simon Kuznets, *National Income and Its Composition, 1919–1938,* no. 4 (New York: National Bureau of Economic Research, 1941).

53. Vilfredo Pareto, *Cours d'économie politique* (Paris, 1896–97) and A. C. Pigou, *Wealth and Welfare* (1920; London: Macmillan, 1960).

54. Wassily Leontief, *The Structure of the American Economy, 1919–1929,* 2nd ed. (New York: Oxford University Press, 1951).

55. John Maynard Keynes, *The General Theory of Employment, Interest and Money* (1936; London: Macmillan, 1973).

56. Milo Keynes, ed., *Essays on John Maynard Keynes* (Cambridge: Cambridge University Press, 1975); Michael Stewart, *Keynes and After* (Harmondsworth: Pelican, 1962); D. E. Moggridge, *John Maynard Keynes* (Harmondsworth: Penguin, 1976).

57. Edward S. Flash, Jr., *Economic Advice and Presidential Leadership* (New York: Columbia University Press, 1965), p. vii.

58. Charles J. Hitch and Roland N. McKean, eds., *The Economics of Defense in the Nuclear Age* (Cambridge, Mass.: Harvard University Press, 1961). See also R. N. McKean, "Economics of Defense," in *The International Encyclopedia of the Social Sciences,* ed. David L. Sills, vol. IV (New York: Free Press, 1977), pp. 485–491.

59. Hitch and McKean, eds., *The Economics of Defense in the Nuclear Age,* p. 2.

60. Bernard Brodie, "The Scientific Strategists," in *Science and National Public Policy Making,* eds. Robert Gilpin and Christopher Wright (New York: Columbia University Press, 1964), p. 254.

61. R. C. Wood, "The Rise of an Apolitical Elite," in ibid., pp. 41–72. This assertion was reinforced at the time by the culmination of a process which began in the late nineteenth century with the establishment of scientific bureaus, such as

the Geological Survey (1879), the Weather Bureau (1890), the National Bureau of Standards (1901), and the Food and Drug Administration (1906), and was accelerated again during World War II with the establishment of the Institute of Health and after with the establishment of the Atomic Energy Commission and the Council of Economic Advisers (1946), the President's Science Advisory Committee (1951), the National Aeronautics and Space Administration (1958), and the Office of Science and Technology (1962). On these developments see Hunter A. Dupree, *Science in the Federal Government* (Cambridge, Mass.: Belknap Press of Harvard University Press, 1952).

62. Albert O. Hirschman, "Rise and Decline of Development Economics," in his *Essays in Trespassing: Economics to Politics and Beyond* (Cambridge: Cambridge University Press, 1981), p. 24.

63. Ibid., pp. 123–129.

64. On the origins of these ideas in Renaissance political thought, see Walter Ullmann, *Medieval Foundations of Renaissance Humanism* (London: Paul Elek, 1977).

65. See David E. Apter, *Politics of Modernization* (Chicago: University of Chicago Press, 1965); and Chaim I. Waxman, ed., *The End of Ideology Debate* (New York: Funk and Wagnalls, 1968).

66. Waxman, *The End of Ideology Debate;* S. M. Lipset, "The End of Ideology and the Ideology of Intellectuals," in J. Ben David and T. N. Clark, *Culture and Its Creators* (Chicago: University of Chicago Press, 1977), pp. 15–42. See also Robert E. Lane, "The Decline of Politics and Ideology in a Knowledgeable Society," *American Sociological Review* 31 (October 1966), 649–662; Bertram M. Gross, "Preface" and "The State of the Nation: Social Systems Accounting," in *Social Indicators*, ed. Raymond A. Bauer (Cambridge, Mass.: MIT Press, 1966), pp. ix–xvii, 255.

67. Robert Luther Thompson, *Wiring a Continent: The History of the Telegraph Industry in the United States, 1832–1866* (Princeton, N.J.: Princeton University Press, 1947).

68. Michael Schudson, *Discovering the News* (New York: Basic Books, 1973).

69. Philip Fisher, "Appearing and Disappearing in Public: Social Space in Late-Nineteenth-Century Literature and Culture," in *Reconstructing American Literary History*, ed. Sacvan Bercovitch (Cambridge, Mass.: Harvard University Press, 1986), p. 164.

70. Ibid.

71. Alan Trachtenberg, *Reading American Photographs: Images as History, Mathew Brady to Walker Evans* (New York: Hill and Wang, 1989).

72. Fisher, "Appearing and Disappearing in Public," pp. 155–188. Important European antecedents of Eakin's *Gross Clinic* or *Agnew Clinic*, like Rembrandt's famous *Operation by Dr. Tulp*, for example, reflect the theatrical aspect of the legitimation of modern science already in its incipient stages in the seventeenth century. See William S. Heckscher, *Rembrandt's Anatomy of Dr. Nicolaas Tulp* (New York: New York University Press, 1958).

73. On the general tensions between political expectations and political actions in the American democracy, see Huntington, *The Promise of Disharmony.*

74. Walter Lippmann, *The Phantom Public* (New York: Harcourt Brace and Company, 1925).

75. On the possible discrepancy between apparent failure and substantive success, see, for instance, Sar A. Levitan and Robert Taggart, "The Great Society Did Succeed," *Political Science Quarterly* 91 (Winter 1976–77), 601–618.

76. On these "scripts" and their political careers, see L. Rainwater and L. W. Yancey, *The Moynihan Report and the Politics of Controversy* (Cambridge, Mass.: MIT Press, 1962); D. P. Moynihan, *Maximum Feasible Misunderstanding* (New York: Free Press, 1970); Edward Banfield, *The Unheavenly City* (Boston: Little, Brown, 1970); Paul Starr, *The Social Transformation of American Medicine* (New York: Basic Books, 1982); *Environment, Heredity and Intelligence*, reprint ser. no. 2, *Harvard Educational Review* (June 1969); Charles Frankel, ed., *Controversies and Decisions* (New York: Russell Sage Foundation, 1976), pp. 123–170.

77. Zhores A. Medvedev, *The Rise and Fall of I. D. Lysenko* (New York: Columbia University Press, 1969). See also Loren G. Graham, *The Soviet Academy of Science and the Communist Party, 1922–1932* (Princeton, N.J.: Princeton University Press, 1962).

78. Thomas A. Baylis, *The Technical Intelligentsia and the East German Elite* (Berkeley: University of California Press, 1979), pp. 52, 154.

79. Ibid., p. 168.

80. For a philosophical discussion of some of the principal arguments against any claim of objective, ultimately correct way of viewing, describing or interpreting the world, see Richard Rorty, *Contingency, Irony and Solidarity* (Cambridge: Cambridge University Press, 1989).

10. From the Politics of Meliorism to the Politics of Equilibrium

1. Robert Lane, "The Decline of Politics and Ideology in the Knowledgeable Society," *The American Sociological Review* 31 (October 1966), 649–662.

2. Sacvan Bercovitch, "The Problem of Ideology in American Literary History," *Critical Inquiry* 12 (Summer 1986), 646.

3. Dennis Meadows et al., *The Limits to Growth* (Washington, D.C.: Potomac Associates, 1972); John McDermott, "Technology: The Opiate of the Intellectuals," *The New York Review of Books,* July 31, 1969; Paul Goodman, *The New Reformation: Notes of a Neolithic Conservative* (New York: Random House, 1969); Thomas Kuhn, *The Structure of Scientific Revolutions,* 2nd ed. (Chicago: University of Chicago Press, 1970); Paul Feyerabend, *Against Method: Outline of an Anarchistic Theory of Knowledge* (London: Verso, 1978); Don K. Price, *America's Unwritten Constitution* (Baton Rouge: Louisiana State University Press, 1983); Michael Oakeshott, *Rationalism in Politics* (New York: Basic Books, 1962); Robert Bellah et al., *Habits of the Heart: Individualism and Commitment in American Life* (Berkeley: University of California Press, 1985); Alasdair MacIntyre, *After Virtue* (Notre Dame, Ind.: University of Notre Dame Press, 1981); Donald A. Schon, *The Reflective Practitioner* (New York: Basic Books, 1983).

4. See Yaron Ezrahi, "Utopian and Pragmatic Rationalism: The Political

Context of Scientific Advice," *Minerva* 18 (Spring 1980), 111–131; and Yaron Ezrahi, "Political Contexts of Science Indicators," in *Toward a Metric of Science: The Advent of Science Indicators,* eds. Y. Elkana, J. Lederberg, R. K. Merton, D. Thackray, and H. Zuckerman (New York: Wiley, 1978), pp. 285–327.

5. Schon, *The Reflective Practitioner.*

6. Although the Watergate scandal was in many respects a case of the penetration of the attestive public eye behind the public face of political leadership, it was a moral drama which focused on the integrity of the chief executive and the question of whether he lied rather than on the question of his competence as an instrumentally effective leader.

7. Mary Douglas, *Risk Acceptability According to the Social Sciences* (London: Routledge & Kegan Paul, 1986), pp. 5–11; Mary Douglas and Aaron Wildavsky, *Risk and Culture* (Berkeley: University of California Press, 1982).

8. Note also the recent impact of computers on the socially entrenched images of the machine and its cultural uses as metaphor. David Bolter notes, for example, the specific immaterial properties of the electronic computer, the fact that unlike the clock this modern machine is not a fixed mechanism consisting of mechanically moveable parts and is often used as a metaphor for the brain, the least mechanistically conceived element of the human body. See Bolter, *Turings' Man: Western Culture in the Computer Age* (Chapel Hill: University of North Carolina Press, 1984). I am indebted to Seymour Mauskopf for this reference.

9. See Albert H. Teich, *Technology and the Future,* 4th ed. (New York: St. Martin's Press, 1986).

10. This has been a partial reversal of the earlier tendency in twentieth century America indicated by John Higham, "Hanging Together: Divergent Unities in American History," *Journal of American History* 61 (June 1974), 23–24; and Daniel J. Boorstin, *The Americans: The Democratic Experience* (New York: Random House, 1974), pp. 238–244.

11. Stanley Cavell, *The World Viewed: Reflections on the Ontology of Film* (New York: Viking Press, 1971); Alan Trachtenberg, *Reading American Photographs: Images as History, Mathew Brady to Walker Evans* (New York: Hill and Wang, 1989).

12. John Szarkowski, *Mirrors and Windows: American Photography since 1960* (New York: Museum of Modern Art, 1978). On the related criticism of the rhetoric of objectivity in journalism, see Michael Schudson, *Discovering the News: A Social History of American Newspapers* (New York: Basic Books, 1978), pp. 176–194.

13. Szarkowski, *Mirrors and Windows,* pp. 20–25.

14. See, for instance, E. F. Schumacher, *Small Is Beautiful: Economics as if People Mattered* (New York: Basic Books, 1978), pp. 176–194. The adaptation of the modern computer to personal data processing is another example.

15. The omnipresence of the television drama as a mode of constructing and experiencing both the real and the imaginary is connected with this shift toward a focus on the individual and a deemphasis of social processes or forces. See Horace Newcomb, *TV: The Most Popular Art* (Garden City, N.Y.: Anchor Books, 1974).

16. See Yaron Ezrahi, "Utopian and Pragmatic Rationalism: The Political Context of Scientific Advice," *Minerva* 18 (Spring 1980), 111–131.

17. Clifford Geertz, "Blurred Genres: The Refiguration of Social Thought," in his *Local Knowledge* (New York: Basic Books, 1983), pp. 34–35.

18. Richard Rorty, *Consequences of Pragmatism* (Minneapolis: University of Minnesota Press, 1982), p. 203.

19. D. P. Walker, *The Decline of Hell: Seventeenth-Century Discussions of Eternal Torment* (Chicago: University of Chicago Press, 1964), pp. 3–4.

20. Ibid. For a discussion of the fear of the political consequences of declining social trust in knowledge and rationality, see Richard Rorty, *Contingency, Irony and Solidarity* (Cambridge: Cambridge University Press, 1989), pp. 73–95.

21. John Rawls, "Justice as Fairness: Political Not Metaphysical," *Philosophy and Public Affairs* 14 (1985), 225.

22. Ibid., 246.

23. J. G. A. Pocock, *The Machiavellian Moment: Florentine Political Thought and the Atlantic Republican Tradition* (Princeton, N.J.: Princeton University Press, 1975), p. 545.

24. George Armstrong Kelly, "Faith, Freedom and Disenchantment: Politics and American Religious Consciousness," *Daedalus* 3 (Winter 1982), 142.

25. Robert Hughes, *The Shock of the New* (New York: Alfred A. Knopf, 1981), p. 211.

26. Edward Purcell, *The Crisis in Democratic Theory* (Lexington: University Press of Kentucky, 1973); C. B. MacPherson, *The Life and Times of Liberal Democracy* (Oxford: Oxford University Press, 1980).

27. On the reformative impulse in American politics, see Samuel P. Huntington, *American Politics: The Promise of Disharmony* (Cambridge, Mass.: Belknap Press of Harvard University Press, 1981), p. 121; on the challenge of European dictatorships, see Purcell, *The Crisis of Democratic Theory*, pp. 117–138.

28. David Dickson, *The New Politics of Science* (New York: Pantheon Books, 1984).

29. Huntington, *The Promise of Disharmony*.

30. Dickson, *The New Politics of Science*, p. 52; and M. L. Goggin, ed., *Governing Science and Technology in a Democracy* (Knoxville: University of Tennessee Press, 1986).

31. Dickson, *The New Politics of Science*, p. 104.

32. Ibid., pp. 261–306.

33. Ibid.

34. Richard Rorty, "The Contingency of Selfhood," *London Review of Books,* May 8, 1986, pp. 11–15.

35. Sacvan Bercovitch, "Rites of Assent: Rhetoric, Ritual, and the Ideology of the American Consensus," in *The American Self,* ed. Sam B. Girgus (Albuquerque: University of New Mexico Press, 1981), p. 9.

36. Bellah et al., *Habits of the Heart,* p. 142.

37. Peter L. Berger, *The Capitalist Revolution* (New York: Basic Books, 1986), p. 106.

38. Bellah et al., *Habits of the Heart.*

39. Benjamin Barber, *Strong Democracy: Participatory Politics for a New Age* (Berkeley: University of California Press, 1984).

40. Ibid.; and Yaron Ezrahi, "Science and Utopia in Late-Twentieth-Century

Pluralist Democracy," in *Nineteen Eighty-Four: Science between Utopia and Dystopia*, eds. E. Mendelsohn and H. Nowotny, Sociology of the Sciences, vol. VIII (Dordrecht: D. Reidel, 1984), pp. 273–290.

41. Barber, *Strong Democracy*, p. 248.

42. R. Inglehart, *The Silent Revolution: Changing Values and Political Styles among Western Publics* (Princeton, N.J.: Princeton University Press, 1977); R. Inglehart "The Renaissance of Political Culture," *American Political Science Review* 82 (December 1988), 1226; Samuel H. Barnes et al., *Political Action: Mass Participation in Western Democracies* (Beverly Hills: Sage Publications, 1979).

43. Paul Starr, *The Social Transformation of American Medicine* (New York: Basic Books, 1982), p. 379; Seymour M. Lipset and William Schneider, *The Confidence Gap: Business, Labor, and Government in the Public Mind* (New York: Free Press, 1983).

44. The observation is supported by a series of unpublished papers delivered in a conference entitled The Learned Professions: Towards a New Social Contract, held in September 1985 in New York under the sponsorship of the Russell Sage Foundation.

45. Starr, *The Social Transformation of American Medicine*, pp. 391–392.

46. Michel J. Crozier, Samuel Huntington, and Joji Watanuki, eds., *The Crisis of Democracy* (New York: New York University Press, 1975), pp. 40–43, 74, 161, 165.

47. Ibid., p. 166; Morris P. Fiorina, "The Decline of Collective Responsibility in American Politics," *Daedalus* 109 (Summer 1980), 25.

48. Fiorina, "The Decline of Collective Responsibility," p. 44; see also Crozier et al., eds., *The Crisis of Democracy*, pp. 165–166.

49. Fiorina, "The Decline of Collective Responsibility," p. 43; Barnes et al., *Political Action*.

50. MacPherson, *The Life and Times of Liberal Democracy*, p. 20.

51. Benjamin I. Page, "The Theory of Political Ambiguity," *American Political Science Review* 70 (September 1976), 742–752.

52. Fiorina, "The Decline of Collective Responsibility," 43.

53. Inglehart, *The Silent Revolution*; Barnes et al., *Political Action*; K. L. Baker, R. J. Dalton, and K. Hildebrandt, *Germany Transformed: Political Culture and the New Politics* (Cambridge, Mass.: Harvard University Press, 1981).

54. Reprinted in *The New Left: A Documentary History*, ed. Massino Teodori (Indianapolis, Ind.: Bobbs-Merrill, 1969), p. 167. See also Donald W. Keim, "Participation in Contemporary Democratic Theories," in *Participation in Politics*, eds. J. R. Pennock and J. W. Chapman (New York: Lieber-Atherton, 1975).

55. For a criticism of the idea that neutral or objective standards are a constraint upon disorganized political participation, see Benjamin Barber, *Strong Democracy: Participatory Politics for a New Age* (Berkeley: University of California, 1984). For a 1960s critique of science and technology and their effects on society and politics, see T. Roszak, *The Making of a Counter-Culture* (Garden City, N.Y.: Anchor Books, 1969).

56. Inglehart, *The Silent Revolution*, p. 320; Barnes et al., *Political Action*.

57. Arthur M. Okun, *Equality and Efficiency: The Big Tradeoff* (Washington, D.C.: Brookings Institution, 1975), 48.

58. Fiorina, "The Decline of Collective Responsibility," 44; see also Crozier et al., eds., *The Crisis of Democracy,* pp. 165–166.

59. Cited in Judith N. Shklar, "Learning without Knowing," in "Intellect and Imagination," *Daedalus* 109 (Spring 1980), 53–72.

60. See Shklar's illuminating discussion of this theme in ibid.

61. Thomas Jefferson's letter to James Madison, September 6, 1789, in *The Portable Thomas Jefferson,* ed. M. D. Peterson (New York: Viking Press, 1975), p. 449.

62. On the "immortality" of society compared to the perishability of the individual, see Emile Durkheim, *The Elementary Forms of the Religious Life* (1915; New York: Free Press, 1965).

63. Lindsay Rogers, *The Pollsters: Public Opinion, Politics, and Democratic Leadership* (New York: Alfred A. Knopf, 1949).

64. George Gallup, *A Guide to Public Opinion Polls* (Princeton, N.J.: Princeton University Press, 1948), p. 4.

65. Lord Bryce, *Modern Democracies,* vol. I (New York: Macmillan, 1921), p. 153.

66. For a view of public opinion formation as a problematic concept from the perspective of liberal-democratic notions of autonomous individual judgments, see Elisabeth Noelle-Neumann, *The Spiral of Silence* (Chicago: University of Chicago Press, 1982).

67. Arthur Maass, *Congress and the Common Good* (New York: Basic Books, 1983), pp. 55–63, 121, 122–123.

68. Ibid., p. 126.

69. See *1970 National Science Foundation Authorization,* Hearings before the Subcommittee on Science, Research and Development of the House Committee on Science and Astronautics, 91st Cong., 1st sess. (Washington, D.C.: U.S. Government Printing Office, 1969).

70. See Edward Shils, ed., *Criteria for Scientific Development: Public Policy and National Goals* (Cambridge, Mass.: MIT Press, 1968).

71. *1970 National Science Foundation Authorization,* pp. 25–87. See also Yaron Ezrahi, "The Political Resources of American Science," *Science Studies* 1 (1971). On the effects of commercial values on basic research in such fields as molecular biology, see Malcolm L. Goggin, ed., *Governing Science and Technology in Democracy* (Knoxville: University of Tennessee Press, 1986).

72. See John P. Gilbert et al., "Statistics and Ethics," *Science* 198 (1977), 687. The American author Sinclair Lewis, son of a country doctor, illustrated this tension between the cultures and the norms of research and treatment in his novel *Arrowsmith* as early as 1925. Arrowsmith is a medical scientist who is sent to a remote region stricken by a deadly epidemic disease as part of a research effort to develop and test a new inoculation. Confronted by the hysteria of the epidemic, Arrowsmith concedes the integrity of his research procedure and yields to the pressures to give the untested medical treatment to hundreds of desperate patients. Sinclair Lewis, *Arrowsmith* (New York: New American Library, 1925).

The compassion and the moral pressure that demand responsiveness to the plight of the living eclipse the imperatives of medical research, the need to make some sacrifices in the present in order to "save millions" in the future. Lewis, as Charles Rosenberg points out, juxtaposes the idealism of the research scientist with the limits imposed by the pressure of society's current needs. "As able, self-sacrificing, and understanding as the best physician might be he could never transcend the social relationships which formed the fabric of his professional existence. And to Lewis the essence of heroism, the measure of a man's stature lay in the extent to which he was able to disengage himself from the confining pressures of American society. His heroic protagonist had to be a scientist; he could not be a physician. And certainly not an American physician." Charles E. Rosenberg, "Martin Arrowsmith: The Scientist as a Hero," in his *No Other Gods: On Science and American Social Thought* (Baltimore: Johns Hopkins University Press, 1978), pp. 123–131. (Toward the closing decades of the twentieth century, the ideal of heroic disengagement from social pressures has in fact been largely replaced by the ideal of public accountable science. Public support for basic research is largely purchased by promises of short term relevance and payoffs.)

73. See Lee J. Cronbach et al., *Toward Reform of Program Evaluation* (San Francisco: Jossey Bass, 1980); Carol H. Weiss, ed., *Evaluating Action Programs* (Boston: Allyn & Bacon, 1972).

74. Stuart W. Cook, "Ethical Issues in the Conduct of Research in Social Relations," in *Research Methods in Social Relations,* eds. C. Sellitz, L. S. Wrightsman, and S. W. Cook (New York: Holt, Rinehart and Winston, 1977), pp. 199–249. On ethical issues in biological research, see Watson Fuller, ed., *The Social Impact of Modern Biology* (London: Routledge & Kegan Paul, 1971).

75. *Science,* May 13, 1983 (editorial).

76. Bertrand de Jouvenel, "The Political Consequences of the Rise of Science," *Bulletin of Atomic Scientists* 19 (December 1963), 2–8.

77. Alexis de Tocqueville, *Democracy in America,* vol. II, ed. Phillips Bradley (New York: Vintage Books, 1945), p. 106.

78. Ibid., p. 135.

79. Jacques Maritain, *Man and the State* (Chicago: University of Chicago Press, 1951), pp. 57–58.

80. Shklar, "Learning without Knowing," 59–60.

81. Hannah Arendt, *Between Past and Future* (Cleveland: Meridian Books, 1963), pp. 72, 74.

82. Frederick J. Hoffman, *The Mortal No: Death and the Modern Imagination* (Princeton, N.J.: Princeton University Press, 1964), p. 4.

83. Leo Bobrov, *Grounds For Optimism,* trans. H. C. Creighton (Moscow: Mir Publishers, 1974), pp. 35, 166–167.

84. Karl R. Popper, *The Poverty of Historicism* (1936; London: Routledge & Kegan Paul, 1961).

85. See particularly Garry Wills, *Reagan's America: Innocents at Home* (New York: Doubleday Company, 1987).

86. Ibid.

87. Ibid., p. 343.

88. Ibid., p. 300.

89. Ibid., p. 44.

90. See note 58 above.

91. Flora Lewis, "Who Are They?" *New York Times*, October 16, 1988.

11. Science and the Decline of Public Culture

1. John Dewey, *Liberalism and Social Action* (1935; New York: Perig e Books, 1980), p. 51.

2. Yaron Ezrahi, "Utopian and Pragmatic Rationalism: The Political Context of Scientific Advice," *Minerva* 18 (Spring 1980), 111–131.

3. James G. March and Herbert A. Simon, *Organizations* (New York: John Wiley & Sons, 1958), p. 139.

4. Ibid., pp. 140–141.

5. Herbert A. Simon, *Administrative Behavior*, 2nd ed. (New York: Macmillan, 1961). See also his "Rationality as Process and as Product of Thought," Richard T. Ely lecture, *American Economic Review* 68 (May 1978), 1–16.

6. Charles E. Lindblom, "The Science of Muddling Through," *Public Administration Review* 19 (Spring 1959), 79–88.

7. Ibid.

8. David Braybrook and Charles E. Lindblom, *A Strategy of Decision* (New York: Free Press, 1970).

9. March and Simon, *Organizations;* and Karl Popper, *The Poverty of Historicism* (London: Routledge & Kegan Paul, 1961).

10. Braybrook and Lindblom, *A Strategy of Decision*, p. 48.

11. Ibid., pp. 42–52, 61–79.

12. Amos Tversky and Daniel Kahneman, "Judgment under Uncertainty: Heuristics and Biases," *Science* 185 (1974), 1124–31; Amos Tversky and Daniel Kahneman, "The Framing of Decisions and the Psychology of Choice," *Science* 211 (1981), 453–458; Irving Janis, *Victims of Groupthink* (Boston: Houghton Mifflin, 1972).

13. Kenneth J. Arrow, *Social Choice and Individual Values* (1951; New Haven, Conn.: Yale University Press, 1975).

14. Abram Bergson, "On the Concept of Social Welfare," *Quarterly Journal of Economics* 68 (May 1954), 233–252 (cited in ibid., p. 107).

15. Arrow, *Social Choice and Individual Values*, p. 120. See also his "Values and Collective Decision-Making," in *Philosophy, Politics and Society*, eds. Peter Laslett and W. G. Runciman (Oxford: Basil Blackwell, 1967).

16. Kenneth Arrow, *The Limits of Organization* (New York: Norton, 1974), pp. 24–25. Questions about the intellectual foundations of the claim that rational group decisions can be constructed from data about individual preferences were raised also in discussions of joint actions that satisfy the requirements of the "pareto optimal," a point at which no improvement in the condition of any individual is possible without a worsening in the position of at least one other individual. Howard Raiffa, *Decision Analysis* (Reading, Mass.: Addison-Wesley, 1970), pp. 199, 203, 208, 218, 229, 233, 237. Powerful criticisms of the analytical possibility of unambiguously fixing one such point consistently with liberal values, and more generally of the shaky foundations of social choice theory, and doubts about the technical value of Keynesian remedies for economic problems

are only a few of the intellectual developments which appear to render the attempt to harmonize the welfare state with democratic administrative centralism increasingly indefensible. See Amartya Sen, "The Impossibility of a Paretian Liberal," *Journal of Political Economy* 78 (January/February 1970), 152–157; J. Elster and A. Hylland, eds., *Foundations of Social Choice Theory* (New York: Cambridge University Press, 1986); Thomas Schwartz, *The Logic of Collective Choice* (New York: Columbia University Press, 1986).

17. Robert L. Heilbroner, "On the Limited 'Relevance' of Economics," *The Public Interest* 21 (Fall 1970), 80–93.

18. Aaron Wildavsky, *The Politics of the Budgetary Process* (Boston: Little, Brown, 1964).

19. *The Behavioral and Social Sciences: Outlooks and Needs,* National Academy of Science Report (Washington, D.C.: National Academy Press, 1969).

20. For an assessment of this development see J. S. Coleman, *Policy Research and the Social Sciences* (Morristown, N.J.: General Learning Press, 1972); Ezrahi, "Utopian and Pragmatic Rationalism"; Graham Allison, *The Essence of Decision* (Boston: Little, Brown, 1971); W. J. Barber, "The U.S.: Economists in a Pluralistic Policy," in *Economists in Government,* ed. A. W. Coats (Durham, N.C.: Duke University Press, 1971), pp. 1978–79; J. D. Steinbruner, *The Cybernetic Theory of Decision* (Princeton, N.J.: Princeton University Press, 1974).

21. Charles Lindblom and David Cohen, *Usable Knowledge: Social Science and Social Problem Solving* (New Haven, Conn.: Yale University Press, 1979), p. 100.

22. Coleman, Policy Research and the Social Sciences; Lee J. Cronbach et al., *Towards Reform of Program Evaluation* (San Francisco: Jossey-Bass Publishers, 1980).

23. Bertrand de Jouvenelle, *The Pure Theory of Politics* (Cambridge: Cambridge University Press, 1963), p. 189.

24. See Edward Banfield, *The Unheavenly City* (Boston: Little, Brown, 1968); and Daniel Moynihan, *Maximum Feasible Misunderstanding* (New York: Free Press, 1970).

25. Banfield, *The Unheavenly City,* p. 239.

26. Ibid., p. 256.

27. Robert A. Packenham, *Liberal America and the Third World: Political Development Ideas in Foreign Aid and Social Science* (Princeton, N.J.: Princeton University Press, 1973), p. 191; Deepak Lal, *The Poverty of "Development Economics"* (Cambridge, Mass.: Harvard University Press, 1985).

28. See Irene L. Gendzier, *Managing Political Change: Social Scientists and the Third World* (Boulder: Westview Press, 1985).

29. C. Wright Mills, "Letter to the New Left," *New Left Review* 5 (1960). See also Chaim I. Waxman, ed., *The End of Ideology Debate* (New York: Funk and Wagnalls, 1968).

30. Raymond Aron, "On the Proper Use of Ideologies," *Culture and Its Creators,* eds. Joseph Ben David and Terry Clark (Chicago: University of Chicago Press, 1972), p. 14. See also in the same volume S. M. Lipset, "The End of Ideology and the Ideology of Intellectuals," pp. 15–42.

31. Ibid., pp. 5, 9.

32. Don K. Price, *America's Unwritten Constitution* (Baton Rouge: Louisiana State University Press, 1983), p. xiii.

33. William T. Golden, ed., *Scientific Advice to the President* (New York: Pergamon Press, 1980), p. 214. (On the effects of such factors on the disestablishment of the scientific advisory structure at the White House under President Richard Nixon, see p. 213.) See also Herbert I. Fusfeld and Carmela S. Haklisch, eds., *Science and Technology Policy Perspectives for the 1980s,* Annals of the New York Academy of Science, vol. 1 (1979); and Harold Orlans, "Academic Social Scientists and the Presidency: From Wilson to Nixon," *Minerva* 24 (Summer-Autumn 1986), 172–204. Orlans describes the history of academic social scientists in the White House as a series of failures to rationalize public policy. From my perspective it would be more appropriate to construe this experience as a series of often successful attempts to use the social sciences in order to build up and legitimate the uses of political power and authority by the Executive Branch. For another example of a "rationalistic" account of a "failure" of a social science, see David Ricci, *The Tragedy of Political Science* (New Haven, Conn.: Yale University Press, 1986).

34. See the useful discussions of this issue in Richard Rorty, *Philosophy and the Mirror Metaphor* (Princeton, N.J.: Princeton University Press, 1979); Nelson Goodman, *Ways of Worldmaking* (Sussex: Harvester Press, 1978); and Thomas Nagel, *The View from Nowhere* (New York: Oxford University Press, 1986).

35. See Chapter 7.

36. Werner Heisenberg, *Philosophic Problems of Nuclear Science,* trans. F. C. Hayes (London: Faber and Faber, 1934), p. 21.

37. Ibid., p. 36.

38. Ibid., p. 39.

39. Ibid., pp. 68–69.

40. Denis Diderot, "d'Alembert's Dream," in *Rameau's Nephew and Other Works,* trans. Jacques Barzun and Ralph H. Bowen (Indianapolis, Ind.: Bobbs-Merrill, 1964), p. 101.

41. Emile Zola, "The Experimental Novel" and "Naturalism in the Theatre," in *Documents of Modern Literary Realism,* ed. George J. Becker, (Princeton, N.J.: Princeton University Press, 1963), pp. 162–229.

42. Linda Nochlin, *Realism* (New York: Penguin, 1971), pp. 40–45.

43. *The Autobiography of Lincoln Steffens,* vol. II (New York: Harcourt, Brace & World, 1958), p. 389.

44. C. K. Ogden and I. A. Richards, *The Meaning of Meaning* (London: Routledge & Kegan Paul, 1923); Stuart Chase, *The Tyranny of Words* (New York: Harcourt, Brace, 1939).

45. Heisenberg, *Philosophic Problems,* p. 71.

46. Ibid., p. 68. See also Peter Galison, "Bubble Chambers and the Experimental Workplace," in *Observation, Experiment and Hypothesis in Modern Physical Science,* eds. Peter Achinstein and Owen Hannaway (Cambridge, Mass.: MIT Press, 1985), pp. 309–371.

47. Ibid., p. 117.

48. David Gooding, Trevor Pinch, and Simon Schaffer, eds., *The Uses of Experiment* (Cambridge: Cambridge University Press, 1989).

49. Albert Einstein, "The Common Language of Science" in his *Out of My*

Later Years (New York: Philosophical Library, 1950), pp. 111–112; Banesh Hoffman with the collaboration of Helen Dukas, *Albert Einstein: Creator and Rebel* (New York: Viking Press, 1972), p. 261; Einstein, "Physics and Reality," in his *Out of My Later Years*, p. 69.

50. John Dewey, *The Quest for Certainty* (New York: Putnam's Sons, 1929), p. 291.

51. Stephen Toulmin, *The Return to Cosmology: Postmodern Science and the Theology of Nature* (Berkeley: University of California Press, 1982), p. 231. For examples of the changing perspectives on the practice of science, see also Karin D. Knorr-Cetina, *The Manufacture of Knowledge: An Essay on Constructivist and Contextual Nature of Science* (Oxford: Pergamon Press, 1981); Bruno Latour and Steve Woolgar, *Laboratory Life: The Social Construction of Scientific Facts* (Beverly Hills: Sage Publications, 1979).

52. Nagel, *The View from Nowhere.*

53. James B. Conant, *Modern Science and Modern Man* (Garden City, N.Y.: Doubleday, Anchor Books, 1953), pp. 35–36.

54. Heisenberg, *Philosophic Problems,* pp. 117–118.

55. Einstein, "The Common Language of Science," pp. 111–112.

56. Although the term "objective" stems, of course, from visual culture which acknowledges the dichotomy between object and subject, it is used here to suggest the quality of being certifiable in a wider sense.

57. Renato Poggioli, *The Theory of the Avant-Garde,* trans. G. Fitzgerald (Cambridge, Mass.: Belknap Press of Harvard University Press, 1968); Jean-François Lyotard, *The Post-Modern Condition: A Report on Knowledge* (Minneapolis: University of Minnesota Press, 1986).

58. E. G. Gombrich, *The Story of Art* (London: Phaidon Press, 1951), p. 418.

59. Ibid., p. 432.

60. Ibid., p. 445.

61. Meyer Schapiro, *Modern Art: Nineteenth and Twentieth Centuries* (New York: George Braziller, 1968), p. 223.

62. The declining role of spectators as informed witnesses of scientific truths is not "balanced" by their conversion into amateur scientists. Distrusting the notion of the world as a scientifically observed object implies a regression from the ideal of science as a form of public knowledge to another social variant of pre-Enlightenment esoteric knowledge. The liberal social usage of the term "scientific research" suggests, of course, a very loose definition which may cover almost any simple collection of facts. Moreover, the very shift in emphasis from "knowledge" to "information" as a basis for rational decisions and actions implies a turn toward a more inclusive concept of competence. The community of the informed is considerably wider than the community of the knowledgeable. On the sociological aspects of the differences between knowledge and information, see Robert K. Merton, *Social Theory and Social Structure* (New York: Free Press, 1968), pp. 493–500. It is important to stress, however, that as a highly organized and technically demanding activity, science is more resistant than art to the pressures of democratization in the sense of enlarged access and participation. Hence the decline of the spectator as an authoritative witness to the works and claims of scientists is not counterbalanced in fact by increased access to more loosely defined "research" activities parallel to the shift from "art" to "the arts." Moreover,

unlike artistic experience, scientific research or scientific knowledge cannot be individually subjectivized. In the context of science, "private knowledge" or "subjective research" is a contradiction in terms.

63. Daniel Dayan and Elihu Katz, "Performing Media Events," in *Impacts & Influences*, eds. J. Curran, A. Smith, and P. Wingate (London: Methuen, 1987), pp. 174–197.

64. Tom Stoppard, *The Real Inspector Hound* (London: Faber and Faber, 1970). I am indebted to Stephen Toulmin for this reference and the analogy. See Toulmin, *The Return to Cosmology*, pp. 237–238. The capacity of distant and passive spectators to break away from their isolation, enter the space of public affairs, and appear as actors on the television screen has, in fact, been one of the most symbolically powerful expressions of late-twentieth-century democratic revolutions—particularly in Eastern Europe.

65. For the "reactive" effects of scientific gazing on social behavior, see "The Hawthorn Effect," in Fritz J. Roethlisberger and William J. Dickson, *Management and the Worker* (Cambridge, Mass.: Harvard University Press, 1939), p. 61.

66. See, for instance, Thomas S. Kuhn, *The Structure of Scientific Revolutions*, 2nd ed. (Chicago: University of Chicago Press, 1970); Imre Lakatos and Alan Musgrave, eds., *Criticism and the Growth of Knowledge* (Cambridge: Cambridge University Press, 1970); Paul Feyerabend, *Against Method* (London: Verso, 1978); Latour and Woolgar, *Laboratory Life;* Martin J. S. Rudwick, *The Great Devonian Controversy,* (Chicago: University of Chicago Press, 1985).

67. See, for example, W. G. Runciman, *A Treatise on Social Theory,* The Methodology of Social Theory, vol. 1 (Cambridge: Cambridge University Press, 1983).

68. On modern pluralistic concepts of reality, see Martin Hollis and Steven Lukes, eds., *Rationality and Relativism* (Oxford: Basil Blackwell, 1982); Goodman, *Ways of Worldmaking;* Imre Lakatos and Alan Musgrave, *Criticism and the Growth of Knowledge* (Cambridge: Cambridge University Press, 1970).

69. Stephen Toulmin, *Philosophy of Science* (London: Hutchinson University Library, 1962), esp. pp. 26–29, 60–61, 70–72, 77–78, 94.

70. For an attempt to defend the classical distinction between fact and fiction as a foundation of liberal politics, see J. D. Barber, *The Pulse of Politics: Electing Presidents in the Media Age* (New York: W. W. Norton, 1980), esp. pp. 311–322. See also Theodore Draper, "Journalism, History and Journalistic History," *New York Times Book Review,* December 9, 1984, pp. 3, 32, 24; Yaron Ezrahi, "Science and the Civil Religion of Liberal Democracy," in *Civil Religion and Political Theology,* ed. Leroy S. Rouner (Notre Dame, Ind.: University of Notre Dame Press, 1986), pp. 59–75.

71. See, for instance, Stuart Chase, *The Tyranny of Words* (New York: Putnam, 1939).

12. Postmodern Science and Postmodern Politics

1. The expression "neutral cosmos" is used in Mary Douglas, *Risk Acceptability According to the Social Sciences* (London: Routledge & Kegan Paul, 1986), p. 94.

2. See Chapter 1.

3. On the breakdown of the grand narrative as a mode of cultural unification of experience, see Jean-François Lyotard, *The Post Modern Condition: A Report on Knowledge* (Minneapolis: University of Minnesota Press, 1986).

4. J. G. A. Pocock, *The Machiavellian Moment* (Princeton, N.J.: Princeton University Press, 1975), p. 545. The anti-instrumentalist mood is reflected in a host of works, such as Robert Nozick, *Anarchy, State and Utopia* (New York: Basic Books, 1974); Richard Rorty, *Contingency, Irony, and Solidarity* (Cambridge: Cambridge University Press, 1989). On some of the cultural aspects of this trend, see also the essays of Milan Kundera, *The Art of the Novel* (New York: Harper and Row, 1988).

5. Joseph Raz, *The Morality of Freedom* (Oxford: Clarendon Press, 1986); and Benjamin R. Barber, *Strong Democracy* (Berkeley: University of California Press, 1984).

6. On this development see Yaron Ezrahi, "Science and Utopia in Late-Twentieth-Century Pluralist Democracy," *Sociology of the Sciences* 8 (1984), 273–290.

7. See Chapters 3, 4, 5, and 6.

8. On the inescapability of aesthetic responses to "documentary photography," see Susan Sontag, *On Photography* (New York: Dell Publications, 1977).

9. On "specified ignorance" as a kind of knowledge, see Robert Merton, "Three Fragments from a Sociologist's Notebooks," *Annual Review of Sociology* 73 (1987), 7–28.

Index